In Tun

Fullness of Peace, Power and Plenty

What All the World's A-Seeking

This Mystical Life of Ours

The Greatest Thing Ever Known

by

Ralph Waldo Trine

COMPASS CIRCLE

In Tune With The Infinite Or, Fullness of Peace, Power and Plenty (1897); What All the World's A-Seeking (1896); This Mystical Life of Ours (1907); The Greatest Thing Ever Known (1898).

The Classic Ralph Waldo Trine Book Collection (Deluxe Edition) - In Tune With The Infinite; What All the World's A-Seeking; This Mystical Life of Ours; The Greatest Thing Ever Known.
Current edition published by Compass Circle in 2018.

Published by Compass Circle
A Division of Garcia & Kitzinger Pty Ltd
Cover copyright ©2018 by Compass Circle.

For information contact :
compasscircle@garciakitzinger.com

In order to enjoy life
one must be a master of life—
for to be a slave
to its inconsistencies can only
mean torment;
and in order to enjoy the senses
one must be master of them.

RALPH WALDO TRINE

SECRET WISDOM OF THE AGES SERIES

Life presents itself, it advances in a fast way. Life indeed never stops. It never stops until the end. The most diverse questions peek and fade in our minds. Sometimes we seek for answers. Sometimes we just let time go by.

The book you have now in your hands has been waiting to be discovered by you. This book may reveal the answers to some of your questions.

Books are friends. Friends who are always by your side and who can give you great ideas, advice or just comfort your soul.

A great book can make you see things in your soul that you have not yet discovered, make you see things in your soul that you were not aware of.

Great books can change your life for the better. They can make you understand fascinating theories, give you new ideas, inspire you to undertake new challenges or to walk along new paths.

Life philosophies like the one of Wallace Wattles are indeed a secret to many, but for those of us lucky enough to have discovered them, by one way or another, these books can enlighten us. They can open a wide range of possibilities to us. Because achieving greatness requires knowledge.

The series SECRET WISDOM OF THE AGES presented by Compass Circle try to bring you the great timeless masterpieces of personal development, positive thinking, and the law of attraction.

We welcome you to discover with us fascinating works by Wallace Wattles, Thomas Troward, James Allen, among others.

Contents

This Mystical Life Of Ours   257

The Greatest Thing Ever Known   405

In Tune With The Infinite

Or,

Fullness of Peace, Power and Plenty

Preface

There is a golden thread that runs through every religion in the world. There is a golden thread that runs through the lives and the teachings of all the prophets, seers, sages, and saviours in the world's history, through the lives of all men and women of truly great and lasting power. All that they have ever done or attained to has been done in full accordance with law. What one has done, all may do.

This same golden thread must enter into the lives of all who today, in this busy work-a-day world of ours, would exchange impotence for power, weakness and suffering for abounding health and strength, pain and unrest for perfect peace, poverty of whatever nature for fullness and plenty.

Each is building his own world. We both build from within and we attract from without. Thought is the force with which we build, for thoughts are forces. Like builds like and like attracts like. In the degree that thought is spiritualized does it become more subtle and powerful in its workings. This spiritualizing is in accordance with law and is within the power of all.

Everything is first worked out in the unseen before it is manifested in the seen, in the ideal before it is realized in the real, in the spiritual before it shows forth in the material. The realm of the unseen is the realm of cause. The realm of the seen is the realm of effect. The nature of effect is always determined and conditioned by the nature of its cause.

To point out the great facts in connection with, and the great laws underlying the workings of the interior, spiritual, thought forces, to point them out so simply and so clearly that even a child can understand, is the author's aim. To point them out so simply and so clearly that all can grasp them, that all can take them and infuse them into every-day life, so as to mould it in all its details in accordance with what they would have it, is his purpose. That life can be thus moulded by them is not a matter of mere speculation or theory with him, but a matter of positive knowledge.

There is a divine sequence running throughout the universe. Within and above and below the human will incessantly works the Divine will. To come into harmony with it and thereby with all the higher laws and forces, to come then into league and to work in conjunction with them, in order that they can work in league and in conjunction with us, is to come into the chain of this wonderful sequence. This is the secret of all success. This is to come into the possession of unknown riches, into the realization of undreamed-of powers.

R.W.T.

I

Prelude

Fullness Of Peace, Power, And Plenty

The optimist is right. The pessimist is right. The one differs from the other as the light from the dark. Yet both are right. Each is right from his own particular point of view, and this point of view is the determining factor in the life of each. It determines as to whether it is a life of power or of impotence, of peace or of pain, of success or of failure.

The optimist has the power of seeing things in their entirety and in their right relations. The pessimist looks from a limited and a one-sided point of view. The one has his understanding illumined by wisdom, the understanding of the other is darkened by ignorance. Each is building his world from within, and the result of the building is determined by the point of view of each. The optimist, by his superior wisdom and insight, is making his own heaven, and in the degree that he makes his own heaven is he helping to make one for all the world beside. The pessimist, by virtue of his limitations, is making his own hell, and in the degree that he makes his own hell is he helping to make one for all mankind.

You and I have the predominating characteristics of an optimist or the predominating characteristics of a pessimist. We then are making, hour by hour, our own heaven or our own hell; and in the degree that we are making the one or the other for ourselves are we helping make it for all the world beside.

The word heaven means harmony. The word hell is from the

old English *hell*, meaning to build a wall around, to separate; to be *helled* was to be shut off from. Now if there is such a thing as harmony there must be that something one can be in right relations with; for to be in right relations with anything is to be in harmony with it. Again, if there is such a thing as being *helled*, shut off, separated from, there must be that something from which one is held, shut off, or separated.

II

The Supreme Fact Of The Universe

The great central fact of the universe is that Spirit of Infinite Life and Power that is behind all, that animates all, that manifests itself in and through all; that self-existent principle of life from which all has come, and not only from which all has come, but from which all is continually coming. If there is an individual life, there must of necessity be an infinite source of life from which it comes. If there is a quality or a force of love, there must of necessity be an infinite source of love whence it comes. If there is wisdom, there must be the all-wise source behind it from which it springs. The same is true in regard to peace, the same in regard to power, the same in regard to what we call material things.

There is, then, this Spirit of Infinite Life and Power behind all which is the source of all. This Infinite Power is creating, working, ruling through the agency of great immutable laws and forces that run through all the universe, that surround us on every side. Every act of our every-day lives is governed by these same great laws and forces. Every flower that blooms by the wayside, springs up, grows, blooms, fades, according to certain great immutable laws. Every snowflake that plays between earth and heaven, forms, falls, melts, according to certain great unchangeable laws.

In a sense there is nothing in all the great universe but law. If this is true there must of necessity be a force behind it all that is the maker of these laws and a force greater than the laws that are made. This Spirit of Infinite Life and Power that is behind all is what I call God. I care not what term you may use, be it Kindly Light, Providence, the Over Soul, Omnipotence, or whatever term may be most convenient. I care not what the term may be as long as we are agreed in regard to the great central fact itself.

God, then, is this Infinite Spirit which fills all the universe with Himself alone, so that all is from Him and in Him, and there is nothing that is outside. Indeed and in truth, then, in Him we live and move and have our being. He is the life of our life, our very life itself. We have received, we are continually receiving our life from Him. We are partakers of the life of God; and though we differ from Him in that we are individualized spirits, while He is the Infinite Spirit including us as well as all else beside, *yet in essence the life of God and the life of man are identically the same, and so are one.* They differ not in essence, in quality; they differ in degree.

There have been and are highly illumined souls who believe that we receive our life from God after the manner of a divine inflow. And again, there have been and are those who believe that our life is one with the life of God, and so that God and man are one. Which is right? Both are right; both right when rightly understood.

In regard to the first: if God is the Infinite Spirit of Life behind all, whence all comes, then clearly our life as individualized spirits is continually coming from this Infinite Source by means of this divine inflow. In the second place, if our lives as individualized spirits are directly from, are parts of this Infinite Spirit of Life, then the degree of the Infinite Spirit that is manifested in the life of each must be identical in quality with that Source, the same as a drop of water taken from the ocean is, in nature, in characteristics, identical with that ocean, its source. And how could it be otherwise? The liability to misunderstanding in this latter case, however, is this: in that although the life of God and the life of man in essence are identically the same, the life of God so far transcends the life of individual man that it includes all else beside. In other words, so far as the quality of life is concerned, in essence they are the same;

so far as the degree of life is concerned, they are vastly different.

In this light is it not then evident that both conceptions are true? and more, that they are one and the same? Both conceptions may be typified by one and the same illustration.

There is a reservoir in a valley which receives its supply from an inexhaustible reservoir on the mountain side. It is then true that the reservoir in the valley receives its supply by virtue of the inflow of the water from the larger reservoir on the mountain side. It is also true that the water in this smaller reservoir is in nature, in quality, in characteristics identically the same as that in the larger reservoir which is its source. The difference, however, is this: the reservoir on the mountain side, in the *amount* of its water, so far transcends the reservoir in the valley that it can supply an innumerable number of like reservoirs and still be unexhausted.

And so in the life of man. If, as I think we have already agreed, however we may differ in regard to anything else, there is this Infinite Spirit of Life behind all, the life of all, and so, from which all comes, then the life of individual man, your life and mine, must come by a divine inflow from this Infinite Source. And if this is true, then the life that comes by this inflow to man is necessarily the same in essence as is this Infinite Spirit of Life. There is a difference. It is not a difference in essence. It is a difference in degree.

If this is true, does it not then follow that in the degree that man opens himself to this divine inflow does he approach to God? If so, it then necessarily follows that in the degree that he makes this approach does he take on the God-powers. And if the God-powers are without limit, does it not then follow that the only limitations man has are the limitations he sets to himself, by virtue of not knowing himself?

III

The Supreme Fact Of Human Life

From the great central fact of the universe in regard to which we have agreed, namely, this Spirit of Infinite Life that is behind all and from which all comes, we are led to inquire as to what is the great central fact in human life. From what has gone before, the question almost answers itself.

The great central fact in human life, in your life and in mine, is the coming into a conscious, vital realization of our oneness with this Infinite Life, and the opening of ourselves fully to this divine inflow. This is the great central fact in human life, for in this all else is included, all else follows in its train. In just the degree that we come into a conscious realization of our oneness with the Infinite Life, and open ourselves to this divine inflow, do we actualize in ourselves the qualities and powers of the Infinite Life.

And what does this mean? It means simply this: that we are recognizing our true identity, that we are bringing our lives into harmony with the same great laws and forces, and so opening ourselves to the same great inspirations, as have all the prophets, seers, sages, and saviours in the world's history, all men of truly great and mighty power. For in the degree that we come into this realization and connect ourselves with this Infinite Source, do we make it possible for the higher powers to play, to work, to manifest through us.

We can keep closed to this divine inflow, to these higher forces and powers, through ignorance, as most of us do, and thus hinder or even prevent their manifesting through us. Or we can intention-

9

ally close ourselves to their operations and thus deprive ourselves of the powers to which, by the very nature of our being, we are rightful heirs. On the other hand, we can come into so vital a realization of the oneness of our real selves with this Infinite Life, and can open ourselves so fully to the incoming of this divine inflow, and so to the operation of these higher forces, inspirations, and powers, that we can indeed and in truth become what we may well term, God-men.

And what is a God-man? One in whom the powers of God are manifesting, though yet a man. No one can set limitations to a man or a woman of this type; for the only limitations he or she can have are those set by the self. Ignorance is the most potent factor in setting limitations to the majority of mankind; and so the great majority of people continue to live their little, dwarfed, and stunted lives simply by virtue of the fact that they do not realize the larger life to which they are heirs. They have never as yet come into a knowledge of the real identity of their true selves.

Mankind has not yet realized that the real self is one with the life of God. Through its ignorance it has never yet opened itself to the divine inflow, and so has never made itself a channel through which the infinite powers and forces can manifest. When we know ourselves merely as men, we live accordingly, and have merely the powers of men. When we come into the realization of the fact that we are God-men, then again we live accordingly, and have the powers of God-men. *In the degree that we open ourselves to this divine inflow are we changed from mere men into God-men.*

A friend has a beautiful lotus pond. A natural basin on his estate—his farm as he always calls it—is supplied with water from a reservoir in the foothills some distance away. A gate regulates the flow of the water from the main that conducts it from the reservoir to the pond. It is a spot of transcendent beauty. There, through the days of the perfect summer weather, the lotus flowers lie full blown upon the surface of the clear, transparent water. The June roses and other wild flowers are continually blooming upon its banks. The birds come here to drink and to bathe, and from early until late one can hear the melody of their song. The bees are continually at work in this garden of wild flowers. A beautiful grove, in which many kinds of wild berries and many varieties of brakes and ferns grow, stretches back of the pond as far as the eye can reach.

Our friend is a man, nay more, a God-man, a lover of his kind, and as a consequence no notice bearing such words as "Private grounds, no trespassing allowed," or "Trespassers will be prosecuted," stands on his estate. But at the end of a beautiful by-way that leads through the wildwood up to this enchanting spot, stands a notice bearing the words "All are welcome to the Lotus Pond." All love our friend. Why? They can't help it. He so loves them, and what is his is theirs.

Here one may often find merry groups of children at play. Here many times tired and weary looking men and women come, and somehow, when they go their faces wear a different expression,— the burden seems to be lifted; and now and then I have heard them when leaving, sometimes in a faint murmur, as if uttering a benediction, say, "God bless our brother-friend." Many speak of this spot as the Garden of God. My friend calls it his Soul Garden, and he spends many hours in quiet here. Often have I seen him after the others have gone, walking to and fro, or sitting quietly in the clear moonlight on an old rustic bench, drinking in the perfume of the wild flowers. He is a man of a beautifully simple nature. He says that here the real things of life come to him, and that here his greatest and most successful plans, many times as by a flash of inspiration, suggest themselves to him.

Everything in the immediate vicinity seems to breathe a spirit of kindliness, comfort, good-will, and good cheer. The very cattle and sheep as they come to the old stone-fence at the edge of the grove and look across to this beautiful spot seem, indeed, to get the same enjoyment that the people are getting. They seem almost to smile in the realization of their contentment and enjoyment; or perhaps it seems so to the looker-on, because he can scarcely help smiling as he sees the manifested evidence of their contentment and pleasure.

The gate of the pond is always open wide enough to admit a supply of water so abundant that it continually overflows a quantity sufficient to feed a stream that runs through the fields below, giving the pure mountain water in drink to the cattle and flocks that are grazing there. The stream then flows on through the neighbors' fields.

Not long ago our friend was absent for a year. He rented his estate during his absence to a man who, as the world goes, was of a very "practical" turn of mind. He had no time for anything that did not bring him direct "practical" returns. The gate connecting the reservoir with the lotus pond was shut down, and no longer had the crystal mountain water the opportunity to feed and overflow it. The notice of our friend, "All are welcome to the Lotus Pond," was removed, and no longer were the gay companies of children and of men and women seen at the pond. A great change came over everything. On account of the lack of the life-giving water the flowers in the pond wilted, and their long stems lay stretched upon the mud in the bottom. The fish that formerly swam in its clear water soon died and gave an offensive odor to all who came near. The flowers no longer bloomed on its banks. The birds no longer came to drink and to bathe. No longer was heard the hum of the bees; and more, the stream that ran through the fields below dried up, so that the cattle and the flocks no longer got their supply of clear mountain water.

The difference between the spot now and the lotus pond when our friend gave it his careful attention was caused, as we readily see, by the shutting of the gate to the pond, thus preventing the water from the reservoir in the hills which was the source of its life, from entering it. And when this, the source of its life, was shut off, not only was the appearance of the lotus pond entirely changed, but the surrounding fields were deprived of the stream to whose banks the flocks and cattle came for drink.

In this do we not see a complete parallel so far as human life is concerned? In the degree that we recognize our oneness, our connection with the Infinite Spirit which is the life of all, and in the degree that we open ourselves to this divine inflow, do we come into harmony with the highest, the most powerful, and the most beautiful everywhere. And in the degree that we do this do we overflow, so that all who come in contact with us receive the effects of this realization on our part. This is the lotus pond of our friend, he who is in love with all that is truest and best in the universe. And in the degree that we fail to recognize our oneness with this Infinite Source, and so close, shut ourselves to this divine inflow, do we come into that state where there seems to be with us nothing of good, nothing of beauty, nothing of power; and when this is true, those who come in contact with us receive not good, but harm. This is the spot of the lotus pond while the farm was in the hands of a renter.

There is this difference between the lotus pond and your life and mine. It has no power in itself of opening the gate to the inflow of the water from the reservoir which is its source. In regard to this it is helpless and dependent upon an outside agency. You and I have the power, the power within us, to open or to close ourselves to this divine inflow exactly as we choose. This we have through the power of mind, through the operation of thought.

There is the soul life, direct from God. This it is that relates us to the Infinite. There is, then, the physical life. This it is that relates us to the material universe about us. The thought life connects the one with the other. It is this that plays between the two.

Before we proceed farther let us consider very briefly the nature of thought. Thought is not, as is many times supposed, a mere indefinite abstraction, or something of a like nature. It is, on the contrary, a vital, living force, the most vital, subtle, and irresistible force there is in the universe.

In our very laboratory experiments we are demonstrating the great fact that thoughts are forces. They have form, and quality, and substance, and power, and we are beginning to find that there is what we may term a *science of thought*. We are beginning also to find that through the instrumentality of our thought forces we have creative power, not merely in a figurative sense, but creative power in reality.

Everything in the material universe about us, everything the universe has ever known, had its origin first in thought. From this it took its form. Every castle, every statue, every painting, every piece of mechanism, everything had its birth, its origin, first in the mind of the one who formed it before it received its material expression or embodiment. The very universe in which we live is the result of the thought energies of God, the Infinite Spirit that is back of all. And if it is true, as we have found, that we in our true selves are in essence the same, and in this sense are one with the life of this Infinite Spirit, do we not then see that in the degree that we come into a vital realization of this stupendous fact, *we, through the operation of our interior, spiritual, thought forces, have in like sense creative power?*

Everything exists in the unseen before it is manifested or realized in the seen, and in this sense it is true that the unseen things are the real, while the things that are seen are the unreal. The unseen things are *cause*; the seen things are *effect*. The unseen things are the eternal; the seen things are the changing, the transient.

The *"power of the word"* is a literal scientific fact. Through the operation of our thought forces we have creative power. The spoken word is nothing more nor less than the outward expression of the workings of these interior forces. The spoken word is then, in a sense, the means whereby the thought forces are focused and directed along any particular line; and this concentration, this giving them direction, is necessary before any outward or material manifestation of their power can become evident.

Much is said in regard to "building castles in the air," and one who is given to this building is not always looked upon with favor. But castles in the air are always necessary before we can have castles on the ground, before we can have castles in which to live. The trouble with the one who gives himself to building castles in the air is not that he builds them in the air, but that he does not go farther and actualize in life, in character, in material form, the castles he thus builds. He does a part of the work, a very necessary part; but another equally necessary part remains still undone.

There is in connection with the thought forces what we may term, the drawing power of mind, and the great law operating here is one with that great law of the universe, that like attracts like. We are continually attracting to us from both the seen and the unseen side of life, forces and conditions most akin to those of our own thoughts.

This law is continually operating whether we are conscious of it or not. We are all living, so to speak, in a vast ocean of thought, and the very atmosphere around us is continually filled with the thought forces that are being continually sent or that are continually going out in the form of thought waves. We are all affected, more or less, by these thought forces, either consciously or unconsciously; and in the degree that we are more or less sensitively organized, or in the degree that we are negative and so are open to outside influences, rather than positive, thus determining what influences shall enter into our realm of thought, and hence into our lives.

There are those among us who are much more sensitively organized than others. As an organism their bodies are more finely, more sensitively constructed. These, generally speaking, are people who are always more or less affected by the mentalities of those with whom they come in contact, or in whose company they are. A friend, the editor of one of our great journals, is so sensitively organized that it is impossible for him to attend a gathering, such as a reception, talk and shake hands with a number of people during the course of the evening, without taking on to a greater or less extent their various mental and physical conditions. These affect him to such an extent that he is scarcely himself and in his best condition for work until some two or three days afterward.

Some think it unfortunate for one to be sensitively organized. By no means. It is a good thing, for one may thus be more open and receptive to the higher impulses of the soul within, and to all higher forces and influences from without. It may, however be unfortunate and extremely inconvenient to be so organized unless one recognize and gain the power of closing himself, of making himself positive to all detrimental or undesirable influences. This power every one, however sensitively organized he may be, can acquire.

This he can acquire through the mind's action. And, moreover, there is no habit of more value to anyone, be he sensitively or less sensitively organized, than that of occasionally taking and holding himself continually in the attitude of mind—I close myself, I make myself positive to all things below, and open and receptive to all higher influences, to all things above. By taking this attitude of mind consciously now and then, it soon becomes a habit, and if one is deeply in earnest in regard to it, it puts into operation silent but subtle and powerful influences in effecting the desired results. In this way all lower and undesirable influences from both the seen and the unseen side of life are closed out, while all higher influences are invited, and in the degree that they are invited will they enter.

And what do we mean by the unseen side of life? First, the thought forces, the mental and emotional conditions in the atmosphere about us that are generated by those manifesting on the physical plane through the agency of physical bodies. Second, the same forces generated by those who have dropped the physical body, or from whom it has been struck away, and who are now manifesting through the agency of bodies of a different nature.

"The individual existence of man *begins* on the sense plane of the physical world, but rises through successive gradations of ethereal and celestial spheres, corresponding with his ever unfolding deific life and powers, to a destiny of unspeakable grandeur and glory. Within and above every physical planet is a corresponding ethereal planet, or soul world, as within and above every physical organism is a corresponding ethereal organism, or soul body, of which the physical is but the external counterpart and materialized expression. From this etherealized or soul planet, which is the immediate home of our arisen humanity, there rises or deepens in infinite gradations spheres within and above spheres, to celestial heights of spiritualized existence utterly inconceivable to the sense man. Embodiment, accordingly, is two-fold,—the physical being but the temporary husk, so to speak, in and by which the real and permanent ethereal organism is individualized and perfected, somewhat as 'the full corn in the ear' is reached by means of its husk, for which there is no further use. By means of this indestructible ethereal body and the corresponding ethereal spheres of environment with the social life and relations in the spheres, the individuality and personal life is preserved forever."

The fact of life in whatever form means the continuance of life, even though the form be changed. Life is the one eternal principle of the universe and so always continues, even though the form of the agency through which it manifests be changed. "In my Father's house are many mansions." And surely, because the individual has dropped, has gone out of the physical body, there is no evidence at all that the life does not go right on the same as before, not commencing,—for there is no cessation,—but commencing in the other form, exactly where it has left off here; for all life is a continuous evolution, step by step; there one neither skips nor jumps.

There are in the other form, then, mentalities and hence lives of all grades and influences, the same as there are in the physical form. If, then, the great law that like attracts like is ever operating, we are continually attracting to us from this side of life influences and conditions most akin to those of our own thoughts and lives. A grewsome thought that we should be so influenced, says one. By no means, all life is one; we are all bound together in the one common and universal life, and especially not when we take into consideration the fact that we have it entirely in our own hands to determine the order of thought we entertain, and consequently the order of influences we attract, and are not mere willowy creatures of circumstance, unless indeed we choose to be.

In our mental lives we can either keep hold of the rudder and so determine exactly what course we take, what points we touch, or we can fail to do this, and failing, we drift, and are blown hither and thither by every passing breeze. And so, on the contrary, welcome should be the thought, for thus we may draw to us the influence and the aid of the greatest, the noblest, and the best who have lived on the earth, whatever the time, wherever the place.

We cannot rationally believe other than that those who have labored in love and with uplifting power here are still laboring in the same way, and in all probability with more earnest zeal, and with still greater power.

"And Elisha prayed, and said, Lord, I pray thee, open his eyes, that he may see. And the Lord opened the eyes of the young man; and he saw: and, behold, the mountain *was full of horses and chariots of fire* round about Elisha."

While riding with a friend a few days ago, we were speaking of the great interest people are everywhere taking in the more vital things of life, the eagerness with which they are reaching out for a knowledge of the interior forces, their ever increasing desire to know themselves and to know their true relations with the Infinite. And in speaking of the great spiritual awakening that is so rapidly coming all over the world, the beginnings of which we are so clearly seeing during the closing years of this, and whose ever increasing proportions we are to witness during the early years of the coming century, I said, "How beautiful if Emerson, the illumined one so far in advance of his time, who labored so faithfully and so fearlessly to bring about these very conditions, how beautiful if he were with us today to witness it all! how he would rejoice!" "How do we know," was the reply, "that he is not witnessing it all? and more, that he is not having a hand in it all,—a hand even greater, perhaps, than when we *saw* him here?" Thank you, my friend, for this reminder. And, truly, "are they not all ministering spirits sent forth to minister to those who shall be heirs of salvation?"

As science is so abundantly demonstrating today,—the things that we see are but a very small fraction of the things that are. The real, vital forces at work in our own lives and in the world about us

18

are not seen by the ordinary physical eye. Yet they are the causes of which all things we see are merely the effects. Thoughts are forces; like builds like, and like attracts like. For one to govern his thinking, then, is to determine his life.

Says one of deep insight into the nature of things: "The law of correspondences between spiritual and material things is wonderfully exact in its workings. People ruled by the mood of gloom attract to them gloomy things. People always discouraged and despondent do not succeed in anything, and live only by burdening some one else. The hopeful, confident, and cheerful attract the elements of success. A man's front or back yard will advertise that man's ruling mood in the way it is kept. A woman at home shows her state of mind in her dress. A slattern advertises the ruling mood of hopelessness, carelessness, and lack of system. Rags, tatters, and dirt are always in the mind before being on the body. The thought that is most put out brings its corresponding visible element to crystallize about you as surely and literally as the visible bit of copper in solution attracts to it the invisible copper in that solution. A mind always hopeful, confident, courageous, and determined on its set purpose, and keeping itself to that purpose, attracts to itself out of the elements things and powers favorable to that purpose.

"Every thought of yours has a literal value to you in every possible way. The strength of your body, the strength of your mind, your success in business, and the pleasure your company brings others, depends on the nature of your thoughts. . . . In whatever mood you set your mind does your spirit receive of unseen substance in correspondence with that mood. It is as much a chemical law as a spiritual law. Chemistry is not confined to the elements we see. The elements we do not see with the physical eye outnumber ten thousand times those we do see. The Christ injunction, 'Do good to those who hate you,' is based on a scientific fact and a natural law. So, to do good is to bring to yourself all the elements in nature of power and good. To do evil is to bring the contrary destructive elements. When our eyes are opened, self-preservation will make us stop all evil thought. Those who live by hate will die by hate: that is, 'those who live by the sword will die by the sword.' Every evil thought is as a sword drawn on the person to whom it is directed. If a sword is drawn in return, so much the worse for both."

And says another who knows full well whereof he speaks: "The law of attraction works universally on every plane of *action*, and we attract whatever we desire or expect. If we desire one thing and expect another, we become like houses divided against themselves, which are quickly brought to desolation. Determine resolutely to expect only what you desire, then you will attract only what you wish for. . . . Carry any kind of thought you please about with you, and so long as you retain it, no matter how you roam over land or sea, you will unceasingly attract to yourself, knowingly or inadvertently, exactly and only what corresponds to your own dominant quality of thought. Thoughts are our private property, and we can regulate them to suit our taste entirely by steadily recognizing our ability so to do."

We have just spoken of the drawing power of mind. Faith is nothing more nor less than the operation of the *thought forces* in the form of an earnest desire, coupled with expectation as to its fulfillment. And in the degree that faith, the earnest desire thus sent out, is continually held to and watered by firm expectation, in just that degree does it either draw to itself, or does it change from the unseen into the visible, from the spiritual into the material, that for which it is sent.

Let the element of doubt or fear enter in, and what would otherwise be a tremendous force will be so neutralized that it will fail of its realization. Continually held to and continually watered by firm expectation, it becomes a force, a drawing power, that is irresistible and absolute, and the results will be absolute in direct proportion as it is absolute.

We shall find, as we are so rapidly beginning to find today, that the great things said in regard to faith, the great promises made in connection with it, are not mere vague sentimentalities, but are all great scientific facts, and rest upon great immutable laws. Even in our very laboratory experiments we are beginning to discover the laws underlying and governing these forces. We, are now beginning, some at least, to use them understandingly and not blindly, as has so often and so long been the case.

Much is said today in regard to the will. It is many times spoken of as if it were a force in itself. But will is a force, a power, only in so far as it is a particular form of the manifestation of the thought forces; for it is by what we call the "will" that thought is focused and given a particular direction, and in the degree that thought is thus focused and given direction, is it effective in the work it is sent out to accomplish.

In a sense there are two kinds of will,—the human and the divine. The human will is the will of what, for convenience' sake, we may term the lower self. It is the will that finds its life merely in the realm of the mental and the physical,—the sense will. It is the will of the one who is not yet awake to the fact that there is a life that far transcends the life of merely the intellect and the physical senses, and which when realized and lived, does not do away with or minify these, but which, on the contrary, brings them to their highest perfection and to their powers of keenest enjoyment. The divine will is the will of the higher self, the will of the one who recognizes his oneness with the Divine, and who consequently brings his will to work in harmony, in conjunction with the divine will. "The Lord thy God *in the midst of thee* is mighty."

The human will has its limitations. So far and no farther, says the law. The divine will has no limitations. It is supreme. All things are open and subject to you, says the law, and so, in the degree that the human will is transmuted into the divine, in the degree that it comes into harmony with and so, acts in conjunction with the divine, does it become supreme. Then it is that "Thou shalt decree a thing and it shall be established unto thee." The great secret of life and of power, then, is to make and to keep one's conscious connection with this Infinite Source.

The power of every life, the very life itself, is determined by

21

what it relates itself to. God is immanent as well as transcendent. He is creating, working, ruling in the universe today, in your life and in mine, just as much as He ever has been. We are too apt to regard Him after the manner of an absentee landlord, one who has set into operation the forces of this great universe, and then taken Himself away.

In the degree, however, that we recognize Him as immanent as well as transcendent, are we able to partake of His life and power. For in the degree that we recognize Him as the Infinite Spirit of Life and Power that is today, at this very moment, working and manifesting in and through all, and then, in the degree that we come into the realization of our oneness with this life, do we become partakers of, and so do we actualize in ourselves the qualities of His life. *In the degree that we open ourselves to the inflowing tide of this immanent and transcendent life, do we make ourselves channels through which the Infinite Intelligence and Power can work.*

It is through the instrumentality of the mind that we are enabled to connect the real soul life with the physical life, and so enable the soul life to manifest and work through the physical. The thought life needs *continually* to be illumined from within. This illumination can come in just the degree that through the agency of the mind we recognize our oneness with the Divine, of which each soul is an individual form of expression.

This gives us the inner guiding which we call intuition. "Intuition is to the spiritual nature and understanding practically what sense perception is to the sensuous nature and understanding. It is an inner spiritual sense through which man is opened to the direct revelation and knowledge of God, the secrets of nature and life, and through which he is brought into conscious unity and fellowship with God, and made to realize his own deific nature and supremacy of being as the son of God. Spiritual supremacy and illumination thus realized through the development and perfection of intuition under divine inspiration, gives the perfect inner vision and direct insight into the character, properties, and purpose of all things to which the attention and interest are directed. . . . It is, we repeat, a spiritual sense opening inwardly, as the physical senses open outwardly; and because it has the capacity to perceive, grasp, and know the truth at first hand, independent of all external sources of information, we call it intuition. All inspired teaching and spiritual revelations are based upon the recognition of this spiritual faculty of the soul, and its power to receive and appropriate them. . . . Conscious unity of man in spirit and purpose with the Father, born out of his supreme desire and trust, opens his soul through this inner sense to immediate inspiration and enlightenment from the Divine Omniscience, and the co-operative energy of the Divine Omnipotence, under which he becomes a seer and a master.

"On this higher plane of realized spiritual life in the flesh the mind holds the impersonal attitude and acts with unfettered freedom and unbiased vision, grasping truth at first hand, independent of all external sources of information. Approaching all beings and things from the divine side, they are seen in the light of the Divine Omniscience. God's purpose in them, and so the truth concerning them, as it rests in the mind of God, are thus revealed by direct illumination from the Divine Mind, to which the soul is opened inwardly through this spiritual sense we call intuition." Some call it the voice of the soul; some call it the voice of God; some call it the sixth sense. It is our inner spiritual sense.

In the degree that we come into the recognition of our own *true* selves, into the realization of the oneness of our life with the Infinite Life, and in the degree that we open ourselves to this divine inflow, does this voice of intuition, this voice of the soul, this voice of God, speak clearly; and in the degree that we recognize, listen to, and obey it, does it speak ever more clearly, until by-and-by there comes the time when it is unerring, *absolutely unerring*, in its guidance.

23

IV

Fullness Of Life—Bodily Health And Vigor

God is the Spirit of Infinite Life. If we are partakers of this life, and have the power of opening ourselves fully to its divine inflow, it means more, so far as even the physical life is concerned, than we may at first think. For very clearly, the life of this Infinite Spirit, from its very nature, can admit of no disease; and if this is true, no disease can exist in the body where it freely enters, through which it freely flows.

Let us recognize at the outset that, so far as the physical life is concerned, *all life is from within out*. There is an immutable law which says: "As within, so without; cause, effect." In other words, the thought forces, the various mental states and the emotions, all have in time their effects upon the physical body.

Some one says: "I hear a great deal said today in regard to the effects of the mind upon the body, but I don't know as I place very much confidence in this." Don't you? Some one brings you sudden news. You grow pale, you tremble, or perhaps you fall into a faint. It is, however, through the channel of your mind that the news is imparted to you. A friend says something to you, perhaps at the table, something that seems very unkind. You are hurt by it, as we say. You have been enjoying your dinner, but from this moment your appetite is gone. But what was said entered into and affected you through the channel of your mind.

Look! yonder goes a young man, dragging his feet, stumbling

24

over the slightest obstruction in the path. Why is it? Simply that he is weak-minded, an idiot. In other words, *a falling state of mind is productive of a falling condition of the body*. To be sure minded is to be sure footed. To be uncertain in mind is to be uncertain in step.

Again, a sudden emergency arises. You stand trembling and weak with fear. Why are you powerless to move? Why do you tremble? And yet you believe that the mind has but little influence upon the body. You are for a moment dominated by a fit of anger. For a few hours afterwards you complain of a violent headache. And still you do not seem to realize that the thoughts and emotions have an effect upon the body.

A day or two ago, while conversing with a friend, we were speaking of worry. "My father is greatly given to worry," he said. "Your father is not a healthy man," I said. "He is not strong, vigorous, robust, and active." I then went on to describe to him more fully his father's condition and the troubles which afflicted him. He looked at me in surprise and said, "Why, you do not know my father?" "No," I replied. "How then can you describe so accurately the disease with which he is afflicted?" "You have just told me that your father is greatly given to worry. When you told me this you indicated to me cause. In describing your father's condition I simply connected with the cause its own peculiar effects."

Fear and worry have the effect of closing up the channels of the body, so that the life forces flow in a slow and sluggish manner. Hope and tranquillity open the channels of the body, so that the life forces go bounding through it in such a way that disease can rarely get a foothold.

Not long ago a lady was telling a friend of a serious physical trouble. My friend happened to know that between this lady and her sister the most kindly relations did not exist. He listened attentively to her delineation of her troubles, and then, looking her squarely in the face, in a firm but kindly tone said: "Forgive your sister." The woman looked at him in surprise and said: "I can't forgive my sister." "Very well, then," he replied, "keep the stiffness of your joints and your kindred rheumatic troubles."

25

A few weeks later he saw her again. With a light step she came toward him and said: "I took your advice. I saw my sister and forgave her. We have become good friends again, and I don't know how it is, but somehow or other from the very day, as I remember, that we became reconciled, my troubles seemed to grow less, and today there is not a trace of the old difficulties left; and really, my sister and I have become such good friends that now we can scarcely get along without one another." Again we have effect following cause.

We have several well-authenticated cases of the following nature: A mother has been dominated for a few moments by an intense passion of anger, and the child at her breast has died within an hour's time, so poisoned became the mother's milk by virtue of the poisonous secretions of the system while under the domination of this fit of anger. In other cases it has caused severe illness and convulsions.

The following experiment has been tried a number of times by a well-known scientist: Several men have been put into a heated room. Each man has been dominated for a moment by a particular passion of some kind; one by an intense passion of anger, and others by different other passions. The experimenter has taken a drop of perspiration from the body of each of these men, and by means of a careful chemical analysis he has been able to determine the particular passion by which each has been dominated. Practically the same results revealed themselves in the chemical analysis of the saliva of each of the men.

Says a noted American author, an able graduate of one of our greatest medical schools, and one who has studied deeply into the forces that build the body and the forces that tear it down: "The mind is the natural protector of the body. . . . Every thought tends to reproduce itself, and ghastly mental pictures of disease, sensuality, and vice of all sorts, produce scrofula and leprosy in the soul, which reproduces them in the body. Anger changes the chemical properties of the saliva to a poison dangerous to life. It is well known that sudden and violent emotions have not only weakened the heart in a few hours, but have caused death and insanity. It has been discovered by scientists that there is a chemical difference between that sudden cold exudation of a person under a deep sense of guilt and the ordinary perspiration; and the state of the mind can sometimes be determined by chemical analysis of the perspiration of a criminal, which, when brought into contact with selenic acid, produces a distinctive pink color. It is well known that fear has killed thousands of victims; while, on the other hand, *courage is a great invigorator.*

"Anger in the mother may poison a nursing child. Rarey, the celebrated horse-tamer, said that an angry word would sometimes raise the pulse of a horse ten beats in a minute. If this is true of a beast, what can we say of its power upon human beings, especially upon a child? Strong mental emotion often causes vomiting. Extreme anger or fright may produce jaundice. A violent paroxysm of rage has caused apoplexy and death. Indeed, in more than one instance, a single night of mental agony has wrecked a life. Grief, long-standing jealousy, constant care and corroding anxiety sometimes tend to develop insanity. Sick thoughts and discordant moods are the natural atmosphere of disease, and crime is engendered and thrives in the miasma of the mind."

From all this we get the great fact we are scientifically demonstrating today,—that the various mental states, emotions, and passions have their various peculiar effects upon the body, and each induces in turn, if indulged in to any great extent, its own peculiar forms of disease, and these in time become chronic.

Just a word or two in regard to their mode of operation. If a person is dominated for a moment by, say a passion of anger, there is set up in the physical organism what we might justly term a bodily thunder-storm, which has the effect of souring, or rather of corroding, the normal, healthy, and life-giving secretions of the body, so that instead of performing their natural functions they become poisonous and destructive. And if this goes on to any great extent, by virtue of their cumulative influences, they give rise to a particular form of disease, which in turn becomes chronic. So the emotion opposite to this, that of kindliness, love, benevolence, good-will, tends to stimulate a healthy, purifying, and life-giving flow of all the bodily secretions. All the channels of the body seem free and open; the life forces go bounding through them. And these very forces, set into a bounding activity, will in time counteract the poisonous and disease-giving effects of their opposites.

A physician goes to see a patient. He gives no medicine this morning. Yet the very fact of his going makes the patient better. He has carried with him the spirit of health; he has carried brightness of tone and disposition; he has carried hope into the sick chamber; he has left it there. In fact, the very hope and good cheer he has carried with him has taken hold of and has had a subtle but powerful influence upon the mind of the patient; and this mental condition imparted by the physician has in turn its effects upon the patient's body, and so through the instrumentality of this mental suggestion the healing goes on.

> "Know, then, whatever cheerful and serene
> Supports the mind, supports the body, too.
> Hence the most vital movement mortals feel
> Is *hope*; the balm and life-blood of the soul."

We sometimes hear a person in weak health say to another, "I always feel better when you come." There is a deep scientific reason underlying the statement. "The tongue of the wise is health." The power of suggestion so far as the human mind is concerned is a most wonderful and interesting field of study. Most wonderful and powerful forces can be set into operation through this agency. One of the world's most noted scientists, recognized everywhere as one of the most eminent anatomists living, tells us that he has proven from laboratory experiments that the entire human structure can be completely changed, made over, within a period of less than one year, and that some portions can be entirely remade within a period of a very few weeks.

"Do you mean to say," I hear it asked, "that the body can be changed from a diseased to a healthy condition through the operation of the interior forces?" Most certainly; and more, this is the natural method of cure. The method that has as its work the application of drugs, medicines and external agencies is the artificial method. The only thing that any drug or any medicine can do is to remove obstructions, that the life forces may have simply a better chance to do their work. *The real healing process must be performed by the operation of the life forces within.* A surgeon and physician of world-wide fame recently made to his medical associates the following declaration: "For generations past the most important influence that plays upon nutrition, the *life principle* itself, has remained an unconsidered element in the medical profession, and the almost exclusive drift of its studies and remedial paraphernalia has been confined to the action of matter over mind. This has seriously interfered with the evolutionary tendencies of the doctors themselves, and consequently the psychic factor in professional life is still in a rudimentary or comparatively undeveloped state. But the light of the nineteenth century has dawned, and so the march of mankind in general is taken in the direction of the hidden forces of nature. Doctors are now compelled to join the ranks of students in psychology and follow their patrons into the broader field of mental therapeutics. There is no time for lingering, no time for skepticism or doubt or hesitation. *He who lingers is lost, for the entire race is enlisted in the movement.*"

I am aware of the fact that in connection with the matter we are now considering there has been a great deal of foolishness during the past few years. Many absurd and foolish things have been claimed and done; but this says nothing against, and it has absolutely nothing to do with the great underlying laws themselves. The same has been true of the early days of practically every system of ethics or philosophy or religion the world has ever known. But as time has passed, these foolish, absurd things have fallen away, and the great eternal principles have stood out ever more and more clearly defined.

I know *personally* of many cases where an entire and permanent cure has been effected, in some within a remarkably short period of time, through the operation of these forces. Some of them are cases that had been entirely given up by the regular practice, *materia medica*. We have numerous accounts of such cases in all times and in connection with all religions. And why should not the power of effecting such cures exist among us today? The *power does exist,* and it will be actualized in just the degree that we recognize the same great laws that were recognized in times past.

One person may do a very great deal in connection with the healing of another, but this almost invariably implies co-operation on the part of the one who is thus treated. In the cures that Christ performed he most always needed the co-operation of the one who appealed to him. His question almost invariably was, "Dost thou believe?" He thus stimulated into activity the life-giving forces within the one cured. If one is in a very weak condition, or if his nervous system is exhausted, or if his mind through the influence of the disease is not so strong in its workings, it may be well for him for a time to seek the aid and co-operation of another. But it would be far better for such a one could he bring himself to a vital realization of the omnipotence of his own interior powers.

One may cure another, but to be *permanently healed* one must do it himself. In this way another may be most valuable as a teacher by bringing one to a clear realization of the power of the forces within, but in every case, in order to have a permanent cure, the work of the self is necessary. Christ's words were almost invariably,—Go and sin no more, or, thy sins are forgiven thee, thus pointing out the one eternal and never-changing fact,—that all disease and its consequent suffering is the direct or the indirect result of the violation of law, either consciously or unconsciously, either intentionally or unintentionally.

Suffering is designed to continue only so long as sin continues, sin not necessarily in the theological, but always in the philosophical sense, though many times in the sense of both. The moment the violation ceases, the moment one comes into perfect harmony with the law, the cause of the suffering ceases; and though there may be residing within the cumulative effects of past violation, the cause is removed, and consequently there can be no more effects in the form of additions, and even the diseased condition that has been induced from past violation will begin to disappear as soon as the right forces are set into activity.

There is nothing that will more quickly and more completely bring one into harmony with the laws under which he lives than this vital realization of his oneness with the Infinite Spirit, which is the life of all life. In this there can be no disease, and nothing will more readily remove from the organism the obstructions that have accumulated there, or in other words, the disease that resides there, than this full realization and the complete opening of one's self to this divine inflow. "I shall put My spirit in you, and ye shall live."

The moment a person realizes his oneness with the Infinite Spirit he recognizes himself as a spiritual being, and no longer as a mere physical, material being. He then no longer makes the mistake of regarding himself as body, subject to ills and diseases, but he realizes the fact that he is spirit, spirit now as much as he ever will or can be, and that he is the builder and so the master of the body, the house in which he lives; and the moment he thus recognizes his power as master he ceases in any way to allow it the mastery over him. He no longer fears the elements or any of the forces that he now in his ignorance allows to take hold of and affect the body. The moment he realizes his own supremacy, instead of fearing them as he did when he was out of harmony with them, he learns to love them. He thus comes into harmony with them; or rather, he so orders them that they come into harmony with him. He who formerly was the slave has now become the master. The moment we come to love a thing it no longer carries harm for us.

There are almost countless numbers today, weak and suffering in body, who would become strong and healthy if they would only give God an opportunity to do His work. To such I would say, *Don't shut out the divine inflow.* Do anything else rather than this. Open yourselves to it. Invite it. In the degree that you open yourselves to it, its inflowing tide will course through your bodies a force so vital that the old obstructions that are dominating them today will be driven out before it. "My words are life to them that find them, and health to all their flesh."

There is a trough through which a stream of muddy water has been flowing for many days. The dirt has gradually collected on its sides and bottom, and it continues to collect as long as the muddy water flows through it. Change this. Open the trough to a swift-flowing stream of clear, crystal water, and in a very little while even the very dirt that has collected on its sides and bottom will be carried away. The trough will be entirely cleansed. It will present an aspect of beauty and no longer an aspect of ugliness. And more, the water that now courses through it will be of value; it will be an agent of refreshment, of health and of strength to those who use it.

Yes, in just the degree that you realize your oneness with this Infinite Spirit of Life, and thus actualize your latent possibilities and powers, you will exchange dis-ease for ease, inharmony for harmony, suffering and pain for abounding health and strength. And in the degree that you realize this wholeness, this abounding health and strength in yourself, will you carry it to all with whom you come in contact; for *we must remember that health is contagious as well as disease.*

I hear it asked, What can be said in a concrete way in regard to the practical application of these truths, so that one can hold himself in the enjoyment of perfect bodily health; and more, that one may heal himself of any existing disease? In reply, let it be said that the chief thing that can be done is to point out the great underlying principle, and that each individual must make his own application; one person cannot well make this for another.

First let it be said, that the very fact of one's holding the thought of perfect health sets into operation vital forces which will in time be more or less productive of the effect,—perfect health. Then speaking more directly in regard to the great principle itself, from its very nature, it is clear that more can be accomplished through the process of realization than through the process of affirmation, though for some affirmation may be a help, an aid to realization.

In the degree, however, that you come into a vital realization of your oneness with the Infinite Spirit of Life, whence all life in individual form has come and is continually coming, and in the degree that through this realization you open yourself to its divine inflow, do you set into operation forces that will sooner or later bring even the physical body into a state of abounding health and strength. For to realize that this Infinite Spirit of Life can from its very nature admit of no disease, and to realize that this, then, is the life in you, by realizing your oneness with it, you can so open yourself to its more abundant entrance that the diseased bodily conditions—effects—will respond to the influences of its all-perfect power, this either quickly or more tardily, depending entirely upon yourself.

There have been those who have been able to open themselves so fully to this realization that the healing has been instantaneous and permanent. The degree of intensity always eliminates in like degree the element of time. *It must, however, be a calm, quiet, and expectant intensity, rather than an intensity that is fearing, disturbed, and non-expectant.* Then there are others who have come to this realization by degrees.

Many will receive great help, and many will be entirely healed by a practice somewhat after the following nature: With a mind at peace, and with a heart going out in love to all, go into the quiet of your own interior self, holding the thought,—I am one with the Infinite Spirit of Life, the life of my life. I then as spirit, I a spiritual being, can in my own real nature admit of no disease. I now open my body, in which disease has gotten a foothold, I open it fully to the inflowing tide of this Infinite Life, and it now, even now, is pouring in and coursing through my body, and the healing process is going on. Realize this so fully that you begin to feel a quickening and a warming glow imparted by the life forces to the body. Believe the healing process is going on. Believe it, and hold continually to it. Many people greatly desire a certain thing, but expect something else. They have greater faith in the power of evil than in the power of good, and hence remain ill.

If one will give himself to this meditation, realization, treatment, or whatever term it may seem best to use, at stated times, as often as he may choose, and then *continually hold himself in the same attitude of mind*, thus allowing the force to work continually, he will be surprised how rapidly the body will be exchanging conditions of disease and inharmony for health and harmony. There is no particular reason, however, for this surprise, for in this way he is simply allowing the Omnipotent Power to do the work, which will have to do it ultimately in any case.

If there is a local difficulty, and one wants to open this particular portion, in addition to the entire body, to this inflowing life, he can hold this particular portion in thought, for to fix the thought in this way upon any particular portion of the body stimulates or increases the flow of the life forces in that portion. It must always be borne in mind, however, that whatever healing may be thus accomplished, effects will not permanently cease until causes have been removed. In other words, *as long as there is the violation of law, so long disease and suffering will result.*

This realization that we are considering will have an influence not only where there is a diseased condition of the body, but even where there is not this condition it will give an increased bodily life, vigor, and power.

We have had many cases, in all times and in all countries, of healing through the operation of the interior forces, entirely independent of external agencies. Various have been the methods, or rather, various have been the names applied to them, but the great law underlying all is one and the same, and the same today. When the Master sent his followers forth, his injunction to them was to heal the sick and the afflicted, as well as to teach the people. The early church fathers had the power of healing, in short, it was a part of their work.

And why should we not have the power today, the same as they had it then? Are the laws at all different? Identically the same. Why, then? Simply because, with a few rare exceptions here and there, we are unable to get beyond the mere letter of the law into its real vital spirit and power. It is the letter that killeth, it is the spirit that giveth life and power. Every soul who becomes so individualized that he breaks through the mere letter and enters into the real vital spirit, *will have the power*, as have all who have gone before, and when he does, he will also be the means of imparting it to others, for he will be one who will move and who will speak with authority.

We are rapidly finding today, and we shall find even more and more, as time passes, that practically all disease, with its consequent suffering, has its origin in perverted mental and emotional states and conditions. *The mental attitude we take toward anything determines to a greater or less extent its effects upon us.* If we fear it, or if we antagonize it, the chances are that it will have detrimental or even disastrous effects upon us. If we come into harmony with it by quietly recognizing and inwardly asserting our superiority over it, in the degree that we are able successfully to do this, in that degree will it carry with it no injury for us.

No disease can enter into or take hold of our bodies unless it find therein something corresponding to itself which makes it possible. And in the same way, no evil or undesirable condition of any kind can come into our lives unless there is already in them that which invites it and so makes it possible for it to come. The sooner we begin to look within ourselves for the cause of whatever comes to us, the better it will be, for so much the sooner will we begin to make conditions within ourselves such that only *good* may enter.

We, who from our very natures should be masters of all conditions, by virtue of our ignorance are mastered by almost numberless conditions of every description.

Do I fear a draft? There is nothing in the draft—a little purifying current of God's pure air—to cause me trouble, to bring on a cold, perhaps an illness. The draft can affect me only in the degree that *I myself* make it possible, only in the degree that I allow it to affect me. We must distinguish between causes and mere occasions. The draft is not cause, nor does it carry cause with it.

Two persons are sitting in the same draft. The one is injuriously affected by it, the other experiences not even an inconvenience, but he rather enjoys it. The one is a creature of circumstances; he fears the draft, cringes before it, continually thinks of the harm it is doing him. In other words, he opens every avenue for it to enter and take hold of him, and so it—harmless and beneficent in itself—brings to him exactly what he has empowered it to bring. The other recognizes himself as the master over and not the creature of circumstances. He is not concerned about the draft. He puts himself into harmony with it, makes himself positive to it, and instead of experiencing any discomfort, he enjoys it, and in addition to its doing him a service by bringing the pure fresh air from without to him, it does him the additional service of hardening him even more to any future conditions of a like nature. But if the draft was cause, it would bring the same results to both. The fact that it does not, shows that it is not a cause, but a condition, and it brings to each, effects which correspond to the conditions it finds within each.

Poor draft! How many thousands, nay millions of times it is made the scapegoat by those who are too ignorant or too unfair to look their own weaknesses square in the face, and who instead of becoming imperial masters, remain cringing slaves. Think of it, what it means! A man created in the image of the eternal God, sharer of His life and power, born to have dominion, fearing, shaking, cringing before a little draft of pure life-giving air. But scapegoats are convenient things, even if the only thing they do for us is to aid us in our constant efforts at self-delusion.

The best way to disarm a draft of the bad effects it has been accustomed to bring one, is first to bring about a pure and healthy set of conditions within, then, to change one's mental attitude toward it. Recognize the fact that of itself it has no power, it has only the power you invest it with. Thus you will put yourself into harmony with it, and will no longer sit in fear of it. Then sit in a draft a few times and get hardened to it, as every one, by going at it judiciously, can readily do. "But suppose one is in delicate health, or especially subject to drafts?" Then be simply a little judicious at first; don't seek the strongest that can be found, especially if you do not as yet in your own mind feel equal to it, for if you do not, it signifies that you still fear it. That supreme regulator of all life, *good common sense*, must be used here, the same as elsewhere.

If we are born to have dominion, and that we are is demonstrated by the fact that some have attained to it,—and what one *has* done, soon or late all *can* do,—then it is not necessary that we live under the domination of any physical agent. In the degree that we recognize our own interior powers, then are we rulers and able to dictate; in the degree that we fail to recognize them, we are slaves, and are dictated to. We build whatever we find within us; we attract whatever comes to us, and all in accordance with spiritual law, for all natural law is spiritual law.

The whole of human life is cause and effect; there is no such thing in it as chance, nor is there even in all the wide universe. Are we not satisfied with whatever comes into our lives? The thing to do, then, is not to spend time in railing against the imaginary something we create and call fate, but to look to the within, and change the causes at work there, in order that things of a different nature may come, for there will come exactly what we cause to come. This is true not only of the physical body, but of all phases and conditions of life. We invite whatever comes, and did we not invite it, either consciously or unconsciously, it could not and it would not come. This may undoubtedly be hard for some to believe, or even to see, at first. But in the degree that one candidly and open-mindedly looks at it, and then studies into the silent, but subtle and, so to speak, omnipotent workings of the thought forces, and as he traces their effects within him and about him, it becomes clearly evident, and easy to understand.

And then whatever does come to one depends for its effects entirely upon his mental attitude toward it. Does this or that occurrence or condition cause you annoyance? Very well; it causes you annoyance, and so disturbs your peace merely because you allow it to. You are born to have absolute control over your own dominion, but if you voluntarily hand over this power, even if for a little while, to some one or to some thing else, then you of course, become the creature, the one controlled.

To live undisturbed by passing occurrences you must first find your own centre. You must then be firm in your own centre, and so rule the world from within. He who does not himself condition circumstances allows the process to be reversed, and becomes a conditioned circumstance. Find your centre and live in it. Surrender it to no person, to no thing. In the degree that you do this will you find yourself growing stronger and stronger in it. And how can one find his centre? By realizing his oneness with the Infinite Power, and by living continually in this realization.

But if you do not rule from your own centre, if you invest this or that with the power of bringing you annoyance, or evil, or harm, then take what it brings, but cease your railings against the eternal goodness and beneficence of all things.

> "I swear the earth shall surely be complete
> To him or her who shall be complete;
> The earth remains jagged and broken
> Only to him who remains jagged and broken."

If the windows of your soul are dirty and streaked, covered with matter foreign to them, then the world as you look out of them will be to you dirty and streaked and out of order. Cease your complainings, however; keep your pessimism, your "poor, unfortunate me" to yourself, lest you betray the fact that your windows are badly in need of something. But know that your friend, who keeps his windows clean, that the Eternal Sun may illumine all within and make visible all without,—know that he lives in a different world from yours.

Then, go wash your windows, and instead of longing for some other world, you will discover the wonderful beauties of this world; and if you don't find transcendent beauties on every hand here, the chances are that you will never find them anywhere.

"The poem hangs on the berry-bush
When comes the poet's eye,
And the whole street is a masquerade
When Shakspeare passes by."

This same Shakspeare, whose mere passing causes all this commotion, is the one who put into the mouth of one of his creations the words: "The fault, dear Brutus, is not in our stars, but in ourselves, that we are underlings." And the great work of his own life is right good evidence that he realized full well the truth of the facts we are considering. And again he gave us a great truth in keeping with what we are considering when he said:

"Our doubts are traitors,
And make us lose the good we oft might win
By *fearing* to attempt."

There is probably no agent that brings us more undesirable conditions than fear. We should live in fear of nothing, nor will we when we come fully to know ourselves. An old French proverb runs

"Some of your griefs you have cured,
And the sharpest you still have survived;
But what *torments of pain* you endured
From evils that never arrived."

Fear and lack of faith go hand in hand. The one is born of the other. Tell me how much one is given to fear, and I will tell you how much he lacks in faith. Fear is a most expensive guest to entertain, the same as worry is: so expensive are they that no one can afford to entertain them. *We invite what we fear, the same as, by a different attitude of mind, we invite and attract the influences and conditions we desire.* The mind dominated by fear opens the door for the entrance of the very things, for the actualization of the very conditions it fears.

"Where are you going?" asked an Eastern pilgrim on meeting the plague one day. "I am going to Bagdad to kill five thousand people," was the reply. A few days later the same pilgrim met the plague returning. "You told me you were going to Bagdad to kill five thousand people," said he, "but instead, you killed fifty thousand." "No," said the plague. "*I killed only five thousand*, as I told you I would; *the others died of fright.*"

Fear can paralyze every muscle in the body. Fear affects the flow of the blood, likewise the normal and healthy action of all the life forces. Fear can make the body rigid, motionless, and powerless to move.

Not only do we attract to ourselves the things we fear, but we also aid in attracting to others the conditions we in our own minds hold them in fear of. This we do in proportion to the strength of our own thought, and in the degree that they are sensitively organized and so influenced by our thought, and this, although it be unconscious both on their part and on ours.

Children, and especially when very young, are, generally speaking, more sensitive to their surrounding influences than grown people are. Some are veritable little sensitive plates, registering the influences about them, and embodying them as they grow. How careful in their prevailing mental states then should be those who have them in charge, and especially how careful should a mother be during the time she is carrying the child, and when every thought, every mental as well as emotional state has its direct influence upon the life of the unborn child. Let parents be careful how they hold a child, either younger or older, in the thought of fear. This is many times done, unwittingly on their part, through anxiety, and at times through what might well be termed over-care, which is fully as bad as under-care.

I know of a number of cases where a child has been so continually held in the thought of fear lest this or that condition come upon him, that the very things that were feared have been drawn to him, which probably otherwise never would have come at all. Many times there has been no adequate basis for the fear. In case there is a basis, then far wiser is it to take exactly the opposite attitude, so as to neutralize the force at work, and then to hold the child in the thought of wisdom and strength that it may be able to meet the condition and master it, instead of being mastered by it.

But a day or two ago a friend was telling me of an experience of his own life in this connection. At a period when he was having a terrific struggle with a certain habit, he was so continually held in the thought of fear by his mother and the young lady to whom he was engaged,—the engagement to be consummated at the end of a certain period, the time depending on his proving his mastery,— that he, very sensitively organized, *continually* felt the depressing and weakening effects of their negative thoughts. He could always tell exactly how they felt toward him; he was continually influenced and weakened by their fear, by their questionings, by their suspicions, all of which had the effect of lessening the sense of his own power, all of which had an endeavor-paralyzing influence upon him. And so instead of their begetting courage and strength in him, they brought him to a still greater realization of his own weakness and the almost worthless use of struggle.

Here were two who loved him dearly, and who would have done anything and everything to help him gain the mastery, but who, ignorant of the silent, subtle, ever-working and all-telling power of the
thought forces, instead of imparting to him courage, instead of adding to his strength, disarmed him of this, and then added an additional weakness from without. In this way the battle for him was made harder in a three-fold degree.

Fear and worry and all kindred mental states are too expensive for any person, man, woman, or child, to entertain or indulge in. Fear paralyzes healthy action, worry corrodes and pulls down the organism, and will finally tear it to pieces. Nothing is to be gained by it, but everything to be lost. Long-continued grief at any loss will do the same. Each brings its own peculiar type of ailment. An inordinate love of gain, a close-fisted, hoarding disposition will have kindred effects. Anger, jealousy, malice, continual fault-finding, lust, has each its own peculiar corroding, weakening, tearing-down effects.

We shall find that not only are happiness and prosperity con-
comitants of righteousness,—living in harmony with the higher
laws, but bodily health as well. The great Hebrew seer enunciated
a wonderful chemistry of life when he said,—"As righteousness
tendeth to life, so he that pursueth evil, pursueth it to his own
death." On the other hand, "In the way of righteousness is life;
and in the pathway thereof there is no death." The time will come
when it will be seen that this means far more than most people
dare *even to think as yet.* "It rests with man to say whether his soul
shall be housed in a stately mansion of ever-growing splendor and
beauty, or in a hovel of his own building,—a hovel at last ruined
and abandoned to decay."

The bodies of almost untold numbers, living their one-sided,
unbalanced lives, are every year, through these influences, weakening and falling by the wayside long before their time. Poor, poor
houses! Intended to be beautiful temples, brought to desolation
by their ignorant, reckless, deluded tenants. Poor houses!

A close observer, a careful student of the power of the thought
forces, will soon be able to read in the voice, in the movements, in
the features, the effects registered by the prevailing mental states
and conditions. Or, if he is told the prevailing mental states and
conditions, he can describe the voice, the movements, the features,
as well as describe, in a general way, the peculiar physical ailments
their possessor is heir to.

We are told by good authority that a study of the human body,
its structure, and the length of time it takes it to come to maturity,
in comparison with the time it takes the bodies of various animals
and their corresponding longevity, reveals the fact that its natural
age should be nearer a hundred and twenty years than what we
commonly find it today. But think of the multitudes all about us
whose bodies are aging, weakening, breaking, so that they have
to abandon them long before they reach what ought to be a long
period of strong, vigorous middle life.

Then, the natural length of life being thus shortened, it comes
to be what we might term a race belief that this shortened period

is the natural period. And as a consequence many, when they approach a certain age, seeing that as a rule people at this period of life begin to show signs of age, to break and go down hill as we say, they, thinking it a matter of course and that it must be the same with them, by taking this attitude of mind, many times bring upon themselves these very conditions long before it is necessary. Subtle and powerful are the influences of the mind in the building and rebuilding of the body. As we understand them better it may become the custom for people to look forward with pleasure to the teens of their second century.

There comes to mind at this moment a friend, a lady well on to eighty years of age. An old lady, some, most people in fact, would call her, especially those who measure age by the number of the seasons that have come and gone since one's birth. But to call our friend old, would be to call black white. She is no older than a girl of twenty-five, and indeed younger, I am glad to say, or I am sorry to say, depending upon the point of view, than *many* a girl of this age. Seeking for the good in all people and in all things, she has found the good everywhere. The brightness of disposition and of voice that is hers today, that attracts all people to her and that makes her so beautifully attractive to all people, has characterized her all through life. It has in turn carried brightness and hope and courage and strength to hundreds and thousands of people through all these years, and will continue to do so, apparently, for many years yet to come.

No fears, no worryings, no hatreds, no jealousies, no sorrowings, no grievings, no sordid graspings after inordinant [Transcriber's note: inordinate?] gain, have found entrance into her realm of thought. As a consequence her mind, free from these abnormal states and conditions, has not externalized in her body the various physical ailments that the great majority of people are lugging about with them, thinking in their ignorance, that they are natural, and that it is all in accordance with the "eternal order of things" that they should have them. Her life has been one of varied experiences, so that all these things would have found ready entrance into the

realm of her mind and so into her life were she ignorant enough
to allow them entrance. On the contrary she has been wise enough
to recognize the fact that in one kingdom at least she is ruler,—
the kingdom of her mind, and that it is hers to dictate as to what
shall and what shall not enter there. She knows, moreover, that in
determining this she is determining all the conditions of her life.
It is indeed a pleasure as well as an inspiration to see her as she
goes here and there, to see her sunny disposition, her youthful
step, to hear her joyous laughter. Indeed and in truth, Shakspeare
knew whereof he spoke when he said,—"It is the mind that makes
the body rich."

With great pleasure I watched her but recently as she was walking along the street, stopping to have a word and so a part in the
lives of a group of children at play by the wayside, hastening her
step a little to have a word with a washerwoman toting her bundle
of clothes, stopping for a word with a laboring man returning with
dinner pail in hand from his work, returning the recognition from
the lady in her carriage, and so imparting some of her own rich
life to all with whom she came in contact.

And as good fortune would have it, while still watching her,
an old lady passed her,—really old, this one, though at least ten
or fifteen years younger, so far as the count by the seasons is
concerned. Nevertheless she was bent in form and apparently stiff
in joint and muscle. Silent in mood, she wore a countenance of
long-faced sadness, which was intensified surely several fold by
a black, sombre headgear with an immense heavy veil still more
sombre looking if possible. Her entire dress was of this description.
By this relic-of-barbarism garb, combined with her own mood and
expression, she continually proclaimed to the world two things,—
her own personal sorrows and woes, which by this very method
she kept continually fresh in her mind, and also her lack of faith
in the eternal goodness of things, her lack of faith in the love and
eternal goodness of the Infinite Father.

Wrapped only in the thoughts of her own ailments, and sorrows,
and woes, she received and she gave nothing of joy, nothing of

hope, nothing of courage, nothing of value to those whom she passed or with whom she came in contact. But on the contrary she suggested to all and helped to intensify in many, those mental states all too prevalent in our common human life. And as she passed our friend one could notice a slight turn of the head which, coupled with the expression in her face, seemed to indicate this as her thought,—Your dress and your conduct are not wholly in keeping with a lady of your years. Thank God, then, thank God they are not. And may He in His great goodness and love send us an innumerable company of the same rare type; and may they live a thousand years to bless mankind, to impart the life-giving influences of their own royal lives to the numerous ones all about us who stand so much in need of them.

Would you remain always young, and would you carry all the joyousness and buoyancy of youth into your maturer years? Then have care concerning but one thing,—how you live in your thought world. This will determine all. It was the inspired one, Gautama, the Buddha, who said,—"The mind is everything; what you think you become." And the same thing had Ruskin in mind when he said,—"Make yourself nests of pleasant thoughts. None of us as yet know, for none of us have been taught in early youth, what fairy palaces we may build of beautiful thought,—*proof against all adversity.*"

And would you have in your body all the elasticity, all the strength, all the beauty of your younger years? Then live these in your mind, making no room for unclean thought, and you will externalize them in your body. In the degree that you keep young in thought will you remain young in body. And you will find that your body will in turn aid your mind, for body helps mind the same as mind builds body.

You are continually building, and so externalizing in your body conditions most akin to the thoughts and emotions you entertain. And not only are you so building from within, but you are also continually drawing from without, forces of a kindred nature. Your particular kind of thought connects you with a similar order of thought from without. If it is bright, hopeful, cheerful, you connect yourself with a current of thought of this nature. If it is sad, fearing, despondent, then this is the order of thought you connect yourself with.

If the latter is the order of your thought, then perhaps unconsciously and by degrees you have been connecting yourself with it. You need to go back and pick up again a part of your child nature, with its careless and cheerful type of thought. "The minds of the group of children at play are unconsciously concentrated in drawing to their bodies a current of playful thought. Place a child by itself, deprive it of its companions, and soon it will mope and become slow of movement. It is cut off from that peculiar thought current and is literally 'out of its element.'

"You need to bring again this current of playful thought to you which has gradually been turned off. You are too serious or sad, or absorbed in the serious affairs of life. You can be playful and cheerful without being puerile or silly. You can carry on business all the better for being in the playful mood when your mind is off your business. There is nothing but ill resulting from the permanent mood of sadness and seriousness,—the mood which by many so long maintained makes it actually difficult for them to smile at all.

"At eighteen or twenty you commenced growing out of the more playful tendency of early youth. You took hold of the more serious side of life. You went into some business. You became more or less involved in its cares, perplexities and responsibilities. Or, as man or woman, you entered on some phase of life involving care or trouble. Or you became absorbed in some game of business which, as you followed it, left no time for play. Then as you associated with older people you absorbed their old ideas, their mechanical methods of thinking, their acceptance of errors without question or thought of question. In all this you opened your mind to a heavy, care-laden current of thought. Into this you glided unconsciously. That thought is materialized in your blood and flesh. The seen of your body is a deposit or crystallization of the unseen element ever flowing to your body from your mind. Years pass on and you find that your movements are stiff and cumbrous,—that you can with difficulty climb a tree, as at fourteen. Your mind has all this time been sending to your body these heavy, inelastic elements, making your body what now it is. . . .

"Your change for the better must be gradual, and can only be accomplished by bringing the thought current of an all-round symmetrical strength to bear on it,—by demanding of the Supreme Power to be led in the best way, by diverting your mind from the many unhealthy thoughts which habitually have been flowing into it without your knowing it, to healthier ones. . . .

"Like the beast, the bodies of those of our race have in the past weakened and decayed. This will not always be. Increase of spiritual knowledge will show the cause of such decay, and will show, also, how to take advantage of a Law or Force to build us up, renew ever the body and give it greater and greater strength, instead of blindly using that Law or Force, as has been done in the past, to weaken our bodies and finally destroy them."

Full, rich, and abounding health is the normal and the natural condition of life. Anything else is an abnormal condition, and abnormal conditions as a rule come through perversions. God never created sickness, suffering, and disease; they are man's own creations. They come through his violating the laws under which he lives. So used are we to seeing them that we come gradually, if not to think of them as natural, then to look upon them as a matter of course.

The time will come when the work of the physician will not be to treat and attempt to heal the body, but to heal the mind, which in turn will heal the body. In other words, the true physician will be a teacher; his work will be to keep people well, instead of attempting to make them well after sickness and disease comes on; and still beyond this there will come a time when each will be his own physician. In the degree that we live in harmony with the higher laws of our being, and so, in the degree that we become better acquainted with the powers of the mind and spirit, will we give less attention to the body,—no less *care*, but less *attention*.

The bodies of thousands today would be much better cared for if their owners gave them less thought and attention. As a rule, those who think least of their bodies enjoy the best health. Many are kept in continual ill health by the abnormal thought and attention they give them.

Give the body the nourishment, the exercise, the fresh air, the sunlight it requires, keep it clean, and then think of it as little as possible. In your thoughts and in your conversation never dwell upon the negative side. Don't talk of sickness and disease. By talking of these you do yourself harm and you do harm to those who listen to you. Talk of those things that will make people the better for listening to you. Thus you will infect them with health and strength and not with weakness and disease.

To dwell upon the negative side is always destructive. This is true of the body the same as it is true of all other things. The following from one whose thorough training as a physician has been supplemented by extensive study and observations along the lines of the powers of the interior forces, are of special significance and value in this connection: "We can never gain health by contemplating disease, any more than we can reach perfection by dwelling upon imperfection, or harmony through discord. We should keep a high ideal of health and harmony constantly before the mind. . . .

"Never affirm or repeat about your health what you do not wish to be true. Do not dwell upon your ailments, nor study your symptoms. Never allow yourself to be convinced that you are not complete master of yourself. Stoutly affirm your superiority over bodily ills, and do not acknowledge yourself the slave of any inferior power. . . . I would teach children early to build a strong barrier between themselves and disease, by healthy habits of thought, high thinking, and purity of life. I would teach them to expel all thoughts of death, all images of disease, all discordant emotions, like hatred, malice, revenge, envy, and sensuality, as they would banish a temptation to do evil. I would teach them that

48

bad food, bad drink, or bad air makes bad blood; that bad blood makes bad tissue, and bad flesh bad morals. I would teach them that healthy thoughts are as essential to healthy bodies as pure thoughts to a clean life. I would teach them to cultivate a strong will power, and to brace themselves against life's enemies in every possible way. I would teach the sick to have hope, confidence, cheer. Our thoughts and imaginations are the only real limits to our possibilities. No man's success or health will ever reach beyond his own confidence; as a rule, we erect our own barriers.

"Like produces like the universe through. Hatred, envy, malice, jealousy, and revenge all have children. Every bad thought breeds others, and each of these goes on and on, ever reproducing itself, until our world is peopled with their offspring. The true physician and parent of the future will not medicate the body with drugs so much as the mind with principles. The coming mother will teach her child to assuage the fever of anger, hatred, malice, with the great panacea of the world,—Love. The coming physician will teach the people to cultivate cheerfulness, good-will, and noble deeds for a health tonic as well as a heart tonic; and that a merry heart doeth good like a medicine."

The health of your body, the same as the health and strength of your mind, depends upon what you relate yourself with. This Infinite Spirit of Life, this Source of all Life, can from its very nature, we have found, admit of no weakness, no disease. Come then into the full, conscious, vital realization of your oneness with this Infinite Life, open yourself to its more abundant entrance, and full and ever-renewing bodily health and strength will be yours.

> "And good may ever conquer ill,
> Health walk where pain has trod;
> 'As a man thinketh, so is he,'
> Rise, then, and think with God."

The whole matter may then be summed up in the one sentence, "God is well and so are you." You must awaken to the knowledge of your *real being*. When this awakening comes, you will have, and you will see that you have, the power to determine what conditions are externalized in your body. You must recognize, you must realize yourself as one with Infinite Spirit. God's will is then your will; your will is God's will, and "with God all things are possible." When we are able to do away with all sense of separateness by living continually in the realization of this oneness, not only will our bodily ills and weaknesses vanish, but all limitations along all lines.

Then "delight thyself in the Lord, and He shall give thee the desires of thine heart." Then will you feel like crying all the day long, "The lines are fallen unto me in pleasant places; yea, I have a goodly heritage." Drop out of mind your belief in good things and good events coming to you in the future. Come *now* into the real life, and coming, appropriate and actualize them *now*. Remember that only the best is good enough for one with a heritage so royal as yours.

> "We buy ashes for bread;
> We buy diluted wine;
> Give me the true,—
> Whose ample leaves and tendrils curled
> Among the silver hills of heaven,
> Draw everlasting dew."

V

The Secret, Power, And Effects Of Love

This is the Spirit of Infinite Love. The moment we recognize ourselves as one with it we become so filled with love that we see only the good in all. And when we realize that we are all one with this Infinite Spirit, then we realize that in a sense we are all one with each other. When we come into a recognition of this fact, we can then do no harm to any one, to any thing. We find that we are all members of the one great body, and that no portion of the body can be harmed without all the other portions suffering thereby.

When we fully realize the great fact of the oneness of all life,— that all are partakers from this one Infinite Source, and so that the same life is the life in each individual, then prejudices go and hatreds cease. Love grows and reigns supreme. Then, wherever we go, whenever we come in contact with the fellow-man, we are able to recognize the God within. We thus look only for the good, and we find it. It always pays.

There is a deep scientific fact underlying the great truth, "He that takes the sword shall perish by the sword." The moment we come into a realization of the subtle powers of the thought forces, we can quickly see that the moment we entertain any thoughts of hatred toward another, he gets the effects of these diabolical forces that go out from us, and has the same thoughts of hatred aroused in him, which in turn return to the sender. Then when we understand the effects of the passion, hatred or anger, even upon the physical body, we can see how detrimental, how expensive this is. The same is true in regard to all kindred thoughts or passions, envy, criticism, jealousy, scorn. In the ultimate we shall find that in entertaining feelings of this nature toward another, we always suffer far more than the one toward whom we entertain them.

And then when we fully realize the fact that selfishness is at the root of all error, sin, and crime, and that ignorance is the basis of all selfishness, with what charity we come to look upon the acts of all. It is the ignorant man who seeks his own ends at the expense of the greater whole. It is the ignorant man, therefore, who is the selfish man. The truly wise man is never selfish. He is a seer, and recognizes the fact that he, a single member of the one great body, is benefited in just the degree that the entire body is benefited, and so he seeks nothing for himself that he would not equally seek for all mankind.

If selfishness is at the bottom of all error, sin, and crime, and ignorance is the basis of all selfishness, then when we see a manifestation of either of these qualities, if we are true to the highest within us, we will look for and will seek to call forth the good in each individual with whom we come in contact. When God speaks to God, then God responds, and shows forth as God. But when devil speaks to devil, then devil responds, and the devil is always to pay.

I sometimes hear a person say, "I don't see any good in him." No? Then you are no seer. Look deeper and you will find the very God in every human soul. But remember it takes a God to recognize a God. Christ always spoke to the highest, the truest, and the best in men. He knew and he recognized the God in each because he had first realized it in himself. He ate with publicans and sinners. Abominable, the Scribes and Pharisees said. They were so wrapped up in their own conceits, their own self-centredness, hence their own ignorance, that they had never found the God in themselves, and so they never dreamed that it was the real life of even publicans and sinners.

In the degree that we hold a person in the thought of evil or of error, do we suggest evil and error to him. In the degree that he is sensitively organized, or not well individualized, and so, subject to the suggestions of the thought forces from others, will he be influenced; and so in this way we may be sharers in the very evildoing in which we hold another in thought. In the same way when we hold a person in the thought of the right, the good, and the true, righteousness, goodness, and truth are suggested to him, and thus we have a most beneficent influence on his life and conduct. If our hearts go out in love to all with whom we come in contact, we inspire love, and the same ennobling and warming influences of love always return to us from those in whom we inspire them. There is a deep scientific principle underlying the precept—If you would have all the world love you, you must first love all the world.

In the degree that we love will we be loved. Thoughts are forces. Each creates of its kind. Each comes back laden with the effect that corresponds to itself and of which it is the cause.

> "Then let your secret thoughts be fair—
> They have a vital part, and share
> In shaping words and moulding fate;
> God's system is so intricate."

I know of no better practice than that of a friend who continually holds himself in an attitude of mind that he continually sends out his love in the form of the thought,—"Dear everybody, I love you." And when we realize the fact that a thought invariably produces its effect before it returns, or before it ceases, we can see how he is continually breathing out a blessing not only upon all with whom he comes in contact, but upon all the world. These same thoughts of love, moreover, tokened in various ways, are continually coming to him from all quarters.

Even animals feel the effects of these forces. Some animals are much more sensitively organized than many people are, and consequently they get the effects of our thoughts, our mental states, and emotions much more readily than many people do.

Therefore whenever we meet an animal we can do it good by sending out to it these thoughts of love. It will feel the effects whether we simply entertain or whether we voice them. And it is often interesting to note how quickly it responds, and how readily it gives evidence of its appreciation of this love and consideration on our part.

What a privilege and how enjoyable it would be to live and walk in a world where we meet only Gods. In such a world you can live. In such a world I can live. For in the degree that we come into this higher realization do we see only the God in each human soul; and when we are thus able to see Him in every one we meet, we then live in such a world.

And when we thus recognize the God in every one, we by this recognition help to call it forth ever more and more. What a privilege,—this privilege of yours, this privilege of mine! That hypocritical judging of another is something then with which we can have nothing to do; for we have the power of looking beyond the evolving, changing, error-making self, and seeing the real, the changeless, the eternal self which by and by will show forth in the full beauty of holiness. We are then large enough also to realize the fact that when we condemn another, by that very act we condemn ourselves.

This realization so fills us with love that we continually overflow it, and all with whom we come in contact feel its warming and life-giving power. These in turn send back the same feelings of love to us, and so we continually attract love from all quarters. Tell me how much one loves and I will tell you how much he has seen of God. Tell me how much he loves and I will tell you how much he lives with God. Tell me how much he loves and I will tell you how far into the Kingdom of Heaven,—the kingdom of harmony, he has entered, for "love is the fulfilling of the law."

And in a sense love is everything. It is the key to life, and its influences are those that move the world. Live only in the thought of love for all and you will draw love to you from all. Live in the thought of malice or hatred, and malice and hatred will come back to you.

"For evil poisons; malice shafts
Like boomerangs return,
Inflicting wounds that will not heal
While rage and anger burn."

Every thought you entertain is a force that goes out, and every thought comes back laden with its kind. This is an immutable law. Every thought you entertain has moreover a direct effect upon your body. Love and its kindred emotions are the normal and the natural, those in accordance with the eternal order of the universe, for "God is love." These have a life-giving, health-engendering influence upon your body, besides beautifying your countenance, enriching your voice, and making you ever more attractive in every way. And as it is true that in the degree that you hold thoughts of love for all, you call the same from them in return, and as these have a direct effect upon your mind, and through your mind upon your body, it is as so much life force added to your own from without. You are then continually building this into both your mental and your physical life, and so your life is enriched by its influence.

Hatred and all its kindred emotions are the unnatural, the abnormal, the perversions, and so, out of harmony with the eternal order of the universe. For if love is the fulfilling of the law, then these, its opposites, are direct violations of law, and there can never be a violation of law without its attendant pain and suffering in one form or another. There is no escape from this. And what is the result of this particular form of violation? When you allow thoughts of anger, hatred, malice, jealousy, envy, criticism, or scorn to exercise sway, they have a corroding and poisoning effect upon the organism; they pull it down, and if allowed to continue will eventually tear it to pieces by externalizing themselves in the particular forms of disease they give rise to. And then in addition to the destructive influences from your own mind you are continually calling the same influences from other minds, and these come as destructive forces augmenting your own, thus aiding in the tearing down process.

And so love inspires love; hatred breeds hatred. Love and good will stimulate and build up the body; hatred and malice corrode and tear it down. Love is a savor of life unto life; hatred is a savor of death unto death.

> "There are loyal hearts, there are spirits brave,
> There are souls that are pure and true;
> Then give to the world the best you have,
> And the best will come back to you.
>
> "Give love, and love to *your* heart will flow,
> A strength in your utmost need;
> Have faith, and a score of hearts will show
> Their faith in *your* word and deed."

I hear it said,—How in regard to one who bears me hatred, towards whom I have entertained no such thoughts and feelings, and so have not been the cause of his becoming my enemy? This may be true, but the chances are that you will have but few enemies if there is nothing of an antagonistic nature in your own mind and heart. Be sure there is nothing of this nature. But if hatred should come from another without apparent cause on your part, then meet it from first to last with thoughts of love and good-will. In this way you can, so to speak, so neutralize its effects that it cannot reach you and so cannot harm you. Love is positive, and stronger than hatred. Hatred can always be conquered by love.

On the other hand, if you meet hatred with hatred, you simply intensify it. You add fuel to the flame already kindled, upon which it will feed and grow, and so you increase and intensify the evil conditions. Nothing is to be gained by it, everything is to be lost. By sending love for hatred you will be able so to neutralize it that it will not only have no effect upon you, but will not be able even to reach you. But more than this, you will by this course sooner or later be able literally to transmute the enemy into the friend. Meet hatred with hatred and you degrade yourself. Meet hatred with love and you elevate not only yourself but also the one who bears you hatred.

The Persian sage has said, "Always meet petulance with gentleness, and perverseness with kindness. A gentle hand can lead even an elephant by a hair. Reply to thine enemy with gentleness. Opposition to peace is sin." The Buddhist says, "If a man foolishly does me wrong I will return him the protection of my ungrudging love. The more evil comes from him the more good shall go from me." "The wise man avenges injuries by benefits," says the Chinese. "Return good for evil, overcome anger by love; hatred never ceases by hatred, but by love," says the Hindu.

The truly wise man or woman will recognize no one as an enemy. Occasionally we hear the expression, "Never mind; I'll get even with him." Will you? And how will you do it? You can do it in one of two ways. You can, as you have in mind, deal with him as he deals, or apparently deals, with you,—pay him, as we say, in his own coin. If you do this you will get even with him by sinking yourself to his level, and both of you will suffer by it. Or, you can show yourself the larger, you can send him love for hatred, kindness for ill-treatment, and so get even with him by raising him to the higher level. But remember that you can never help another without by that very act helping yourself; and if forgetful of self, then in most all cases the value to you is greater than the service you render another. If you are ready to treat him as he treats you, then you show clearly that there is in you that which draws the hatred and ill-treatment to you; you deserve what you are getting and should not complain, nor would you complain if you were wise. By following the other course you most effectually accomplish your purpose,—you gain a victory for yourself, and at the same time you do a great service for him, for which it is evident he stands greatly in need.

Thus you may become his saviour. He in turn may become the saviour of other error-making, and consequently care-encumbered men and women. Many times the struggles are greater than we can ever know. We need more gentleness and sympathy and compassion in our common human life. Then we will neither blame nor condemn. Instead of blaming or condemning we will sympathize, and all the more we will

"Comfort one another,
For the way is often dreary,
And the feet are often weary,
And the heart is very sad.
There is a heavy burden bearing,
When it seems that none are caring,
And we half forget that ever we were glad

"Comfort one another
With the hand-clasp close and tender,
With the sweetness love can render,
And the looks of friendly eyes.
Do not wait with grace unspoken,
While life's daily bread is broken—
Gentle speech is oft like manna from the skies."

When we come fully to realize the great fact that all evil and error and sin with all their consequent sufferings come through ignorance, then wherever we see a manifestation of these in whatever form, if our hearts are right, we will have compassion, sympathy and compassion for the one in whom we see them. Compassion will then change itself into love, and love will manifest itself in kindly service. Such is the divine method. And so instead of aiding in trampling and keeping a weaker one down, we will hold him up until he can stand alone and become the master. But all life-growth is from within out, and one becomes a true master in the degree that the knowledge of the divinity of his own nature dawns upon his inner consciousness and so brings him to a knowledge of the higher laws; and in no way can we so effectually hasten this dawning in the inner consciousness of another, as by showing forth the divinity within ourselves simply by the way we live.

By example and not by precept. By living, not by preaching. By doing, not by professing. By living the life, not by dogmatizing as to how it should be lived. There is no contagion equal to the contagion of life. Whatever we sow, that shall we also reap, and each thing sown produces of its kind. We can kill not only by doing another bodily injury directly, but we can and we do kill by every antagonistic thought. Not only do we thus kill, but while we kill we suicide. Many a man has been made sick by having the ill thoughts of a number of people centred upon him; some have been actually killed. Put hatred into the world and we make it a literal hell. Put love into the world and heaven with all its beauties and glories becomes a reality.

Not to love is not to live, or it is to live a living death. The life that goes out in love to all is the life that is full, and rich, and continually expanding in beauty and in power. Such is the life that becomes ever more inclusive, and hence larger in its scope and influence. The larger the man and the woman, the more inclusive they are in their love and their friendships. The smaller the man and the woman, the more dwarfed and dwindling their natures, the more they pride themselves upon their "exclusiveness." Any one—a fool or an idiot—can be exclusive. It comes easy. It takes and it signifies a large nature to be universal, to be inclusive. Only the man or the woman of a small, personal, self-centred, self-seeking nature is exclusive. The man or the woman of a large, royal, unself-centred nature never is. The small nature is the one that continually strives for effect. The larger nature never does. The one goes here and there in order to gain recognition, in order to attach himself to the world. The other stays at home and draws the world *to him.* The one loves merely himself. The other loves all the world; but in his larger love for all the world he finds himself included.

Verily, then, the more one loves the nearer he approaches to God, for God is the spirit of infinite love. And when we come into the realization of our oneness with this Infinite Spirit, then divine love so fills us that, enriching and enrapturing our own lives, from them it flows out to enrich the life of all the world.

In coming into the realization of our oneness with the Infinite Life, we are brought at once into right relations with our fellowmen.

We are brought into harmony with the great law, that we find our own lives in losing them in the service of others. We are brought to a knowledge of the fact that all life is one, and so that we are all parts of the one great whole. We then realize that we can't do for another without at the same time doing for ourselves. We also realize that we cannot do harm to another without by that very act doing harm to ourselves. We realize that the man who lives to himself alone lives a little, dwarfed, and stunted life, because he has no part in this larger life of humanity. But the one who in service loses his own life in this larger life, has his own life increased and enriched a thousand or a million fold, and every joy, every happiness, everything of value coming to each member of this greater whole comes as such to him, for he has a part in the life of each and all.

And here let a word be said in regard to true service. Peter and John were one day going up to the temple, and as they were entering the gate they were met by a poor cripple who asked them for alms. Instead of giving him something to supply the day's needs and then leaving him in the same dependent condition for the morrow and the morrow, Peter did him a real service, and a real service for all mankind by saying, Silver and gold have I none, but such as I have I give unto thee. *And then he made him whole.* He thus brought him into the condition where he could help himself. In other words, the greatest service we can do for another is to help him to help himself. To help him directly might be weakening, though not necessarily. It depends entirely upon circumstances. But to help one to help himself is never weakening, but always encouraging and strengthening, because it leads him to a larger and stronger life.

There is no better way to help one to help himself than to bring him to a knowledge of himself. There is no better way to bring one to a knowledge of himself than to lead him to a knowledge of the powers that are lying dormant within his own soul. There is nothing that will enable him to come more readily or more completely into an awakened knowledge of the powers that are lying dormant within his own soul, than to bring him into the conscious, vital realization of his oneness with the Infinite Life and Power, so that he may open himself to it in order that it may work and manifest through him.

We will find that these same great truths lie at the very bottom of the solution of our social situation; and we will also find that we will never have a full and permanent solution of it until they are fully recognized and built upon.

VI

Wisdom And Interior Illumination

This is the Spirit of Infinite Wisdom, and in the degree that we open ourselves to it does the highest wisdom manifest itself to and through us. We can in this way go to the very heart of the universe itself and find the mysteries hidden to the majority of mankind,—hidden to them, though not hidden of themselves.

In order for the highest wisdom and insight we must have absolute confidence in the Divine guiding us, but not through the channel of some one else. And why should we go to another for knowledge and wisdom? With God is no respect of persons. Why should we seek these things second hand? Why should we thus stultify our own innate powers? Why should we not go direct to the Infinite Source itself? "If any man lack wisdom let him ask of God." "Before they call I will answer, and while they are yet speaking, I will hear."

When we thus go directly to the Infinite Source itself we are no longer slaves to personalities, institutions, or books. We should always keep ourselves open to suggestions of truth from these agencies. We should always regard them as agencies, however, and never as sources. We should never recognize them as masters, but simply as teachers. With Browning, we must recognize the great fact that—

"Truth is within ourselves; it takes no rise
From outward things, whate'er you may believe.
There is an inmost centre in us all,
Where truth abides in fullness."

There is no more important injunction in all the world, nor one with a deeper interior meaning, than "To thine own self be true." In other words, be true to your own soul, for it is through your own soul that the voice of God speaks to you. This is the interior guide. This is the light that lighteth every man that cometh into the world. This is conscience. This is intuition. This is the voice of the higher self, the voice of the soul, the voice of God. "Thou shalt hear a voice behind thee, saying: This is the way, walk ye in it."

When Moses was on the mountain it was after the various physical commotions and manifestations that he heard the "still, small voice," the voice of his own soul, through which the Infinite God was speaking. If we will but follow this voice of intuition, it will speak ever more clearly and more plainly, until by and by it will be absolute and unerring in its guidance. The great trouble with us is that we do not listen to and do not follow this voice within our own souls, and so we become as a house divided against itself. We are pulled this way and that, and we are never *certain* of anything. I have a friend who listens so carefully to this inner voice, who, in other words, always acts so quickly and so fully in accordance with his intuitions, and whose life as a consequence is so absolutely guided by them, that he always does the right thing at the right time and in the right way. He always knows when to act and how to act, and he is never in the condition of a house divided against itself.

But some one says, "May it not be dangerous for us to act always upon our intuitions? Suppose we should have an intuition to do harm to some one?" We need not be afraid of this, however, for the voice of the soul, this voice of God speaking through the soul, will never direct one to do harm to another, nor to do anything that is not in accordance with the highest standards of right, and truth, and justice. And if you at any time have a prompting of this kind, know that it is not the voice of intuition; it is some characteristic of your lower self that is prompting you.

Reason is not to be set aside, but it is to be continually illumined by this higher spiritual perception, and in the degree that it is thus illumined will it become an agent of light and power. When one becomes thoroughly individualized he enters into the realm of all knowledge and wisdom; and to be individualized is to recognize no power outside of the Infinite Power that is back of all. When one recognizes this great fact and opens himself to this Spirit of Infinite Wisdom, he then enters upon the road to the true education, and mysteries that before were closed now reveal themselves to him. This must indeed be the foundation of all true education, this evolving from within, this evolving of what has been involved by the Infinite Power.

All things that it is valuable for us to know will come to us if we will but open ourselves to the voice of this Infinite Spirit. It is thus that we become seers and have the power of seeing into the very heart of things. There are no new stars, there are no new laws or forces, but we can so open ourselves to this Spirit of Infinite Wisdom that we can discover and recognize those that have not been known before; and in this way they become new to us. When in this way we come into a knowledge of truth we no longer need facts that are continually changing. We can then enter into the quiet of our own interior selves. We can open the window and look out, and thus gather the facts as we choose. This is true wisdom. "Wisdom is the knowledge of God." Wisdom comes by intuition. It far transcends knowledge. Great knowledge, knowledge of many things, may be had by virtue simply of a very retentive memory. It comes by tuition. But wisdom far transcends knowledge, in that knowledge is a mere incident of this deeper wisdom.

He who would enter into the realm of wisdom must first divest himself of all intellectual pride. He must become as a little child. Prejudices, preconceived opinions and beliefs always stand in the way of true wisdom. Conceited opinions are always suicidal in their influences. They bar the door to the entrance of truth.

All about us we see men in the religious world, in the world of science, in the political, in the social world, who through intellectual pride are so wrapped in their own conceits and prejudices that larger and later revelations of truth can find no entrance to them; and instead of growing and expanding, they are becoming dwarfed and stunted, and still more incapable of receiving truth. Instead of actively aiding in the progress of the world, they are as so many dead sticks in the way that would retard the wheels of progress. This, however, they can never do. Such always in time get bruised, broken, and left behind, while God's triumphal car of truth moves steadily onward.

When the steam engine was still being experimented with, and before it was perfected sufficiently to come into practical use, a well-known Englishman—well known then in scientific circles—wrote an extended pamphlet proving that it would be impossible for it ever to be used in ocean navigation, that is, in a trip involving the crossing of the ocean, because it would be utterly impossible for any vessel to carry with it sufficient coal for the use of its furnace. And the interesting feature of the whole matter was that the very first steam vessel that made the trip from England to America, had among its cargo a part of the first edition of this carefully prepared pamphlet. There was only the one edition. Many editions might be sold now.

This seems indeed an amusing fact; but far more amusing is the man who voluntarily closes himself to truth because, forsooth, it does not come through conventional, or orthodox, or heretofore accepted channels; or because it may not be in full accord with, or possibly may be opposed to, established usages or beliefs. On the contrary—

"Let there be many windows in your soul,
That all the glory of the universe
May beautify it. Not the narrow pane
Of one poor creed can catch the radiant rays
That shine from countless sources. Tear away

The blinds of superstition: let the light
Pour through fair windows, broad as truth itself
And high as heaven. . . . Tune your ear
To all the worldless music of the stars
And to the voice of nature, and your heart

Shall turn to truth and goodness as the plant
Turns to the sun. A thousand unseen hands
Reach down to help you to their peace-crowned heights,
And all the forces of the firmament
Shall fortify your strength. Be not afraid
To thrust aside half-truths and grasp the whole."

There is a great law in connection with the coming of truth. It is this: Whenever a man or a woman shuts himself or herself to the entrance of truth on account of intellectual pride, preconceived opinions, prejudices, or for whatever reason, there is a great law which says that truth *in its fullness* will come to that one from no source. And on the other hand, when a man or a woman opens himself or herself fully to the entrance of truth from *whatever* source it may come, there is an equally great law which says that truth will flow in to him or to her from all sources, from all quarters. Such becomes the free man, the free woman, for it is the truth that makes us free. The other remains in bondage, for truth has had no invitation and will not enter where it is not fully and freely welcomed.

And where truth is denied entrance the rich blessings it carries with it cannot take up their abode. On the contrary, when this is the case, it sends an envoy carrying with it atrophy, disease, death, physically and spiritually as well as intellectually. And the man who would rob another of his free and unfettered search for truth, who would stand as the interpreter of truth for another, with the intent of remaining in this position, rather than endeavoring to lead him to the place where he can be his own interpreter, is more to be shunned than a thief and a robber. The injury he works is far greater, for he is doing direct and positive injury to the very life of the one he thus holds.

Who has ever appointed any man, whoever he may be, as the keeper, the custodian, the dispenser of God's illimitable truth? Many indeed are moved and so are called to be teachers of truth; but the true teacher will never stand as the interpreter of truth for another. The *true teacher* is the one whose endeavor is to bring the one he teaches to a true knowledge of himself and hence of his own interior powers, that he may become his own interpreter. All others are, generally speaking, those animated by purely personal motives, self-aggrandizement, or personal gain. Moreover, he who would claim to have all truth and the only truth, is a bigot, a fool, or a knave.

In the Eastern literature is a fable of a frog. The frog lived in a well, and out of his little well he had never been. One day a frog whose home was in the sea came to his well. Interested in all things, he went in. "Who are you? Where do you live?" said the frog in the well. "I am so and so, and my home is in the sea." "The sea? What is that? Where is that?" "It is a very large body of water, and not far away." "How big is your sea?" "Oh, very big." "As big as this?" pointing to a little stone lying near. "Oh, much bigger." "As big as this?" pointing to the board upon which they were sitting. "Oh, much bigger." "How much bigger, then?" "Why, the sea in which I live is bigger than your entire well; it would make millions of wells such as yours." "Nonsense, nonsense; you are a deceiver and a falsifier. Get out of my well. Get out of my well. I want nothing to do with any such frogs as you."

"Ye shall know the truth and the truth shall make you free," is the promise. Ye shall close yourselves to truth, ye shall live in your own conceits, and your own conceits shall make fools and idiots of you, would be a statement applicable to not a few, and to not a few who pride themselves upon their superior intellectual attainments.

Idiocy is arrested mental growth. Closing one's self for whatever reason to truth and hence to growth, brings a certain type of idiocy, though it may not be called by this name. And on the other hand, another type is that arrested growth caused by taking all things for granted, without proving them for one's self, merely because they come from a particular person, a particular book, a particular institution. This is caused by one's always looking without instead of being true to the light within, and carefully tending it that it may give an ever-clearer light.

With brave and intrepid Walt Whitman, we should all be able to say—

> "From this hour I ordain myself loos'd of limits
> and imaginary lines,
> Going where I list, my own master total and
> absolute,
> Listening to others, considering well what they say,
> Pausing, searching, receiving, contemplating,
> Gently, but with undeniable will divesting myself
> of the holds that would hold me."

Great should be the joy that God's boundless truth is open to all, open *equally* to all, and that it will make each one its dwelling place in proportion as he earnestly desires it and opens himself to it.

And in regard to the wisdom that guides us in our daily life, there is nothing that it is right and well for us to know that may not be known when we recognize the law of its coming, and are able wisely to use it. Let us know that all things are ours as soon as we know how to appropriate them.

> "I hold it as a changeless law,
> From which no soul can sway or swerve,
> We have that in us which will draw
> Whate'er we need or most deserve."

If the times come when we know not what course to pursue, when we know not which way to turn, the fault lies in ourselves.

If the fault lies in ourselves then the correction of this unnatural condition lies also in ourselves. It is never necessary to come into such a state if we are awake and remain awake to the light and the powers within us. The light is ever shining, and the only thing that it is necessary for us diligently to see to is that we permit neither this thing nor that to come between us and the light. "With Thee is the fountain of life; in Thy light shall we see light."

Let us hear the words of one of the most highly illumined men I have ever known, and one who as a consequence is never in the dark, when the time comes, as to what to do and how to do it. "Whenever you are in doubt as to the course you should pursue, after you have turned to every outward means of guidance, *let the inward eye see, let the inward ear hear*, and allow this simple, natural, beautiful process to go on unimpeded by questionings or doubts. . . . In all dark hours and times of unwonted perplexity we need to follow one simple direction, found, as all needed directions can be found, in the dear old gospel, which so many read, but alas, *so few interpret.* 'Enter into thine inner chamber and shut the door.' Does this mean that we must literally betake ourselves to a private closet with a key in the door? If it did, then the command could never be obeyed in the open air, on land or sea, and the Christ loved the lakes and the forests far better than the cramping rooms of city dwelling houses; still his counsels are so wide-reaching that there is no spot on earth and no conceivable situation in which any of us may be placed where we cannot follow them.

"One of the most intuitive men we ever met had a desk in a city office where several other gentlemen were doing business constantly and often talking loudly. Entirely undisturbed by the many various sounds about him, this self-centred, faithful man would, in any moment of perplexity, draw the curtains of privacy so completely about him that he would be as fully enclosed in his own psychic aura, and thereby as effectually removed from all distractions as though he were alone in some primeval wood. Taking his difficulty with him into the mystic silence in the form of a direct question, to which he expected a certain answer, he would remain utterly passive until the reply came, and never once through many years' experience did he find himself disappointed or misled. Intuitive perceptions of truth are the daily bread to satisfy our daily hunger; they come like the manna in the desert day by day; each day brings adequate supply for that day's need only. They must be followed instantly, for dalliance with them means their obscuration, and the more we dally the more we invite erroneous impressions to cover intuition with a pall of conflicting moral phantasy born of illusions of the terrence will.

"One condition is imposed by *universal law*, and this we must obey. Put all wishes aside save the one desire to know *truth*; couple with this one demand the fully consecrated determination to follow what is distinctly perceived as truth immediately it is revealed. No other affection must be permitted to share the field with this all-absorbing love of *truth* for its own sake. Obey this one direction and never forget that expectation and desire are bride and bridegroom and forever inseparable, and you will soon find your hitherto darkened way grow luminous with celestial radiance, for with the heaven within, all heavens without incessantly co-operate." This may be termed going into the "silence." This it is to perceive and to be guided by the light that lighteth every man that cometh into the world. This it is to listen to and be guided by the voice of your own soul, the voice of your higher self.

The soul is divine and in allowing it to become translucent to the Infinite Spirit it reveals all things to us. As man turns away from the Divine Light do all things become hidden. There is nothing hidden of itself. When the spiritual sense is opened, then it transcends all the limitations of the physical senses and the intellect. And in the degree that we are able to get away from the limitations set by them, and realize that so far as the real life is concerned it is one with the Infinite Life, then we begin to reach the place where this voice will always speak, where it will never fail us, if we follow it, and as a consequence where we will always have the divine illumination and guidance. To know this and to live in this realization is not to live in heaven hereafter, but to live in heaven here and now, *today and every day.*

No human soul need be without it. When we turn our face in the right direction it comes as simply and as naturally as the flower blooms and the winds blow. It is not to be bought with money or with price. It is a condition waiting simply to be realized, by rich and by poor, by king and by peasant, by master and by servant the world over. All are equal heirs to it. And so the peasant, if he find it first, lives a life far transcending in beauty and in real power the life of his king. The servant, if he find it first, lives a life surpassing the life of his master.

If you would find the highest, the fullest, and the richest life that not only this world but that any world can know, then do away with the sense of the separateness of your life from the life of God. Hold to the thought of your oneness. In the degree that you do this you will find yourself realizing it more and more, and as this life of realization is lived, you will find that no good thing will be withheld, for all things are included in this. Then it will be yours, without fears or forebodings, simply to do today what your hands find to do, and so be ready for tomorrow, *when it comes*, knowing that tomorrow will bring tomorrow's supplies for the mental, the spiritual, and the physical life. Remember, however, that tomorrow's supplies are not needed until tomorrow comes.

If one is willing to trust himself *fully* to the Law, the Law will never fail him. It is the half-hearted trusting to it that brings uncertain, and so, unsatisfactory results. Nothing is firmer and surer than Deity. It will never fail the one who throws himself wholly upon it. The secret of life then, is to live continually in this realization, whatever one may be doing, wherever one may be, by day and by night, both waking and sleeping. It can be lived in while we are sleeping no less than when we are awake. And here shall we consider a few facts in connection with sleep, in connection with receiving instruction and illumination while asleep?

During the process of sleep it is merely the physical body that is at rest and in quiet; the soul life with all its activities goes right on. Sleep is nature's provision for the recuperation of the body, for the rebuilding and hence the replacing of the waste that is continually going on during the waking hours. It is nature's great restorer. If sufficient sleep is not allowed the body, so that the rebuilding may equalize the wasting process, the body is gradually depleted and weakened, and any ailment or malady, when it is in this condition, is able to find a more ready entrance. It is for this reason that those who are subject to it will take a cold, as we term it, more readily when the body is tired or exhausted through loss of sleep than at most any other time. The body is in that condition where outside influences can have a more ready effect upon it, than when it is in its normal condition. And when they do have an effect they always go to the weaker portions first.

Our bodies are given us to serve far higher purposes than we ordinarily use them for. Especially is this true in the numerous cases where the body is master of its owner. In the degree that we come into the realization of the higher powers of the mind and spirit, in that degree does the body, through their influence upon it, become less gross and heavy, finer in its texture and form. And then, because the mind finds a kingdom of enjoyment in itself, and in all the higher things it becomes related to, *excesses* in eating and drinking, as well as all others, naturally and of their own accord fall away. There also falls away the desire for the heavier, grosser, less valuable kinds of food and drink, such as the flesh of animals, alcoholic drinks, and all things of the class that stimulate the body and the passions rather than build the body and the brain into a strong, clean, well-nourished, enduring, and fibrous condition. In the degree that the body thus becomes less gross and heavy, finer in its texture and form, is there less waste, and what there is is more easily replaced, so that it keeps in a more regular and even condition. When this is true, less sleep is actually required. And even the amount that is taken does more for a body of this finer type than it can do for one of the other nature.

As the body in this way grows finer, in other words, as the process of its evolution is thus accelerated, it in turn helps the mind and the soul in the realization of ever higher perceptions, and thus body helps mind the same as mind builds body. It was undoubtedly this fact that Browning had in mind when he said:

> "Let us cry 'All good things
> Are ours, nor soul helps flesh, more now,
> Than flesh helps soul.'"

Sleep, then, is for the resting and the rebuilding of the body. The soul needs no rest, and while the body is at rest in sleep the soul life is active the same as when the body is in activity.

There are some, having a deep insight into the soul's activities, who say that we travel when we sleep. Some are able to recall and bring over into the conscious, waking life the scenes visited, the information gained, and the events that have transpired. Most people are not able to do this and so much that might otherwise be gained is lost. They say, however, that it is in our power, in proportion as we understand the laws, to go where we will, and to bring over into the conscious, waking life all the experiences thus gained. Be this, however, as it may, it certainly is true that while sleeping we have the power, in a perfectly normal and natural way, to get much of value by way of light, instruction, and growth that the majority of people now miss.

If the soul life, that which relates us to Infinite Spirit, is always active, even while the body is at rest, why may not the mind so direct conditions as one falls asleep, that while the body is at rest, it may continually receive illumination from the soul and bring what it thus receives over into the conscious, waking life? This, indeed, can be done, and is done by some to great advantage; and many times the highest inspirations from the soul come in this way, as would seem most natural, since at this time all communications from the outer, material world no longer enter. I know those who do much work during sleep, the same as they get much light along desired lines. By charging the mind on going to sleep as to a particular time for waking, it is possible, as many of us know, to wake on the very minute. Not infrequently we have examples of difficult problems, problems that defied solution during waking hours, being solved during sleep.

A friend, a well-known journalist, had an extended newspaper article clearly and completely worked out for her in this way. She frequently calls this agency to her aid. She was notified by the managing editor one evening to have the article ready in the morning,—an article requiring more than ordinary care, and one in which quite a knowledge of facts was required. It was a matter in connection with which she knew scarcely anything, and all her efforts at finding information regarding it seemed to be of no avail.

She set to work, but it seemed as if even her own powers defied her. Failure seemed imminent. Almost in desperation she decided to retire, and putting the matter into her mind in such a way that she would be able to receive the greatest amount of aid while asleep, she fell asleep and slept soundly until morning. When she awoke her work of the previous evening was the first thing that came into her mind. She lay quietly for a few minutes, and as she lay there, the article, completely written, seemed to stand before her mind. She ran through it, arose, and without dressing took her pen and transcribed it on to paper, literally acting simply as her own amanuensis.

The mind acting intently along a particular line will continue so to act until some other object of thought carries it along another line. And since in sleep only the body is in quiet while the mind and soul are active, then the mind on being given a certain direction when one drops off to sleep, will take up the line along which it is directed, and can be made, in time, to bring over into consciousness the results of its activities. Some will be able very soon to get results of this kind; for some it will take longer. Quiet and continued effort will increase the faculty.

Then by virtue of the law of the drawing power of mind, since the mind is always active, we are drawing to us even while sleeping, influences from the realms kindred to those in which we in our thoughts are living before we fall asleep. In this way we can put ourselves into relation with what ever kinds of influence we choose and accordingly gain much during the process of sleep. In many ways the interior faculties are more open and receptive while we are in sleep than while we are awake. Hence the necessity of exercising even greater care as to the nature of the thoughts that occupy the mind as we enter into sleep, for there can come to us only what we by our own order of thought attract. We have it entirely in our own hands.

And for the same reason,—this greater degree of receptivity during this period,—we are able by understanding and using the law, to gain much of value more readily in this way than when the physical senses are fully open to the material world about us. Many will find a practice somewhat after the following nature of value: When light or information is desired along any particular line, light or information you feel it is right and wise for you to have, as, for example, light in regard to an uncertain course of action, then as you retire, first bring your mind into the attitude of peace and good-will for all. You in this way bring yourself into an harmonious condition, and in turn attract to yourself these same peaceful conditions from without.

Then resting in this sense of peace, quietly and calmly send out your earnest desire for the needed light or information; cast out of your mind all fears or forebodings lest it come not, for "in quietness and in confidence shall be your strength." Take the expectant attitude of mind, firmly believing and expecting that when you awake the desired results will be with you. Then on awaking, before any thoughts or activities from the outside world come in to absorb the attention, remain for a little while receptive to the intuitions or the impressions that come. When they come, when they manifest themselves clearly, then act upon them without delay. In the degree that you do this, in that degree will the power of doing it ever more effectively grow.

Or, if for unselfish purposes you desire to grow and develop any of your faculties, or to increase the health and strength of your body, take a corresponding attitude of mind, the form of which will readily suggest itself in accordance with your particular needs or desires. In this way you will open yourself to, you will connect yourself with, and you will set into operation within yourself, the particular order of forces that will make for these results. Don't be afraid to voice your desires. In this way you set into operation vibratory forces which go out and which make their impress felt somewhere, and which, arousing into activity or uniting with other forces, set about to actualize your desires. No good thing shall be withheld from him who lives in harmony with the higher laws and forces. There are no desires that shall not be satisfied to the one who knows and who wisely uses the powers with which he or she is endowed.

Your sleep will be more quiet, and peaceful, and refreshing, and so your power increased mentally, physically, and spiritually, simply by sending out as you fall asleep, thoughts of love and good-will, thoughts of peace and harmony for all. In this way you are connecting yourself with all the forces in the universe that make for peace and harmony.

A friend who is known the world over through his work along humane lines, has told me that many times in the middle of the night he is awakened suddenly and there comes to his mind, as a flash of inspiration, a certain plan in connection with his work. And as he lays there quietly and opens himself to it, the methods for its successful carrying out all reveal themselves to him clearly. In this way many plans are entered upon and brought to a successful culmination that otherwise would never be thought of, plans that seem, indeed, marvelous to the world at large. He is a man with a sensitive organism, his life in thorough harmony with the higher laws, and given wholly and unreservedly to the work to which he has dedicated it. Just how and from what source these inspirations come he does not fully know. Possibly no one does, though each may have his theory. But this we do know, and it is all we need to know now, at least,—that to the one who lives in harmony with the higher laws of his being, and who opens himself to them, they come.

Visions and inspirations of the highest order will come in the degree that we make for them the right conditions. One who has studied deeply into the subject in hand has said: "To receive education spiritually while the body is resting in sleep is a perfectly normal and orderly experience, and would occur definitely and satisfactorily in the lives of all of us, if we paid more attention to internal and consequently less to external states with their supposed but unreal necessities. . . . Our thoughts make us what we are here and hereafter, and our thoughts are often busier by night than by day, for when we are asleep to the exterior we can be wide awake to the interior world; and the unseen world is a substantial place, the conditions of which are entirely regulated by mental and moral attainments. When we are not deriving information through outward avenues of sensation, we are receiving instruction through interior channels of perception, and when this fact is understood for what it is worth, it will become a universal custom for persons to take to sleep with them the special subject on which they most earnestly desire particular instruction. The Pharaoh type of person dreams, and so does his butler and baker; but the Joseph type, which is that of the truly gifted seer, both dreams and interprets."

But why had not Pharaoh the power of interpreting his dreams? Why was Joseph the type of the "truly gifted seer?" Why did he not only dream, but had also the power to interpret both his own dreams and the dreams of others? Simply read the lives of the two. He who runs may read. In all true power it is, after all, living the life that tells. And in proportion as one lives the life does he not only attain to the highest power and joy for himself, but he also becomes of ever greater service to all the world. One need remain in no hell longer than he himself chooses to; and the moment he chooses not to remain longer, not all the powers in the universe can prevent his leaving it. One can rise to any heaven he himself chooses; and when he chooses so to rise, all the higher powers of the universe combine to help him heavenward.

When one awakes from sleep and so returns to conscious life, he is in a peculiarly receptive and impressionable state. All relations with the material world have for a time been shut off, the mind is in a freer and more natural state, resembling somewhat a sensitive plate, where impressions can readily leave their traces. This is why many times the highest and truest impressions come to one in the early morning hours, before the activities of the day and their attendant distractions have exerted an influence. This is one reason why many people can do their best work in the early hours of the day.

But this fact is also a most valuable one in connection with the moulding of every-day life. The mind is at this time as a clean sheet of paper. We can most valuably use this quiet, receptive, impressionable period by wisely directing the activities of the mind along the highest and most desirable paths, and thus, so to speak, set the pace for the day.

Each morning is a fresh beginning. We are, as it were, just beginning life. We have it *entirely* in our own hands. And when the morning with its fresh beginning comes, all yesterdays should be yesterdays, with which we have nothing to do. Sufficient is it to know that the way we lived our yesterday has determined for us our today. And, again, when the morning with its fresh beginning comes, all tomorrows should be tomorrows, with which we have nothing to do. Sufficient to know that the way we live our today determines our tomorrow.

"Every day is a fresh beginning,
Every morn is the world made new;
You who are weary of sorrow and sinning,
Here is a beautiful hope for you,
A hope for me and a hope for you.

"All the past things are past and over,
The tasks are done, and the tears are shed.
Yesterday's errors let yesterday cover;
Yesterday's wounds, which smarted and bled,
Are healed with the healing which might has shed.

78

* * * * * * * * * *

"Let them go, since we cannot relieve them,
Cannot undo and cannot atone.
God in His mercy receive, forgive them!
Only the new days are our own.
Today is ours, and today alone.

"Here are the skies all burnished brightly;
Here is the spent earth all reborn;
Here are the tired limbs springing lightly
To face the sun and to share with the morn
In the chrism of dew and the cool of dawn.

"Every day is a fresh beginning,
Listen, my soul, to the glad refrain,
And, spite of old sorrow and older sinning,
And puzzles forecasted, and possible pain,
Take heart with the day and begin again."

Simply the first hour of this new day, with all its richness and glory, with all its sublime and eternity-determining possibilities, and each succeeding hour as it comes, but *not before* it comes. This is the secret of character building. This simple method will bring any one to the realization of the highest life that can be even conceived of, and there is nothing in this connection that can be conceived of that cannot be realized somehow, somewhen, somewhere.

This brings such a life within the possibilities of *all*, for there is *no one*, if really in earnest and if he really desires it, who cannot live to his highest for a single hour. But even though there should be, if he is *only earnest in his endeavor*, then, through the law that like builds like, he will be able to come a little nearer to it the next hour, and still nearer the next, and the next, until sooner or later comes the time when it becomes the natural, and any other would require the effort.

In this way one becomes in love and in league with the highest and best in the universe, and as a consequence, the highest and best in the universe becomes in love and in league with him. They aid him at every turn; they seem literally to move all things his way, because forsooth, he has first moved their way.

VII

The Realization Of Perfect Peace

This is the Spirit of Infinite Peace, and the moment we come into harmony with it there comes to us an inflowing tide of peace, for peace is harmony. A deep interior meaning underlies the great truth, "To be spiritually minded is life and peace." To recognize the fact that we are spirit, and to live in this thought, is to be spiritually minded, and so to be in harmony and peace. Oh, the thousands of men and women all about us weary with care, troubled and ill at ease, running hither and thither to find peace, weary in body, soul, and mind; going to other countries, traveling the world over, coming back, and still not finding it. Of course they have not found it and they never will find it in this way, because they are looking for it where it is not. They are looking for it without when they should look within. Peace is to be found only within, and unless one find it there he will never find it at all.

Peace lies not in the external world. It lies within one's own soul. We may travel over many different avenues in pursuit of it, we may seek it through the channels of the bodily appetites and passions, we may seek it through all the channels of the external, we may chase for it hither and thither, but it will always be just beyond our grasp, because we are searching for it where it is not. In the degree, however, that we order the bodily appetites and passions in accordance with the promptings of the soul within will the higher forms of happiness and peace enter our lives; but in the degree that we fail in doing this will disease, suffering, and discontent enter in.

To be at one with God is to be at peace. The child simplicity is the greatest agency in bringing this full and complete realization, the child simplicity that recognizes its true relations with the Father's life. There are people I know who have come into such a conscious realization of their oneness with this Infinite Life, this Spirit of Infinite Peace, that their lives are fairly bubbling over with joy. I have particularly in mind at this moment a comparatively young man who was an invalid for several years, his health completely broken with nervous exhaustion, who thought there was nothing in life worth living for, to whom everything and everybody presented a gloomy aspect, and he in turn presented a gloomy aspect to all with whom he came in contact. Not long ago he came into such a vital realization of his oneness with this Infinite Power, he opened himself so completely to its divine inflow, that today he is in perfect health, and frequently as I meet him now he cannot resist the impulse to cry out, "Oh, it is a joy to be alive."

I know an officer on our police force who has told me that many times when off duty and on his way home in the evening, there comes to him such a vivid and vital realization of his oneness with this Infinite Power, and this Spirit of Infinite Peace so takes hold of and so fills him, that it seems as if his feet could scarcely keep to the pavement, so buoyant and so exhilarated does he become by reason of this inflowing tide.

He who comes into this higher realization never has any fear, for he has always with him a sense of protection, and the very realization of this makes his protection complete. Of him it is true,— "No weapon that is formed against thee shall prosper;" "There shall no ill come nigh thy dwelling;" "Thou shalt be in league with the stones of the field, and the beasts of the field shall be at peace with thee."

These are the men and the women who seem to live charmed lives. The moment we fear anything we open the door for the entrance of the actualization of the very thing we fear. An animal will never harm a person who is absolutely fearless in regard to it.

The instant he fears he opens himself to danger; and some animals, the dog for example, can instantly detect the element of fear, and this gives them the courage to do harm. In the degree that we come into a full realization of our oneness with this Infinite Power do we become calm and quiet, undisturbed by the little occurrences that before so vex and annoy us. We are no longer disappointed in people, for we always read them aright. We have the power of penetrating into their very souls and seeing the underlying motives that are at work there.

A gentleman approached a friend the other day, and with great show of cordiality grasped him by the hand and said, "Why, Mr. ———, I am so glad to see you." Quick as a flash my friend read him, and looking him steadily in the eye, replied, "No, you are mistaken, you are not glad to see me; but you are very much disconcerted, so much so that you are now blushing in evidence of it." The gentleman replied, "Well, you know in this day and age of conventionality and form we have to put on the show and sometimes make believe what we do not really feel." My friend once more looked him in the face and said, "Again you are mistaken. Let me give you one little word of advice: You will always fare better and will think far more of yourself, always to recognize and to tell the truth rather than to give yourself to any semblance of it."

As soon as we are able to read people aright we will then cease to be disappointed in them, we will cease to place them on pedestals, for this can never be done without some attendant disappointment. The fall will necessarily come, sooner or later, and moreover, we are thus many times unfair to our friends. When we come into harmony with this Spirit of Peace, evil reports and apparent bad treatment, either at the hands of friends or of enemies, will no longer disturb us. When we are conscious of the fact that in our life and our work we are true to that eternal principle of right, of truth, of justice that runs through all the universe, that unites and governs all, that always eventually prevails, then nothing of this kind can come nigh us, and come what may we will always be tranquil and undisturbed.

The things that cause sorrow, and pain, and bereavement will not be able to take the hold of us they now take, for true wisdom will enable us to see the proper place and know the right relations of all things. The loss of friends by the transition we call death will not cause sorrow to the soul that has come into this higher realization, for he knows that there is no such thing as death, for each one is not only a partaker, but an eternal partaker, of this Infinite Life. He knows that the mere falling away of the physical body by no means affects the real soul life. With a tranquil spirit born of a higher faith he can realize for himself, and to those less strong he can say—

> "Loving friends! be wise and dry
> Straightway every weeping eye;
> What you left upon the bier
> Is not worth a single tear;
> 'Tis a simple sea-shell, one
> Out of which the pearl has gone.
> The shell was nothing, leave it there;
> The pearl—the soul—was all, is here."

And so far as the element of separation is concerned, he realizes that to spirit there are no bounds, and that spiritual communion, whether between two persons in the body, or two persons, one in the body and one out of the body, is within the reach of all. In the degree that the higher spiritual life is realized can there be this higher spiritual communion.

The things that we open ourselves to always come to us. People in the olden times expected to see angels and they saw them; but there is no more reason why they should have seen them than that we should see them now; no more reason why they should come and dwell with them than that they should come and dwell with us, for the great laws governing all things are the same today as they were then. If angels come not to minister unto us it is because we do not invite them, it is because we keep the door closed through which they otherwise might enter.

In the degree that we are filled with this Spirit of Peace by thus opening ourselves to its inflow does it pour through us, so that we carry it with us wherever we go. In the degree that we thus open ourselves do we become magnets to attract peace from all sources; and in the degree that we attract and embody it in ourselves are we able to give it forth to others. We can in this way become such perfect embodiments of peace that wherever we go we are continually shedding benedictions. But a day or two ago I saw a woman grasp the hand of a man (his face showed the indwelling God), saying, "Oh, it does me so much good to see you. I have been in anxiety and almost in despair during the past few hours, but the very sight of you has rolled the burden entirely away." There are people all around us who are continually giving out blessings and comfort, persons whose mere presence seems to change sorrow into joy, fear into courage, despair into hope, weakness into power.

It is the one who has come into the realization of his own true self who carries this power with him and who radiates it wherever he goes,—the one who, as we say, has found his centre. And in all the great universe there is but one centre,—the Infinite Power that is working in and through all. The one who then has found his centre is the one who has come into the realization of his oneness with this Infinite Power, the one who recognizes himself as a spiritual being, for God is spirit.

Such is the man of power. Centred in the Infinite, he has thereby, so to speak, connected himself with, he has attached his belts to, the great power-house of the universe. He is constantly drawing power to himself from all sources. For, thus centred, knowing himself, conscious of his own power, the thoughts that go from his mind are thoughts of strength; and by virtue of the law that like attracts like, he by his thoughts is continually attracting to himself from all quarters the aid of all whose thoughts are thoughts of strength, and in this way he is linking himself with this order of thought in the universe.

And so to him that hath, to him shall be given. This is simply the working of a natural law. His strong, positive, and hence constructive thought is continually working success for him along all lines, and continually bringing to him help from all directions. The things that he sees, that he creates in the ideal, are through the agency of this strong constructive thought continually clothing themselves, taking form, manifesting themselves in the material. Silent, unseen forces are at work which will sooner or later be made manifest in the visible.

Fear and all thoughts of failure never suggest themselves to such a man; or if they do, they are immediately sent out of his mind, and so he is not influenced by this order of thought from without. He does not attract it to him. He is in another current of thought. Consequently the weakening, failure-bringing thoughts of the fearing, the vacillating, the pessimistic about him, have no influence upon him. The one who is of the negative, fearing kind not only has his energies and his physical agents weakened, or even paralyzed through the influence of this kind of thought that is born within him, but he also in this way connects himself with this order of thought in the world about him. And in the degree that he does this does he become a victim to the weak, fearing, negative minds all around him. Instead of growing in power, he increases in weakness. He is in the same order of thought with those of whom it is true,—and even that which they have shall be taken away from them. This again is simply the working of a natural law, the same as is its opposite. Fearing lest I lose even what I have I hide it away in a napkin. Very well. I must then pay the price of my "fearing lest I lose."

Thoughts of strength both build strength from within and attract it from without. Thoughts of weakness actualize weakness from within and attract it from without. Courage begets strength, fear begets weakness. And so courage begets success, fear begets failure. It is the man or the woman of faith, and hence of courage, who is the master of circumstances, and who makes his or her power felt in the world. It is the man or the woman who lacks faith and who as a consequence is weakened and crippled by fears and forebodings, who is the creature of all passing occurrences.

Within each one lies the cause of whatever comes to him. Each has it in his own hands to determine what comes. Everything in the visible, material world has its origin in the unseen, the spiritual, the thought world. This is the world of cause, the former is the world of effect. The nature of the effect is always in accordance with the nature of the cause. What one lives in his invisible, thought world, he is continually actualizing in his visible, material world. If he would have any conditions different in the latter he must make the necessary change in the former. A clear realization of this great fact would bring success to thousands of men and women who all about us are now in the depths of despair. It would bring health, abounding health and strength to thousands now diseased and suffering. It would bring peace and joy to thousands now unhappy and ill at ease.

And oh, the thousands all about us who are continually living in the slavery of fear. The spirits within that should be strong and powerful, are rendered weak and impotent. Their energies are crippled, their efforts are paralyzed. "Fear is everywhere,—fear of want, fear of starvation, fear of public opinion, fear of private opinion, fear that what we own today may not be ours tomorrow, fear of sickness, fear of death. Fear has become with millions a fixed habit. The thought is everywhere. The thought is thrown upon us from every direction. . . . To live in continual dread, continual cringing, continual fear of anything, be it loss of love, loss of money, loss of position or situation, is to take the readiest means to lose what we fear we shall."

By fear nothing is to be gained, but on the contrary, everything is to be lost. "I know this is true," says one, "but I am given to fear; it's natural to me and I can't help it." Can't help it! In saying this you indicate one great reason of your fear by showing that you do not even know yourself as yet. You must know yourself in order to know your powers, and not until you know them can you use them wisely and fully. Don't say you can't help it. If you think you can't, the chances are that you can't. If you think you can, and act in accordance with this thought, then not only are the chances that you can, but if you act fully in accordance with it, that you can and that you will is an absolute certainty. It was Virgil who in describing the crew which in his mind would win the race, said of them,—They can because they think they can. In other words, this very attitude of mind on their part will infuse a spiritual power into their bodies that will give them the strength and endurance which will enable them to win.

Then take the thought that you *can*; take it merely as a seed-thought, if need be, plant it in your consciousness, tend it, cultivate it, and it will gradually reach out and gather strength from all quarters. It will focus and make positive and active the spiritual force within you that is now scattered and of little avail. It will draw to itself force from without. It will draw to your aid the influence of other minds of its own nature, minds that are fearless, strong, courageous. You will thus draw to yourself and connect yourself with this order of thought. If earnest and faithful, the time will soon come when all fear will loose its hold; and instead of being an embodiment of weakness and a creature of circumstances, you will find yourself a tower of strength and a master of circumstances.

We need more faith in every-day life,—faith in the power that works for good, faith in the Infinite God, and hence faith in ourselves created in His image. And however things at times may seem to go, however dark at times appearances may be, the knowledge of the fact that "the Supreme Power has us in its charge as it has the suns and endless systems of worlds in space," will give us the supreme faith that all is well with us, the same as all is well with the world. "Thou wilt keep him in perfect peace whose mind is stayed on Thee."

There is nothing firmer, and safer, and surer than Deity. Then, as we recognize the fact that we have it in our own hands to open ourselves ever more fully to this Infinite Power, and call upon it to manifest itself in and through us, we will find in ourselves an ever increasing sense of power. For in this way we are working in conjunction with it, and it in turn is working in conjunction with us. We are then led into the full realization of the fact that all things work together for good to those that love the good. Then the fears and forebodings that have dominated us in the past will be transmuted into faith, and faith when rightly understood and rightly used is a force before which nothing can stand.

Materialism leads naturally to pessimism. And how could it do otherwise? A knowledge of the Spiritual Power working in and through us as well as in and through all things, a power that works for righteousness, leads to optimism. Pessimism leads to weakness. Optimism leads to power. The one who is centred in Deity is the one who not only outrides every storm, but who through the faith, and so, the conscious power that is in him, faces storm with the same calmness and serenity that he faces fair weather; for he knows well beforehand what the outcome will be. He knows that underneath are the everlasting arms. He it is who realizes the truth of the injunction, "Rest in the Lord, wait patiently for Him and He shall give thee thy heart's desire." All shall be given, simply given, to him who is ready to accept it. Can anything be clearer than this?

In the degree, then, that we work in conjunction with the Supreme Power do we need the less to concern ourselves about results. To live in the full realization of this fact and all that attends it brings peace, a full, rich, abiding peace,—a peace that makes the present complete, and that, going on before, brings back the assurance that as our days, so shall our strength be. The one who is thus centred, even in the face of all the unrest and the turmoil about us, can realize and say—

* * * * * * * * * *

"I stay my haste, I make delays,
For what avails this eager pace?
I stand amid eternal ways,
And what is mine shall know my face.
  "Asleep, awake, by night or day,
The friends I seek are seeking me;
No wind can drive my bark astray,
Nor change the tide of destiny.

* * * * * * * * * *

  "The waters know their own, and draw
The brooks that spring in yonder height;
So flows the good with equal law
Unto the soul of pure delight
  "The stars come nightly to the sky;
The tidal wave unto the sea;
Nor time, nor space, nor deep, nor high,
Can keep my own away from me."

VIII

Coming Into Fullness Of Power

This is the Spirit of Infinite Power, and in the degree that we open ourselves to it does power become manifest in us. With God all things are possible,—that is, in conjunction with God all things are possible. The true secret of power lies in keeping one's connection with the God who worketh all things; and in the degree that we keep this connection are we able literally to rise above every conceivable limitation.

Why, then, waste time in running hither and thither to acquire power? Why waste time with this practice or that practice? Why not go directly to the mountain top itself, instead of wandering through the by-ways, in the valleys, and on the mountain sides? That man has absolute dominion, as taught in all the scriptures of the world, is true not of physical man, but of *spiritual man*. There are many animals, for example, larger and stronger, over which from a physical standpoint he would not have dominion, but he can gain supremacy over even these by calling into activity the higher mental, psychic, and spiritual forces with which he is endowed.

Whatever can't be done in the physical can be done in the spiritual. And in direct proportion as a man recognizes himself as spirit, and lives accordingly, is he able to transcend in power the man who recognizes himself merely as material. All the sacred literature of the world is teeming with examples of what we call miracles. They are not confined to any particular times or places. There is no age of miracles in distinction from any other period

91

that may be an age of miracles. Whatever has been done in the world's history can be done again through the operation of the same laws and forces. These miracles were performed not by those who were more than men, but by those who through the recognition of their oneness with God became God-men, so that the higher forces and powers worked through them.

For what, let us ask, is a miracle? Is it something supernatural? Supernatural only in the sense of being above the natural, or rather, above that which is natural to man in his ordinary state. A miracle is nothing more nor less than this. One who has come into a knowledge of his true identity, of his oneness with the all-pervading Wisdom and Power, thus makes it possible for laws higher than the ordinary mind knows of to be revealed to him. These laws he makes use of; the people see the results, and by virtue of their own limitations, call them miracles and speak of the person who performs these apparently supernatural works as a supernatural being. But they as supernatural beings could themselves perform these supernatural works if they would open themselves to the recognition of the same laws, and consequently to the realization of the same possibilities and powers. And let us also remember that the supernatural of yesterday becomes, as in the process of evolution we advance from the lower to the higher, from the more material to the more spiritual, the common and the natural of today, and what seems to be the supernatural of today becomes in the same way the natural of tomorrow, and so on through the ages. Yes, it is the God-man who does the things that appear supernatural, the man who by virtue of his realization of the higher powers transcends the majority and so stands out among them. But any power that is possible to one human soul is possible to another. The same laws operate in every life. We can be men and women of power or we can be men and women of impotence. The moment one vitally grasps the fact that he can rise he will rise, and he can have absolutely no limitations other than the limitations he sets to himself. Cream always rises to the top. It rises simply because *it is the nature of cream to rise.*

We hear much said of "environment." We need to realize that environment should never be allowed to make the man, but that man should always, *and always can,* condition the environment. When we realize this we will find that many times it is not necessary to take ourselves out of any particular environment, because we may yet have a work to do there; but by the very force we carry with us we can so affect and change matters that we will have an entirely new set of conditions in an old environment.

The same is true in regard to "hereditary" traits and influences. We sometimes hear the question asked, "Can they be overcome?" Only the one who doesn't yet know himself can ask a question such as this. If we entertain and live in the belief that they cannot be overcome, then the chances are that they will always remain. The moment, however, that we come into a realization of our true selves, and so of the tremendous powers and forces within,—the powers and forces of the mind and spirit,—hereditary traits and influences that are harmful in nature will begin to lessen, and will disappear with a rapidity directly in proportion to the completeness of this realization.

> "There is no thing we cannot overcome;
> Say not thy evil instinct is inherited,
> Or that some trait inborn makes thy whole life forlorn,
> And calls down punishment that is not merited.
> "Back of thy parents and grandparents lies
> The Great Eternal Will! That too is thine
> Inheritance,—strong, beautiful, divine,
> Sure lever of success for one who tries.

*   *   *   *   *   *   *   *   *   *

"There is no noble height thou canst not climb;
All triumphs may be thine in Time's futurity,
If, whatso'er thy fault, thou dost not faint or halt;
But lean upon the staff of God's security.

"Earth has no claim the soul cannot contest;
Know thyself part of the Eternal Source;
Naught can stand before thy spirit's force;
The soul's Divine Inheritance is best."

Again there are many who are living far below their possibilities because they are continually handing over their individualities to others. Do you want to be a power in the world? Then be yourself. Don't class yourself, don't allow yourself to be classed among the second-hand, among the *they-say* people. Be true to the highest within your own soul, and then allow yourself to be governed by no customs or conventionalities or arbitrary man-made rules that are not founded upon *principle*. Those things that are founded upon principle will be observed by the right-minded, the right-hearted man or woman, in any case.

Don't surrender your individuality, which is your greatest agent of power, to the customs and conventionalities that have gotten their life from the great mass of those who haven't enough force to preserve their individualities,—those who in other words have given them over as ingredients to the "mush of concession" which one of our greatest writers has said characterizes our modern society. If you do surrender your individuality in this way, you simply aid in increasing the undesirable conditions; in payment for this you become a slave, and the chances are that in time you will be unable to hold even the respect of those whom you in this way try to please.

If you preserve your individuality then you become a master, and if wise and discreet, your influence and power will be an aid in bringing about a higher, a better, and a more healthy set of conditions in the world. All people, moreover, will think more of you, will honor you more highly for doing this than if you show your weakness by contributing yourself to the same "mush of concession" that so many of them are contributing themselves to. With all classes of people you will then have an influence. "A great style of hero draws equally all classes, all extremes of society to him, till we say the very dogs believe in him."

To be one's self is the only worthy, and by all means the only satisfactory, thing to be. "May it not be good policy," says one, "to be governed sometimes by one's surroundings?" What is good policy? To be yourself, first, last, and always.

> "This above all,—to thine own self be true;
> And it must follow, as the night the day,
> Thou canst not then be false to any man."

"When we appeal to the Supreme and our life is governed by a principle, we are not governed either by fear of public opinion or loss of others' approbation, and we may be sure that the Supreme will sustain us. If in any way we try to live to suit others we never shall suit them, and the more we try the more unreasonable and exacting do they become. The government of your life is a matter that lies entirely between God and yourself, and when your life is swayed and influenced from any other source you are on the wrong path." When we find the kingdom within and become centred in the Infinite, then we become a law unto ourselves. When we become a law unto ourselves, then we are able to bring others to a knowledge of laws higher than they are governed or many times even enslaved by.

When we have found this centre, then that beautiful simplicity, at once the charm and the power of a truly great personality, enters into our lives. Then all striving for effect,—that sure indicator of weakness and a lack of genuine power,—is absent. This striving for effect that is so common is always an indicator of a lack of something. It brings to mind the man who rides behind a dock-tailed horse. Conscious of the fact that there is not enough in *himself* to attract attention, in common with a number of other weaklings, he adopts the brutal method of having his horse's tail sawed off, that its unnatural, odd appearance may attract from

95

people the attention that he of himself is unable to secure.

But the one who strives for effect is always fooled more than he succeeds in fooling others. The man and the woman of true wisdom and insight can always see the causes that prompt, the motives that underlie the acts of all with whom he or she comes in contact. "He is great who is what he is from nature and who never reminds us of others."

The men and the women who are truly awake to the real powers within are the men and women who seem to be doing so little, yet who in reality are doing so much. They seem to be doing so little because they are working with higher agencies, and yet are doing so much because of this very fact. They do their work on the higher plane. They keep so completely their connection with the Infinite Power that *It* does the work for them and they are relieved of the responsibility. They are the care-less people. They are care-less because it is the Infinite Power that is working through them, and with this Infinite Power they are simply co-operating.

The secret of the highest power is simply the uniting of the outer agencies of expression with the Power that works from within. Are you a painter? Then in the degree that you open yourself to the power of the forces within will you become great instead of mediocre. You can never put into permanent form inspirations higher than those that come through your own soul. In order for the higher inspirations to come through it, you must open your soul, you must open it fully to the Supreme Source of all inspiration. Are you an orator? In the degree that you come into harmony and work in conjunction with the higher powers that will speak through you will you have the real power of moulding and of moving men. If you use merely your physical agents, you will be simply a demagogue. If you open yourself so that the voice of God can speak through and use your physical agents, you will become a great and true orator, great and true in just the degree that you so open yourself.

Are you a singer? Then open yourself and let the God within pour forth in the spirit of song. You will find it a thousand times easier than all your long and studied practice without this, and other things being equal, there will come to you a power of song so enchanting and so enrapturing that its influence upon all who hear will be irresistible.

When my cabin or tent has been pitched during the summer on the edge or in the midst of a forest, I have sometimes lain awake on my cot in the early morning, just as the day was beginning to break. Silence at first. Then an intermittent chirp here and there. And as the unfolding tints of the dawn became faintly perceptible, these grew more and more frequent, until by and by the whole forest seemed to burst forth in one grand chorus of song. Wonderful! wonderful! It seemed as if the very trees, as if every grass-blade, as if the bushes, the very sky above, and the earth beneath, had part in this wonderful symphony. Then, as I have listened as it went on and on, I have thought. What a study in the matter of song! If we could but learn from the birds. If we could but open ourselves to the same powers and allow them to pour forth in us, what singers, what movers of men we might have! Nay, what singers and what movers of men *we would have!*

Do you know the circumstances under which Mr. Sankey sang for the first time "The Ninety and Nine?" Says one of our able journals: "At a great meeting recently in Denver, Mr. Ira W. Sankey, before singing 'The Ninety and Nine,' which, perhaps, of all his compositions is the one that has brought him the most fame, gave an account of its birth. Leaving Glasgow for Edinburg with Mr. Moody, he stopped at a news-stand and bought a penny religious paper. Glancing over it as they rode on the cars, his eye fell on a few little verses in the corner of the page. Turning to Mr. Moody he said, 'I've found my hymn.' But Mr. Moody was busily engaged and did not hear a word. Mr. Sankey did not find time to make a tune for the verses, so he pasted them in his music scrapbook.

"One day they had an unusually impressive meeting in Edin-burg, in which Dr. Bonar had spoken with great effect on 'The Good Shepherd.' At the close of the address Mr. Moody beckoned to his partner to sing. He thought of nothing but the Twenty-third

Psalm, but that he had sung so often. His second thought was to sing the verses he had found in the newspaper, but the third thought was, how could it be done when he had no tune. Then a fourth thought came, and that was to sing them anyway. He put the verses before him, touched the keys of the organ, opened his mouth and sang, not knowing where he was going to come out. He finished the first verse amid profound silence. He took a long breath and wondered if he could sing the second the same way. He tried and succeeded; after that it was easy to sing it. When he finished the hymn the meeting was all broken down and the throngs were crying. Mr. Sankey says it was the most intense moment of his life. Mr. Moody said he never heard a song like it. It was sung at every meeting, and was soon going over the world."

When we open ourselves to the highest inspirations they never fail us. When we fail to do this we fail in attaining the highest results, whatever the undertaking.

Are you a writer? Then remember that the one great precept underlying all successful literary work is, *Look into thine own heart and write. Be true. Be fearless. Be loyal to the promptings of your own soul.* Remember that an author can never write more than he himself is. If he would write more, then he must be more. He is simply his own amanuensis. He in a sense writes himself into his book. He can put no more into it than he himself is.

If he is one of a great personality, strong in purpose, deep in feeling, open always to the highest inspirations, a certain indefinable something gets into his pages that makes them breathe forth a vital, living power, a power so great that each reader gets the same inspirations as those that spoke through the author. That that's written between the lines is many times more than that that's written in the lines. It is the spirit of the author that engenders this power. It is this that gives that extra twenty-five or thirty per cent that takes a book out of the class called medium and lifts it into the class called superior,—that extra per cent that makes it the one of the hundred that is truly successful, while the ninety-nine never see more than their first edition.

It is this same spiritual power that the author of a great personality puts into his work, that causes it to go so rapidly from reader to reader; for the only way that any book circulates in the ultimate is from mouth to mouth, any book that reaches a large circulation. It is this that many times causes a single reader, in view of its value to himself, to purchase numbers of copies for others. "A good poem," says Emerson, "goes about the world offering itself to reasonable men, who read it with joy and carry it to their reasonable neighbors. Thus it draws to it the *wise and generous souls*, confirming their secret thoughts, and through their sympathy *really publishing itself*."

This is the type of author who writes not with the thought of having what he writes become literature, but he writes with the sole thought of reaching the hearts of the people, giving them something of vital value, something that will broaden, sweeten, enrich, and beautify their lives; that will lead them to the finding of the higher life and with it the higher powers and the higher joys. It most always happens, however, that if he succeeds in thus reaching the people, the becoming literature part somehow takes care of itself, and far better than if he aimed for it directly.

The one, on the other hand, who fears to depart from beaten paths, who allows himself to be bound by arbitrary rules, limits his own creative powers in just the degree that he allows himself so to be bound. "My book," says one of the greatest of modern authors, "shall smell of the pines and resound with the hum of insects. The swallow over my window shall interweave that thread or straw he carries in his bill into my web also." Far better, gentle sage, to have it smell of the pines and resound with the hum of insects than to have it sound of the rules that a smaller type of man gets by studying the works of a few great, fearless writers like yourself, and formulating from what he thus gains a handbook of rhetoric. "Of no use are the men who study to do exactly as was done before, who can never understand that *today is a new day*."

When Shakspeare is charged with debts to his authors, Landor replies: "Yet he was more original than his originals. He breathed upon dead bodies and brought them into life." This is the type of man who doesn't move the world's way, but who moves the world his way.

I had rather be an amanuensis of the Infinite God, as it is my privilege literally to be, than a slave to the formulated rules of any rhetorician, or to the opinions of any critic. Oh, the people, the people over and over! Let me give something to them that will lighten the every-day struggles of our common life, something that will add a little sweetness here, a little hope there, something that will make more thoughtful, kind, and gentle this thoughtless, animal-natured man, something that will awaken into activity the dormant powers of this timid, shrinking little woman, powers that when awakened will be irresistible in their influence and that will surprise even herself. Let me give something that will lead each one to the knowledge of the divinity of every human soul, something that will lead each one to the conscious realization of *his own divinity*, with all its attendant riches, and glories, and powers,—let me succeed in doing this, and I can then well afford to be careless as to whether the critics praise or whether they blame. If it is blame, then under these circumstances it is as the cracking of a few dead sticks on the ground below, compared to the matchless music that the soft spring gale is breathing through the great pine forest.

Are you a minister, or a religious teacher of any kind? Then in the degree that you free yourself from the man-made theological dogmas that have held and that are holding and limiting so many, and in the degree that you open yourself to the Divine Breath, will you be one who will speak with authority. In the degree that you do this will you study the prophets less and be in the way of becoming a prophet yourself. The way is open for you exactly the same as it has ever been open for anyone.

If when born into the world you came into a family of the English-speaking race, then in all probability you are a Christian. To be a Christian is to be a follower of the *teachings* of Jesus, the Christ; to live in harmony with the same laws he lived in harmony with: in brief, *to live his life*. The great central fact of his teaching was this conscious union of man with the Father. It was the complete realization of this oneness with the Father on his part that made Jesus the Christ. It was through this that he attained to the power he attained to, that he spake as never man spake.

He never claimed for himself anything that he did not claim equally for all mankind. "The mighty works performed by Jesus were not exceptional, they were the natural and necessary concomitants of his state; he declared them to be in accordance with unvarying order; he spoke of them as no unique performances, but as the outcome of a state to which all might attain if they chose. As a teacher and demonstrator of truth, according to his own confession, he did nothing for the purpose of proving his solitary divinity. . . . The life and triumph of Jesus formed an epoch in the history of the race. His coming and victory marked a new era in human affairs; he introduced a new because a more complete ideal to the earth, and when his three most intimate companions saw in some measure what the new life really signified, they fell to the earth, speechless with awe and admiration."

By coming into this complete realization of his oneness with the Father, by mastering, absolutely mastering every circumstance that crossed his path through life, even to the death of the body, and by pointing out to us the great laws which are the same for us as they were for him, he has given us an ideal of life, an ideal for us to attain to *here and now*, that we could not have without him.*One has conquered first; all may conquer afterward.* By completely realizing it first for himself, and then by pointing out to others this great law of the at-one-ment with the Father, he has become probably the world's greatest saviour.

Don't mistake his mere person for his life and his teachings, an error that has been made in connection with most all great teachers by their disciples over and over again. And if you have been among the number who have been preaching a dead Christ, then for humanity's sake, for Christ's sake, for God's sake, and I speak most reverently, don't steal the people's time any longer, don't waste your own time more, in giving them stones in place of bread, dead form for the spirit of living truth. In his own words, "let the dead bury their dead." Come out from among them. Teach as did Jesus, *the living Christ.* Teach as did Jesus, *the Christ within.* Find this in all its transcendent beauty and power,—find it as Jesus found it, then you also will be one who will speak with authority. Then you will be able to lead large numbers of others to its finding. This is the pearl of great price.

It is the type of preacher whose soul has never as yet even perceived the *vital spirit* of the teachings of Jesus, and who as a consequence instead of giving this to the people, is giving them old forms and dogmas and speculations, who is emptying our churches. This is the type whose chief efforts seem to be in getting men ready to die. The Germans have a saying, Never go to the second thing first. We need men who will teach us first how to live. Living quite invariably precedes dying. This also is true, that when we once know how to live, and live in accordance with what we know, then the dying, as we term it, will in a wonderfully beautiful manner take care of itself. It is in fact the only way in which it can be taken care of.

It is on account of this emptying of our churches, for the reason that the people are tiring of mere husks, that many short-sighted people are frequently heard to say that religion is dying out. Religion dying out? How can anything die before it is really born? And so far as the people are concerned, religion is just being born, or rather they are just awaking to a vital, every-day religion. We are just beginning to get beyond the mere letter into its real, vital spirit. Religion dying out? Impossible even to conceive of. Religion is as much a part of the human soul as the human soul is a part of God. And as long as God and the human soul exist, religion will never die.

Much of the dogma, the form, the ceremony, the mere letter that has stood as religion,—and honestly, many times, let us be fair enough to say,—this, thank God, is rapidly dying out, and never so rapidly as it is today. By two methods it is dying. There is, first, a large class of people tired of or even nauseated with it all, who conscientiously prefer to have nothing rather than this. They are simply abandoning it, the same as a tree abandons its leaves when the early winter comes. There is, second, a large class in whom the Divine Breath is stirring, who are finding the Christ within in all its matchless beauty and redeeming power. And this new life is pushing off the old, the same as in the spring the newly awakened life in the tree pushes off the old, lifeless leaves that have clung on during the winter, to make place for the new ones. And the way this old dead leaf religion is being pushed off on every hand is indeed most interesting and inspiring to witness.

Let the places of those who have been emptying our churches by reason of their attempts to give stones for bread, husks and chaff for the life-giving grain, let their places be taken even for but a few times by those who are open and alive to these higher inspirations, and then let us again question those who feel that religion is dying out. "It is the live coal that kindles others, not the dead." Let their places be taken by those who have caught the inspiration of the Divine Breath, who as a consequence have a message of mighty value and import for the people, who by virtue of this same fact are able to present it with a beauty and a power so enrapturing that it takes captive the soul. Then we will find that the churches that today are dotted here and there with a few dozen people will be filled to overflowing, and there will not be even room enough for all who would enter. "Let the shell perish that the pearl may appear." We need no new revelations as yet. We need simply to find the vital spirit of those we already have. Then in due time, when we are ready for them, new ones will come, but not before.

"What the human soul, all the world over, needs," says John Pulsford, "is not to be harangued, however eloquently, about the old, accepted religion, but to be permeated, charmed, and taken captive by *a warmer and more potent Breath of God than they ever felt before.* And I should not be true to my personal experience if I did not bear testimony that this Divine Breath is as exquisitely adapted to the requirements of the soul's nature as a June morning to the planet. Nor does the morning breath leave the trees freer to delight themselves and develop themselves under its influence than the Breath of God allows each human mind to unfold according to its genius. Nothing stirs the central wheel of the soul like the Breath of God. The whole man is quickened, his senses are new senses, his emotions new emotions; his reason, his affections, his imagination, are all new-born. The change is greater than he knows; he marvels at the powers in himself which the Breath is opening and calling forth. He finds his nature to be an unutterable thing; he is sure therefore that the future must have inconceivable surprises in store. And herein lies the evidence, which I commend to my readers, of the existence of God, and of the Eternal human Hope. Let God's Breath kindle new spring-time in the soul, start into life its deeply buried germs, lead in heaven's summer; you will then have as clear evidence of God from within as you have of the universe from without. Indeed, your internal experience of life, and illimitable Hope in God will be nearer to you, and more prevailing, than all your external and superficial experience of nature and the world."

There is but one source of power in the universe. Whatever then you are, painter, orator, musician, writer, religious teacher, or whatever it may be, know that to catch and take captive the secret of power is so to work in conjunction with the Infinite Power, in order that it may continually work and manifest through you. If you fail in doing this, you fail in everything. If you fail in doing this, your work, whatever it may be, will be third or fourth rate, possibly at times second rate, but it positively never can be first rate. Absolutely impossible will it be for you ever to become a master.

Whatever estimate you put upon yourself will determine the effectiveness of your work along any line. As long as you live merely in the physical and the intellectual, you set limitations to yourself that will hold you as long as you so live. When, however, you come into the realization of your oneness with the Infinite

Life and Power, and open yourself that it may work through you, you will find that you have entered upon an entirely new phase of life, and that an ever increasing power will be yours. Then it will be true that your strength will be as the strength of ten because your heart is pure.

> "O God! I am one forever
>   With Thee by the glory of birth;
> The celestial powers proclaim it
>   To the utmost bounds of the earth.
> "I think of this birthright immortal,
>   And my being expands like a rose,
> As an odorous cloud of incense
>   Around and above me flows.
> "A glorious song of rejoicing
>   In an innermost spirit I hear,
> And it sounds like heavenly voices,
>   In a chorus divine and clear.
> "And I feel a power uprising,
>   Like the power of an embryo god;
> With a glorious wall it surrounds me,
>   And lifts me up from the sod."

IX

Plenty Of All Things—The Law Of Prosperity

This is the Spirit of Infinite Plenty, the Power that has brought, that is continually bringing, all things into expression in material form. He who lives in the realization of his oneness with this Infinite Power becomes a magnet to attract to himself a continual supply of whatsoever things he desires.

If one hold himself in the thought of poverty, he will be poor, and the chances are that he will remain in poverty. If he hold himself, whatever present conditions may be, continually in the thought of prosperity, he sets into operation forces that will sooner or later bring him into prosperous conditions. The law of attraction works unceasingly throughout the universe, and the one great and never changing fact in connection with it is, as we have found, that like attracts like. If we are one with this Infinite Power, this source of all things, then in the degree that we live in the realization of this oneness, in that degree do we actualize in ourselves a power that will bring to us an abundance of all things that it is desirable for us to have. In this way we come into possession of a power whereby we can actualize at all times those conditions that we desire.

As all truth exists *now*, and awaits simply our perception of it, so all things necessary for present needs exist *now*, and await simply the power in us to appropriate them. God holds all things in His hands. His constant word is, My child, acknowledge me in all your ways, and in the degree that you do this, in the degree that you live this, then what is mine is yours. Jehovah-jireh,—the Lord will provide. "He giveth to all men liberally and upbraideth not." He giveth liberally to all men who put themselves in the right attitude to receive from Him. He forces no good things upon any one.

The old and somewhat prevalent idea of godliness and poverty has absolutely no basis for its existence, and the sooner we get away from it the better. It had its birth in the same way that the idea of asceticism came into existence, when the idea prevailed that there was necessarily a warfare between the flesh and the spirit. It had its origin therefore in the minds of those who had a distorted, a one-sided view of life. True godliness is in a sense the same as true wisdom. The one who is truly wise, and who uses the forces and powers with which he is endowed, to him the great universe always opens her treasure house. The supply is always equal to the demand,—equal to the demand when the demand is rightly, wisely made. When one comes into the realization of these higher laws, then the fear of want ceases to tyrannize over him.

Are you out of a situation? Let the fear that you will not get another take hold of and *dominate* you, and the chances are that it may be a long time before you will get another, or the one that you do get may be a very poor one indeed. Whatever the circumstances, you must realize that you have within you forces and powers that you can set into operation that will triumph over any and all apparent or temporary losses. Set these forces into operation and you will then be placing a magnet that will draw to you a situation that may be far better than the one you have lost, and the time may soon come when you will be even thankful that you lost the old one.

Recognize, working in and through you, the same Infinite Power that creates and governs all things in the universe, the same Infinite Power that governs the endless systems of worlds in space. Send out your thought,—thought is a force, and it has occult power of unknown proportions when rightly used and wisely directed,—

send out your thought that the right situation or the right work will come to you at the right time, in the right way, and that you will recognize it when it comes. Hold to this thought, never allow it to weaken, hold to it, and continually water it with firm expectation. You in this way put your advertisement into a psychical, a spiritual newspaper, a paper that has not a limited circulation, but one that will make its way not only to the utmost bounds of the earth, but of the very universe itself. It is an advertisement, moreover, which if rightly placed on your part, will be far more effective than any advertisement you could possibly put into any printed sheet, no matter what claims are made in regard to its being "the great advertising medium." In the degree that you come into this realization and live in harmony with the higher laws and forces, in that degree will you be able to do this effectively.

If you wish to look through the "want" columns of the newspapers, then do it not in the ordinary way. Put the higher forces into operation and thus place it on a higher basis. As you take up the paper, take this attitude of mind: If there is here an advertisement that it will be well for me to reply to, the moment I come to it I will recognize it. Affirm this, believe it, expect it. If you do this in full faith you will somehow feel the intuition the moment you come to the right one, and this intuition will be nothing more nor less than your own soul speaking to you. When it speaks then act at once.

If you get the situation and it does not prove to be exactly what you want, if you feel that you are capable of filling a better one, then the moment you enter upon it take the attitude of mind that this situation is the stepping-stone that will lead you to one that will be still better. Hold this thought steadily, affirm it, believe it, expect it, and all the time be faithful, *absolutely faithful* to the situation in which you are at present placed. If you are *not* faithful to it then the chances are that it will not be the stepping-stone to something better, but to something poorer. If you are faithful to it, the time may soon come when you will be glad and thankful, when you will rejoice, that you lost your old position.

This is the law of prosperity: When apparent adversity comes, be not cast down by it, but make the best of it, and always look forward for better things, for conditions more prosperous. To hold yourself in this attitude of mind is to set into operation subtle, silent, and irresistible forces that sooner or later will actualize in material form that which is today merely an idea. But ideas have occult power, and ideas, when rightly planted and rightly tended, are the seeds that actualize material conditions.

Never give a moment to complaint, but utilize the time that would otherwise be spent in this way in looking forward and actualizing the conditions you desire. Suggest prosperity to yourself. See yourself in a prosperous condition. Affirm that you will before long be in a prosperous condition. Affirm it calmly and quietly, but strongly and confidently. Believe it, believe it absolutely. Expect it,—keep it continually watered with expectation. You thus make yourself a magnet to attract the things that you desire. Don't be afraid to suggest, to affirm these things, for by so doing you put forth an ideal which will begin to clothe itself in material form. In this way you are utilizing agents among the most subtle and powerful in the universe. If you are particularly desirous for anything that you feel it is good and right for you to have, something that will broaden your life or that will increase your usefulness to others, simply hold the thought that at the right time, in the right way, and through the right instrumentality, there will come to you or there will open up for you the way whereby you can attain what you desire.

I know of a young lady who a short time ago wanted some money very badly. She wanted it for a good purpose; she saw no reason why she shouldn't have it. She is one who has come into an understanding of the power of the interior forces. She took and held herself in the attitude of mind we have just pointed out. In the morning she entered into the silence for a few moments. In this way she brought herself into a more complete harmony with the higher powers. Before the day closed a gentleman called, a member of a family with which she was acquainted. He asked her if she would do for the family some work that they wanted done. She was a little surprised that they should ask her to do this particular kind of work, but she said to herself, "Here is a call. I will respond and see what it will lead to." She undertook the work. *She did it well.* When she had completed it there was put into her hands an amount of money far beyond what she had expected. She felt that it was an amount too large for the work she had done. She protested. They replied, "No; you have done us a service that transcends in value the amount we offer to pay you." The sum thus received was more than sufficient for the work she wished to accomplish.

This is but one of many instances in connection with the wise and effective use of the higher powers. It also carries a lesson,— Don't fold your hands and expect to see things drop into your lap, but set into operation the higher forces and then take hold of the first thing that offers itself. Do what your hands find to do, *and do it well.* If this work is not thoroughly satisfactory to you, then affirm, believe, and expect that it is the agency that will lead you to something better. "The basis for attracting the best of all the world can give to you is to first surround, own, and live in these things in mind, or what is falsely called imagination. All so-called imaginings are realities and forces of unseen element. Live in mind in a palace and gradually palatial surroundings will gravitate to you. But so living is *not* pining, or longing, or complainingly wishing. It is when you are 'down in the world,' calmly and persistently seeing yourself as up. It is when you are now compelled to eat from a tin plate, regarding that tin plate as only the certain step to one of silver. It is not envying and growling at other people who have silver plate. That growling is just so much capital stock taken from the bank account of mental force."

A friend who knows the power of the interior forces, and whose life is guided in every detail by them, has given a suggestion in this form: When you are in the arms of the bear, even though he is hugging you, look him in the face and laugh, but all the time keep your eye on the bull. If you allow all of your attention to be given to the work of the bear, the bull may get entirely out of your sight. In other words, if you yield to adversity the chances are that it will master you, but if you recognize in yourself the power of mastery over conditions then adversity will yield to you, and will be changed into prosperity. If when it comes you calmly and quietly recognize it, and use the time that might otherwise be spent in regrets, and fears, and forebodings, in setting into operation the powerful forces within you, it will soon take its leave.

Faith, absolute dogmatic faith, is the only law of true success. When we recognize the fact that a man carries his success or his failure with him, and that it does not depend upon outside conditions, we will come into the possession of powers that will quickly change outside conditions into agencies that make for success. When we come into this higher realization and bring our lives into complete harmony with the higher laws, we will then be able so to focus and direct the awakened interior forces, that they will go out and return laden with that for which they are sent. We will then be great enough to attract success, and it will not always be apparently just a little ways ahead. We can then establish in ourselves a centre so strong that instead of running hither and thither for this or that, we can stay at home and draw to us the conditions we desire. If we firmly establish and hold to this centre, things will seem continually to come our way.

The majority of people of the modern world are looking for things that are practical and that can be utilized in every-day life. The more carefully we examine into the laws underlying the great truths we are considering, the more we will find that they are not only eminently practical, but in a sense, and in the deepest and truest sense, they are the only practical things there are.

There are people who continually pride themselves upon being exceedingly "practical," but many times those who of themselves think nothing about this are the most practical people the world knows. And, on the other hand, those who take great pride in speaking of their own practicality are many times the least practical. Or again, in some ways they may be practical, but so far as

life in its totality is concerned, they are absurdly impractical.

What profit, for example, can there be for the man who, materially speaking, though he has gained the whole world, has never yet become acquainted with his own soul? There are multitudes of men all about us who are entirely missing the real life, men who have not learned even the a, b, c of true living. Slaves they are, abject slaves to their temporary material accumulations. Men who thinking they possess their wealth are on the contrary completely possessed by it. Men whose lives are comparatively barren in service to those about them and to the world at large. Men who when they can no longer hold the body,—the agency by means of which they are related to the material world,—will go out poor indeed, pitiably poor. Unable to take even the smallest particle of their accumulations with them, they will enter upon the other form of life naked and destitute.

The kindly deeds, the developed traits of character, the realized powers of the soul, the real riches of the inner life and unfoldment, all those things that become our real and eternal possessions, have been given no place in their lives, and so of the real things of life they are destitute. Nay, many times worse than destitute. We must not suppose that habits once formed are any more easily broken off in the other form of life than they are in this. If one voluntarily grows a certain mania here, we must not suppose that the mere dropping of the body makes all conditions perfect. All is law, all is cause and effect. As we sow, so shall we also reap, not only in this life but in all lives.

He who is enslaved with the sole desire for material possessions here will continue to be enslaved even after he can no longer retain his body. Then, moreover, he will have not even the means of gratifying his desires. Dominated by this habit, he will be unable to set his affections, for a time at least, upon other things, and the desire, without the means of gratifying it will be doubly torturing to him. Perchance this torture may be increased by his seeing the accumulations he thought were his now being scattered and wasted by spendthrifts. He wills his property, as we say, to others, but he can have no word as to its use.

How foolish, then, for us to think that any material posses-sions *are ours*. How absurd, for example, for one to fence off a number of acres of God's earth and say they are *his*. Nothing is ours that we cannot retain. The things that come into our hands come not for the purpose of being possessed, as we say, much less for the purpose of being hoarded. They come into our hands to be used, to be wisely used. We are stewards merely, and as stew-ards we shall be held accountable for the way we use whatever is entrusted to us. That great law of compensation that runs through all life is wonderfully exact in its workings, although we may not always fully comprehend it, or even recognize it when it operates in connection with ourselves.

The one who has come into the realization of the higher life no longer has a desire for the accumulation of enormous wealth, any more than he has a desire for any other *excess*. In the degree that he comes into the recognition of the fact that he is wealthy within, external wealth becomes less important in his estimation. When he comes into the realization of the fact that there is a source within from which he can put forth a power to call to him and actualize in his hands at any time a sufficient supply for all his needs, he no longer burdens himself with vast material accumulations that require his constant care and attention, and thus take his time and his thought from the real things of life. In other words, he first finds the *kingdom*, and he realizes that when he has found this, all other things follow in full measure.

It is as hard for a rich man to enter into the kingdom of heaven, said the Master,—he who having nothing had everything,—as it is for a camel to pass through the eye of a needle. In other words, if a man give all his time to the accumulation, the hoarding of outward material possessions far beyond what he can possibly ever use, what time has he for the finding of that wonderful kingdom, which when found, brings all else with it. Which is better, to have millions of dollars, and to have the burden of taking care of it all,—for the one always involves the other,—or to come into the knowledge of such laws and forces that every need will be supplied in good time, to know that no good thing shall be withheld, to know that we have it in our power to make the supply always equal to the demand?

The one who enters into the realm of this higher knowledge, never cares to bring upon himself the species of insanity that has such a firm hold upon so many in the world today. He avoids it as he would avoid any loathsome disease of the body. When we come into the realization of the higher powers, we will then be able to give more attention to the real life, instead of giving so much to the piling up of vast possessions that hamper rather than help it. It is the medium ground that brings the true solution here, the same as it is in all phases of life.

Wealth beyond a certain amount cannot be used, and when it cannot be used it then becomes a hindrance rather than an aid, a curse rather than a blessing. All about us are persons with lives now stunted and dwarfed who could make them rich and beautiful, filled with a perennial joy, if they would begin wisely to use that which they have spent the greater portion of their lives in accumulating.

The man who accumulates during his entire life, and who leaves even all when he goes out for "benevolent purposes," comes far short of the ideal life. It is but a poor excuse of a life. It is not especially commendable in me to give a pair of old, worn-out shoes that I shall never use again to another who is in need of shoes. But it is commendable, if indeed doing anything we ought to do can be spoken of as being commendable, it is commendable for me to give a good pair of strong shoes to the man who in the midst of a severe winter is practically shoeless, the man who is exerting every effort to earn an honest living and thereby take care of his family's needs. And if in giving the shoes I also give myself, he then has a double gift, and I a double blessing.

There is no wiser use that those who have great accumulations can make of them than wisely to put them into life, into character, *day by day while they live*. In this way their lives will be continually enriched and increased. The time will come when it will be regarded as a disgrace for a man to die and leave vast accumulations behind him.

Many a person is living in a palace today who in the real life is poorer than many a one who has not even a roof to cover him. A man may own and live in a palace, but the palace for him may be a pool-house still.

Moth and rust are nature's wise provisions—God's methods— for disintegrating and scattering, in this way getting ready for use in new forms, that which is hoarded and consequently serving no use. There is also a great law continually operating whose effects are to dwarf and deaden the powers of true enjoyment, as well as all the higher faculties of the one who hoards.

Multitudes of people are continually keeping away from them higher and better things because they are forever clinging on to the old. If they would use and pass on the old, room would be made for new things to come. Hoarding always brings loss in one form or another. Using, wisely using, brings an ever renewing gain.

If the tree should as ignorantly and as greedily hold on to this year's leaves when they have served their purpose, where would be the full and beautiful new life that will be put forth in the spring? Gradual decay and finally death would be the result. If the tree is already dead, then it may perhaps be well enough for it to cling on to the old, for no new leaves will come. But as long as the life in the tree is active, it is *necessary* that it rid itself of the old ones, that room may be made for the new.

Opulence is the law of the universe, an abundant supply for every need if nothing is put in the way of its coming. The natural and the normal life for us is this,—To have such a fullness of life and power by living so continually in the realization of our oneness with the Infinite Life and Power that we find ourselves in the constant possession of an abundant supply of all things needed.

Then not by hoarding but by wisely using and ridding ourselves of things as they come, an ever renewing supply will be ours, a supply far better adapted to present needs than the old could possibly be. In this way we not only come into possession of the richest treasures of the Infinite Good ourselves, but we also become open channels through which they can flow to others.

X

How Men Have Become Prophets, Seers, Sages, And Saviours

I have tried thus far to deal fairly with you in presenting these vital truths, and have spoken of everything on the basis of our own reason and insight. It has been my aim to base nothing on the teachings of others, though they may be the teachings of those inspired. Let us now look for a moment at these same great truths in the light of the thoughts and the teachings as put forth by some of the world's great thinkers and inspired teachers.

The sum and substance of the thought presented in these pages is, you will remember, that the great central fact in human life is the coming into a conscious, vital realization of our oneness with the Infinite Life, and the opening of ourselves fully to this divine inflow. I and the Father are one, said the Master. In this we see how he recognized his oneness with the Father's life. Again he said, The words that I speak unto you I speak not of myself: but the Father that dwelleth in me, He doeth the works. In this we see how clearly he recognized the fact that he of himself could do nothing, only as he worked in conjunction with the Father. Again, My Father works and I work. In other words, my Father sends the power, I open myself to it, and work in conjunction with it.

Again he said, Seek ye first the kingdom of God and His righteousness, and all these things shall be added unto you. And he left us not in the dark as to exactly what he meant by this, for again he said. Say not Lo here nor lo there, know ye not that the kingdom of heaven is within you? According to his teaching, the kingdom of God and the kingdom of heaven were one and the same. If, then, his teaching is that the kingdom of heaven is within us, do we not clearly see that, putting it in other words, his injunction is nothing more nor less than, Come ye into a conscious realization of your oneness with the Father's life. As you realize this oneness you find the kingdom, and when you find this, all things else shall follow.

The story of the prodigal son is another beautiful illustration of this same great teaching of the Master. After the prodigal had spent everything, after he had wandered in all the realms of the physical senses in the pursuit of happiness and pleasure, and found that this did not satisfy but only brought him to the level of the animal creation, he then came to his senses and said, I will arise and go to my Father. In other words, after all these wanderings, his own soul at length spoke to him and said, You are not a mere animal. You are your Father's child. Arise and go to your Father, who holds all things in His hands. Again, the Master said, Call no man your Father upon the earth: for one is your Father, which is in heaven. Here he recognized the fact that the real life is direct from the life of God. Our fathers and our mothers are the agents that give us the bodies, the houses in which we live, but the real life comes from the Infinite Source of Life, God, who is our Father.

One day word was brought to the Master that his mother and his brethren were without, wishing to speak with him. Who is my mother and who are my brethren? said he. Whosoever shall do the will of my Father which is in heaven, the same is my brother, and my sister, and mother.

Many people are greatly enslaved by what we term ties of relationship. It is well, however, for us to remember that our true relatives are not necessarily those who are connected with us by ties of blood. Our truest relatives are those who are nearest akin to us in mind, in soul, in spirit. Our nearest relatives may be those living on the opposite side of the globe,—people whom we may never have seen as yet, but to whom we will yet be drawn, either in this form of life or in another, through that ever working and never failing law of attraction.

When the Master gave the injunction, Call no man your father upon the earth: for one is your Father, which is in heaven, he here gave us the basis for that grand conception of the fatherhood of God. And if God is equally the Father of all, then we have here the basis for the brotherhood of man. But there is, in a sense, a conception still higher than this, namely, the oneness of man and God, and hence the oneness of the whole human race. When we realize this fact, then we clearly see how in the degree that we come into the realization of our oneness with the Infinite Life, and so, every step that we make Godward, we aid in lifting all mankind up to this realization, and enable them, in turn, to make a step God-ward.

The Master again pointed out our true relations with the Infinite Life when he said, Except ye become as little children ye shall not enter into the kingdom of heaven. When he said, Man shall not live by bread alone, but by every word that proceedeth out of the mouth of God, he gave utterance to a truth of far greater import than we have as yet commenced fully to grasp. Here he taught that even the physical life can not be maintained by material food alone, but that one's connection with this Infinite Source determines to a very great extent the condition of even the bodily structure and activities. Blessed are the pure in heart for they shall see God. In other words, blessed are they who in all the universe recognize only God, for by such God shall be seen.

Said the great Hindu sage, Manu, He who in his own soul perceives the Supreme Soul in all beings, and acquires equanimity toward them all, attains the highest bliss. It was Athanasius who said, Even we may become Gods walking about in the flesh. The same great truth we are considering is the one that runs through the life and the teachings of Gautama, he who became the Buddha. People are in bondage, said he, because they have not yet removed the idea of *I*. To do away with all sense of separateness, and to recognize the oneness of the self with the Infinite, is the spirit that breathes through all his teachings. Running through the lives of all the mediaeval mystics was this same great truth,—union with God.

Then, coming nearer to our own time, we find the highly illumined seer, Emanuel Swedenborg, pointing out the great laws in connection with what he termed, the divine influx, and how we may open ourselves more fully to its operations. The great central fact in the religion and worship of the Friends is, the inner light,—God in the soul of man speaking directly in just the degree that the soul is opened to Him. The inspired one, the seer who when with us lived at Concord, recognized the same great truth when he said, We are all inlets to the great sea of life. And it was by opening himself so fully to its inflow that he became one inspired.

All through the world's history we find that the men and the women who have entered into the realm of true wisdom and power, and hence into the realm of true peace and joy, have lived in harmony with this Higher Power. David was strong and powerful and his soul burst forth in praise and adoration in just the degree that he listened to the voice of God and lived in accordance with his higher promptings. Whenever he failed to do this we hear his soul crying out in anguish and lamentation. The same is true of every nation or people. When the Israelites acknowledged God and followed according to His leadings they were prosperous, contented, and powerful, and nothing could prevail against them. When they depended upon their own strength alone and failed to recognize God as the source of their strength, we find them overcome, in bondage, or despair.

A great immutable law underlies the truth, Blessed are they that hear the word of God and do it. Then follows all. We are wise in the degree that we live according to the higher light.

All the prophets, seers, sages, and saviours in the world's history became what they became, and consequently had the powers they had, through an entirely natural process. They all recognized and came into the conscious realization of their oneness with the Infinite Life. God is no respecter of persons. He doesn't create prophets, seers, sages, and saviours as such. He creates men. But here and there one recognizes his true identity, recognizes the oneness of his life with the Source whence it came. He lives in the realization of this oneness, and in turn becomes a prophet, seer, sage, or saviour. Neither is God a respecter of races or of nations. He has no chosen people; but here and there a race or nation becomes a respecter of God and hence lives the life of a chosen people.

There has been no age or place of miracles in distinction from any other age or place. What we term miracles have abounded in all places and at all times where conditions have been made for them. They are being performed today just as much as they ever have been when the laws governing them are respected. Mighty men, we are told they were, mighty men who walked with God; and in the words "who walked with God" lies the secret of the words "mighty men." Cause, effect.

The Lord never prospers any man, but the man prospers because he acknowledges the Lord, and lives in accordance with the higher laws. Solomon was given the opportunity of choosing whatever he desired; his better judgment prevailed and he chose wisdom. But when he chose wisdom he found that it included all else beside. We are told that God hardened Pharaoh's heart. I don't believe it. God never hardens any one's heart. Pharaoh hardened his own heart and God was blamed for it. But when Pharaoh hardened his heart and disobeyed the voice of God, the plagues came. Again, cause, effect. Had he, on the contrary, listened,—in other words, had he opened himself to and obeyed the voice of God, the plagues would not have come.

We can be our own best friends or we can be our own worst enemies. In the degree that we become friends to the highest and best within us, we become friends to all; and in the degree that we become enemies to the highest and best within us, do we become enemies to all. In the degree that we open ourselves to the higher powers and let them manifest through us, then by the very inspirations we carry with us do we become in a sense the saviours of our fellow-men, and in this way we all are, or may become, the saviours one of another. In this way you may become, indeed, one of the world's redeemers.

XI

The Basic Principle Of All Religions—The Universal Religion

The great truth we are considering is the fundamental principle running through all religions. We find it in every one. In regard to it all agree. It is, moreover, a great truth in regard to which all people can agree, whether they belong to the same or to different religions. People always quarrel about the trifles, about their personal views of minor insignificant points. They always come together in the presence of great fundamental truths, the threads of which run through all. The quarrels are in connection with the lower self, the agreements are in connection with the higher self.

A place may have its factions that quarrel and fight among themselves, but let a great calamity come upon the land, flood, famine, pestilence, and these little personal differences are entirely forgotten and all work shoulder to shoulder in the one great cause. The changing, the evolving self gives rise to quarrels; the permanent, the soul self unites all in the highest efforts of love and service.

Patriotism is a beautiful thing; it is well for me to love my country, but why should I love my own country more than I love all others? If I love my own and hate others, I then show my limitations, and my patriotism will stand the test not even for my own. If I love my own country and in the same way love all other countries, then I show the largeness of my nature, and a patriotism of this kind is noble and always to be relied upon.

The view of God in regard to which we are agreed, that He is the Infinite Spirit of Life and Power that is back of all, that is working in and through all, that is the life of all, is a matter in regard to which all men, all religions can agree. With this view there can be no infidels or atheists. There are atheists and infidels in connection with many views that are held concerning God, and thank God there are. Even devout and earnest people among us attribute things to God that no respectable men or women would permit to be attributed to themselves. This view is satisfying to those who cannot see how God can be angry with his children, jealous, vindictive. A display of these qualities always lessens our respect for men and women, and still we attribute them to God.

The earnest, sincere heretic is one of the greatest friends true religion can have. Heretics are among God's greatest servants. They are among the true servants of mankind. Christ was one of the greatest heretics the world has ever known. He allowed himself to be bound by no established or orthodox teachings or beliefs. Christ is preëminently a type of the universal. John the Baptist is a type of the personal. John dressed in a particular way, ate a particular kind of food, belonged to a particular order, lived and taught in a particular locality, and he himself recognized the fact that he must decrease while Christ must increase. Christ, on the other hand, gave himself absolutely no limitations. He allowed himself to be bound by nothing. He was absolutely universal and as a consequence taught not for his own particular day, but for all time.

This mighty truth which we have agreed upon as the great central fact of human life is the golden thread that runs through all religions. When we make it the paramount fact in our lives we will find that minor differences, narrow prejudices, and all these laughable absurdities will so fall away by virtue of their very insignificance, that a Jew can worship equally as well in a Catholic cathedral, a Catholic in a Jewish synagogue, a Buddhist in a Christian church, a Christian in a Buddhist temple. Or all can worship equally well about their own hearth-stones, or out on the hillside, or while pursuing the avocations of every-day life. For true worship, only God and the human soul are necessary. It does not depend upon times, or seasons, or occasions. Anywhere and at any time God and man in the bush may meet.

This is the great fundamental principle of the universal religion upon which all can agree. This is the great fact that is permanent. There are many things in regard to which all cannot agree. These are the things that are personal, non-essential, and so as time passes they gradually fall away. One who doesn't grasp this great truth, a Christian, for example, asks "But was not Christ inspired?" Yes, but he was not the only one inspired. Another who is a Buddhist asks, "Was not Buddha inspired?" Yes, but he was not the only one inspired. A Christian asks, "But is not our Christian Bible inspired?" Yes, but there are other inspired scriptures. A Brahmin or a Buddhist asks, "Are not the Vedas inspired?" Yes, but there are other inspired sacred books. Your error is not in believing that your particular scriptures are inspired, but your error is—and you show your absurdly laughable limitations by it—your inability to see that other scriptures are also inspired.

The sacred books, the inspired writings, all come from the same source,—God, God speaking through the souls of those who open themselves that He may thus speak. Some may be more inspired than others. It depends entirely on the relative degree that this one or that one opens himself to the Divine voice. Says one of the inspired writers in the Hebrew scriptures, Wisdom is the breath of the power of God, and *in all ages* entering into holy souls she maketh them friends of God and prophets.

Let us not be among the number so dwarfed, so limited, so bigoted as to think that the Infinite God has revealed Himself to one little handful of His children, in one little quarter of the globe, and at one particular period of time. This isn't the pattern by which God works. Of a truth I perceive that God is no respecter of persons, but in every nation he that revereth God and worketh righteousness is accepted of Him, says the Christian Bible.

When we fully realize this truth we will then see that it makes but little difference what particular form of religion one holds to, but it does make a tremendous difference how true he is to the *vital* principles of this one. In the degree that we love self less and love truth more, in that degree will we care less about converting people to our particular way of thinking, but all the more will we care to aid them in coming into the full realization of truth through the channels best adapted to them. The doctrine of our master, says the Chinese, consisted solely in integrity of heart. We will find as we search that this is the doctrine of every one who is at all worthy the name of master.

The great fundamental principles of all religions are the same. They differ only in their minor details according to the various degrees of unfoldment of different people. I am sometimes asked, "To what religion do you belong?" What religion? Why, bless you, there is only one religion,—the religion of the living God. There are, of course, the various creeds of the same religion arising from the various interpretations of different people, but they are all of minor importance. The more unfolded the soul the less important do these minor differences become. There are also, of course, the various so-called religions. There is in reality, however, but one religion.

The moment we lose sight of this great fact we depart from the real, vital spirit of true religion and allow ourselves to be limited and bound by form. In the degree that we do this we build fences around ourselves which keep others away from us, and which also prevent our coming into the realization of universal truth; there is nothing worthy the name of truth that is not universal.

There is only one religion. "Whatever road I take joins the highway that leads to Thee," says the inspired writer in the Persian scriptures. "Broad is the carpet God has spread, and beautiful the colors he has given it." "The pure man respects every form of faith," says the Buddhist. "My doctrine makes no difference between high and low, rich and poor; like the sky, it has room for all, and like the water, it washes all alike." "The broad minded see the truth in different religions; the narrow minded see only the differences," says the Chinese. The Hindu has said, "The narrow minded ask, 'Is this man a stranger, or is he of our tribe?' But to those in whom love dwells, the whole world is but one family." "Altar flowers are of many species, but all worship is one." "Heaven is a palace with many doors, and each may enter in his own way." "Are we not all children of one Father?" says the Christian. "God has made of one blood all nations, to dwell on the face of the earth." It was a latter-day seer who said, "That which was profitable to the soul of man the Father revealed to the ancients; that which is profitable to the soul of man today revealeth He this day."

It was Tennyson who said, "I dreamed that stone by stone I reared a sacred fane, a temple, neither pagoda, mosque, nor church, but loftier, simpler, always open-doored to every breath from heaven, and Truth and Peace and Love and Justice came and dwelt therein."

Religion in its true sense is the most joyous thing the human soul can know, and when the real religion is realized, we will find that it will be an agent of peace, of joy, and of happiness, and never an agent of gloomy, long-faced sadness. It will then be attractive to all and repulsive to none. Let our churches grasp these great truths, let them give their time and attention to bringing people into a knowledge of their true selves, into a knowledge of their relations, of their oneness, with the Infinite God, and such joy will be the result, and such crowds will flock to them, that their very walls will seem almost to burst, and such songs of joy will continually pour forth as will make all people in love with the religion that makes for every-day life, and hence the religion that is true and vital. Adequacy for life, adequacy for everyday life here and now, must be the test of all true religion. If it does not bear this test, then it simply is not religion. We need an everyday, a this-world religion. All time spent in connection with any other is worse than wasted. The eternal life that we are now living will be well lived if we take good care of each little period of time as it presents itself day after day. If we fail in doing this, we fail in everything.

XII

Entering Now Into The Realization Of The Highest Riches

I hear the question, What can be said in a concrete way in regard to the method of coming into this realization? The facts underlying it are, indeed, most beautiful and true, but how can we actualize in ourselves the realization that carries with it such wonderful results?

The method is not difficult if we do not of ourselves make it difficult. The principal word to be used is the word,—Open. Simply to open your mind and heart to this divine inflow which is waiting only for the opening of the gate, that it may enter. It is like opening the gate of the trough which conducts the water from the reservoir above into the field below. The water, by virtue of its very nature, will rush in and irrigate the field if the gate is but opened. As to the realization of our oneness with this Infinite Life and Power, after seeing, as I think we have clearly seen by this time, the relations it bears to us and we to it, the chief thing to be said is simply,—Realize your oneness with it. The open mind and heart whereby one is brought into the receptive attitude is the first thing necessary. Then the earnest, sincere desire.

It may be an aid at first to take yourself for a few moments each day into the quiet, into the silence, where you will not be agitated by the disturbances that enter in through the avenues of the physical senses. There in the quiet alone with God, put yourself into the receptive attitude. Calmly, quietly, and expectantly desire

129

that this realization break in upon and take possession of your soul. As it breaks in upon and takes possession of the soul, it will manifest itself to your mind, and from this you will feel its manifestations in every part of your body. Then in the degree that you open yourself to it you will feel a quiet, peaceful, illuminating power that will harmonize body, soul, and mind, and that will then harmonize these with all the world. You are now on the mountain top, and the voice of God is speaking to you. *Then, as you descend, carry this realization with you.* Live in it, waking, working, thinking, walking, sleeping. In this way, although you may not be continually on the mountain top, you will nevertheless be continually living in the realization of all the beauty, and inspiration, and power you have felt there.

Moreover, the time will come when in the busy office or on the noisy street you can enter into the silence by simply drawing the mantle of your own thoughts about you and realizing that there and everywhere the Spirit of Infinite Life, Love, Wisdom, Peace, Power, and Plenty is guiding, keeping, protecting, leading you. This is the spirit of continual prayer. This it is to pray without ceasing. This it is to know and to walk with God. *This it is to find the Christ within.* This is the new birth, the second birth. First that which is natural, then that which is spiritual. It is thus that the old man Adam is put off and the new man Christ is put on. This it is to be saved unto life eternal, whatever one's form of belief or faith may be; for it is life eternal to know God. "The Sweet By and By" will be a song of the past. We will create a new song—"The Beautiful Eternal Now."

This is the realization that you and I can come into this very day, this very hour, this very minute, if we desire and if we will it. And if now we merely set our faces in the right direction, it is then but a matter of time until we come into the full splendors of this complete realization. To set one's face in the direction of the mountain and then simply to journey on, whether rapidly or more slowly, will bring him to it. But unless one set his face in the right direction and make the start, he will not reach it. It was

Goethe who said:

> "Are you in earnest? Seize this very minute:
> What you can do, or dream you can, begin it;
> Boldness has genius, power, and magic in it.
> Only engage and then the mind grows heated;
> Begin and then the work will be completed."

Said the young man, Gautama Siddhârtha, I have awakened to the truth and I am resolved to accomplish my purpose,—Verily I shall become a Buddha. It was this that brought him into the life of the Enlightened One, and so into the realization of Nirvana right here in this life. That this same realization and life is within the possibilities of all here and now was his teaching. It was this that has made him the Light Bearer to millions of people.

Said the young man, Jesus, Know ye not that I must be about my Father's business? Making this the one great purpose of his life he came into the full and complete realization,—I and the Father are one. He thus came into the full realization of the Kingdom of Heaven right here in this life. That all could come into this same realization and life here and now was his teaching. It was this that has made him the Light Bearer to millions of people.

And so far as practical things are concerned, we may hunt the wide universe through and we shall find that there is no injunction more practical than, Seek ye first the kingdom of God and His righteousness and all other things shall be added unto you. And in the light of what has gone before, I think there is no one who is open to truth and honest with himself who will fail to grasp the underlying reason and see the great laws upon which it is based.

Personally I know lives that have so fully entered into the kingdom through the realization of their oneness with the Infinite Life and through the opening of themselves so fully to its divine guidance, that they are most wonderful concrete examples of the reality of this great and all-important truth. They are people whose lives are in this way guided not only in a general way, but literally in every detail. They simply live in the realization of their oneness with this Infinite Power, continually in harmony with it, and so continually in the realization of the kingdom of heaven. An abundance of all things is theirs. They are never at a loss for anything. The supply seems always equal to the demand. They never seem at a loss in regard to what to do or how to do it. Their lives are care-less lives. They are lives free from care because they are continually conscious of the fact that the higher powers are doing the guiding, and they are relieved of the responsibility. To enter into detail in connection with some of these lives, and particularly with two or three that come to my mind at this moment, would reveal facts that no doubt to some would seem almost incredible if not miraculous. But let us remember that what is possible for one life to realize is possible for all. This is indeed the natural and the normal life, that which will be the every-day life of every one who comes into and who lives in this higher realization and so in harmony with the higher laws. This is simply getting into the current of that divine sequence running throughout the universe; and when once in it, life then ceases to be a plodding and moves along day after day much as the tides flow, much as the planets move in their courses, much as the seasons come and go.

All the frictions, all the uncertainties, all the ills, the sufferings, the fears, the forebodings, the perplexities of life come to us because we are out of harmony with the divine order of things. They will continue to come as long as we so live. Rowing against the tide is hard and uncertain. To go with the tide and thus to take advantage of the working of a great natural force is safe and easy. To come into the conscious, vital realization of our oneness with the Infinite Life and Power is to come into the current of this divine sequence. Coming thus into harmony with the Infinite, brings us in turn into harmony with all about us, into harmony with the life of the heavens, into harmony with all the universe. And above all, it brings us into harmony with ourselves, so that body, soul, and mind become perfectly harmonized, and when this is so, life becomes full and complete.

The sense life then no longer masters and enslaves us. The

physical is subordinated to and ruled by the mental; this in turn is subordinated to and continually illumined by the spiritual. Life is then no longer the poor, one-sided thing it is in so many cases; but the three-fold, the all-round life with all its beauties and ever increasing joys and powers is entered upon. Thus it is that we are brought to realize that the middle path is the great solution of life; neither asceticism on the one hand nor license and perverted use on the other. Everything is for use, but all must be wisely used in order to be fully enjoyed.

As we live in these higher realizations the senses are not ignored but are ever more fully perfected. As the body becomes less gross and heavy, finer in its texture and form, all the senses become finer, so that powers we do not now realize as belonging to us gradually develop. Thus we come, in a perfectly natural and normal way, into the super-conscious realms whereby we make it possible for the higher laws and truths to be revealed to us. As we enter into these realms we are then not among those who give their time in speculating as to whether this one or that one had the insight and the powers attributed to him, but we are able *to know* for ourselves. Neither are we among those who attempt to lead the people upon the hearsay of some one else, but we know whereof we speak, and only thus can we speak with authority. There are many things that we cannot know until by living the life we bring ourselves into that state where it is possible for them to be revealed to us. "If any man will do His will, he shall know of the doctrine." It was Plotinus who said, The mind that wishes to behold God must itself become God. As we thus make it possible for these higher laws and truths to be revealed to us, we will in turn become enlightened ones, channels through which they may be revealed to others.

When one is fully alive to the possibilities that come with this higher awakening, as he goes here and there, as he mingles with his fellow-men, he imparts to all an inspiration that kindles in them a feeling of power kindred to his own. We are all continually giving out influences similar to those that are playing in our own lives. We do this in the same way that each flower emits its own peculiar odor. The rose breathes out its fragrance upon the air and all who come near it are refreshed and inspired by this emanation from the soul of the rose. A poisonous weed sends out its obnoxious odor; it is neither refreshing nor inspiring in its effects, and if one remain near it long he may be so unpleasantly affected as to be made even ill by it.

The higher the life the more inspiring and helpful are the emanations that it is continually sending out. The lower the life the more harmful is the influence it continually sends out to all who come in contact with it. Each one is continually radiating an atmosphere of one kind or the other.

We are told by the mariners who sail on the Indian Seas, that many times they are able to tell their approach to certain islands long before they can see them by the sweet fragrance of the sandal-wood that is wafted far out upon the deep. Do you not see how it would serve to have such a soul playing through such a body that as you go here and there a subtle, silent force goes out from you that all feel and are influenced by; so that you carry with you an inspiration and continually shed a benediction wherever you go; so that your friends and all people will say,—His coming brings peace and joy into our homes, welcome his coming; so that as you pass along the street, tired, and weary, and even sin-sick men and women will feel a certain divine touch that will awaken new desires and a new life in them; that will make the very horse as you pass him turn his head with a strange, half-human, longing look? Such are the subtle powers of the human soul when it makes itself translucent to the Divine. To know that such a life is within our living here and now is enough to make one burst forth with songs of joy. And when the life itself is entered upon, the sentiment of at least one song will be:

"Oh! I stand in the Great Forever,
  All things to me are divine;
I eat of the heavenly manna,
  I drink of the heavenly wine.

"In the gleam of the shining rainbow
   The Father's Love I behold,
As I gaze on its radiant blending
   Of crimson and blue and gold.
"In all the bright birds that are singing,
   In all the fair flowers that bloom,
Whose welcome aromas are bringing
   Their blessings of sweet perfume;
"In the glorious tint of the morning,
   In the gorgeous sheen of the night,
Oh! my soul is lost in rapture,
   My senses are lost in sight."

As one comes into and lives continually in the full, conscious realization of his oneness with the Infinite Life and Power, then all else follows. This it is that brings the realization of such splendors, and beauties, and joys as a life that is thus related with the Infinite Power alone can know. This it is to come into the realization of heaven's richest treasures while walking the earth. This it is to bring heaven down to earth, or rather to bring earth up to heaven. This it is to exchange weakness and impotence for strength; sorrows and sighings for joy; fears and forebodings for faith; longings for realizations. This it is to come into fullness of peace, power, and plenty. This it is to be in tune with the Infinite.

What All The World's
A-Seeking

Preface

There are two reasons the author has for putting forth this little volume: he feels that the time is, as it always has been, ripe for it; and second, his soul has ever longed to express itself upon this endless theme. It therefore comes from the heart—the basis of his belief that it will reach the heart.

R. W. T.

I

The Principle

Would you find that wonderful life supernal,
That life so abounding, so rich, and so free?
Seek then the laws of the Spirit Eternal,
With them bring your life into harmony.

How can I make life yield its fullest and best? How can I know the true secret of power? How can I attain to a true and lasting greatness? How can I fill the whole of life with a happiness, a peace, a joy, a satisfaction that is ever rich and abiding, that ever increases, never diminishes, that imparts to it a sparkle that never loses its lustre, that ever fascinates, never wearies?

No questions, perhaps, in this form or in that have been asked oftener than these. Millions in the past have asked them. Millions are asking them to-day. They will be asked by millions yet unborn. Is there an answer, a true and safe one for the millions who are eagerly and longingly seeking for it in all parts of the world to-day, and for the millions yet unborn who will as eagerly strive to find it as the years come and go? Are you interested, my dear reader, in the answer? The fact that you have read even thus far in this little volume whose title has led you to take it up, indicates that you are,—that you are but one of the innumerable company already mentioned.

It is but another way of asking that great question that has come through all the ages—What is the *summum bonum* in life? and there have been countless numbers who gladly would have given all they possessed to have had the true and satisfactory answer. Can we then find this answer, true and satisfactory to ourselves, surely the brief time spent together must be counted as the most precious and valuable of life itself. *There is an answer:* follow closely, and that our findings may be the more conclusive, take issue with me at every step if you choose, but tell me finally if it is not true and satisfactory.

There is one great, one simple principle, which, if firmly laid hold of, and if made the great central principle in one's life, around which all others properly arrange and subordinate themselves, will make that life a grand success, truly great and genuinely happy, loved and blessed by all in just the degree in which it is laid hold upon,—a principle which, if universally made thus, would wonderfully change this old world in which we live,—ay, that would transform it almost in a night, and it is for its coming that the world has long been waiting; that in place of the gloom and despair in almost countless numbers of lives would bring light and hope and contentment, and no longer would it be said as so truly to-day, that "man's inhumanity to man makes countless thousands mourn"; that would bring to the life of the fashionable society woman, now spending her days and her nights in seeking for nothing but her own pleasure, such a flood of true and genuine pleasure and happiness and satisfaction as would make the poor, weak something she calls by this name so pale before it, that she would quickly see that she hasn't known what true pleasure is, and that what she has been mistaking for the real, the genuine, is but as a baser metal compared to the purest of gold, as a bit of cut glass compared to the rarest of diamonds, and that would make this same woman who scarcely deigns to notice the poor woman who washes her front steps, but who, were the facts known, may be living a much grander life, and consequently of much more value to the world than she herself, see that this poor woman is after all her sister, because child of the same Father; and that would make the humble life of this same poor woman beautiful and happy and sweet in its humility; that would give us a nation of statesmen in place of,

140

with now and then an exception, a nation of politicians, each one bent upon his own personal aggrandizement at the expense of the general good; that would go far, ay, very far toward solving our great and hard-pressing social problems with which we are already face to face; that, in short, would make each man a prince among men, and each woman a queen among women.

I have seen the supreme happiness in lives where this principle has been caught and laid hold of, some, lives that seemed not to have much in them before, but which under its wonderful influences have been so transformed and so beautified, that have been made so sweet and so strong, so useful and so precious, that each day seems to them all too short, the same time that before, when they could scarcely see what was in life to make it worth the living, dragged wearily along. So there are countless numbers of people in the world with lives that seem not to have much in them, among the wealthy classes and among the poorer, who might under the influence of this great, this simple principle, make them so precious, so rich, and so happy that time would seem only . too short, and they would wonder why they have been so long running on the wrong track, for it is true that much the larger portion of the world to-day is on the wrong track in the pursuit of happiness; but almost all are there, let it be said, not through choice, but by reason of not knowing the right, the true one.

The fact that really great, true, and happy lives have been lived in the past and are being lived to-day gives us our starting-point. Time and again I have examined such lives in a most careful endeavor to find what has made them so, and have found that in *each and every* individual case this that we have now come to has been the great central principle upon which they have been built. I have also found that in numbers of lives where it has not been, but where almost every effort apart from it has been made to make them great, true, and happy, they have not been so; and also that no life built upon it in sufficient degree, other things being equal, has failed in being thus.

Let us then to the answer, examine it closely, see if it will stand every test, if it is the true one, and if so, rejoice that we have found it, lay hold of it, build upon it, tell others of it. The last four words have already entered us at the open door. The idea has prevailed in the past, and this idea has dominated the world, that *self* is the great concern,—that if one would find success, greatness, happiness, he must give all attention to self, and to self alone. This has been the great mistake, this the fatal error, this the *direct* opposite of the right, the true as set forth in the great immutable law that—*we find our own lives in losing them in the service of others*, in longer form—the more of our lives we give to others, the fuller and the richer, the greater and the grander, the more beautiful and the more happy our own lives become. It is as that great and sweet soul who when with us lived at Concord said,—that generous giving or losing of your life which saves it.

This is an expression of one of the greatest truths, of one of the greatest principles of practical ethics the world has thus far seen. In a single word, it is *service*,—not self, but the other self. We shall soon see, however, that our love, our service, our helpfulness to others, invariably comes back to us, intensified sometimes a hundred or a thousand or a thousand thousand fold, and this by a great, immutable law.

The Master Teacher, he who so many years ago in that far-away Eastern land, now in the hill country, now in the lake country, as the people gathered round him, taught them those great, high-born, and tender truths of human life and destiny, the Christ Jesus, said identically this when he said and so continually repeated,—"He that is greatest among you shall be your servant"; and his whole life was but an embodiment of this principle or truth, with the result that the greatest name in the world to-day is his,—the name of him who as his life-work, healed the sick; clothed the naked; bound up the broken-hearted; sustained the weak, the faltering; befriended and aided the poor, the needy; condemned the proud, the vain, the selfish; and through it all taught the people to love justice and mercy and service, to live in their higher, their diviner selves,—in brief, to *live* his life, the Christ-life, and who has helped in making it possible for this greatest principle of practical ethics the world has thus far seen to be enunciated, to be laid hold of, to be lived by to-day. "He that is greatest among you shall be your servant," or, he who would be truly great and recognized as such must find it in the capacity of a servant.

And what, let us ask, is a servant? One who renders service. To himself? Never. To others? Alway. Freed of its associations and looked at in the light of its right and true meaning, than the word "servant" there is no greater in the language; and in this right use of the term, as we shall soon see, every life that has been really true, great, and happy has been that of a servant, and apart from this no such life *ever has been or ever can be lived.*

O you who are seeking for power, for place, for happiness, for contentment in the ordinary way, tarry for a moment, see that you are on the wrong track, grasp this great eternal truth, lay hold of it, and you will see that your advance along this very line will be manifold times more rapid. Are you seeking, then, to make for yourself a name? Unless you grasp this mighty truth and make your life accordingly, as the great clock of time ticks on and all things come to their proper level according to their merits, as all invariably, inevitably do, you will indeed be somewhat surprised to find how low, how very low your level is. Your name and your memory will be forgotten long ere the minute-hand has passed even a single time across the great dial; while your fellow-man who has grasped this simple but this great and all-necessary truth, and who accordingly is forgetting himself in the service of others, who is making his life a part of a hundred or a thousand or a million lives, thus illimitably intensifying or multiplying his own, instead of living as you in what otherwise would be his own little, diminutive self, will find himself ascending higher and higher until he stands as one among the few, and will find a peace, a happiness, a satisfaction so rich and so beautiful, compared to which yours will be but a poor miserable something, and whose name and memory when his life here is finished, will live in the minds and hearts of his fellow-men and of mankind fixed and eternal as the stars.

A corollary of the great principle already enunciated might be formulated thus: *there is no such thing as finding true happiness by searching for it directly.* It must come, if it come at all, indirectly, or by the service, the love, and the happiness we give to others. So, *there is no such thing as finding true greatness by searching for it directly.* It always, without a single exception has come indirectly in this same way, and it is not at all probable that this great eternal law is going to be changed to suit any particular case or cases. Then recognize it, put your life into harmony with it, and reap the rewards of its observance, or fail to recognize it and pay the penalty accordingly; for the law itself will remain unchanged.

The men and women whose names we honor and celebrate are invariably those with lives founded primarily upon this great law. Note if you will, every *truly* great life in the world's history, among those living and among the so-called dead, and tell me if in *every* case that life is not a life spent in the service of others, either directly, or indirectly as when we say—he served his country. Whenever one seeks for reputation, for fame, for honor, for happiness directly and for his own sake, then that which is true and genuine never comes, at least to any degree worthy the name. It may seem to for a time, but a great law says that such an one gets so far and no farther. Sooner or later, generally sooner, there comes an end.

Human nature seems to run in this way, seems to be governed by a great paradoxical law which says, that whenever a man self-centred, thinking of, living for and in himself, is very desirous for place, for preferment, for honor, the very fact of his being thus is of itself a sufficient indicator that he is too small to have them, and mankind refuses to accord them. While the one who forgets self, and who, losing sight of these things, makes it his chief aim in life to help, to aid, and to serve others, by this very fact makes it known that he is large enough, is great enough to have them, and his fellow-men instinctively bestow them upon him. This is a great law which many would profit by to recognize. That it is true is attested by the fact that the praise of mankind instinctively and universally goes out to a hero; but who ever heard of a hero who became such by doing something for himself? Always something he has done for others. By the fact that monuments and statues are gratefully erected to the memory of those who have helped and served their fellow-men, not to those who have lived to themselves alone.

I have seen many monuments and statues i erected to the memories of philanthropists, but I never yet have seen one erected to a miser; many to generous-hearted, noble-hearted men, but never yet to one whose whole life was that of a sharp bargain-driver, and who clung with a sort of semi-idiotic grasp to all that came thus into his temporary possession. I have seen many erected to statesmen,—statesmen,—but never one to mere politicians; many to true orators, but never to mere demagogues; many to soldiers and leaders, but never to men who were not willing, when necessary, to risk all in the service of their country. No, you will find that the world's monuments and statues have been erected and its praises and honors have gone out to those who were large and great enough to forget themselves in the service of others, who have been servants, true servants of mankind, who have been true to the great law that we find our own lives in losing them in the service of others. Not honor for themselves, but service for others. But notice the strange, wonderful, beautiful transformation as it returns upon itself,—*honor for themselves, because of service to others.*

It would be a matter of exceeding great interest to verify the truth of what has just been said by looking at a number of those who are regarded as the world's great sons and daughters,—those to whom its honors, its praises, its homage go out,—to see why it is, upon what their lives have been founded that they have become so great and are so honored. Of all this glorious company that would come up, we must be contented to look at but one or two.

There comes to my mind the name and figure of him the celebration of whose birthday I predict will soon be made a national holiday,—he than whom there is no greater, whose praises are sung and whose name and memory are honored and blessed by millions in all parts of the world to-clay, and will be by millions yet unborn, our beloved and sainted Lincoln. And then I ask, Why is this? Why is this? One sentence of his tells us what to look to for the answer. During that famous series of public debates in Illinois with Stephen A. Douglas in 1858, speaking at Freeport, Mr. Douglas at one place said, "I care not whether slavery in the Territories be voted up or whether, it be voted down, it makes not a particle of difference with me." Mr. Lincoln, speaking from the fulness of his great and royal heart, in reply said, with emotion, "I am sorry to perceive that my friend Judge Douglas is so constituted that he does not feel the lash the least bit when it is laid upon another man's back." Thoughts upon self? Not for a moment. Upon others? Always. He at once recognized in those black men four million brothers for whom he had a service to perform.

It would seem almost grotesque to use the word *self-ish* in connection with this great name. He very early, and when still in a very humble and lowly station in life, either consciously or unconsciously grasped this great truth, and in making the great underlying principle of his life to serve, to help his fellow-men, he adopted just that course that has made him one of the greatest of the sons of men, our royal-hearted elder brother. He never spent time in asking what he could do to attain to greatness, to popularity, to power, what to perpetuate his name and memory. He simply asked how he could help, how he could be of service to his fellow-men, and continually did all his hands found to do.

He simply put his life into harmony with this great principle; and in so doing he adopted the best means,—the *only* means to secure that which countless numbers seek and strive for directly, and every time so woefully fail in finding.

There comes to my mind in this same connection another princely soul, one who loved all the world, one whom all the world loves and delights to honor. There comes to mind also a little incident that will furnish an insight into the reason of it all. On an afternoon not long ago, Mrs. Henry Ward Beecher was telling me of some of the characteristics of Brooklyn's great preacher. While she was yet speaking of some of those along the very lines we are considering, an old gentleman, a neighbor, came into the room bearing in his hands something he had brought from Mr. Beecher's grave. It was the day next following Decoration Day. His story was this: As the great procession was moving into the cemetery with its bands of rich music, with its carriages laden with sweet and fragrant flowers, with its. waving flags, beautiful in the sunlight, a poor and humble-looking woman with two companions, by her apparent nervousness attracted the attention of the gate-keeper. He kept her in view for a little while, and presently saw her as she gave something she had partially concealed to one of her companions, who, leaving the procession, went over to the grave of Mr. Beecher, and tenderly laid it there. Reverently she stood for a moment or two, and then, retracing her steps, joined her two companions, who with bowed heads were waiting by the wayside.

It was this that the old gentleman had brought,—a gold frame, and in it a poem cut from a volume, a singularly beautiful poem through which was breathed the spirit of love and service and self-devotion to the good and the needs of others. At one or two places where it fitted, the pen had been drawn across a word and Mr. Beecher's name inserted, which served to give it a still more real, vivid, and tender meaning. At the bottom this only was written, "From a poor Hebrew woman to the immortal friend of the Hebrews." There was no name, but this was sufficient to tell the whole story. Some poor, humble woman, but one out of a mighty number whom he had at some time befriended or helped or cheered, whose burden he had helped to carry, and soon perhaps had forgotten all about it. When we remember that this was his life, is it at all necessary to seek farther why all the world delights to honor this, another royal-hearted elder brother? and, as we think of this simple, beautiful, and touching incident, how true and living becomes the thought in the old, old lines!—

"Cast thy bread upon the waters, waft it on with praying breath,

*In some distant, doubtful moment it may save a soul from death.
When you sleep in solemn silence, 'neath the morn and evening dew,
Stranger hands which you have strengthened may strew lilies over you."*

Our good friend, Henry Drummond, in one of his most beautiful and valuable little works says—and how admirably and how
truly!—that "love is the greatest thing in the world." Have you this
greatest thing? Yes. How, then, does it manifest itself? In kindliness, in helpfulness, in service, to those around you? If so, well
and good, you have it. If not, then I suspect that what you have
been calling love is something else; and you have indeed been
greatly fooled. In fact, I am sure it is; for if it does not manifest
itself in this way, it cannot be true love, for this is the one grand
and never-failing test. Love is the statics, helpfulness and service
the dynamics, the former necessary to the latter, but the latter the
more powerful, as action is always more powerful than potential-
ity; and, were it not for the dynamics, the statics might as well not
be. Helpfulness, kindliness, service, is but the expression of love.
It is love in action; and unless love thus manifests itself in action, it
is an indication that it is of that weak and sickly nature that needs
exercise, growth, and development, that it may grow and become
strong, healthy, vigorous, and true, instead of remaining a little,
weak, indefinite, sentimental something or nothing.

It was but yesterday that I heard one of the world's greatest
thinkers and speakers, one of our keenest observers of human
affairs, state as his opinion that selfishness is the root of all evil.
Now, if it is possible for any one thing to be the root of all evil,
then I think there is a world of truth in the statement. But, leaving
out of account for the present purpose whether it is true or not, it
certainly is true that he who can't get beyond self robs his life of its
chief charms, and more, defeats the very ends he has in view. It is a
well-known law in the natural world about us that whatever hasn't
use, that whatever serves no purpose, shrivels up. So it is a law of
our own being that he who makes himself of no use, of no service
to the great body of mankind, who is concerned only with his own

small self, finds that self, small as it is, growing smaller and smaller, and those finer and better and grander qualities of his nature, those that give the chief charm and happiness to life, shrivelling up. Such an one lives, keeps constant company with his own diminutive and stunted self; while he who, forgetting self, makes the object of his life service, helpfulness, and kindliness to others, finds his whole nature growing and expanding, himself becoming large-hearted, magnanimous, kind, loving, sympathetic, joyous, and happy, his life becoming rich and beautiful. For instead of his own little life alone he has entered into and has part in a hundred, a thousand, ay, in countless numbers of other lives; and every success, every joy, every happiness coming to each of these comes as such to him, for he has a part in each and all. And thus it is that one becomes a prince among men, a queen among women.

Why, one of the very fundamental principles of life is, so much love, so much love in return; so much love, so much growth; so much love, so much power; so much love, so much life,—strong, healthy, rich, exulting, and abounding life. The world is beginning to realize the fact that love, instead of being a mere indefinite something, is a vital and living force, the same as electricity is a force, though perhaps of a different nature. The same great fact we are learning in regard to thought,—that thoughts are things, that *thoughts are forces, the most vital and powerful in the universe*, that they have form and substance and power, the quality of the power determined as it is by the quality of the life in whose organism the thoughts are engendered; and so, when a thought is given birth, it does not end there, but takes form, and as a force it goes out and has its effect upon other minds and lives, the effect being determined by its intensity and the quality of the prevailing emotions, and also by the emotions dominating the person at the time the thoughts are engendered and given form.

Science, while demonstrating the great facts it is to-day demonstrating in connection with the mind in its relations to and effects upon the body, is also finding from its very laboratory experiments that each particular kind of thought and emotion has its own peculiar qualities, and hence its own peculiar effects or influences; and these it is classifying with scientific accuracy. A very general classification in just a word would be—those of a higher and those of a lower nature.

Some of the chief ones among those of the lower nature are anger, hatred, jealousy, malice, rage. Their effect, especially when violent, is to emit a poisonous substance into the system, or rather, to set up a corroding influence which transforms the healthy and life-giving secretions of the body into the poisonous and the destructive. When one, for example, is dominated, even if for but a moment by a passion of anger or rage, there is set up in the system what might be justly termed a bodily thunder-storm, which has the effect of souring or corroding the normal and healthy secretions of the body and making them so that instead of life-giving they become poisonous. This, if indulged in to any extent, sooner or later induces the form of disease that this particular state of mind and emotion or passion gives birth to; and it in turn becomes chronic.

We shall ultimately find, as we are beginning to so rapidly today, that practically all disease has its origin in perverted mental states or emotions; that anger, hatred, fear, worry, jealousy, lust, as well as all milder forms of perverted mental states and emotions, has each its own peculiar poisoning effects and induces each its own peculiar form of disease, for all life is from within out.

Then some of the chief ones belonging to the other class— mental states and emotions of the higher nature—are love, sympathy, benevolence, kindliness, and good cheer. These are the natural and the normal; and their effect, when habitually entertained, is to stimulate a vital, healthy, bounding, purifying, and life-giving action, the exact opposite of the others; and these very forces, set into a bounding activity, will in time counteract and heal the disease-giving effects of their opposites. Their effects upon the countenance and features in inducing the highest beauty that can dwell there are also marked and all-powerful. So much, then, in regard to the effects of one's thought forces upon the self. A word more in regard to their effects upon others.

Our prevailing thought forces determine the mental atmosphere we create around us, and all who come within its influence are affected in one way or another, according to the quality of that atmosphere; and, though they may not always get the exact thoughts, they nevertheless get the effects of the emotions dominating the originator of the thoughts, and hence the creator of this particular mental atmosphere, and the more sensitively organized the person the more sensitive he or she is to this atmosphere, even at times to getting the exact and very thoughts. So even in this the prophecy is beginning to be fulfilled,—there is nothing hid that shall not be revealed.

If the thought forces sent out by any particular life are those of hatred or jealousy or malice or fault-finding or criticism or scorn,. these same thought forces are aroused and sent back from others, so that one is affected not only by reason of the unpleasantness of having such thoughts from others, but they also in turn affect one's own mental states, and through these his own bodily conditions, so that, so far as even the welfare of self is concerned, the indulgence in thoughts and emotions of this nature are most expensive, most detrimental, most destructive.

If, on the other hand, the thought forces sent out be those of love, of sympathy, of kindliness, of cheer and good will, these same forces are aroused and sent back, so that their pleasant, ennobling, warming, and life-giving effects one feels and is influenced by; and so again, so far even as the welfare of self is concerned, there is nothing more desirable, more valuable and life-giving. There comes from others, then, exactly what one sends to and hence calls forth from them.

And would we have all the world love us, we must first then love all the world,—merely a great scientific fact. Why is it that all people instinctively dislike and shun the little, the mean, the self-centred, the selfish, while all the world instinctively, irresistibly, loves and longs for the company of the great-hearted, the tender-hearted, the loving, the magnanimous, the sympathetic, the brave? The mere answer—because—will not satisfy. There is a deep, scientific reason for it, either this or it is not true.

Much has been said, much written, in regard to what some have been pleased to call personal magnetism, but which, as is so commonly true in cases of this kind, is even to-day but little understood. But to my mind personal magnetism in its true sense, and as distinguished from what may be termed a purely animal magnetism, is nothing more nor less than the thought forces sent out by a great-hearted, tender-hearted, magnanimous, loving, sympathetic man or woman; for, let me ask, have you ever known of any great personal magnetism in the case of the little, the mean, the vindictive, the self-centred? Never, I venture to say, but always in the case of the other.

Why, *there is nothing that can stand before this wonderful transmuting power of love.* So. far even as the enemy is concerned, I may not be to blame if I have an enemy; but I am to blame if I keep him as such, especially after I know of this wonderful transmuting power. Have I then an enemy, I will refuse, absolutely refuse, to recognize him as such; and instead of entertaining the thoughts of him that he entertains of me, instead of sending him like thought forces, I will send him only thoughts of love, of sympathy, of brotherly kindness, and magnanimity. But a short time it will be until he feels these, and is influenced by them. Then in addition I will watch my opportunity, and whenever I can, I will even go out of my way to do him some little kindnesses. Before these forces he cannot stand, and by and by I shall find that he who to-day is my bitterest enemy is my warmest friend and it may be my staunchest supporter. No, the wise man is he who by that wonderful alchemy of love transmutes the enemy into the friend,—transmutes the bitterest enemy into the warmest friend and supporter. Certainly this is what the Master meant when he said: "Love your enemies, do good to them that hate you and despitefully use you: thou shalt thereby be heaping coals of fire upon their heads." Ay, thou shalt melt them: before this force they cannot stand. Thou shalt melt them, and transmute them into friends.

"You never can tell what your thoughts will do
In bringing you hate or love;
For thoughts are things, and their airy wings
Are swifter than carrier doves.
They follow the law of the universe,
Each thing must create its kind;
And they speed o'er the track to bring you back
Whatever went out from your mind."

Yes, science to-day, at the close of this nineteenth century, in the laboratory is discovering and scientifically demonstrating the great, immutable laws upon which the inspired and illuminated ones of all ages have based all their teachings, those who by ordering their lives according to the higher laws of their being get in a moment of time, through the direct touch of inspiration, what it takes the physical investigator a whole lifetime or a series of investigators a series of lifetimes to discover and demonstrate.

II

The Application

Are you seeking for greatness, O brother of mine,
As the full, fleeting seasons and years glide away?
If seeking directly and for self alone,
The true and abiding you never can stay.
But all self forgetting, know well the law,
It's the hero, and not the self-seeker, who's crowned.
Then go lose your life in the service of others,
And, lo! with rare greatness and glory 'twill abound.

Is it your ambition to become great in any particular field, to attain to fame and honor, and thereby to happiness and contentment? Is it your ambition, for example, to become a great *orator*, to move great masses of men, to receive their praise, their plaudits? Then remember that there never has been, there never will, in brief, there never can be a truly great orator without a great *purpose*, a great cause behind him. You may study in all the best schools in the country, the best universities and the best schools of oratory. You may study until you exhaust all these, and then seek the best in other lands. You may study thus until your hair is beginning to change its color, but this of itself will *never* make you a great orator. You may become a demagogue, and, if self-centred, you inevitably will; for this is exactly what a demagogue is,—a great demagogue, if you please, than which it is hard for one to call to mind a more contemptible animal, and the greater the more contemptible. But without laying hold of and building upon this great principle you never can become a great orator.

154

Call to mind the greatest in the world's history, from Demosthenes—Men of Athens, march against Philip, your country and your fellow-men will be in early bondage unless you give them your best service now—down to our own Phillips and Gough,—Wendell Phillips against the traffic in human blood, John B. Gough against a slavery among his fellow-men more hard and galling and abject than the one just spoken of; for by it the body merely is in bondage, the mind and soul are free, while in this, body, soul, and mind are enslaved. So you can easily discover the great *purpose*, the great cause for *service*, behind each and every one.

The man who can't get beyond himself, his own aggrandizement and interests, must of necessity be small, petty, personal, and at once marks his own limitations; while he whose life is a life of service and self-devotion has no limits, for he thus puts himself at once on the side of the *Universal*, and this more than all else combined gives a tremendous power in oratory. Such a one can mount as on the wings of an eagle, and Nature herself seems to come forth and give a great soul of this kind means and material whereby to accomplish his purposes, whereby the great universal truths go direct to the minds and hearts of his hearers to mould them, to move them; for the orator is he who moulds the minds and hearts of his hearers in the great moulds of universal and eternal truth, and then moves them along a definite line of action, not he who merely speaks pieces to them.

How thoroughly Webster recognized this great principle is admirably shown in that brief but powerful description of eloquence of his; let us pause to listen to a sentence or two: "True eloquence indeed does not consist in speech. . . . Words and phrases may be marshalled in every way, but they cannot compass it. . . . Affected passion, intense expression, the pomp of declamation, all may aspire to it; they cannot reach it. . . . The graces taught in the schools, the costly ornaments and studied contrivances of speech, shock and disgust men when their own lives and the fate of their wives and their children and their country hang on the decision of the hour. Then words have lost their power, rhetoric is vain, and all elaborate oratory contemptible. Even genius itself then feels rebuked and subdued, as in the presence of higher qualities. Then patriotism is eloquent, then self-devotion is eloquent. The clear conception, outrunning the deductions of logic, the high purpose, the firm resolve, the dauntless spirit speaking on the tongue, beaming from the eye, informing every feature and urging the whole man onward, right onward to his object,—this, this is eloquence." And note some of the chief words he has used,—*self-devotion, patriotism, high purpose.* The self-centred man can never know these, and much less can he make use of them.

True, things that one may learn, as the freeing of the bodily agents, the developing of the voice, and so on, that all may become the *true reporters of the soul,* instead of limiting or binding it down, as is so frequently the case in public speakers,—these are all valuable, ay, are very important and very necessary, unless one is content to live below his highest possibilities, and he is wise who recognizes this fact; but these in themselves are but as trifles when compared to those greater, more powerful, and all-essential qualities.

Is it your ambition to become a great *states-man?* Note the very first thing, then, the word itself,—*states-man,* a man who gives his life to the service of the State. And do you not recognize the fact that, when one says—a man who gives his life to the service of the State, it is but another way of saying—a man who gives his life to the service of his fellow-men; for what, after all, is any country, any State, in the true sense of the term, but the aggregate, the great body of its individual citizenship. And he who lives for and unto himself, who puts the interests of his own small self before the interests of the thousands, can never become a states-man; for a statesman must be a larger man than this.

Call to your mind the greatest of the world, among those living and among the so-called dead, and you will quickly see that the life of each and every one has been built upon this great principle, and that all have been great and are held as such in just the degree in which it has been. Two of the greatest among Americans, both passed away, would to-day and even more as time goes on, be counted still greater, had they been a little larger in one aspect of their natures,—large enough to have recognized to its fullest extent the eternal truth and importance of this great principle, and had they given the time to the service of their fellow-men that was spent in desiring the Presidency and in all too plainly making it known. Having gained it could have made them no greater, and having so plainly shown their eager and childish desire for it has made them less great. Of the many thousands of men who have been in our American Congress since its beginning, and of the very, very small number comparatively that you are able to call to mind, possibly not over fifty, which would be about one out of every six hundred or more, you will find that you are able to call to mind each one of this very small number on account of his standing for some measure or principle that would to the highest degree increase the human welfare, thus truly fulfilling the great office of a *statesman*.

The one great trouble with our country to-day is that we have but few statesmen. We have a great swarm, a great hoard of politicians; but it is only now and then that we find a man who is large enough truly to deserve the name—statesman. The large majority in public life to-day are there not for the purpose of serving the best interests of those whom they are supposed to represent, but they are there purely for self, purely for self-aggrandizement in this form or in that, as the case may be.

Especially do we find this true in our municipalities. In some, the government instead of being in the hands of those who would make it such in truth, those who would make it serve the interests it is designed to serve, it is in the hands of those who are there purely for self, little whelps, those who will resort to any means to secure their ends, at times even to honorable means, should they seem to serve best the particular purpose in hand. We have but to look around us to see that this is true. The miserable, filthy, and deplorable condition of affairs the Lexow Committee in its investigations not so long ago laid bare to public gaze had its root in what?. In the fact that the offices in that great municipality have been and are filled by men who are there to serve in the highest degree the public welfare or by men who are there purely for self-aggrandizement? But let us pass on. This degraded condition of affairs exists not only in this great city, but there are scarcely any that are free from it entirely. Matters are not always to continue thus, however. The American people will learn by and by what they ought fully to realize to-day—that the moment the honest people, the citizens, in distinction from the barnacles, mass themselves and stay massed, the notorious, filthy political rings cannot stand before them for a period of even twenty-four hours. *The right, the good, the true, is all-powerful, and will inevitably conquer sooner or later when brought to the front.* Such is the history of civilization.

Let our public offices—municipal, state, and federal—be filled with men who are in love with the human kind, large men, men whose lives are founded upon this great law of service, and we will then have them filled with statesmen. Never let this glorious word be disgraced, degraded, by applying it to the little, self-centred whelps who are unable to get beyond the politician stage. Then enter public life; but enter it as a man, not as a barnacle: enter it as a statesman, not as a politician.

Is it your ambition to become a great *preacher*, or better yet, with the same meaning, a great *teacher*? Then remember that the greatest of the world have been those who have given themselves in thorough self-devotion and service to their fellow-men, who have given themselves so thoroughly to all they have come in contact with that there has been no room for self. They have not peen seekers after fame, or men who have thought so much of their own particular dogmatic ways of thinking as to spend the greater part of their time in discussing dogma, creed, theology, in order, as is so generally true in cases of this kind, to prove that the *ego* you see before you is right in his particular ways of thinking, and that his chief ambition is to have this fact clearly understood,—an abomination, I verily believe, in the sight of God himself, whose children in the mean time are starving, are dying for the bread of life, and an abomination I am sure, in the sight of the great majority of mankind. Let us be thankful, however, for mankind is finding less use for such year by year, and the time will soon come when they will scarcely be tolerated at all.

It is to a very great extent on account of men of this kind, especially in the early history, that the true spirit of religion, of Christianity, has been lost sight of in the mere form. The basket in which it has been deemed necessary to carry it has been held as of greater import than the rare and divinely beautiful fruit itself. The true spirit, that that quickeneth and giveth life and power, has had its place taken by the mere letter, that that alone blighteth and killeth. Instead of running after these finely spun, man-made theories, this stuff,—for stuff is the word,—this that we outgrow once every few years in our march onward and upward, and then stand and laugh as we look back to think that such ideas have ever been held, instead of this, thinking that thus you will gain power, act the part of the wise man, and go each day into the *silence*, there commune with the Infinite, there dwell for a season with the Infinite Spirit of all life, of all power; for you can get *true power* in no other way.

Instead of running about here and there to have your cup filled at these little stagnant pools, dried up as they generally are by the continual rays of a constantly shining egoistic sun, go direct to the great fountain-head, and there drink of the water of life that is poured. out freely to every one if he will but go there for it. One can't, however, send and have it brought by another.

Go, then, into the *silence*, even if it be but for a short period,—a period of not more than a quarter or a half-hour a day,—and there come into contact with the Great Source of all life, of all power. *Send out your earnest desires for whatsoever you will; and whatsoever you will, if continually watered by expectation, will sooner or later come to you.* All knowledge, all truth, all power, all wisdom, all things whatsoever, are yours, if you will but go in this way for them. It has been tried times without number, and has never yet once failed where the motives have been high, where the knowledge of the results beforehand has been sufficiently great. Within a fortnight you can know the truth of this for yourself if you will but go in the right way.

All the truly great teachers in the world's history have gotten their powers in this way. You remember the great soul who left us not long ago, he who ministered so faithfully at Trinity, the great preacher of such wonderful. powers, the one so truly inspired. It was but .an evening or two since, when in conversation with a member of his congregation, we were talking in regard to Phillips Brooks. She was telling of his beautiful and powerful spirit, and said that they were all continually conscious of the fact that he had a power they hadn't, but that all longed for; that he seemed to have a great secret of power they hadn't, but that they often tried to find. She continued, and in the very next sentence went on to tell of a fact,—one that I knew full well,—the fact that during a certain period of each day he took himself alone into a little, silent room, he fastened the door behind him, and during this period under no circumstances could he be seen by any one. The dear lady knew these two things, she knew and was influenced by his great soul power, she also knew of his going thus into the silence each day; but, bless her heart, it had never once occurred to her to put the two together.

It is in this way that great soul power is grown; and the men of this great power are the men who move the world, the men who do the great work in the world along all lines, and against whom no man, no power, can stand. Call to mind a number of the world's greatest preachers, or, using again the better term, teachers, and bear in mind I do not mean creed, dogma, form, but religious teachers,—and the one class differs from the other even as the night from the day,—and you will find two great facts in the life of each and all,—great soul power, grown chiefly by much time spent in the silence, and the fact that the life of each has been built upon this one great and all-powerful principle of love, service, and helpfulness for all mankind.

Is it your ambition to become a great *writer*? Very good. But remember that unless you have something to give to the world, something you feel mankind must have, something that will aid them in their march upward and onward, unless you have some service of this kind to render, then you had better be wise, and not take up the pen; for, if your object in writing is merely fame or money, the number of your readers may be exceedingly small, possibly a few score or even a few dozen may be a large estimate.

What an author writes is, after all, the sum total of his life, his habits, his characteristics, his experiences, his purposes. *He never can write more than he himself is.* He can never pass beyond his limitations; and unless he have a purpose higher than writing merely for fame or self-aggrandizement, he thereby marks his own limitations, and what he seeks will never come. While he who writes for the world, because he feels he has something that it needs and that will be a help to mankind, if it is something it needs, other things being equal, that which the other man seeks for directly, and so never finds, will come to him in all its fulness. This is the way it comes, and this way only. *Mankind cares nothing for you until you have shown that you care for mankind.*

Note this statement from the letter of a now well-known writer, one whose very first book met with instant success, and that has been followed by others all similarly received. She says, "I never thought of writing until two years and a half ago, when, in order to disburden my mind of certain thoughts that clamored for utterance, I produced," etc. In the light of this we cannot wonder at the remarkable success of her very first and all succeeding books. She had something she felt the world needed and must have; and, with no thought of self, of fame, or of money, she gave it. The world agreed with her; and, as she was large enough to seek for neither, it has given her both.

Note this also: "I write for the love of writing, not for money or reputation. The former I have without exertion, the latter is not worth a pin's point in the general economy of the vast universe. Work done for the love of working brings its own reward far more quickly and surely than work done for mere payment." This is but the formulated statement of what all the world's greatest writers and authors have said or would say,—at least so far as I have come in contact with their opinions in regard to it.

So, unless you are large enough to forget self for the good, for the service of mankind, thus putting yourself on the side of the universal and making it possible for you to give something that will in turn of itself bring fame, you had better be wise, and not lift the pen at all; for what you write will not be taken up, or, if it is, will soon be let fall again.

One of our most charming and most noted American authors says in regard to her writing, "I press my soul upon the white paper"; and let me tell you the reason it in turn makes its impression upon so many thousands of other souls is because hers is so large, so tender, so sympathetic, so loving, that others cannot resist the impression, living as she does not for self, but for the service of others, her own life thus having a part in countless numbers of other lives.

It is only that that comes from the heart that can reach the heart. Take from their shelves the most noted, the greatest works in any library, and you will find that their authors have made them what they are not by a study of the rules and principles of rhetoric, for this of itself never has made and never can make a great writer. They are what they are because the author's very soul has been fired by some great truth or fact that the world has needed, that has been a help to mankind. Large souls they have been, souls in love with all the human kind.

Is it your ambition to become a great *actor*? Then remember that if you make it the object of your life to play to influence the hearts, the lives, and so the destinies of men, this same great law of nature that operates in the case of the orator will come to your assistance, will aid you in your growth and development, and will enable you to attain to heights you could never attain to or even dream of, in case you play for the little *ego* you otherwise would stand for. In the latter case you may succeed in making a third or a fourth rate actor, possibly a second rate; but you can never become one of the world's greatest, and the chances are you may succeed in making not even a livelihood, and thus have your wonderment satisfied why so many who try fail.

In the other case, other things being equal, the height you may attain to is unbounded, depending upon the degree you are able to forget yourself in influencing the minds and the souls, and thus the lives and the destinies of men.

Is it your ambition to become a great *singer*? Then remember that if your thought is only of self, you may never sing at all, unless, indeed, you enjoy singing to yourself,—this, or you will be continually anxious as to the size of your audience. If, on the other hand, you choose this field of work because here you can be of the greatest service to mankind, if your ambition is to sing to the hearts and the lives of men, then this same great law of nature will come to assist you in your growth and development and efforts, and other things being equal, instead of singing to yourself or being anxious as to the size of your audience, you will seldom find time for the first, and your anxiety will be as to whether the place has an audience-chamber large enough to accommodate even a small portion of the people who will seek admittance. You remember Jenny Lind.

Is it your ambition to become a *fashionable society woman*, this and nothing more, intent only upon your own pleasure and satisfaction? Then stop and meditate, if only for a moment; for if this is the case, you never will, ay, you never can find the true and the genuine, for you fail to recognize the great law that there is no such thing as finding true happiness by searching for it *directly*, and the farther on you go the more flimsy and shallow and unsatisfying that imitation you are willing to accept for the genuine will become. You will thereby rob life of its chief charms, defeat the very purpose you have in view. And, while you are at this moment meditating, oh grasp the truth of the great law that you will find your own life only in losing it in the service of others,—that the more of your life you so give, the fuller and the richer, the greater and the grander, the more beautiful and the more happy your own life will become.

And with your abundant means and opportunities build your life upon this great law of service, and experience the pleasure of growing into that full, rich, ever increasing and satisfying life that will result, and that will make you better known, more honored and blessed, than the life of any mere society woman can be, or any life, for that matter; for you are thus living a life the highest this world can know. And you will thus hasten the day when, standing and looking back and seeing the emptiness and the littleness of the other life as compared with this, you will bless the time that your better judgment prevailed and saved you from it. Or, if you chance to be in it already, delay not, but commence now to build upon this true foundation.

Instead of discharging your footman, as did a woman of whom I chance to know, because he finally refused to stand in the rain by the side of her carriage, with his arms folded just so, standing immovable like a mummy (I had almost said like a fool), daring to look neither to one side nor the other, but all the time in the direction of her so-called ladyship, while she spent an hour or two in doing fifteen or twenty minutes' shopping in her desire to make it known that this is Mrs. Q.'s carriage, and this is the footman that goes with it,—instead of doing this, give him an umbrella if necessary, and take him to aid you as you go on your errands of mercy and cheer and service and loving kindness to the innumerable ones all about you who so stand in need of them.

Is there any comparison between the appellation "Lady Bountiful" and "a proud, selfish, pleasure-seeking woman"? And, much more, do you think there is any comparison whatever between the real pleasure and happiness and satisfaction in the lives of the two?

Is it the ambition of your life to *accumulate great wealth*, and thus to acquire a great name, and along with it happiness and satisfaction? Then remember that whether these will come to you will depend *entirely* upon the use and disposition you make of your wealth. If you regard it as a *private trust* to be used for the highest good of mankind, then well and good, these will come to you. If your object, however, is to pile it up, to hoard it, then neither will come; and you will find it a life as unsatisfactory as one can live.

There is, there can be, no greatness in things, in material things, of themselves. The greatness is determined entirely by the use and disposition made of them. The greatest greatness and the only *true* greatness in the world is unselfish love and service and self-devotion to one's fellow-men.

Look at the matter carefully, and tell me candidly if there can be anything more foolish than a man's spending all the days of his life piling up and hoarding money, too mean and too stingy to use any but what is absolutely necessary, accumulating many times more than he can possibly ever use, always eager for more, growing still more eager and grasping the nearer he comes to life's end, then lying down, dying, and leaving it. It seems to me about as sensible for a man to have as the great aim and ambition of life the piling up of an immense pile of old iron in the middle of a large field, and sitting on it day after day because he is so wedded to it that it has become a part of his life and lest a fragment disappear, denying himself and those around him many of the things that go to make life valuable and pleasant, and finally dying there, himself, the soul, so dwarfed and so stunted that he has really a hard time to make his way out of the miserable old body. There is not such a great difference, if you will think of it carefully,—one a pile of old iron, the other a pile of gold or silver, but all belonging to the same general class.

It is a great law of our being that we become like those things we contemplate. If we contemplate those that are true and noble and elevating, we grow in the likeness of these. If we contemplate merely material things, as gold or silver or copper or iron, our souls, our natures, and even our faces become like them, hard and flinty, robbed of their finer and better and grander qualities. Call to mind the person or picture of the miser, and you will quickly see that this is true. Merely nature's great law. He thought he was going to be a master: he finds himself the slave. Instead of possessing his wealth, his wealth possesses him. How often have

I seen persons of nearly or quite this kind! Some can be found almost anywhere. You can call to mind a few, perhaps many.

During the past two or three years two well-known millionaires in the United States, millionaires many times over, have died. The one started into life with the idea of acquiring a great name by accumulating great wealth. These two things he had in mind,—self and great wealth. And, as he went on, he gradually became so that he could see nothing but these. The greed for gain soon made him more and more the slave i and he, knowing nothing other than obedience to his master, piled and accumulated and hoarded, and after spending all his days thus, he then lay down and died, taking not so much as one poor little penny with him, only a soul dwarfed compared to what it otherwise might have been. For it might have been the soul of a royal master instead of that of an abject slave.

The papers noted his death with seldom even a single word of praise. It was regretted by few, and he was mourned by still fewer. And even at his death he was spoken of by thousands in words far from complimentary, all uniting in saying what he might have been and done, what a tremendous power for good, how he might have been loved and honored during his life, and at death mourned and blessed by the entire nation, the entire world. A pitiable sight, indeed, to see a human mind, a human soul, thus voluntarily enslave itself for a few temporary pieces of metal.

The other started into life with the principle that a man's success is to be measured by his *direct usefulness* to his fellow-men, to the world in which he lives, and by this alone; that private wealth is merely a *private trust* to be used for the highest good of mankind. Under the benign influences of this mighty principle of service, we see him great, influential, wealthy; his whole nature expanding, himself growing large-hearted, generous, magnanimous, serving his State, his country, his fellow-men, writing his name on the hearts of all he comes in contact with, so that his name is never thought of by them without feelings of gratitude and praise.

Then as the chief service to his fellow-men, next to his own personal influence and example, he uses his vast fortune, this vast private trust, for the founding and endowing of a great institution of learning, using his splendid business capacities in its organization, having uppermost in mind in its building that young men and young women may there have every advantage at the least possible expense to fit themselves in turn for the greatest *direct usefulness* to their fellow-men while they live in the world.

In the midst of these activities the news comes of his death. Many hearts now are sad. The true, large-hearted, sympathizing friend, the servant of rich and poor alike, has gone away. Countless numbers whom he has befriended, encouraged, helped, and served, bless his name, and give thanks that such a life has been lived. His own great State rises up as his pall-bearers, while the entire nation acts as honorary pall-bearers. Who can estimate the influence of a life such as this? But it cannot be estimated; for it will flow from the ones personally influenced to others, and through them to others throughout eternity. He alone who in His righteous balance weighs each human act can estimate it. And his final munificent gift to mankind will make his name remembered and honored and blessed long after the accumulations of mere plutocrats are scattered and mankind forgets that they have ever lived.

Then have as your object the accumulation of great wealth if you choose; but bear in mind that, unless you are able to get beyond self, it will make you not great, but small, and you will rob life of the finer and better things in it. If, on the other hand, you are guided by the principle that private wealth is but a *private trust*, and that *direct usefulness* or service to mankind is the only real measure of true greatness, and bring your life into harmony with it, then you will become and will be counted great; and with it will come that rich joy and happiness and satisfaction that always accompanies a life of true service, and therefore the best and truest life.

One can never afford to forget that personality, life, and character, that there may be the greatest service, are the chief things, and wealth merely the *incident*. Nor can one afford to be among those who are too mean, too small, or too stingy to invest in anything that will grow and increase these.

III

The Unfoldment

If you'd have a rare growth and unfoldment supreme,
And make life one long joy and contentment complete,
Then with kindliness, love, and good will let it teem,
And with service for all make it fully replete.
If you'd have all the world and all heaven to love you,
And that love with its power would you fully convince,
Then love all the world; and men royal and true,
Will make cry as you pass—"God bless him, the prince!"

ONE beautiful feature of this principle of love and service is that this phase of one's personality, or nature, can be grown. I have heard it asked, If one hasn't it to any marked degree naturally, what is to be done? In reply let it be said, Forget self, get out of it for a little while, and, as it comes in your way, do something for some one, some kind service, some loving favor, it makes no difference how *small* it may appear. But a kind look or word to one weary with care, from whose life all worth living for seems to have gone out; a helping hand or little lift to one almost discouraged,—it may be that this is just the critical moment, a helping hand just now may change a life or a destiny. Show yourself a friend to one who thinks he or she is friendless.

Oh, there are a thousand opportunities each day right where you are,—not the great things far away, but the little things right at hand. With a heart full of love do something: experience the rich returns that will come to you, and it will be unnecessary to urge a repetition or a continuance. The next time it will be easier and more natural, and the next. You know of that wonderful reflex-nerve system you have in your body,—that which says that whenever you do a certain thing in a certain way, it is easier to do the same thing the next time, and the next, and the next, until presently it is done with scarcely any effort on your part at all, it has become your second nature. And thus we have what? Habit. This is the way that all habit is, the way that all habit must be formed. And have you ever fully realized that *life is, after all, merely a series of habits*, and that it lies entirely within one's own power to determine just what that series shall be?

I have seen this great principle made the foundation principle in an institution of learning. It is made not a theory merely as I have seen it here and there, but a vital, living truth. And I wish I had time to tell of its wonderful and beautiful influences upon the life and work of that institution, and upon the lives and the work of those who go out from it. A joy indeed to be there. One can't enter within its walls even for a few moments without feeling its benign influences. One can't go out without taking them with him. I have seen purposes and lives almost or quite transformed; and life so rich, so beautiful, and so valuable opened up, such as the persons never dreamed could be, by being but a single year under these beautiful and life-giving influences.

I have also seen it made the foundation principle of a great summer congress, one that has already done an unprecedented work, one that has a far greater work yet before it, and chiefly by reason of this all-powerful foundation upon which it is built,—conceived and put into operation as it was by a rare and highly illumined soul, one thoroughly filled with the love of service for all the human kind. There are no thoughts of money returns, for everything it has to give is as free as the beautiful atmosphere that pervades it. The result is that there is drawn together, by way of its magnificent corps of lectures as well as those in attendance, a company of people of the rarest type, so that everywhere there is a manifestation of that spirit of love, helpfulness, and kindliness, that permeates the entire atmosphere with a deep feeling of peace, that makes every moment of life a joy.

So enchanting does this spirit make the place that very frequently the single day of some who have come for this length of time has lengthened itself into a week, and the week in turn into a month; and the single week of others has frequently lengthened itself, first into a month, then into the entire summer. There is nothing at all strange in this fact, however; for *wherever one finds sweet humanity, he there finds a spot where all people love to dwell.*

Making this the fundamental principle of one's life, around which all others properly arrange and subordinate themselves, is not, as a casual observer might think, and as he sometimes suggests, an argument against one's own growth and development, against the highest possible unfoldment of his entire personality and powers. Rather, on the other hand, is it one of the greatest reasons, one of the greatest arguments, in its favor; for, the stronger the personality and the greater the powers, the greater the influence in the service of mankind. If, then, life be thus founded, can there possibly be any greater incentive to that self-development that brings one up to his highest possibilities? A development merely for self alone can never have behind it an incentive, a power so great; *and after all, there is nothing in the world so great, so effective in the service of mankind, as a strong, noble, and beautiful manhood or womanhood.* It is this that in the ultimate determines the influence of every man upon his fellow-men. *Life, character, is the greatest power in the world, and character it is that gives the power; for in all true power, along whatever line it may be, it is after all, living the life that tells.* This is a great law that but few who would have great power and influence seem to recognize, or, at least, that but few seem to act upon.

Are you a writer? You can never write more than you yourself are. Would you write more? Then broaden, deepen, enrich the life. Are you a minister? You can never raise men higher than you have raised yourself. Your words will have exactly the sound of the life whence they come. Hollow the life? Hollow-sounding and empty will be the words, weak, ineffective, false. Would you have them go with greater power, and thus be more effective? Live the life, the power will come. Are you an orator? The power and effectiveness of your words in influencing and moving masses of men depends entirely upon the altitude from which they are spoken. Would you have them more effective, each one filled with a living power? Then elevate the life, the power will come. Are you in the walks of private life? Then, wherever you move, there goes from you, even if there be no word spoken, a silent but effective influence of an elevating or a degrading nature. Is the life high, beautiful? Then the influences are inspiring, life-giving. Is it low, devoid of beauty? The influences then, are disease-laden, death-dealing. The tones of your voice, the attitude of your body, the character of your face, all are determined by the life you live, all in turn influence for better or for worse all who come within your radius. And if, as one of earth's great souls has said, the only way truly to help a man is to make him better, then the tremendous power of merely the life itself.

Why, I know personally a young man of splendid qualities and gifts, who was rapidly on the way of ruin, as the term goes, gradually losing control of himself day after day, self-respect almost gone,—already the thought of taking his own life had entered his mind,—who was so inspired with the mere presence and bearing of a royal-hearted young man, one who had complete mastery of himself, and therefore a young man of power, that the very sight of him as he went to and fro in his daily work was a power that called his better self to the front again, awakened the God nature within him, so that he again set his face in the direction of the right, the true, the manly; and to-day there is no grander, stronger, more beautiful soul in all the wide country than he. Yes, there is a powerful influence that resolves itself into a service for all in each individual strong, pure, and noble life.

And have the wonderful possibilities of what may be termed an inner or soul development ever come strongly to your notice? Perhaps not, for as yet only a few have begun to recognize under this name a certain great power that has always existed,—a power that has never as yet been fully understood, and so has been called by this term and by that. It is possible so to develop this soul power that, as we stand merely and talk with a person, there goes out from us a silent influence that the person cannot see or hear, but that he feels, and the influences of which he cannot escape; that, as we merely go into a room in which several persons are sitting, there goes out from us a power, a silent influence that all will feel and will be influenced by, even though not a word be spoken. This has been the power of every man, of every woman, of great and lasting influence in the world's history.

It is just beginning to come to us through a few highly illumined souls that this power can be grown, that it rests upon great natural law that the Author of our being has instituted within us and about us. It is during the next few years that we are to see many wonderful developments along this line; for in this, as in many others, the light is just beginning to break. A few, who are far up on the heights of human development, are just beginning to catch the first few faint flushes of the dawn. Then live to your highest. This of itself will make you of great service to mankind, but without this you never can be. Naught is the difference how hard you may try; and know, even so far as your own highest interests are concerned, that *the true joy of existence comes from living to one's highest.*

This life, and this alone, will bring that which I believe to be one of the greatest characteristics of a truly great man,— humility; and when one says humility, he necessarily implies simplicity; for the two always go hand in hand. The one is born of the other. The proud, the vain, the haughty, those striving for effect, are never counted among the world's greatest personages. The very fact of one's striving for effect of itself indicates that there is not enough in him to make him really great; while he who really is so needs never concern himself about it, nor does he ever. I can think of no better way for one to attain to humility and simplicity than for him to have his mind off of *self* in the service of others. Vanity, that most dangerous quality, and especially for young people, is the outcome of one's always regarding self.

Mrs. Henry Ward Beecher once said that, when they lived in the part of Brooklyn known as the Heights, they could always tell when Mr. Beecher was coming in the evening from the voices and the joyous laughter of the children. All the street urchins, as well as the more well-to-do children in the vicinity, knew him, and would often wait for his coming. When they saw him in the distance, they would run and gather around him, get hold of his hands, into those large overcoat pockets for the nuts and the good things he so often filled them with before starting for home, knowing as he did full well what was coming, tug at him to keep him with them as long as they could, he all the time laughing or running as if to get away, never too great—ay, rather let us say, great enough—to join with them in their sports.

That mysterious dignity of a man less great, therefore with less of humility and simplicity, with mind always intent upon self and his own standing, would have told him that possibly this might not be just the "proper thing" to do. But even the children, street urchins as well as those well-to-do, found in this great loving soul a friend. Recall similar incidents in the almost daily life of Lincoln and in the lives of all truly great men. All have that beautiful and ever-powerful characteristic, that simple, childlike nature.

Another most beautiful and valuable feature of this life is its effect upon one's own growth and development. There is a law which says that one can't do a kind act or a loving service for another without its bringing rich returns to his own life and growth. This is an invariable law. Can I then, do a kind act or a loving service for a brother or a sister,—and all indeed are such because children of the same Father,—why, I should be glad—ay, doubly glad of the opportunity. If I do it thus out of love, forgetful of self, for aught I know it may do me more good than the one I do it for, in its influence upon the growing of that rich, beautiful, and happy life it is mine to grow; though the joy and satisfaction resulting from it, the highest, the sweetest, the keenest this life can know, are of themselves abundant rewards.

In addition to all this it scarcely ever fails that those who are thus aided by some loving service may be in a position somehow, some-when, somewhere, either directly or indirectly, and at a time when it may be most needed or most highly appreciated, to do in turn a kind service for him who, with never a thought of any possible return, has dealt kindly with them. So

> *"Cast your bread upon the waters, far and wide your treasures strew,*
> *Scatter it with willing fingers, shout for joy to see it go!*
> *You may think it lost forever; but, as sure as God is true,*
> *In this life and in the other it will yet return to you."*

Have you sorrows or trials that seem very heavy to bear? Then let me tell you that one of the best ways in the world to lighten and sweeten them is to lose yourself in the service of others, in helping to bear and lighten those of a fellow-being whose, perchance, are much more grievous than your own. It is a great law of your being which says you can do this. Try it, and experience the truth for yourself, and know that, when turned in this way, sorrow is the most beautiful soul-refiner of which the world knows, and hence not to be shunned, but to be welcomed and rightly turned.

There comes to my mind a poor widow woman whose life would seem to have nothing in it to make it happy, but, on the other hand, cheerless and tiresome, and whose work would have been very hard, had it not been for a little crippled child she dearly loved and cared for, and who was all the more precious to her on account of its helplessness. Losing herself and forgetting her own hard lot in the care of the little cripple, her whole life was made cheerful and happy, and her work not hard, but easy, because lightened by love and service for another. And this is but one of innumerable cases of this kind.

So you may turn your sorrows, you may lighten your burdens, by helping bear the burdens, if not of a crippled child, then of a brother or a sister who in another sense may be crippled, or who may become so but for your timely service. You can find them all about you: never pass one by.

By building upon this principle, the poor may thus live as

grandly and as happily as the rich, those in humble and lowly walks of life as grandly and as happily as those in what seem to be more exalted stations. Recognizing the truth, as we certainly must by this time, that one is *truly* great only in so far as this is made the fundamental principle of his life, it becomes evident that that longing for greatness for its and for one's own sake falls away, and none but a diseased mind cares for it; for no sooner is it grasped than, as a bubble, it bursts, because it is not the true, the permanent, but the false, the transient. On the other hand, he who forgetting self and this kind of greatness, falsely so called, in the service of his fellow-men, by this very fact puts himself on the right track, the only track for the true, the genuine; and in what degree it will come to him depends entirely upon his adherence to the law.

And do you know the influence of this life in the moulding of the features, that it gives the highest beauty that can dwell there, the beauty that comes from within,—the *soul beauty*, so often found in the paintings of the old masters. *True beauty must cone, must be grown, from within.* That outward veneering, which is so prevalent, can never be even a poor imitation of this type of the true, the genuine. To appreciate fully the truth of this, it is but necessary to look for a moment at that beautiful picture by Sant, the "Soul's Awakening," a face that grows more beautiful each time one looks at it, and that one never tires of looking at, and compare with it the fractional parts of apothecary shops we see now and then—or so often, to speak more truly—on the streets. A face of this higher type carries with it a benediction wherever it goes.

A beautiful little incident came to my notice not long ago. It was a very hot and dusty day. The passengers on the train were weary and tired. The time seemed long and the journey cheerless. A lady with a face that carries a benediction to all who see her entered the car with a little girl, also of that type of beauty that comes from within, and with a voice musical, sweet, and sparkling, such as also comes from this source.

The child, when they were seated, had no sooner spoken a

few words before she began to enlist the attention of her fellow-passengers. She began playing peek-a-boo with a staid and dignified old gentleman in the seat behind her. He at first looked at her over his spectacles, then lowered his paper a little, then a little more, and a little more. Finally, he dropped it altogether, and, apparently forgetting himself and his surroundings, became oblivious to everything in the fascinating pleasure he was having with the little girl. The other passengers soon found themselves following his example. All papers and books were dropped. The younger folks gave way to joyous laughter, and all seemed to vie with. each other in having the honor of receiving a word or a smile from the little one.

The dust, the heat, the tired, cheerless feelings were all forgotten; and when these two left the car, the little girl waving them good-by, instinctively, as one person, all the passengers waved it to her in return, and two otherwise dignified gentlemen, leaving their seats, passed over to the other side, and looked out of the window to see her as long as they could. Something as an electrical spark seemed to have passed through the car. Ali were light-hearted and happy now; and the conditions in the car, compared to what they were before these two entered, would rival the work of the stereopticon, so far as completeness of change is concerned. You have seen such faces and have heard such voices. They result from a life the kind we are considering. They are but its outward manifestations, spontaneous as the water from the earth as it bursts forth a natural fountain.

We must not fail also to notice the effect of this life upon one's manners and bearing. True politeness comes from a life founded upon this great principle, and from this alone. This gives the true gentleman,—*gentle-man*,—a man gentle, kind, loving, courteous from nature. Such a one can't have anything but true politeness, can't be anything but a gentle-man; for one can't truly be anything but himself. So the one always intent upon and thinking of self cannot be the true gentle-man, notwithstanding the artful contrivances and studied efforts to appear so, but which so generally reveal his own shallowness and artificiality, and disgust all with whom he comes in contact.

I sometimes meet a person who, when introduced, will go through a series of stiff, cold, and angular movements, the knee at such a bend, the foot at such an angle, the back with such a bend or hump,—much less pleasant to see than that of a camel or a dromedary, for with these it is natural,—so that I have found myself almost thinking, Poor fellow, I wonder what the trouble is, whether he will get over it all right. It is so very evident that he all the time has his mind upon himself, wondering whether or not he is getting everything just right. What a relief to turn from such a one to one who, instead of thinking always of self, has continually in mind the ease and comfort and pleasure he can give to others, who, in other words, is the true *gentle-man*, and with whom true politeness is natural; for one's every act is born of his thoughts.

It is said that there was no truer gentleman in all Scotland than Robert Burns. And yet he was a farmer all his life, and had never been away from his native little rural village into a city until near the close of his life, when, taking the manuscripts that for some time had been accumulating in the drawer of his writing-table up to Edinburgh, he captivated the hearts of all in the capital. Without studied contrivances, he was the true gentleman, and true politeness was his, because his life was founded upon the principle that continually brought from his pen lines such as:—

> "It's coming yet, for a' that,
> That man to man, the warld o'er,
> Shall brothers be for a' that!"

And under the influence of this principle, he was a gentleman by nature, and one of nature's noblemen, without ever thinking whether he was or not, as he who is truly such never needs to and never does.

And then recall the large-hearted Ben Franklin, when sent to the French court. In his plain gray clothes, unassuming and entirely forgetful of himself, how he captured the hearts of all, of even the giddy society ladies, and how he became and remained while there the centre of attraction in that gay capital! His politeness, his manners, all the result of that great, kind, loving, and helpful nature which made others feel that it was they he was devoting himself to, and not himself.

This little extract from a letter written by Franklin to George Whitefield will show how he regarded the great principle we are considering: "As to the kindness you mention, I wish it could have been of more service to you. But, if it had, the only thanks I should desire is that you would always be equally ready to serve any other person that may need your assistance; and so let good offices go around, for mankind are all of a family. For my own part, when I am employed in serving others, I do not look upon myself as conferring favors, but as paying debts. In my travels, and since my settlement, I have received much kindness from men to whom I shall never have any opportunity of making any direct return, and numberless mercies from God, who is infinitely above being benefited by our services. These kindnesses from men I can, therefore, only return on their fellow-men; and I can only show my gratitude for these mercies from God by a readiness to help his other children and my brethren."

No, true gentlemanliness and politeness always comes from within, and is born of a life of love, kindliness, and service. This is the universal language, known and understood everywhere, even when our words are not. There is, you know, a beautiful old proverb which says, "He who is kind and courteous to strangers thereby shows himself a citizen of the world." And there is nothing so remembered, and that so endears one to all mankind, as this universal language. Even dumb animals understand it and are affected by it. How quickly the dog, for example, knows and makes it known when he is spoken to and treated kindly or the reverse! And here shall not a word be spoken in connection with that great body of our fellow-creatures whom, because we do not understand their language, we are accustomed to call dumb? The attitude we have assumed toward these fellow-creatures, and the treatment they have been subjected to in the past, is something almost appalling.

There are a number of reasons why this has been true. Has not one been on account of a belief in a future life for man, but not for the animal? A few years ago a gentleman left by will some fifty thousand dollars for the work of Henry Bergh's New York Society. His relatives contested the will on the ground of insanity,—on the ground of insanity because he believed in a future life for animals. The judge, in giving his decision sustaining the will, stated that after a very careful investigation, he found that fully half the world shared the same belief. Agassiz thoroughly believed it. An English writer has recently compiled a list of over one hundred and seventy English authors who have so thoroughly believed it as to write upon the subject. The same belief has been shared by many of the greatest thinkers in all parts of the world, and it is a belief that is constantly gaining ground.

Another and perhaps the chief cause has been on account of a supposed inferior degree of intelligence on the part of animals, which in another form would mean, that they are less able to care for and protect themselves. Should this, however, be a reason why they should be neglected and cruelly treated? Nay, on the other hand, should this not be the greatest reason why we should all the more zealously care for, protect, and kindly treat them?

You or I may have a brother or a sister who is not normally endowed as to brain power, who, perchance, may be idiotic or insane, or who, through sickness or mishap, is weak-minded; but do we make this an excuse for neglecting, cruelly treating, or failing to love such a one? On the contrary, the very fact that he or she is not so able to plan for, care for, and protect him or her self, is all the greater reason for all the more careful exercise of these functions on our part. But, certainly, there are many animals around us with far more intelligence, at least manifested intelligence, than this brother or sister. The parallel holds, but the absurd falsity of the position we assume is most apparent. No truer nobility of character can anywhere manifest itself than is shown in one's attitude toward and treatment of those weaker or the so-called inferior, and so with less power to care for and protect themselves. Moreover, I think we shall find that we are many times mistaken in regard to our beliefs in connection with the inferior intelligence of at least many animals. If, instead of using them simply to serve our own selfish ends without a just recompense, without a thought further than as to what we can get out of them, and then many times casting them off when broken or of no further service, and many times looking down upon, neglecting, or even abusing them,—if, instead of this, we would deal equitably with them, love them, train and educate them the same as we do our children, we would be somewhat surprised at the remarkable degree of intelligence the "dumb brutes" possess, and also the remarkable degree of training they are capable of. What, however, can be expected of them when we take the attitude we at present hold toward them?

Page after page might readily be filled with most interesting as well as inspiring portrayals of their superior intelligence, their remarkable capabilities under kind and judicious training, their *faithfulness* and *devotion*. The efforts of such noble and devoted workers as Henry Bergh in New York, of George T. Angell in Massachusetts, and many others in various parts of the country, have already brought about a great change in our attitude toward and relations with this great body of our fellow-creatures, and have made all the world more thoughtful, considerate, and kind. This, however, is just the beginning of a work that is assuming greater and ever greater proportions.

The work of the American Humane Education Society[1] is probably surpassed in its vitality and far-reaching results by the work of no other society in the world to-day. Its chief object is the humane education of the American people; and through one phase of its work alone—its Bands of Mercy, over twenty-five thousand of which have already been formed, giving regular, systematic humane training and instruction to between one and two million

---

[1]Headquarters at Boston, Mass.

children, and these continually increasing in numbers—a most vital work is being done, such as no man can estimate.

The humane sentiment inculcated in one's relations with the animal world, and its resultant feelings of sympathy, tenderness, love, and care, will inevitably manifest itself in one's relations with his fellows; and I for one, would rejoice to see this work carried into every school throughout the length and breadth of the land. In many cases this one phase of the child's training would be of far more vital value and import as he grows to manhood than all the rest of the schooling combined, and it would form a most vital entering wedge in the solution of our social situation.

And why should we not speak to and kindly greet an animal as we pass it, as instinctively as we do a human fellow-being? Though it may not get our words, it will invariably get the attitude and the motive that prompts them, and will be affected accordingly. This it will do every time. Animals in general are marvellously sensitive to the mental conditions, the thought forces, and emotions of people. Some are peculiarly sensitive, and can detect them far more quickly and unerringly than many people can.

It ought to help us greatly in our relations with them ever fully to realize that they with us are parts of the one Universal Life, simply different forms of the manifestation of the One Life, having their part to play in the economy of the great universe the same as we have ours, having their destiny to work out the same as we have ours, and just as important, just as valuable, in the sight of the All in All as we ourselves.

"I saw deep in the eyes of the animals the human soul look out upon me.

"I saw where it was born deep down under feathers and fur, or condemned for a while to roam four-footed among the brambles. I caught the clinging mute glance of the prisoner, and swore I would be faithful.

"Thee my brother and sister I see, and mistake not. Do not be afraid. Dwelling thus for a while, fulfilling thy appointed time, thou, too, shall come to thyself at last.

"Thy half-warm horns and long tongue lapping round my wrist do not conceal thy humanity any more than the learned talk of the pedant conceals his,—for all thou art dumb, we have words and plenty between us.

"Come nigh, little bird, with your half-stretched quivering wings,—within you I behold choirs of angels, and the Lord himself in vista."[2]

But a small thing, apparently, is a kind look, word, or service of some kind; but, oh! who can tell where it may end? It costs the giver comparatively nothing; but who can tell the priceless value to him who receives it? The cup of loving service, be it merely a cup of cold water, may grow and swell into a boundless river, refreshing and carrying life and hope in turn to numberless others, and these to others, and so have no end. This may be just the critical moment in some life. Given now, it may save or change a life or a destiny. So don't withhold the bread that's in your keeping, but
"Scatter it with willing fingers, shout for joy to see it go."
There is no greater thing in life that you can do, and nothing that will bring you such rich and precious returns.
The question is sometimes asked, How can one feel a deep and genuine love, a love sufficient to manifest itself in service for all?—there are some so mean, so small, with so many peculiar, objectionable, or even obnoxious characteristics. True, very true, apparently at least; but another great law of life is that *we find in men and women exactly those qualities, those characteristics, we look for, or that are nearest akin to the predominant qualities or characteristics of our own natures.* If we look for the peculiar, the little, the objectionable, these we shall find; but back of all this, all that is most apparent

---

[2]Toward Democracy.

on the exterior, in the depths of each and every human soul, is the good, the true, the brave, the loving, the divine, the God-like, that that never changes, the very God Himself that at some time or another will show forth His full likeness.

And still another law of life is that others usually manifest to us that which our own natures, or, in other words, our own thoughts and emotions, call forth. The same person, for example, will come to two different people in an entirely different way, because the larger, better, purer, and more universal nature of the one calls forth the best, the noblest, the truest in him; while the smaller, critical, personal nature of the other calls forth the opposite. The wise man is therefore careful in regard to what he has to say concerning this or that one; for, generally speaking, it is a sad commentary upon one's self if he find only the disagreeable, the objectionable. *One lives always in the atmosphere of his own creation.*

Again, it is sometimes said, But such a one has such and such habits or has done so and so, has committed such and such an error or such and such a crime. But who, let it be asked, constituted me a judge of my fellowman? Do I not recognize the fact that the moment I judge my fellow-man, by that very act I judge myself? One of two things, I either judge myself or hypocritically profess that never once in my entire life have I committed a sin, an error of any kind, never have I stumbled, never fallen, and by that very profession I pronounce myself at once either a fool or a knave, or both.

Again, it is said, But even for the sake of helping, of doing some service, I could not for my own sake, for character's, for reputation's sake, I could not afford even to be seen with such a one. What would people, what would my friends, think and say? True, apparently at least, but, if my life, my character, has such a foundation, a foundation so weak, so uncertain, so tottering, as to be affected by anything of this kind, I had better then look well to it, and quietly, quickly, but securely, begin to rebuild it; and, when I am sure that it is upon the true, deep, substantial foundation, the only additional thing then necessary is for me to reach that glorious stage of development which quickly gets one out of the personal into the universal, or rather that indicates that he is already out of the one and into the other, when he can say: They think. What do they think? Let them think. They say. What do they say? Let them say.

And, then, the supreme charity one should have, when he realizes the fact *that the great bulk of the sin and error in the world is committed not through choice, but through ignorance.* Not that the person does not know many times that this or that course of action is wrong, that it is wrong to commit this error or sin or crime; but the ignorance comes in his belief that in this course of conduct he is deriving pleasure and happiness, and his ignorance of the fact that through a different course of conduct he would derive a pleasure, a happiness, much keener, higher, more satisfying and enduring.

Never should we forget that we are all the same in motive,— pleasure and happiness: we differ only in method; and this difference in method is solely by reason of some souls being at any particular time more fully evolved, and thus having a greater knowledge of the great, immutable laws under which we live, and by putting the life into more and ever more complete harmony with these higher laws and forces, and in this way bringing about the highest, the keenest, the most abiding pleasure and happiness instead of seeking it on the lower planes.

While all are the same in essence, all a part of the One Infinite, Eternal, all with the same latent possibilities, all reaching ultimately the same place, it nevertheless is true that at any particular time some are more fully awakened, evolved, unfolded. One should also be careful, if life is continuous, eternal, how he judges any particular life merely from these threescore years and ten; for the very fact of life, in whatever form, means continual activity, growth, advancement, enfoldment, attainment, and, if there is the one, there must of necessity be the other. So in regard to this one or that one, no fears need be entertained.

By the door of my woodland cabin stood during the summer a

magnificent tube-rose stock. The day was when it was just putting into bloom; and then I counted buds—latent flowers—to the number of over a score. Some eight or ten one morning were in full bloom. The ones nearer the' top did not bloom forth until some two and three weeks later, and for some it took quite a month to reach the fully perfected stage. These certainly were not so beautiful, so satisfying, as those already in the perfect bloom, those that had already reached their highest perfection. But should they on this account be despised? Wait, wait and give the element of time an opportunity of doing its work; and you may find that by and by, when these have reached their highest perfection, they may even far transcend in beauty and in fragrance those at present so beautiful, so fragrant, so satisfying, those that we so much admire.

Here we recognize the element of time. How foolish, how childish, how puerile, to fail or even refuse to do the same when it comes to the human soul, with all its Godlike possibilities! And, again, how foolish, because some of the blooms on the rose stock had not reached their perfection as soon as others, to have pronounced them of no value, unworthy, and to have refused them the dews, the warm rains, the life-giving sunshine, the very agencies that hastened their perfected growth! Yet this puerile, unbalanced attitude is that taken by untold numbers in the world to-day toward many human souls on account of their less mature unfoldment at any given time.

Why, the very fact that a fellow-man and a brother has this or that fault, error, undesirable or objectionable characteristic, is of itself the very reason he needs all the more of charity, of love, of kindly help and aid, than is needed by the one more fully developed, and hence more free from these. All the more reason is there why the best in him should be recognized and ever called to the front.

The wise man is he who, when he desires to rid a room of darkness or gloom, does not attempt to drive it out directly, but who throws open the doors and the windows, that the room may be flooded with the golden sunlight; for in its presence darkness and gloom cannot remain. So the way to help a fellowman and a brother to the higher and better life is not by ever prating upon and holding up to view his errors, his faults, his shortcomings, any more than in the case of children, but by recognizing and ever calling forth the higher, the nobler, the divine, the God-like, *by opening the doors and the windows of his own soul*, and thus bringing about a spiritual perception, that he may the more carefully listen to the inner voice, that he may the more carefully follow "the light that lighteth every man that cometh into the world." For in the exact proportion that the interior perception comes will the outer life and conduct accord with it,—so far, and no farther.

Where in all the world's history is to be found a more beautiful or valuable incident than this? A group of men, self-centred, self-assertive, have found a poor woman who, in her blindness and weakness, has committed an error, the same one that they, in all probability, have committed not once, but many times; *for the rule is that they are first to condemn who are most at fault themselves.* They bring her to the Master, they tell him that she has committed a sin,—ay, more, that she has been taken in the very act,—and ask what shall be done with her, informing him that, in accordance with the olden laws, such a one should be stoned.

But, quicker than thought, that great incarnation of spiritual power and insight reads their motives; and, after allowing them to give full expression to their accusations, he turns, and calmly says, "He among you that is *without sin*, let *him* cast the first stone." So saying, he stoops down, as if he is writing in the sand. The accusers, feeling the keen and just rebuke, in the mean time sneak out, until not one remains. The Master, after all have gone, turns to the woman, his sister, and kindly and gently says, "And where are thine accusers? doth no man condemn thee?" "No man, Lord." *"And neither do I condemn thee: go thou, and sin no more."* Oh, the beauty, the soul pathos! Oh, the royal-hearted brother! Oh, the invaluable lesson to us all!

I have no doubt that this gentle, loving admonition, this calling of the higher and the better to the front, set into operation in her interior nature forces that hastened her progress from the purely animal, the unsatisfying, the diminishing, to the higher spiritual, the satisfying, the ever-increasing, or, even more, that made it instantaneous, but that in either case brought about the new birth,- the new birth that comes with the awakening of the soul out of its purely physical sense-life to the higher spiritual perception and knowledge of itself, and thus the birth of the higher out of the lower, as at some time or another comes to each and every human soul.

And still another fact that should make us most charitable toward and slow to judge, or rather refuse to judge, a fellow-man and a brother,—the fact that we cannot know the intense strugglings and fightings he or she may be subjected to, though accompanied, it is true, by numerous stumblings and fallings, though the latter we see, while the former we fail to recognize. Did we, however, know the truth of the matter, it may be that *in the case of ourselves*, who are so quick to judge, had we the same temptations and fightings, the battle would not be half so nobly, so manfully fought, and our stumblings and fallings might be many times the number of his or of hers. Had we infinite knowledge and wisdom, our judgments would be correct; though, had we infinite knowledge and wisdom, we would be spared the task, though perhaps pleasure would seem to be the truer word to use, of our own self-imposed judgments.

Even so, then, if I cannot give myself in thorough love and service and self-devotion to each and all of the Father's other children, to every brother, no matter what the rank, station, or apparent condition, it shows that at least one of several things is radically wrong with self; and it also indicates that I shall never know the full and supreme joy of existence until I am able to and until I regard each case in the light of a rare and golden opportunity, in which I take a supreme delight.

Although what has just been said is true, at the same time there are occasions when it must be taken with wise discretion; and, although there are things it may be right for me to do for the sake of helping another life, at the same time there are things it may be unwise for me to do. I have sympathy for a friend who is lying in the gutter; but it would be very unwise for me to get myself into the same condition, and go and lie with him, thinking that only thus I could show my fullest sympathy, and be of greatest help to him. On the contrary, it is only as I stand on the higher ground that I am able to reach forth the hand that will truly lift him up. The moment I sink myself to the same level, my power to help ceases.

Just as unwise, to use a familiar example, far more unwise, would it be for me, were I a woman, to think of marrying a man who is a drunkard or a libertine, thinking that because I may love him I shall be able to reform him. In the first place, I should find that the desired results could not be accomplished in this way, or, rather, no results that could not be accomplished, and far more readily accomplished otherwise, and at far less expense. In the second place, I could not afford to subject myself to the demands, the influences, of one such, and so either sink myself to his level or, if not, then be compelled to use the greater part of my time, thought, and energy in demonstrating over existing conditions, and keeping myself true to the higher life, the same time that might be used in helping the lives of many others. If I sink myself to his level, I do not help, but aid all the more in dragging him down, or, if I do not sink to his level, then in the degree that I approach it do I lose my power over and influence with that life. Especially would it be unwise on my part if on his part there is no real desire for a different course, and no manifest endeavor to attain to it. Many times it seems necessary for such a one to wallow in the deepest of the mire, until, to use a commonplace phrase, he has his fill. He will then be ready to come out, will then be open to influence. I in the mean time, instead of entering into the mire with him, instead of subjecting my life to his influences, will stand up on the higher ground, and will ever point him upward, will ever reach forth a hand to help him upward, and will thus subject *him* to the higher influences; and, by preserving myself in this attitude, I can do the same for many other lives. In it all there will be no bitterness, no condemnation, no casting off, but the highest charity, sympathy and love; and it is only by this method that I can manifest the highest, only by this method that I can the most truly aid, for only as I am lifted up can I draw others unto me.

In this matter of service, as in all other matters, that supreme regulator of human life and conduct—good common sense— must always be used. There are some natures, for example, whom the more we would do for, the more we would have to do for, who, in other words, would become dependent, losing their sense of self-dependence. For such the highest service one can render is as judiciously and as indirectly as possible to lead them to the sense of self-reliance. Then there are others whose natures are such that, the more they are helped, the more they expect, the more they demand, even as their right, who, in other words, are parasites or vultures of the human kind. In this case, again, the greatest service that can be rendered may be a refusal of service, a refusal of aid in the ordinary or rather expected forms, and a still greater service in the form of teaching them that great principle of justice, of compensation, that runs through all the universe,—that for every service there must be in some form or another an adequate service in return, that the law of compensation in one form or another is absolute, and, in fact, the greatest forms of service we can render any one are, generally speaking, along the lines of teaching him the great laws of his own being, the great laws of his true possibilities and powers, and so the great laws of self-help.

And, again, it is possible for one whose heart goes out in love and service for all, and who, by virtue of lacking that long range of vision or by virtue of not having a grasp of things in their entirety or wholeness, may have his time, his energies so dissipated in what seems to be the highest service that he is continually kept from his own highest enfoldment, powers, and possessions, the very things that in their completeness would make him a thousand-fold more effective and powerful in his own life, and hence in the life of real service and influence. And, in a case of this kind, many times the mark of the most absolute unselfishness is a strong and marked selfishness, which will prove however to be a selfishness only in the seeming.

The self should never be lost sight of. It is the one thing of supreme importance, the greatest factor even in the life of the greatest service.

Being always and necessarily precedes doing: having always and necessarily precedes giving. But this law also holds: that when there is the being, it is all the more increased by the doing; when there is the having, it is all the more increased by the giving. *Keeping to one's self dwarfs and stultifies. Boarding brings loss: using brings even greater gain.* In brief, the more we are, the more we can do; the more we have, the more we can give.

The most truly successful, the most powerful and valuable life, then, is the life that is first founded upon this great, immutable law of love and service, and that then becomes supremely self-centred,—supremely self-centred that it may become all the more supremely unself-centred; in other words, the life that looks well to self, that there may be the ever greater self, in order that there may be the ever greater service.

IV

The Awakening

If you'd live a religion that's noble,
That's God-like and true,
A religion the grandest that men
Or that angels can,
Then live, live the truth
Of the brother who taught you,
It's love to God, service and love
To the fellow-man.

SOCIAL problems are to be among the greatest problem of the generation just moving on to the stage of action. They, above all others, will claim the attention of mankind, as they are already claiming it across the waters even as at home. The attitude of the two classes toward each other, or the separation of the classes, will be by far the chief problem of them all. Already it is imperatively demanding a solution. Gradually, as the years have passed, this separation has been going on, but never so rapidly as of late. Each has come to regard the other as an enemy, with no interests in common, but rather that what is for the interests of the one must necessarily be to the detriment of the other.

The great masses of the people, the working classes, those who as much, if not more than many others ought to be there, are not in our churches to-day. They already feel that they are not wanted there, and that the Church even is getting to be their enemy. There must be a reason for this, for it is impossible to have an effect without its preceding cause. It is indeed time to waken up to these facts and conditions; for they must be *squarely* met. A solution is imperatively demanded, and the sooner it comes, the better; for, if allowed to continue thus, all will come back to be paid for, intensified a thousand-fold,—ay, to be paid for even by many innocent ones.

Let this great principle of service, helpfulness, love, and self-devotion to the interests of one's fellow-men be made the fundamental principle of all lives, and see how simplified these great and all-important questions will become. Indeed, they will almost solve themselves. It is the man all for self, so small and so short sighted that he can't get beyond his own selfish interests, that has done more to bring about this state of affairs than all other causes combined. Let the cause be removed, and then note the results.

For many years it has been a teaching even of political economy that an employer buys his help just as he buys his raw material or any other commodity; and this done, he is in no way responsible for the welfare of those he employs. In fact, the time isn't so far distant when the employed were herded together as animals, and were treated very much as such. But, thanks be to God, a better and a brighter day is dawning. Even the employer is beginning to see that *practical ethics, or true Christianity, and business cannot and must not be divorced*; that the man he employs, instead of being a mere animal whose services he buys, is, after all his fellow-man and his brother, and demands a treatment as such, and that when he fails to recognize this truth, a righteous God steps in, demanding a penalty for its violation.

He is recognizing the fact that whatsoever is for the well-being of the one he employs, that whatever privileges he is enabled to enjoy that will tend to grow and develop his physical, his mental, and his moral life, that will give him an agreeable home and pleasant family relations, that whatever influences tend to elevate him and to make his life more happy, are a direct gain, even from a financial standpoint for himself, by its increasing for him the efficiency of the man's labor. It is already recognized as a fact that the employer who interests himself in these things, other things being equal, is the most successful. Thus the old and the false are breaking away before the right and the true, as all inevitably must sooner or later; and the divinity and the power of the workingman is being ever more fully recognized.

In the very remote history of the race there was one who, violating a great law, having wronged a brother, asked, "Am I my brother's keeper?" Knowing that he was, he nevertheless deceitfully put the question in this way in his desire, if possible, to avoid the responsibility. Many employers in their selfishness and greed for gain have asked this same question in this same way. They have thought they could thus defeat the sure and eternal laws of a Just Ruler, but have thereby deceived themselves the more. These more than any others have to a great degree brought about the present state of affairs in the industrial and social world.

Just as soon as the employer recognizes the falsity of these old teachings and practices, and the fact that he cannot buy his employee's services the same as he buys his raw material, with no further responsibility, but that the two are on vastly different planes, that his employee is his fellow-man and his brother, and that he is his brother's keeper, and will be held responsible as such, that it is to his own highest interests, as well as to the highest interests of those he employs and to society in general, to recognize this; and just as soon as he who is employed fully appreciates his opportunities and makes the highest use of all, and in turn takes an active, personal interest in all that pertains to his employer's welfare,—just that soon will a solution of this great question come forth, and no sooner.

It is not so much a question of legislation as of education and right doing, thus a dealing with the *individual*, and so a prevention and a cure, not merely a suppression and a regulation, which is always sure to fail; for, *in a case of right or wrong no question is ever settled finally until it is settled rightly.*

The individual, dealing with the individual is necessarily at the bottom of all true social progress. There can't be anything worthy the name without it. The truth will at once be recognized by all *that the good of the whole depends upon the good of each, and the good of each makes the good of the whole.* Attend, then, to the individual, and the whole will take care of itself. Let each individual work in harmony with every other, and harmony will pervade the whole. The old theory of competition that in order to have great advancement, great progress, we must have great competition to induce it—is as false as it is savage and detrimental in its nature. We are just reaching that point where the larger men and women are beginning to see its falsity. They are recognizing the fact that, *not competition, but co-operation, reciprocity, is the great, the true power,*—to climb, not by attempting to drag, to keep down one's fellows, but by aiding them, and being in turn aided by them, thus combining, and so multiplying the power of all instead of wasting a large part one against the other.

And grant that a portion do succeed in rising, while the other portion remain in the lower condition, it is of but little value so far as their own peace and welfare are concerned; for they can never be what they would be, were all up together. Each is but a part, a member, of the great civil body; and no member, let alone the entire body, can be perfectly well, perfectly at ease, when any other part is in dis-ease. No one part of the community, no one part of the nation, can stand alone: all are dependent, interdependent. This is the uniform teaching of history from the remotest times in the past right through to the present. A most admirable illustration of this fact—if indeed the word "admirable" can be used in connection with a matter so deplorable—was the unparalleled labor trouble we had in our great Western city but a few summers ago. The wise man is he who learns from experiences of this terrific nature.

No, not until this all-powerful principle is fully recognized, and is built upon so thoroughly that the brotherhood principle, the principle of oneness can enter in, and each one recognizes the fact that his own interests and welfare depend upon the interests, the welfare of each, and therefore of all, that each is but a part of the one great whole, and each one stands shoulder to shoulder in the advance forward, can we hope for any true solution of the great social problems before us, for any permanent elevation of the standard in our national social life and welfare.

This same principle is the solution, and the only true solution, of the charities question, as indeed the whole world during the last few years or so, and during this time only, is beginning to realize. And the splendid and efficient work of the organized charities in all our large cities, as of the Elberfeld system in Germany, is attesting the truth of this. Almost numberless methods have been tried during the past, but all have most successfully failed; and many have greatly increased the wretched condition of matters, and of those it was designed to help. During this length of time only have these all-important questions been dealt with in a true, scientific, Christ-like, common-sense way. It has been found even here that nothing can take the place of the personal and friendly influences of a life built upon this principle of service.

The question of aiding the poor and needy has passed through three distinct phases of development in the world's history. In early times it was, "Each one for himself, and the devil take the hindmost." From the time of the Christ, and up to the last few years it has been, "Help others." Now it is, "*Help others to help themselves.*" The wealthy society lady going down Fifth Avenue in New York, or Michigan Avenue in Chicago, or Charles Street in Baltimore, or Commonwealth Avenue in Boston, who flings a coin to one asking alms, is *not* the one who is doing a true act of charity; but, on the other hand, she may be doing the one she thus gives to and to society in general much more harm than good, as is many times the case. It is but a cheap, a very cheap way of buying ease for her sympathetic nature or her sense of duty. Never let the word "charity," which always includes the elements of interested service, true helpfulness, kindliness, and love, be debased by making it a synonym of mere giving, which may mean the flinging of a quarter in scorn or for show.

Recognizing the great truth that the best and only way to help another is to help him to help himself, and that the neglected classes need not so much alms as friends, the Organized Charities with their several branches in different parts of the city have their staffs of "friendly visitors," almost all voluntary, and from some of the best homes in the land. Then when a case of need comes to the notice of the society, one of these goes to the person or family as a *friend* to investigate, to find what circumstances have brought about these conditions, and, if found worthy of aid, present needs are supplied, an effort is made to secure work, and every effort is made to put them on their feet again, that self-respect may be regained, that hope may enter in; for there is scarcely anything that tends to make one lose his self-respect so quickly and so completely as to be compelled, or of his own accord, to ask for alms.

It is thus many times that a new life is entered upon, brightness and hope taking the place of darkness and despair. This is not the only call the friendly visitor makes; but he or she becomes a *true friend*, and makes regular visits as such. If by this method the one seeking charity is found to be an impostor, as is frequently the case, proper means of exposure are resorted to, that his or her progress in this course may be stopped. The organizations are thus doing a most valuable work, and one that will become more and more valuable as they are enabled to become better organized, the greatest need to-day being more with the true spirit to act as visiting friends.

It is this same great principle that has given birth to our college and university settlements and our neighborhood guilds which are so rapidly increasing, and which are destined to do a great and efficient work. Here a small colony of young women, many from our best homes, and the ablest graduates of our best colleges, and young men, many of them the ablest graduates of our best universities, take up their abode in the poorest parts of our large cities, to try by their personal influence and personal contact to raise the surrounding life to a higher plane. It is in these ways that the poor and the unfortunate are dealt with directly. Thus the classes mingle. Thus that sentimentalism which may do and which has done harm to these great problems, and by which the people it is designed to help may be hindered rather than helped, is done away with. Thus true aid and service are rendered, and the needy are really helped.

The one whose life is built upon this principle will not take up work of this kind as a "fad," or because it is "fashionable," but because it is right, true, Christ-like. The truly great and noble never fear thus to mingle with those poorer and less fortunate. It is only those who would like to be counted as great, but who are too small to be so recognized, and who, therefore, always thinking of self, put forth every effort to appear so. There is no surer test than this.

Very truly has it been said that "the greatest thing a man can do for God is to be kind to some of His other children." All children of the same Father, therefore all brothers, sisters. Man is next to God. Man is God incarnate. Humanity, therefore, cannot be very far from being next to godliness. Many people there are who are greatly concerned about serving God, as they term it. Their idea is to build great edifices with costly ornaments to Him. A great deal of their time is spent in singing songs and hallelujahs to Him, just as if *He* needed or wanted these for Himself, forgetting that He is far above being benefited by anything that we can say or do, forgetting that He doesn't want these, when for lack of them some of His children are starving for bread to eat or are dying for the bread of life.

Can you conceive of a God who is worthy of love and service,—and I speak most reverently,—who under such conditions would take a satisfaction in these things? I confess I am not able to. I can conceive of no way in which I can serve God only as I serve Him through my own life and through the lives of my fellow-men. This, certainly, is the only kind of service He needs or wants, or that is acceptable to Him. At one place we read, "He that says he loves God and loves not his fellow-men, is a liar; and the truth is not in him."

Even in religion I think we shall find that there is nothing greater or more important than this great principle of service, helpfulness, kindliness, and love. Is not Christianity, you ask, greater or more important? Why, bless you, is this any other than Christianity, is Christianity any other than this,—at least, if we take what the Master Teacher himself has said? For what, let us ask, is a Christian,—the real, not merely in name? A follower of Christ, one who does as he did, one who lives as he lived. And, again, who was Christ? He that healed the sick, clothed the naked, bound up the broken-hearted, sustained and encouraged the weak, the faltering, befriended and aided the poor, the needy, condemned the proud and the selfish, taught the people to live nobly, truly, grandly, to live in their higher, diviner selves, that the greatest among them should be their servant, and that his followers were those who lived as he lived. He spent all his time in the service of humanity. He gave his whole life in this way. He it was who went about doing good.

Is it your desire then, to be numbered among his followers, to bear that blessed name, the name "Christian"? Then sit at his feet, and learn of him, love him, do as he did, as he taught you to do, live as he lived, as he taught you to live, and you are a Christian, and not unless you do. True Christianity can be found in no other way.

Naught is the difference what one may call himself; for many call themselves by this name to whom Christ says it will one day be said, "I never knew you: depart from me, ye cursed." Naught is the difference what creeds one may subscribe to, what rites and ceremonies he may observe, how loud and how numerous his professions may be. All of these are but as a vain mockery, unless he is a Christian; and to be a Christian is, as we have found, to be a follower of Christ, to do as he did, to live as he lived. *Then live the Christ life.* Live so as to become at one with God, and dwell continually in this blessed at-one-ment. The trouble all along has been that so many have mistaken the mere person of the Christ, the mere physical Jesus, for his life, his spirit, his teachings, and have succeeded in getting no farther than this as yet, except in cases here and there.

Now and then a rare soul rises up, one with great power, great inspiration, and we wonder at his great power, his great inspiration, why it is. When we look deeply enough, however, we will find that one great fact will answer the question every time. It is living the life that brings the power. He is living the Christ life, not merely standing afar off and looking at it, admiring it, and saying, Yes, I believe, I believe, and ending it there. In other words, he has found the kingdom of heaven. He has found that it is not a place, but a condition; and the song continually arising from his heart is, There is joy, only joy.

The Master, you remember, said: "Seek ye not for the kingdom of heaven in tabernacles or in houses made with hands. Know ye not that the kingdom of heaven is within you?" He told in plain words where and how to find it. He then told how to find *all other* things, when he said, "Seek ye first the kingdom of heaven, and all these other things shall be added unto you." Now, do you wonder at his power, his inspiration, his abundance of all things? The trouble with so many is that they act as if they do not believe what the Master said. They do not take him at his word. They say one thing: they do another. Their acts give the lie to their words. Instead of taking him at his word, and living as if they had faith in him, they prefer to follow a series of old, outgrown, man-made theories, traditions, forms, ceremonies, and seem to be satisfied with the results. No, *to be a Christian is to live the Christ life*, the life of him who went about doing good, the life of him who came not to be ministered unto, but to minister.

We will find that this mighty principle of love and service is the greatest to live by in this life, and also one of the gates whereby all who would must enter the kingdom of heaven.

Again we have the Master's words. In his own and only description of the last judgment, after speaking of the Son of Man coming in all his glory and all the holy angels with him, of his sitting on the throne of his glory with all nations gathered before him, of the separation of this gathered multitude into two parts, the one on his right, the other on his left, he says: "Then shall the King say unto them on his right hand, Come, ye blessed of my Father, inherit the kingdom prepared for you from the foundation of the world. For I was an hungered, and ye gave me meat; I was thirsty, and ye gave me drink; I was a stranger, and ye took me in; naked, and ye clothed me; I was sick, and ye visited me; I was in prison, and ye came unto me. Then shall the righteous answer him, saying, Lord, when saw we *thee* an hungered, and fed *thee*? or thirsty, and gave *thee* drink? When saw we *thee* a stranger, and took thee in? or naked, and clothed *thee*? Or when saw we *thee* sick, or in prison, and came unto *thee*? And the King shall answer, and say unto them, Verily I say unto you, *Inasmuch as ye have done it unto one of the least of these my brethren, ye have done it unto me.*

"Then shall he say unto them on the left hand, Depart from me, ye cursed. For I was an hungered, and ye gave me no meat; I was thirsty, and ye gave me no drink; I was a stranger, and ye took me not in; sick, and in prison, and ye visited me not. Then shall they answer him, saying, Lord, when saw we thee an hungered, or athirst, or a stranger, or naked, or sick, or in prison, and did not minister unto thee? Then shall he answer them, saying, Verily I say unto you, *Inasmuch as ye did it not to one of the least of these, ye did it not to me.*"

After spending the greater portion of his life in many distant climes in a fruitless endeavor to find the Cup of the Holy Grail,[1] thinking that thereby he was doing the greatest service he could for God, Sir Launfal at last returns an old man, gray-haired and bent. He finds that his castle is occupied by others, and that he himself is an outcast. His cloak is torn; and instead of the charger in gilded trappings he was mounted upon when as a young man, he started out with great hopes and ambitions, he is afoot and

[1]"According to the mythology of the Romancers, the Sangreal, or Holy Grail, was the cup out of which Jesus partook of the Last Supper with his disciples. It was brought into England by Joseph of Arimathea, and remained there, an object of pilgrimage and adoration, for many years in the keeping of his lineal descendants. It was incumbent upon those who had charge of it to be chaste in thought, word, and deed; but, one of the keepers having broken this condition, the Holy Grail disappeared. From that time it was a favorite enterprise of the Knights of Sir Arthur's court to go in search of it."—*James Russell Lowell.*

leaning on a staff. While sitting there and meditating, he is met by the same poor and needy leper he passed the morning he started, the one who in his need asked for aid, and to whom he had flung a coin in scorn, as he hurried on in his eager desire to be in the Master's service. But matters are changed now, and he is a wiser man. Again the poor leper says:—

"'For Christ's sweet sake, I beg an alms';—
The happy camels may reach the spring,
But Sir Launfal sees only the grewsome thing,
The leper, lank as the rain-blanched bone,
That cowers beside him, a thing as lone
And white as the ice-isles of Northern seas
In the desolate horror of his disease.

"And Sir Launfal said: 'I behold in thee
An image of Him who died on the tree;
Thou also hast had thy crown of thorns,—
Thou also hast had the world's buffets and scorns,—
And to thy life were not denied
The wounds in the hands and feet and side:
Mild Mary's Son, acknowledge me;
Behold, *through him*, I give to thee!'

"Then the soul of the leper stood up in his eyes
And looked at Sir Launfal, and straightway he
Remembered in what a haughtier guise
He had flung an alms to leprosie,
When he girt his young life up in gilded mail
And set forth in search of the Holy Grail.
The heart within him was ashes and dust;

He parted in twain his single crust,
He broke the ice on the streamlet's brink,
And gave the leper to eat and drink,
'Twas a mouldy crust of coarse brown bread,
'Twas water out of a wooden bowl,—
Yet with fine wheaten bread was the leper fed,
And 'twas red wine he drank with his thirsty soul.

"As Sir Launfal mused with a downcast face,
A light shone round about the place;
The leper no longer crouched at his side,
But stood before him glorified,
Shining and tall and fair and straight
As the pillar that stood by the Beautiful Gate,—
Himself the Gate whereby men can
Enter the temple of God in Man.

"And the voice that was calmer than silence said,
'Lo, it is I, be not afraid!
In many climes, without avail,
Thou hast spent thy life for the Holy Grail;
Behold, it is here,—this cup which thou
Didst fill at the streamlet for me but now;
This crust is my body broken for thee,
This water His blood that died on the tree;
The Holy Supper is kept, indeed,
In whatso we share with another's need;
Not what we give, but what we *share*,—
For the gift without the giver is bare;
Who gives himself with his alms feeds three,—
Himself, his hungering neighbor, and me.'"

The fear is sometimes entertained, and the question is sometimes asked, May not adherence to this principle of helpfulness and service become mere sentimentalism? or still more, may it not be the means of lessening another's sense of self-dependence, and thus may it not at times do more harm than good? In reply let it be said: If the love which impels it be a selfish love, or a weak sentimentalism, or an effort at show, or devoid of good common sense, yes, many times. But if it be a strong, genuine, unselfish love, then no, never. For, *if my love for my fellow-man be the true love, I can never do anything that will be to his or any one's else detriment,—nothing that will not redound to his highest ultimate welfare.* Should he, for example come and ask of me a particular favor, and were it clear to me that granting it would not be for his highest good ultimately, then love at once resolves itself into duty, and compels me to forbear. A true, genuine, unselfish love for on 's fellow-man will never prompt, and much less permit, anything that will not result in his highest ultimate good. Adherence, therefore, to this great principle in its truest sense, instead of being a weak sentimentalism, is, we shall find, of all practical things the *most intensely practical.*

And a word here in regard to the test of true love and service, in distinction from its semblance for show or for vain glory. The test of the true is this: that it goes about and 0' does its good work, it never says anything about it, but lets others do the saying. It not only says nothing about it, but more, it has no desire to have it known; and, the truer it is, the greater the desire to have it unknown save to God and its own true self. In other words, it is not sicklied o'er with a semi-insane desire for notoriety or vainglory, and hence never weakens itself nor harasses any one else by lengthy recitals of its good deeds. It is not the *professional* good-doing. It is simply living its natural life, open-minded, openhearted, doing each day what its hands find to do, and in this finding its own true life and joy. And in this way it unintentionally but irresistibly draws to itself a praise the rarest and divinest I know of,—the praise I heard given but a day or two ago to one who is living simply his own natural life without any conscious effort at anything else, the praise contained in the words: And, oh, it is beautiful, the great amount of good he does and of which the world never hears.

V

The Incoming

O dull, gray grub, unsightly and noisome, unable to roam,
Days pass, God's at work, the slow chemistry's going on,
Behold! Behold!
O brilliant, buoyant life, full winged, all the heaven's thy home!
O poor, mean man, stumbling and falling, e'en shamed by a clod
Years pass, God's at work, spiritual awakening has come,
Behold! Behold!
O regal, royal soul, then image, now the likeness of God.

THE Master Teacher, he who appeals most strongly and comes nearest to us of this western civilization, has told us that the whole and the highest duty of man is comprised in two great, two simple precepts—love to God and love to the fellow-man. The latter we have already fully considered. We have found that in its real and true meaning it is not a mere indefinite or sentimental abstraction, but that it is a vital, living force; and in its manifestation it is life, it is action, it is service. Let us now for a moment to the other,—love to God, which in great measure however let it be said, has been considered in dealing with love to the fellow-man. Let us see, however, what it in its true and full nature reveals.

The question naturally arising at the outset is, Who, what is God? I think no truer, sublimer definition has ever been given in the world's history, in any language, in any clime, than that given by the Master himself when standing by the side of Jacob's well, to the Samaritan woman he said, God is Spirit; and they that worship Him must worship Him in spirit and in truth. God is

Spirit, the Infinite Spirit, the Infinite Life back of all these physical manifestations we see in this changing world about us, and of which all, including we ourselves, is the body or outer form; the one Infinite Spirit which fills all the universe with Himself, so that all is He, since He is all. All is He in the sense of being a part of Him; for, if He is all, there can be nothing that is outside of, that is not a part of Him, so that each one is a part of this Eternal God who is not separate from us, and, if not separate from us, then not afar off, for in Him we live and move and have our being, *He is the life of our life*, our very life itself. The life of God is in us, we are in the life of God; but that life transcends us so that it includes all else,—every person, every animal, every grass-blade, every flower, every particle of earth, every particle of everything, animate and inanimate. So that God is *All*; and, if all, then each individual, you and I, must be a vital part of that all, since there can be nothing separate from it; and, if a part, then the same in nature, in characteristics,—the same as a tumbler of water taken from the ocean is, in nature, in qualities, in characteristics, identical with that ocean, its source. God, then, is the Infinite Spirit of which each one is a part in the form of an individualized spirit. God is Spirit, creating, manifesting, ruling through the agency of great spiritual laws and forces that surround us on every side, that run through all the universe, and that unite all; for in one sense, there is nothing in all this great universe but law. And, oh, the stupendous grandeur of it all! These same great spiritual laws and forces operate within us. They are the laws of our being. By them every act of each individual life is governed.

Now one of the great facts borne ever more and more into the inner consciousness of man is that sublime and transcendent fact that we have just noticed,—that man is one with, that he is part of, the Infinite God, this Infinite Spirit that is the life of all, this Infinite Whole; that he is not a mere physical, material being,—for the physical is but the material which the real inner self, the real life or spirit uses to manifest through,—but that he is this spirit, this spirit, using, living in this physical, material house or body to get the contact, the experience with the material world around him while in this form of life, but spirit nevertheless, and spirit now as much as he ever will or ever can be, except so far of course, as he recognizes more and more his true, his higher self, and so consciously evolves, step by step, into the higher and ever higher realization of the real nature, the real self, the God-self. As I heard it said by one of the world's great thinkers and writers but a few days ago: Men talk of having a soul. I have no soul. I am a soul: I have a body. We are told moreover in the word, that man is created in the image of God. God is Spirit. What then must man be, if that which tells us is true?

Now one of the great errors all along in the past has been that we have mistaken the mere body, the mere house in which we live while in this form of life for a period,—that which comes from the earth and which, in a greater or less time, returns to the earth,—this we have mistaken for the real self. Either we have lost sight of or we have failed to recognize the true identity. The result is that we are at life from the wrong side, from the side of the external, while *all true life is from within out.*

We have taken our lives out of a conscious harmony with the higher laws of our being, with the result that we are going against the great current of the Divine Order of things. Is it any wonder, then, that we find the strugglings, the inharmonies, the sufferings, the fears, the forebodings, the fallings by the wayside, the "strange, inscrutable dispensations of Providence" that we behold on every side? The moment we bring our lives into harmony with the higher laws of our being, and, as a result, into harmony with the current of the Divine Order of things, we shall find that all these will have taken wings; for the cause will have been removed. And as we look down the long vista of such a life, we shall find that each thing fits into all others with a wonderful, a sublime, a perfect, a divine harmony.

This, it will seem to some,—and to many, no doubt,—is claiming a great deal. No more, however, than the Master Teacher warranted us in claiming when he said, and repeated it so often,

Seek ye first the kingdom of heaven, and all these other things shall be added unto you; and he left us not in the dark as to exactly what he meant by the kingdom of heaven, for again he said: Say not, Lo here, nor to there. Know ye not that the kingdom of heaven is within you? *Within you.* The interior spiritual kingdom, the kingdom of the higher self, which is the kingdom of God; the kingdom of harmony,—harmony with the higher laws of your being.

The Master said what he said not for the sake merely of using a phrase of rhetoric, nor even to hear himself talk; for this he never did. But that great incarnation of spiritual insight and power knew of the great spiritual laws and forces under which we live, and also that supreme fact of the universe, that *man is a spiritual being, born to have dominion*, and that, by recognizing the true self and by bringing it into complete and perfect harmony with the higher spiritual laws and forces under which he lives, he can touch these laws and forces so that they will respond at every call and bring him whatsoever he wills,—one of the most stupendous scientific facts of the universe. When he has found and entered into the kingdom, then applies to him the truth of the great precept, Take ye no thought for the morrow; for the things of the morrow will take care of themselves.

Yes, we are at life from the wrong side. We have been giving all time and attention to the mere physical, the material, the external, the mere outward means of expression and the things that pertain thereto, thus missing the real life; and this we have called living, and seem, indeed, to be satisfied with the results. No wonder the cry has gone out again and again from many a human soul, Is life worth the living? But from one who has once commenced to *live*, this cry never has, nor can it ever come; for, *when the kingdom is once found, life then ceases to be a plodding, and becomes an exultation, an ecstasy, a joy.* Yes, you will find that all the evil, all the error, all the disease, all the suffering, all the fears, all the forebodings of life, are on the side of the physical, the material, the transient; while all the peace, all the joy, all the happiness, all the growth, all the life, all the rich, exulting, abounding life, is on the side of the spiritual, the ever-increasing, the eternal,—that that never changes, that has no end. Instead of crying out against the destiny of fate, let us cry out against the destiny of self, or rather against the destiny of the mistaken self; for everything that comes to us comes through causes which we ourselves or those before us have set into operation. Nothing comes by chance, for *in all the wide universe Mere is absolutely no such thing as chance.* We bring whatever comes. Are we not satisfied with the effects, the results? The thing then to do, is to change the causes; for we have everything in our own hands the moment we awake to a recognition of the true self.

We make our own heaven or our own hell, and the only heaven or hell that will ever be ours is that of our own making. The order of the universe is one thing: we take our lives out of harmony with and so pervert the laws under which we live, and make it another. The order is the all good. We pervert the laws, and what we call evil is the result,—simply the result of the violation of law; and we then wonder that a just and loving God could permit such and such things. We wonder at what we term the "strange, inscrutable dispensations of Providence," when all is of our own making. We can be our own best friends or we can be our own worst enemies; and *the only real enemy one can ever have is the self, the very self.*

It is a well-known fact in the scientific world that the great work in the process of evolution is the gradual advancing from the lower to the higher, from the coarser to the finer, or, in other words, from the coarser material to the finer spiritual; and this higher spiritualization of life is the great work before us all. All pass ultimately over the same road in general, some more rapidly, some more slowly. The ultimate destiny of all is the higher life, the finding of the higher self; and to this we are either led or we are pushed,—led, by recognizing and coming into harmony with the higher laws of our being, or pushed, through their violation, and hence through experience, through suffering, and at times through bitter suffering, until through this very agency we learn the laws and come into harmony with them, so that we thus see the economy, the blessedness of even error, shame, and suffering itself, in that, if we are not wise enough to go voluntarily and of our own accord, it all the more quickly brings us to our true, our higher selves.

Moreover, whatever is evolved must as surely first be involved. We cannot conceive even of an evolution without first an involution; and, if this is true, we cannot conclude otherwise than that all that will ever be brought forth through the process of evolution is already within, all the God possibilities of the human soul are now, at this very moment, latent within. This being true, the process of evolution need not, as is many times supposed, take æons or even ages for its accomplishment; for the process is wonderfully accelerated when we have grasped and when we have commenced to actualize the reality of that mighty precept, Know thyself.

It is possible, through an intelligent understanding of the laws of the higher life, to advance in the spiritual awakening and enfoldment even in a single year more than one otherwise would through a whole lifetime, or more in a single day or even hour than in an entire year or series of years otherwise.

This higher spiritualization of life is certainly what the Master had in mind when he said, It is as hard for a rich man to enter into the kingdom of heaven as it is for a camel to pass through the eye of a needle. For, if a man give all his days and his nights merely to the accumulation of outer material possessions, what time has he for the growing, the unfolding, of the interior, the spiritual, what time for finding that wonderful kingdom, the kingdom of heaven, the Christ within?

This certainly is also the significance of the temptation in the wilderness. The temptations were all, you will recall, in connection with the material, the physical, and the things that pertain thereto. Do so and so, said the physical: follow after me, and I will give you bread in abundance, I will give you great fame and notoriety, I will give you vast material possessions. All, you see, a calling away from the real, the interior, the spiritual, the eternal. Dominion over all the kingdoms of the *world* was promised. But what, what is dominion over all the world, with heaven left out?

All, however, was triumphed over. The physical was put into subjection by the spiritual, the victory was gained once for all and forever; and he became the supreme and royal Master, and by this complete and glorious mastery of self he gained the mastery over all else besides, even to material things and conditions.

And by this higher spiritual chemicalization of life thus set into operation the very thought forces of his mind became charged with a living, mighty, and omnipotent power, so as to effect a mastery over all exterior conditions: hence the numerous things called miracles by those who witnessed and who had not entered into a knowledge of the higher laws that can triumph over and master the lower, but which are just as real and as natural on their plane as the lower, and even more real and more natural, because higher and therefore more enduring. But this complete mastery over self during this period of temptation was just the beginning of the path that led from glory unto glory, the path that for you and for me will lead from glory unto glory the same as for him.

It was this new divine and spiritual chemistry of life thus set into operation that transformed the man Jesus, that royal-hearted elder brother, into the Christ Jesus, and forever blessed be his name; for he thus became our Saviour,—he became our Saviour by virtue of pointing out to us the way. This overcoming by the calling of the higher spiritual forces into operation is certainly what he meant when he said, I have overcome the world, and what he would have us understand when he says, Overcome the world, even as I have overcome it.

And in the same sense we are all the saviors one of another, or may become so. A sudden emergency arises, and I stand faltering and weak with fear. My friend beside me is strong and fearless. He sees the emergency. He summons up all the latent powers within him, and springs forth to meet it. This sublime example arouses me, calls my latent powers into activity, when but for him I might not have known them there. I follow his example. I now know my powers, and know them forever after. Thus, in this, my friend has become my savior.

I am weak in some point of character,—vacillating, yielding, stumbling, falling, continually eating the bitter fruit of it all. My friend is strong, he has gained thorough self-mastery. The majesty and beauty of power are upon his brow. I see his example, I love his life, I am influenced by his power. My soul longs and cries out for the same. A supreme effort of will—that imperial master that will take one anywhere when rightly directed—arises within me, it is born at last, and it calls all the soul's latent powers into activity; and instead of stumbling I stand firm, instead of giving over in weakness I stand firm and master, I enter into the joys of full self-mastery, and through this into the mastery of all things besides. And thus my friend has again become my savior.

With the new power I have acquired through the example and influence of my savior-friend, I, in turn, stand before a friend who is struggling, who is stumbling and in despair. He sees, he feels, the power of my strength. He longs for, his soul cries out for the same. *His* interior forces are called into activity, he now knows his powers; and instead of the slave, he becomes the master, and thus I, in turn, have become his savior. Oh, the wonderful sense of sublimity, the mighty feelings of responsibility, the deep sense of power and peace the recognition of this fact should bring to each and all.

God works through the instrumentality of human agency. Then forever away with that old, shrivelling, weakening, dying, and devilish idea that we are poor worms of the dust! We may or we may not be: it all depends upon the self. The moment we believe we are we become such; and as long as we hold to the belief we will be held to this identity, and will act and live as such. The moment, however, we recognize our divinity, our higher, our God-selves, and the fact that we are the saviors of our fellow-men, we become saviors, and stand and move in the midst of a majesty and beauty and power that of itself proclaims us as such.

There is a prevalent idea to the effect that overcoming in this sense necessarily implies more or less of a giving up,—that it means something possibly on the order of asceticism. On the contrary, the highest, truest, keenest pleasures the human soul can know, it finds only after the higher is entered upon and has commenced its work of mastery; and, instead of there being a giving up of any kind, there is a great law which says that the lower always and of its own accord falls away before the higher. And the time soon comes when, as one stands and looks back, he wonders that this or that that he at one time called pleasure ever satisfied him; for what then satisfied him, compared to what now is his hourly peace, satisfaction, and joy, was but as poor brass compared to the finest, purest, and rarest of gold.

From what has been said let it not be inferred that the body, the physical, material life is to be despised or looked down upon. This, rather let it be said, is one of the crying errors of the times, and prolific of a *vast* amount of error, suffering, and shame. On the contrary, it should be thought all the more highly of: it should be loved and developed to its highest perfections, beauties, and powers. God gave us the body not in vain. It is just as holy and beautiful as the spirit itself. It is merely the outward material manifestation of the individualized spirit; and we by our hourly thoughts and emotions are building it, are determining its conditions, its structure, and appearance. And, if there are any conditions we are not satisfied with, we by an understanding of the laws, have it in our power to make it over and change these conditions. Flamarion, the eminent French scientist, member of the Royal Academy of Science, and recognized as one of the most eminent scientists living, tells us that the entire human structure can be made over within a period of less than one year, some eleven months being the length of time required for the more compact and more set portions to respond; while some portions respond much more readily, within a period of from two to three months, and some even within a month.

Every part, every organ, every function of the body is just as clean, just as beautiful, just as sweet, and just as holy as every other part; and it is only by virtue of man's perverted ways of looking at some that they become otherwise, and the moment they so become, abuses, ill uses, suffering, and shame creep in.

Not repression, but elevation. Would that this could be repeated a thousand times over! Not repression, but elevation. Every part, every organ, every function of the body is given for *use*, but not for misuse or abuse; and the moment the latter takes place in connection with any function it loses its higher powers of use, and there goes with this the higher powers of true enjoyment. It is thus that we get that large class known as abnormals, resorting to the methods they resort to for enjoyment, but which, in its true sense, they always fail in finding, because law will admit of no violations; and, if violated, it takes away the very powers of enjoyment, it takes away the very things that through its violation they thought they had secured, or it turns them into ashes in their very hands. God, nature, law, the higher self, is not mocked.

Not repression, but elevation,—repression only in the sense of mastery; but this means—nay, this is—elevation. In other words, we should be the master, and not the body. We should dictate to the body, and should never, even for an instant, allow it to dictate to us.

Oh, the thousands, the hundreds of thousands of men and women who are everywhere being driven hither and thither, led into this and into that which their own better selves would not enter into, simply because they have allowed the body to assume the mastery; while they have taken the place of the weakling, the slave, and all on account of their own weakness,—weakness through ignorance, ignorance of the tremendous forces and powers within, the forces and powers of the mind and spirit.

It would be a right royal plan for those who are thus enslaved by the body,—and we all are more or less, each in his own particular way, and not one is absolutely free,—it would be a good plan to hold immediately, at this very hour, a conversation with the body somewhat after this fashion: Body, we have for some time been dwelling together. Life for neither has been in the highest degree satisfactory. The cause is now apparent to me. The mastery I have voluntarily handed over to you. You have not assumed it of your own accord; but I have given it over to you little by little, and just in the degree that you have appropriated it. Neither one is to blame. It has been by virtue of ignorance. But henceforth we will reverse positions. You shall become the servant, and I the master. From this time forth you shall no longer dictate to me, but I will dictate to you.

I, one with Infinite intelligence, wisdom, and power, longing for a fuller and ever fuller realization of this oneness, will assume control, and will call upon you to help in the fuller and ever fuller external manifestation of this realization. We will thus regain the ground both of us have lost. We will thus be truly married instead of farcically so. And thus we will help each the other to a realization of the highest, most satisfying and most enduring pleasures and joys, possibilities and powers, loves and realizations, that human life can know; and so, hand in hand, we will help each the other to the higher and ever-increasing life instead of degrading each the other to the lower and ever-decreasing. I will become the imperial master, and you the royal companion; and thus we will go forth to an ever larger life of love and service, and so of true enjoyment.

This conversation, if entered into in the spirit, accompanied by an earnest, sincere desire for its fulfilment, re-enforced by the thought forces, and continually attended by that absolute magnet of power, firm expectation, will, if all are firmly and persistently held to, bring the full realization of one's fondest desires with a certainty as absolute as that effect follows cause. The higher self will invariably master when it truly and firmly asserts itself. Much the same attitude can be assumed in connection with the body in disease or in suffering with the same results. Forces can be set into operation which will literally change and make over the diseased, the abnormal portions, and in time transform them into the healthy, the strong, the normal,—this when we once understand and vitally grasp the laws of these mighty forces, and are brought to the full recognition of the absolute control of mind, of spirit, over matter, and all, again let it be said, in accordance with natural spiritual law.

No, a knowledge of the spiritual realities of life prohibits asceticism, repression, the same as it prohibits license and perverted use. To err on the one side is just as contrary to the ideal life as to err on the other. All things are for a purpose, all should be used and enjoyed; but all should be rightly used, that they may be fully enjoyed.

It is the threefold life and development that is wanted,— physical, mental, spiritual. This gives the rounded life, and he or she who fails in any one comes short of the perfect whole. The physical has its uses just the same and is just as important as the others. The great secret of the highly successful life is, however, to infuse the mental and the physical with the spiritual; in other words, to spiritualize all, and so raise all to the highest possibilities and powers.

It is the all-round, fully developed we want,—not the ethereal, pale-blooded man and woman, but the man and woman of flesh and blood, for action and service here and now,—the man and woman strong and powerful, with all the faculties and functions fully unfolded and used, all in a royal and bounding condition, but all rightly subordinated. The man and the woman of this kind, with the imperial hand of mastery upon all,—standing, moving thus like a king, nay, like a very God,—such is the man and such is the woman of power. Such is the ideal life: anything else is one, sided, and falls short of it.

The most powerful agent in character-building is this awakening to the true self, to the fact that man is a spiritual being,—nay, more, that I, this very eternal I, am a spiritual being, right here and now, at this very moment, with the God-powers which can be quickly called forth. With this awakening, life in all its manifold relations becomes wonderfully simplified. And as to the powers, the full realization of the fact that man is a spiritual being and a living as such brings, they are absolutely without limit, increasing in direct proportion as the higher self, the God-self, assumes the mastery, and so as this higher spiritualization of life goes on.

With this awakening and realization one is brought at once *en rapport* with the universe. He feels the power and the thrill of the life universal. He goes out from his own little garden spot, and mingles with the great universe; and the little perplexities, trials, and difficulties of life that to-day so vex and annoy him, fall away of their own accord by reason of their very insignificance. The intuitions become keener and ever more keen and unerring in their guidance. There comes more and more the power of reading men, so that no harm can come from this source. There comes more and more the power of seeing into the future, so that more and more true becomes the old adage,—that coming events cast their shadows before. Health in time takes the place of disease; for all disease and its consequent suffering is merely the result of the violation of law, either consciously or unconsciously, either intentionally or unintentionally. There comes also a spiritual power which, as it is sent out, is adequate for the healing of others the same as in the days of old. The body becomes less gross and heavy, finer in its texture and form, so that it serves far better and responds far more readily to the higher impulses of the soul. Matter itself in time responds to the action of these higher forces; and many things that we are accustomed by reason of our limited vision to call miraculous or supernatural become the normal, the natural, the every-day.

For what, let us ask, is a miracle? Nothing more nor less than this: a highly illumined soul, one who has brought his life into thorough harmony with the higher spiritual laws and forces of his being, and therefore with those of the universe, thus making it possible for the highest things to come to him, has brought to him a law a little higher than the ordinary mind knows of as yet. This he touches, he operates. It responds. The people see the result, and cry out, Miracle! miracle! when it is just as natural, just as fully in accordance with the law on this higher plane, as is the common, the every-day on the ordinary. And let it be remembered that the miraculous, the supernatural of to-day becomes, as in the process of evolution we leave the lower for the higher, the commonplace, the natural, the every-day of to-morrow; and, truly, miracles are being performed in the world to-day just as much as they ever have been.

And why should we not to-day have the powers of the foremost in the days of old? The great universe in which we live is just the same, the great laws under which we live are identically the same, God the same and working in His world now just as then. The only difference we shall find is in ourselves, in that we have taken our lives out of harmony with the higher laws of our being, and consequently have lost the higher powers through not using them. Mighty men we are told they were, mighty men who walked with God,—and in the last clause lies the secret of the first,—men who lived in the spirit, men who followed after the real life instead of giving all time and attention to the mere external, men who lived in the higher stories of their being, and not continually in the basements.

With here and there an exception we reverse the process. We live in the valleys, so to speak, often disease-infected valleys, when we might mount up to the mountain-tops, and there dwell continually in the warm and mellow sunlight of God's, or if you please, of nature's great, unchangeable laws, and find ourselves rising ever higher and higher, and revelations coming new every day.

The Master never claimed for himself anything that he did not claim for all mankind; but, quite to the contrary, he said and continually repeated, Not only shall ye do these things, but greater than these shall ye do; for I have pointed out to you the way,—meaning, though strange as it evidently seems to many, *exactly* what he said.

Of the vital power of thought and the interior forces in moulding conditions, and more, of the supremacy of thought over all conditions, the world has scarcely the faintest grasp, not to say even idea, as yet. The fact that thoughts are forces, and that through them *we have creative power*, is one of the most vital facts of the universe, the most vital fact of man's being. And through this instrumentality we have in our grasp and as our rightful heritage, the power of making life and all its manifold conditions exactly what we will.

Through our thought-forces we have creative power, not in a figurative sense, but in reality. Everything in the material universe about us had its origin first in spirit, in thought, and from this it took its form. The very world in which we live, with all its manifold wonders and sublime manifestations, is the result of the energies of the divine intelligence or mind,—God, or whatever term it comes convenient for each one to use. And God said, Let there be, and there was,—the material world, at least the material manifestation of it, literally spoken into existence, the spoken word, however, but the outward manifestation of the interior forces of the Supreme Intelligence.

Every castle the world has ever seen was first an ideal in the architect's mind. Every statue was first an ideal in the sculptor's mind. Every piece of mechanism the world has ever known was first formed in the mind of the inventor. Here it was given birth to. These same mind-forces then dictated to and sent the energy into the hand that drew the model, and then again dictated to and sent the energy into the hands whereby the first instrument was clothed in the material form of metal or of wood. The lower negative always gives way to the higher when made positive. Mind is positive: matter is negative.

Each individual life is a part of, and hence is one with, the Infinite Life; and the highest intelligence and power belongs to each in just the degree that he recognizes his oneness and lays claim to and uses it. The power of the word is not merely an idle phrase or form of expression. It is a real mental, spiritual, scientific fact, and can become vital and powerful in your hands and in mine in just the degree that we understand the omnipotence of the thought forces and raise all to the higher planes.

The blind, the lame, the diseased, stood before the Christ, who said, Receive thy sight, rise up and walk, or, be thou healed; and lo! *it was so.* The spoken word, however, was but the outward expression and manifestation of his interior thought-forces, the power and potency of which he so thoroughly knew. But the laws governing them are the same to-day as they were then, and it lies in our power to use them the same as it lay in his.

Each individual life, after it has reached a certain age or degree of intelligence, lives in the midst of the surroundings or environments of its own creation; and this by reason of that wonderful power, *the drawing power of mind*, which is continually operating in every life, whether it is conscious of it or not.

We are all living, so to speak, in a vast ocean of thought. The very atmosphere about us is charged with the thought-forces that are being continually sent out. When the thought-forces leave the brain, they go out upon the atmosphere, the subtle conducting ether, much the same as sound-waves go out. It is by virtue of this law that thought transferences is possible, and has become an established scientific fact, by virtue of which a person can so direct his thought-forces that a person at a distance, and in a receptive attitude, can get the thought much the same as sound, for example, is conducted through the agency of a connecting medium.

Even though the thoughts as they leave a particular person, are not consciously directed, they go out; and all may be influenced by them in a greater or less degree, each one in proportion as he or she is more or less sensitively organized, or in proportion as he or she is negative, and so open to forces and influences from without. The law operating here is one with that great law of the universe,—that *like attracts like*, so that one continually attracts to himself forces and influences most akin to those of his own life. And his own life is determined by the thoughts and emotions he habitually entertains, for *each is building his world from within*. As within, so without; cause, effect.

A stalk of wheat and a stock of corn are growing side by side, within an inch of each other. The soil is the same for both; but the wheat converts the food it takes from the soil into wheat, the likeness of itself, while the corn converts the food it takes from the same soil into corn, the likeness of itself. What that which each has taken from the soil is converted into is determined by the soul, the interior life, the interior forces of each. This same grain taken as food by two persons will be converted into the body of a criminal in the one case, and into the body of a saint in the other, each after its kind; and its kind is determined by the inner life of each. And what again determines the inner life of each? The thoughts and emotions that are habitually entertained and that inevitably, sooner or later, manifest themselves in outer material form. Thought is the great builder in human life: it is the determining factor. Continually think thoughts that are good, and your life will show forth in goodness, and your body in health and beauty. Continually think evil thoughts, and your life will show forth in evil, and your body in weakness and repulsiveness. Think thoughts of love, and you will love and will be loved. Think thoughts of hatred, and you will hate and will be hated. Each follows its kind.

It is by virtue of this law that each person creates his own "atmosphere"; and this atmosphere is determined by the character of the thoughts he habitually entertains. It is, in fact, simply his thought atmosphere—the atmosphere which other people detect and are influenced by.

In this way each person creates the atmosphere of his own room; a family, the atmosphere of the house in which they live, so that the moment you enter the door you feel influences kindred to the thoughts and hence to the lives of those who dwell there. You get a feeling of peace and harmony or a feeling of disquietude and inharmony. You get a welcome, want-to-stay feeling or a cold, want-to-get-away feeling, according to their thought attitude toward you, even though but few words be spoken. So the characteristic mental states of a congregation of people who assemble there determine the atmosphere of any given assembly-place, church, or cathedral. Its inhabitants so make, so determine the atmosphere of a particular village or city. The sympathetic thoughts sent out by a vast amphitheatre of people, as they cheer a contestant, carry him to goals he never could reach by his own efforts alone. The same is true in regard to an orator and his audience.

Napoleon's army is in the East. The plague is beginning to make inroads into its ranks. Long lines of men are lying on cots and on the ground in an open space adjoining the army. Fear has taken a vital hold of all, and the men are continually being stricken. Look yonder, contrary to the earnest entreaties of his officers, who tell him that such exposure will mean sure death, Napoleon with a calm and dauntless look upon his face, with a firm and defiant step, is coming through these plague-stricken ranks. He is going up to, talking with, touching the men; and, as they see him, there goes up a mighty shout,—The Emperor.! the Emperor! and from that hour the plague in its inroads is stopped. A marvellous example of the power of a man who, by his own dauntless courage, absolute fearlessness, and power of mind, could send out such forces that they in turn awakened kindred forces in the minds of thousands of others, which in turn dominate their very bodies, so that the plague, and even death itself, is driven from the field. One of the grandest examples of a man of the most mighty and tremendous mind and will power, and at the same time an example of one of the grandest failures, taking life in its totality, the world has ever seen.

Again, as has been said, the great law operating in connection with the thought-forces is one with that great law of the universe,—that like attracts like. We can, by virtue of our ignorance of the powers of the mind forces and the prevailing mental states,—we can take the passive, the negative, fearing, drifting attitude, and thus continually attract to us like influences and conditions from both the seen and the unseen side of life. Or, by a knowledge of the power and potency of these forces, we can take the positive, the active attitude, that of mastery, and so attract the higher and more valuable influences, exactly as we will to.

We are all much more influenced by the thought-forces and mental states of those around us and of the world at large than we have even the slightest conception of. If not self-hypnotized into certain beliefs and practices, we are, so to speak, semi-hypnotized through the influence of the thoughts of others, even though unconsciously both on their part and on ours. We are so influenced and enslaved in just the degree that we fail to recognize the power and omnipotence of our own forces, and so become slaves to custom, conventionality, the opinions of others, and so in like proportion lose our own individuality and powers. He who in his own mind takes the attitude of the slave, by the power of his own thoughts and the forces he thus attracts to him, becomes the slave. He who in his own mind takes the attitude of the master, by the same power of his own thoughts and the forces he thus attracts to him, becomes the master. Each is building his world from within, and, if outside forces play, it is because he allows them to play; and he has it in his own power to determine whether these shall be positive, uplifting, ennobling, strengthening, success-giving, or negative, degrading, weakening, failure-bringing.

Nothing is more subtle than thought, nothing more powerful, nothing more irresistible in its operations, when rightly applied and held to with a faith and fidelity that is unswerving,—a faith and fidelity that never knows the neutralizing effects of doubt and fear. If one have aspirations and a sincere desire for a higher and better condition, so far as advantages, facilities, associates, or any surroundings or environments are concerned, and if he continually send out his highest thought-forces for the realization of these desires, and continually water these forces with firm expectation as to their fulfilment, he will sooner or later find himself in the realization of these desires, and all in accordance with natural laws and forces.

Fear brings its own fulfilment the same as hope. The same law operates, and if, as our good and valued friend, Job, said when the darkest days were setting in upon him,—that which I feared has come upon me,—was true, how much more surely could he have brought about the opposite conditions, those he would have desired, had he have had even the slightest realization of his own powers, and had he acted the part of the master instead of that of the servant, had he have dictated terms instead of being dictated to, and thus suffering the consequences.

If one finds himself in any particular condition, in the midst of any surroundings or environments that are not desirable, that have nothing—at least for any length of time—that is of value to him, for his highest life and unfoldment, he has the remedy entirely within his own grasp the moment he realizes the power and supremacy of the forces of the mind and spirit; and, unless he intelligently use these forces, he drifts. Unless through them he becomes master and dictates, he becomes the slave and is dictated to, and so is driven hither and thither.

Earnest, sincere desire, sincere aspiration for higher and better conditions or means to realize them, the thought-forces actively sent out for their realization, these continually watered by firm expectation without allowing the contrary, neutralizing force of fear ever to enter in,—this, accompanied by rightly directed work and activity, will bring about the fullest realization of one's highest desires and aspirations with a certainty as absolute as that effect follows cause. Each and every one of us can thus make for himself ever higher and higher conditions, can attract ever and ever higher influences, can realize an ever higher and higher ideal in life. These are the forces that are within us, simply waiting to be recognized and used,—the forces that we should infuse into and mould every-day life with. The moment we vitally recognize them, they become our servants and wait upon our bidding.

Are you, for example, a young man or a young woman desiring a college, a university education, or have you certain literary or artistic instincts your soul longs the more fully to realize and actualize, and seems there no way open for you to realize the fulfilment of your desires? But the power is in your hands the moment you recognize it there. Begin at once to set the right forces into operation. Put forth your ideal, which will begin to clothe itself in material form, send out your thought-forces for its realization, continually hold and add to them, always strongly but always calmly, never allow the element of fear, which will keep the realization just so much farther away, to enter in; but, on the contrary, continually water with firm expectation all the forces thus set into operation. Do not then sit and idly fold the hands, expecting to see all things drop into the lap,—God feeds the sparrow, but he does not throw the food into its nest,—but take hold of the first thing that offers itself for you to do,—work in the fields, at the desk, saw wood, wash dishes, tend behind the counter, or whatever it may be,—be faithful to the thing in hand, always expecting something better, and know that this in hand is the thing that will open to you the next higher, and this the next and the next; and so realize that each thing thus taken hold of is but the agency that takes you each time a step nearer the realization of your fondest ideals. You then hold the key; and bolts that otherwise would remain immovable, by this mighty force, will be thrown before you.

We are born to be neither slaves nor beggars, but to dominion and to plenty. This is our rightful heritage, if we will but recognize and lay claim to it. Many a man and many a woman is to-day longing for conditions better and higher than he or she is in, who might be using the same time now spent in vain, indefinite, spasmodic longings, in putting into operation forces which, accompanied by the right personal activity, would speedily bring the fullest realization of his or her fondest dreams. The great universe is filled with an abundance of all things, filled to overflowing. All there is, is in her, waiting only for the touch of the right forces to cast them forth. She is no respecter of persons outside of the fact that she always responds to the demands of the man or the woman who knows and uses the forces and powers he or she is endowed with. And to the demands of such she always opens her treasure-house, for the supply is always equal to the demand. All things are in the hands of him who knows they are there.

Of all known forms of energy, thought is the most subtle, the most irresistible force. It has always been operating; but, so far as the great masses of the people are concerned, it has been operating blindly, or, rather, they have been blind to its mighty power, except in the cases of a few here and there. And these, as a consequence, have been our prophets, our seers, our sages, our saviors, our men of great and mighty power. We are just beginning to grasp the tremendous truth that there is a *science of thought*, and that the laws governing it can be known and scientifically applied. The man who understands and who appropriates this fact has literally all things under his control. Heredity and its attendant circumstances and influences? you ask. Most surely. The barriers which heredity builds, the same as those environment erects, when the awakened interior forces are considered, are as mud walls standing within the range of a Krupp gun: shattered and crumbled they are when the tremendous force is applied.

Thought needs direction to be effective, and upon this effective results depend as much as upon the force itself. This brings us to the will. Will is not as is so often thought, a force in itself; will is the directing power. Thought is the force. Will gives direction. Thought scattered gives the weak, the uncertain, the vacillating, the aspiring, but the never-doing, the I-would-like-to, but the get-no-where, the attain-to-nothing man or woman. Thought steadily directed by the will, gives the strong, the firm, the never-yielding, the never-know-defeat man or woman, the man or woman who uses the very difficulties and hindrances that would dishearten the ordinary person, as stones with which he paves a way over which he triumphantly walks, who, by the very force he carries with him, so neutralizes and transmutes the very obstacles that would bar his way that they fall before him, and in turn aid him on his way; the man or woman who, like the eagle, uses the very contrary wind that would thwart his flight, that would turn him and carry him in the opposite direction, as the very agency upon which he mounts and mounts and mounts, until actually lost to the human eye, and which, in addition to thus aiding him, brings to him an ever fuller realization of his own powers, in other words, an ever greater power.

It is this that gives the man or the woman who in storm or in sunny weather, rides over every obstacle, throws before him every barrier, and, as Browning has said, finally "arrives." Take, for example, the successful business man,—for it is all one, the law is the same in all cases,—the man who started with nothing except his own interior equipments. He has made up his mind to *one* thing,—success. This is his ideal. He thinks success, he sees success. He refuses to see anything else. He expects success: he thus attracts it to him, his thought-forces continually attract to him every agency that makes for success. He has set up the current, so that every wind that blows brings him success. He doesn't expect failure, and so he doesn't invite it. He has no time, no energies, to waste in fears or forebodings. He is dauntless, untiring, in his efforts. Let disaster come to-day, and tomorrow—ay, even yet to-day—he is getting his bearings, he is setting forces anew into operation; and these very forces are of more value to him than the half million dollars of his neighbor who has suffered from the same disaster. We speak of a man's failing in business, little thinking that cue real failure came long before, and that the final crash is but the culmination, the outward visible manifestation, of the real failure that occurred within possibly long ago. *A man carries his success or his failure with him: it is not dependent upon outside conditions.*

Will is the steady directing power: it is concentration. It is the pilot which, after the vessel is started by the mighty force within, puts it on its right course and keeps it true to that course, the pilot under whose control the rudder is which brings the great ocean liner, even through storms and gales, to an exact spot in the Liverpool port within a few minutes of its scheduled time, and at times even upon the very minute. Will is the sun-glass which so concentrates and so focuses the sun's rays that they quickly burn a hole through the paper that is held before it. The same rays, not thus concentrated, not thus focused, would fall upon the paper for days without any effect whatever. Will is the means for the directing, the concentrating, the focusing, of the thought-forces. Thought under wise direction,—this it is that does the work, that brings results, that makes the successful career. One object in mind which we never lose sight of; an ideal steadily held before the mind, never lost sight of, never lowered, never swerved from,—this, with persistence, determines all. Nothing can resist the power of thought, when thus directed by will.

May not this power, then, be used for base as well as for good purposes, for selfish as well as for unselfish ends? The same with this modification,—the more highly thought is spiritualized, the more subtle and powerful it becomes; and the more highly spiritualized the life, the farther is it removed from base, ignoble, selfish ends. But, even if it can be thus used, let him who would so use it be careful, let him never forget that that mighty, searching, omnipotent law of the right, of truth, of justice, that runs through all the universe and that can never be annulled or even for a moment set aside, will drive him to the wall, will crush him with a terrific force if he so use it.

Let him never forget that whatever he may get for self at the expense of some one else, through deception, through misrepresentation, through the exercise of the lower functions and powers, will by a law equally subtle, equally powerful, be turned into ashes in his very hands. The honey he thinks he has secured will be turned into bitterness as he attempts to eat it; the beautiful fruit he thinks is his will be as wormwood as he tries to enjoy it; the rose he has plucked will vanish, and he will find himself clutching a handful of thorns, which will penetrate to the very quick and which will flow the very life-blood from his hands. For through the violation of a higher, an immutable law, though he may get this or that, the power of true enjoyment will be taken away, and what he gets will become as a thorn in his side: either this or it will sooner or later escape from his hands. God's triumphal-car moves in a direction and at a rate that is certain and absolute, and he who would oppose it or go contrary to it must fall and be crushed beneath its wheels; and for him this crushing is necessary, in order that it may bring him the more quickly to a knowledge of the higher laws, to a realization of the higher self.

This brings to our notice two orders of will, which we may term, for convenience' sake, the human and the divine. The human will is the one just noticed, the sense will, the will of the lower self, that which seeks its own ends regardless of its connection with the

228

greater whole. The divine will is the will of the higher self, the god-self, that that never makes an error, that never leads into difficulties. How attain to its realization? How call it into a dominating activity? Through an awakening to and a living in the higher, the god-self, thus making it one with God's will, one with the will of infinite intelligence, infinite love, infinite wisdom, infinite power; and when this is done, no mistakes can be made, any more than limits can be set.

It is thus that the Infinite Power works through and for us—true inspiration—while our part is simply to see that our connection with this power is consciously and perfectly kept. And, when we come to a knowledge of the true nature, a knowledge of the true self, when we come to a conscious realization of the fact that we are one with, a part of, this spirit of infinite life, infinite love, infinite wisdom, infinite power, and infinite plenty, do we not see that we lack for nothing, that all things *are* ours? It is then ours to speak the word: desire induces and gives place to realization. If you are intelligence, if you are power, if you are that all-seeing, all-knowing, all-doing, all-loving, all-having, that eternal self, that eternal one without beginning and without end, the same yesterday, to-day, and forever, then all things *are* yours, and you lack for nothing; and, when you come *consciously to know and to live* this truth, then the whole of life for you is summed up in the one word realization. The striving, the pulling, the running hither and thither to accomplish this or that, that takes place on all planes of life below this highest plane, gives place to this *realization*; and you and your desire become one.

And what does this mean? Simply this: that you have found and have literally entered into the kingdom of heaven, and heaven means harmony, so that you have entered into the kingdom of harmony,—harmony or oneness with the Infinite Life, the Infinite God. And do we not, then, clearly see the rational and scientific basis for the injunction—Seek ye first the kingdom of heaven, and all these other things shall be added unto you? Than this there is nothing in all the wide universe more scientific, nothing more practical; and in the light of this can we not also see how readily follows the injunction—Take ye no thought for the things of the morrow, for the things of the morrow will take care of themselves? This realization gives you that care-less attitude, free from care. The Infinite Power does the work for you, and you are relieved of the responsibility. Your responsibility lies in keeping yourself in a faithful and a never-failing connection with this Infinite Source. Why, I know a few lives that have come into such a conscious oneness with the Infinite Life, and who so continually live in its realization, that all things that have just been said are *absolutely* true in their cases. The solution of all things they thus put into the law, so that, when the time comes, the difficulty is solved, the course is clear, the way is opened, or the means are at hand. When one knows whereof he speaks, of this he can speak with authority.

When this realization comes, fear goes, hope attends, faith dominates,—the faith of to-day which gives place to the realization of tomorrow. We then have nothing to do with the past, nothing to do with the future; for the whole of life is determined by the ever-present to-day. As my life to-day has been determined by the way I lived my yesterday, so my to-morrow is being determined by the way I live my to-day. Let me then live in this *eternal now*, and realize that I am at this very moment living the eternal life as much as I ever shall or can live it. I will then waste no time with the past, except perhaps occasionally to give thanks that its then seeming trials, sorrows, errors, and stumblings have brought me all the sooner into harmony with the laws of the higher life. Let me waste no time with the future, no time in idle dreaming, neither in fears nor forebodings, thus inviting and opening the door for the entrance of their actualizations; but rather let me, by the thoughts and so by the deeds of to-day, make the future exactly what I will.

Every act is preceded and given birth to by a thought, the act repeated forms the habit, the habit determines the character, and character determines the life, the destiny,—a most significant, a most tremendous truth: thought on the one hand, life, destiny, on the other. And how simplified, when we realize that it is merely the thought of the present hour, and the next when it comes, and the next, and the next! so life, destiny, on the one hand, the thoughts of the present hour, on the other. This is the secret of character-building. How wonderfully simple, though what vigilance it demands!

What, shall we ask, is the place, what the value, of prayer? Prayer, as every act of devotion, brings us into an ever greater conscious harmony with the Infinite, the one pearl of great price; for it is this harmony which brings all other things. Prayer is the soul's sincere desire, and thus is its own answer, as the sincere desire made active and accompanied by faith sooner or later gives place to realization; *for faith is an invisible and invincible magnet, and attracts to itself whatever it fervently desires and calmly and persistently expects.* This is absolute, and the results will be absolute in exact proportion as this operation of the thought forces, as this faith is absolute, and relative in exact proportion as it is relative. The Master said, What things soever ye desire, when ye pray, *believe* that ye receive them and ye shall have them. Can any law be more clearly enunciated, can anything be more definite and more absolute than this? According to thy faith be it unto thee. Do we at times fail in obtaining the results we desire? The fault, the failure, lies not in the law but in ourselves. Regarded in its right and true light, than prayer there is nothing more scientific, nothing more valuable, nothing more effective.

This conscious realization of oneness with the Infinite Life is of all things the one thing to be desired; for, when this oneness is realized and lived in, all other things follow in its train, there are no desires that shall not be realized, for God has planted in the human breast no desire without its corresponding means of realization. No harm can come nigh, nothing can touch us, there will be nothing to fear; for we shall thus attract only the good. And whatever changes time may bring, understanding the law, we shall always expect something better, and thus set into operation the forces that will attract that something, realizing that many times angels go out that archangels may enter in; and this is always true in the case of the life of this higher realization. And why should we have any fear whatever,—fear even for the nation, as is many times expressed? *God is behind His world, in love and with infinite care and watchfulness working out his great and almighty plans*; and whatever plans men may devise, He will when the time is ripe either frustrate and shatter, or aid and push through to their most perfect culmination,—frustrate and shatter if contrary to, aid and actualize if in harmony with His.

It will readily be seen what a power the life that is fully awake, that fully grasps and uses the great forces of its own interior self, can be in the service of mankind. One with these forces highly spiritualized will not have to go here and there to do the greatest service for mankind. Such a one can sit in his cabin, in his tent, in his own home, or, as he goes here and there, he can continually send out influences of the most potent and powerful nature,—influences that will have their effect, that will do their work, and that will reach to the uttermost parts of the world. Than this there can be no more valuable, more vital service, nor one of a higher nature.

These facts, the facts relating to the powers that come with the higher awakening, have been dealt with somewhat fully, to show that the matters along the lines of man's interior, intuitive, spiritual, thought, soul life, instead of being, as they are so many times regarded, merely indefinite, sentimental, or impractical, are, on the contrary, powerfully, omnipotently real, and are of all practical things in the world the most practical, and, in the truest and deepest sense, the only truly practical things there are. And pre-eminently is this true when we look with a long range of vision, past the mere to-day, to the final outcome, to the time when that transition we are accustomed to call death takes place, and all accumulations and possessions material are left behind, and the soul takes with it only the unfoldment and growth of the real life; and unless it has this, when all else must be left behind, it goes out poor indeed. And a most wonderful and beautiful fact of it all is this: that all growth, all advancement, all attainment made along the lines of the spiritual, the soul, the real life, is so much made forever, and can never be lost. Hence the great fact in the admonition, Lay not up for yourselves treasures on earth, where moth doth corrupt and where thieves break through and steal; but lay up for yourselves treasures in heaven,—the interior, spiritual kingdom,—where neither moth doth corrupt nor where thieves break through and steal.

What then, again let us ask, is love to God? It is far more, we have found, than a mere sentimental abstraction. It is this awakening to the higher, the god-self, a coming into the conscious realization of the fact that your life is one with, is a part of, the Infinite Life, the full realization of the fact that you are a spiritual being here and now, at this very moment, and a living as such. It is being true to the light that lighteth every man that cometh into the world, and so a finding of the Christ within; a realization of the fact that God is the life of your life, and so not afar off; a realization of a oneness so perfect that you are able to say, as did His other son, "I and my Father are one"—the ultimate destiny of each human soul, each of the Father's children, for all, no matter what differences man may see, are equal in His sight; and He created not one in vain. So love to God in its true expression is not a mere sentimentality, a mere abstraction: it is life, it is growth, it is spiritual awakening and unfoldment, it is realization. Again, it is life: it is the more abundant life.

Then recognize this fact, and so fill your life with an intense, a passionate love for God. Then take this life, so rich, so abundant, and so powerful, and *lose it in the love and service of your fellow-men*, the Father's other children. Fill it with an intense, a passionate love for service; and when this shall have been done, your life is in complete harmony with all the law and the prophets, in complete harmony with the two great and determining facts of human life and destiny,—love to God and love to one's fellow-men,—the two eternal principles upon which the great universal religion, which is slowly and gradually evolving out an almost endless variety and form, is to rest. Do this, and feel once for all the power and the thrill of the life universal. Do this, and find yourself coming into the full realization of such splendors and beauties as all the royal courts of this world combined have never been able even to dream of.

When the step from the personal to the impersonal, from the personal, the individual, to the universal, is once made, the great solution of life has come; and by this same step one enters at once into the realm of all power. When this is done, and one fully realizes the fact that the greatest life is the life spent in the service of all mankind, and then when he vitally grasps that great eternal principle of right, of truth, of justice, that runs through all the universe, and which, though temporarily it may seem to be perverted, always and with never an exception eventually prevails, and that with an omnipotent power,—he then holds the key to all situations.

A king of this nature goes about his work absolutely regardless of what men may say or hear or think or do; for he himself has absolutely nothing to gain or nothing to lose, and nothing of this nature can come near him or touch him, for he is standing not in the personal, but in the universal. He is then in God's work, and the very God-powers are his, and it seems as if the very angels of heaven come to minister unto him and to move things his way; and this is true, very true, for he himself is simply moving God's way, and when this is so, the certainty of the outcome is absolute.

How often did the Master say, "I seek not to do mine own will, but the will of the Father who sent me"! Here is the world's great example of the life out of the personal and in the universal, hence his great power. The same has been true of all the saviors, the prophets, the seers, the sages, and the leaders in the world's history, of all of truly great and lasting power.

He who would then come into the secret of cower must come from the personal into the universal, and with this comes not only great power, but also freedom from the vexations and perplexities that rise from the misconstruing of motives, the opinions of others;

for such a one cares nothing as to what men may say, or hear, or think, or do, so long as he is true to the great principles of right and truth before him. And, if we will search carefully, we shall find that practically all the perplexities and difficulties of life have their origin on the side of the personal.

Much is said to young men to-day about success in life,— success generally though, as the world calls success. It is well, however, always to bear in mind the fact that there is a success which is a miserable, a deplorable failure; while, on the other hand, there is a failure which is a grand, a noble, a God-like success. And one crying need of the age is that young men be taught the true dignity, nobility, and power of such a failure,—such a failure in the eyes of the world to-day, but such a success in the eyes of God and the coming ages. When this is done, there will be among us more prophets, more saviors, more men of grand and noble stature, who with a firm and steady hand will hold the lighted torch of true advancement high up among the people; and they will be those whom the people will gladly follow, for they will be those who will speak and move with authority, true sons of God, true brothers of men. A man may make his millions and his life be a failure still.

The promise was given that our conversation should not be extended; and unless we conclude it now, the promise will not be kept. Our aim at the outset, you will remember, was to find answer to the question—How can I make life yield its fullest and best? how can I know the true secret of power? how can I attain to true greatness? how can I fill the whole of life with a happiness, a peace, a joy, a satisfaction, that is ever rich and abiding, that ever increases, never diminishes?

Two great laws come forward: the one, that we find our own lives in losing them in the service of others,—love to the fellow-man; the other, that all life is one with, is part of, the Infinite Life, that we are not material, but spiritual beings,—spiritual beings here and now, and a living as such, which brings us in turn to a realization of the higher, the god-self, thus bringing us into the realm of all peace, all power, and all plenty,—this is love to God.

And I wonder now if we have found the answer true and satisfactory. We have sat at the feet of the Master Teacher, and he has told us that we have. We have found that through them, and through them alone, *true* greatness, power, and success can come; that through them comes the richest joy, the greatest peace and satisfaction this world can know. We have also found that, if one's desire is to make life narrow, pinched, and of little value, to rob it of its chief charms, the only requirement necessary is to become self-centred, to live continually with the little, stunted self, which will inevitably grow more and more diminutive and shrivelled as time passes, instead of reaching out and having a part in the great life of humanity, thus illimitably intensifying and multiplying his own. For each act of humble service is that divine touching of the ground which enables one to get the spring whereby he leaps to ever greater heights. We have found that a recognition of these two laws enables one to grow and develop the fullest and richest life here, and that they are the two gates whereby all who would must enter the kingdom of heaven.

Around this great and sweet-incensed altar of love, service, and self-devotion to God and the fellow-man, can and do all mankind bow and worship. To it can all religions and creeds subscribe: it is the universal religion.

Then become at one with God, as did His other son, through the awakening to the real self and by living continually in this the higher, the god-self. Become at one with humanity, as did His other son, by bringing your life into harmony with this great, immutable law of love and service and self-devotion, and so feel once for all the power and the thrill of the life universal.

Yours will then be a life the greatest, the grandest, the most joyous this world can know; for you will indeed be living the Christ-life, the life that is beyond compare, the life to which all the world stretches out its eager palms, and innumerable companies will rise up and call you blessed, and give thanks that such a life is the rich heritage of the world. The song continually arising from your lips will then be, There is joy, only joy; for we are all one with the Infinite Life, all parts of the one great whole, and the Spirit of Infinite Goodness and Love is ever ruling over all.

VI

Character-building Thought Power

*A thought,—good or evil,—an act, in time a habit,—so
runs life's law: what you live in your thought-world,
that, sooner or later, you will find objectified in your life.*

UNCONSCIOUSLY we are forming habits every moment of our lives. Some are habits of a desirable nature; some are those of a most undesirable nature. Some, though not so bad in themselves, are exceedingly bad in their cumulative effects, and cause us at times much loss, much pain and anguish, while their opposites would, on the contrary, bring us much peace and joy, as well as a continually increasing power.

Have we it within our power to determine at all times what types of habits shall take form in our lives? In other words, is habit-forming, character-building, a matter of mere chance, or have we it within our own control? We have, entirely and absolutely. "I will be what I will to be," can be said and should be said by every human soul.

After this has been bravely and determinedly said, and not only said, but fully inwardly realized, something yet remains. Something remains to be said regarding the great law underlying habit-forming, character-building; for there is a simple, natural, and thoroughly scientific method that all should know. A method whereby old, undesirable, earth-binding habits can be broken, and new, desirable, heaven-lifting habits can be acquired,—a method whereby life in part or in its totality can be changed, provided one is sufficiently in earnest to know, and, knowing it, to apply the law.

Thought is the force underlying all. And what do we mean by this? Simply this: Your every act—every conscious act—is preceded by a thought. Your dominating thoughts determine your dominating actions. The acts repeated crystallize themselves into the habit. The aggregate of your habits is your character. Whatever, then, you would have your acts, you must look well to the character of the thought you entertain. Whatever act you would not do,—habit you would not acquire,—you must look well to it that you do not entertain the type of thought that will give birth to this act, this habit.

It is a simple psychological law that any type of thought, if entertained for a sufficient length of time, will, by and by, reach the motor tracks of the brain, and finally burst forth into action. Murder can be and many times is committed in this way, the same as all undesirable things are done. On the other hand, the greatest powers are grown, the most God-like characteristics are engendered, the most heroic acts are performed in the same way.

The thing clearly to understand is this: That the thought is always parent to the act. Now, we have it entirely in our own hands to determine exactly what thoughts we entertain. In the realm of our own minds we have absolute control, or we should have, and if at any time we have not, then there is a method by which we can gain control, and in the realm of the mind become thorough masters. In order to get to the very foundation of the matter, let us look to this for a moment. For if thought is always parent to our acts, habits, character, life, then it is first necessary that we know fully how to control our thoughts.

Here let us refer to that law of the mind which is the same as is the law in connection with the reflex nerve system of the body, the law which says that whenever one does a certain thing in a certain way it is easier to do the same thing in the same way the next time, and still easier the next, and the next, and the next, until in time it comes to pass that no effort is required, or no effort worth speaking of; but on the contrary, to do the opposite would re-. quire the effort. The mind carries with it the power that perpetuates its own type of thought, the same as the body carries with it through the reflex nerve system the power which perpetuates and makes continually easier its own particular acts. Thus a simple effort to control one's thoughts, a simple setting about it, even if at first failure is the result, and even if for a time failure seems to be about the only result, will in time, sooner or later, bring him to the point of easy, filll, and complete control.

Each one, then, can grow the power of determining, controlling his thought, the power of determining what types of thought he shall and what types he shall not entertain. For let us never part in mind with this fact, that every earnest *effort* along any line makes the end aimed at just a little easier for each succeeding effort, even if, as has been said, apparent failure is the result of the earlier efforts. This is a case where even failure is success, for the failure is not in the effort, and every earnest effort adds an increment of power that will eventually accomplish the end aimed at. We *can*, then, gain the full and complete power of determining what character, what type of thoughts we entertain Shall we now give attention to some two or three concrete cases? Here is a man, the cashier of a large mercantile establishment, or cashier of a bank. In his morning paper he reads of a man who has become suddenly rich, has made a fortune of half a million or a million dollars in a few hours through speculation on the stock market. Perhaps he has seen an account of another man who has done practically the same thing lately. He is not quite wise enough, however, to comprehend the fact that when he reads of one or two cases of this kind he could find, were he to look into the matter carefully, one or two hundred cases of men who have lost all they had in the same way. He thinks, however, that he will be one of the fortunate ones. He does not fully realize that there are no short cuts to wealth honestly made. He takes a part of his savings, and as is true in practically all cases of this kind, he loses all that he has put in. Thinking now that he sees why he lost, and that had he more money he would be able to get back what he has lost, and perhaps make a handsome sum in addition, and make it quickly, the thought comes to him to use some of the funds he has charge of. In nine cases out of ten, if not in ten cases in every ten, the results that inevitably follow this are known sufficiently well to make it unnecessary to follow him farther. Where is the man's safety in the light of what we have been considering? Simply this: the moment the thought of using for his own purpose funds belonging to others enters his mind, if he is wise he will *instantly* put the thought from his mind. If he is a fool he will entertain it. In the degree in which he entertains it, it will grow upon him; it will become the absorbing thought in his mind; it will finally become master of his will power, and through rapidly succeeding steps, dishonor, shame, degradation, penitentiary, remorse will be his. It is easy for him to put the thought from his mind when it first enters; but as he entertains it, it grows into such proportions that it becomes more and more difficult for him to put it from his mind; and by and by it becomes practically *impossible* for him to do it. The light of the match, which but a little effort of the breath would have extinguished at first, has imparted a flame that is raging through the entire building, and now it is almost, if not quite impossible to conquer it.

Shall we notice another concrete case? a trite case, perhaps, but one in which we can see how habit is formed, and also how the same habit can be unformed. Here is a young man, he may be the son of poor parents, or he may be the son of rich parents; one in the ordinary ranks of life, or one of high social standing, whatever that means. He is good-hearted, one of good impulses, generally speaking,—a good fellow. He is out with some companions, companions of the same general type. They are out for a pleasant evening, out for a good time. They are apt at times to be thoughtless, even careless. The suggestion is made by one of the company, not that they get drunk, no, not at all; but merely that they go and have something to drink together. The young man whom we first mentioned, wanting to be genial, scarcely listens to the suggestion that comes to his inner consciousness—that it will be better for him not to fall in with the others in this. He does not stop long enough to realize the fact that the greatest strength and nobility of character lies always in taking a firm stand on the side of the right, and allow himself to be influenced by nothing that will weaken this stand. He goes, therefore, with his companions to the drinking place. With the same or with other companions this is repeated now and then; and each time it is repeated his power of saying "No" is gradually decreasing. In this way he has grown a little liking for intoxicants, and takes them perhaps now and then by himself. He does not dream, or in the slightest degree realize, what way he is tending, until there comes a day when he wakens to the consciousness of the fact that he hasn't the power nor even the impulse to resist the taste which has gradually grown into a minor form of craving for intoxicants. Thinking, however, that he will be able to stop when he is really in danger of getting into the drink habit, he goes thoughtlessly and carelessly on. We will pass over the various intervening steps and come to the time when we find him a confirmed drunkard. It is simply the same old story told a thousand or even a million times over.

He finally awakens to his true condition; and through the shame, the anguish, the degradation, and the want that comes upon him he longs for a return of the days when he was a free man. But hope has almost gone from his life. It would have been easier for him never to have begun, and easier for him to have stopped before he reached his present condition, but even in his present condition, be it the lowest and the most helpless and hopeless that can be imagined, he has the power to get out of it and be a free man once again. Let us see. The desire for drink comes upon him again. If he entertain the thought, the desire, he is lost again. His only hope, his only means of escape is this: the moment, aye, *the very instant* the thought comes to him, if he will put it out of his mind he will thereby put out the little flame of the match. If he entertain the thought the little flame will communicate itself until almost before he is aware of it a consuming fire is raging, and then effort is almost useless. The thought must be banished from the mind the instant it enters; dalliance with it means failure and defeat, or a fight that will be indescribably fiercer than it would be if the thought is ejected at the beginning.

And here we must say a word regarding a certain great law that we may call the "law of indirectness." A thought can be put out of the mind easier and more successfully, not by dwelling upon it, not by attempting to put it out *directly*, but by throwing the mind on to some other object, by putting some other object of thought into the mind. This may be, for example, the ideal of full and perfect self-mastery, or it may be something of a nature entirely distinct from the thought which presents itself, something to which the mind goes easily and naturally. This will in time become the absorbing thought in the mind, and the danger is past. This same course of action repeated, will gradually grow the power of putting more readily out of mind the thought of drink as it presents itself, and will gradually grow the power of putting into the mind those objects of thought one most desires. The result will be that as time passes the thought of drink will present itself less and less, and when it does present itself it can be put out of the mind more easily . each succeeding time, until the time comes when it can be put out without difficulty, and eventually the time will come when the thought will enter the mind no more at all.

Still another case. You may be more or less of an irritable nature—naturally, perhaps, provoked easily to anger. Some one says something or does something that you dislike, and your first impulse is to show resentment and possibly to give way to anger. In the degree that you allow this resentment to display itself, that you allow yourself to give way to anger, in that degree will it become easier to do the same thing when any cause, even a very slight cause, presents itself. It will, moreover, become continually harder for you to refrain from it, until resentment, anger, and possibly even hatred and revenge become characteristics of your nature, robbing it of its sunniness, its charm, and its brightness for all with whom you come in contact. If, however, the instant the impulse to resentment and anger arises, you check it *then and there*, and throw the mind on to some other object of thought, the power will gradually grow itself of doing this same thing more readily, more easily, as succeeding like causes present themselves, until by and by the time will come when there will be scarcely anything that can irritate you, and nothing that can impel you to anger; until by and by a matchless brightness and charm of nature and disposition will become habitually yours, a brightness and charm you would scarcely think possible to-day. And so we might take up case after case, characteristic after characteristic, habit after habit. The habit of fault-finding and its opposite are grown in identically the same way; the characteristic of jealousy and its opposite; the characteristic of fear and its opposite. In this same way we grow either love or hatred; in this way we come to take a gloomy, pessimistic view of life, which objectifies itself in a nature, a disposition of this type, or we grow that sunny, hopeful, cheerful, buoyant nature that brings with it so much joy and beauty and power for ourselves, as well as so much hope and inspiration and joy for all the world.

There is nothing more true in connection with human life than that we grow into the likeness of those things we contemplate. Literally and scientifically and necessarily true is it that, "as a man thinketh in his heart, so is he." The "is" part is his character. His character is the sum total of his habits. His habits have been formed by his conscious acts; but every conscious act is, as we have found, preceded by a thought. And so we have it—thought on the one hand, character, life, destiny on the other. And simple it becomes when we bear in mind that it is simply the thought of the present moment, and the next moment when it is upon us, and then the next, and so on through all time.

One can in this way attain to whatever ideals he would attain to. Two steps are necessary: first, as the days pass, to form one's ideals; and second, to follow them continually whatever may arise, wherever they may lead him. Always remember that the great and strong character is the one who is ever ready to sacrifice the present pleasure for the future good. He who will thus follow his highest ideals as they present themselves to him day after day, year after year, will find that as Dante, following his beloved from world to world, finally found her at the gates of Paradise, so he will find himself eventually at the same gates. Life is not, we may say, for mere passing pleasure, but for the highest unfoldment that one can attain to, the noblest character that one can grow, and for the greatest service that one can render to all mankind. In this, however, we will find the highest pleasure, for in this the only real pleasure lies. He who would find it by any short cuts, or by entering upon any other paths, will inevitably find that his last state is always worse than his first; and if he proceed upon paths other than these he will find that he will never find real and lasting pleasure at all. The question is not, What are the conditions in our lives? but, How do we meet the conditions that we find there? And whatever the conditions are, it is unwise and profitless to look upon them, even if they are conditions that we would have otherwise, in the attitude of complaint, for complaint will bring depression, and depression will weaken and possibly even kill the spirit that would engender the power that would enable us to bring into our lives an entirely new set of conditions.

In order to be concrete, even at the risk of being personal, I will say that in my own experience there have come at various times into my life circumstances and conditions that I gladly would have run from at the time—conditions that caused at the time humiliation and shame and anguish of spirit. But invariably, as sufficient time has passed, I have been able to look back and see clearly the part which every experience of the type just mentioned had to play in my life. I have seen the lessons it was essential for me to learn; and the result is that now I would not drop a single one of these experiences from my life, humiliating and hard to bear as they were at the time; no, not for the world. And here is also a lesson I have learned: whatever conditions are in my life to-day that are not the easiest and most agreeable, and whatever conditions of this type all coming time may bring, I will take them just as they come, without complaint, without depression, and meet them in the wisest possible way; knowing that they are the best possible conditions that could be in my life at the time, or otherwise they would not be there; realizing the fact that, although I may not at the time see why they are in my life, although I may not see just what part they have to play, the time will Come, and when it comes I will see it all, and thank God for every condition just as it came.

Each one is so apt to think that his own conditions, his own trials or troubles or sorrows, or his own struggles, as the case may be, are greater than those of the great mass of mankind, or possibly greater than those of any one else in the world. He forgets that each one has his own peculiar trials or troubles or sorrows to bear, or struggles in habits to overcome, and that his is but the common lot of all the human race. We are apt to make the mistake in this—in that we see and feel keenly our own trials, or adverse conditions, or characteristics to be overcome, while those of others we do not see so clearly, and hence we are apt to think that they are not at all equal to our own. Each has his own problems to work out. Each must work out his own problems. Each must grow the insight that will enable him to see what the causes are that have brought the unfavorable conditions into his life; each must grow the strength that will enable him to face these conditions, and to set into operation forces that will bring about a different set of conditions. We may be of aid to one another by way of suggestion, by way of bringing to one another a knowledge of certain higher laws and forces,—laws and forces that will make it easier to do that which we would do. The doing, however, must be done by each one for himself.

And so the way to get out of any conditions we have gotten into, either knowingly or inadvertently, either intentionally or unintentionally, is to take time to look the conditions squarely in the face, and to find the law whereby they have come about. And when we have discovered the law, the thing to do is not to rebel against it, not to resist it, but to go with it by working in harmony with it. If we work in harmony with it, it will work for our highest good, and will take us wheresoever we desire. If we oppose it, if we resist it, if we fail to work in harmony with it, it will eventually break us to pieces. The law is immutable in its workings. Go with it, and it brings all things our way; resist it, and it brings suffering, pain, loss, and desolation.

But a few days ago I was talking with a lady; a most estimable lady living on a little New England farm of some five or six acres. Her husband died a few years ago, a good-hearted, industrious man, but one who spent practically all of his earnings in drink. When he died the little farm was unpaid for, and the wife found herself without any visible means of support, with a family of several to care for. Instead of being discouraged with what many would have called her hard lot, instead of rebelling against the circumstances in which she found herself, she faced the matter bravely, firmly believing that there were ways by which she could manage, though she could not see them clearly at the time. She took up her burden where she found it, and went bravely forward. For several years she has been taking care of summer boarders who come to that part of the country, getting up regularly, she told me, at from half-past three to four o'clock in the morning, and working until ten o'clock each night. In the wintertime, when this means of revenue is cut off, she has gone out to do nursing in the country round about. In this way the little farm is now almost paid for; her children have been kept in school, and they are now able to aid her to a greater or less extent. Through it all she has entertained no fears nor forebodings; she has shown no rebellion of any kind. She has not kicked against the circumstances which brought about the conditions in which she found herself, but she has put herself into harmony with the law that would bring her into another set of conditions. And through it all, she told me, she had been continually grateful that she has been able to work, and that whatever her own circumstances have been, she has never yet failed to find some one whose circumstances were still a little worse than hers, and for whom it was not possible for her to render some little service.

Most heartily she appreciates the fact, and most grateful is she for it, that the little home is now almost paid for, and soon no more of her earnings will have to go out in that channel. The dear little home, she said, would be all the more precious to her by virtue of the fact that it was finally hers through her own efforts. The strength and nobility of character that have come to her during these years, the sweetness of disposition, the sympathy and care for others, her faith in the final triumph of all that is honest and true and pure and good, are qualities that thousands and hundreds of thousands of women, yes, of both men and women, who are apparently in better circumstances in life can justly envy. And should the little farm home be taken away to-morrow, she has gained something that a farm of a thousand acres could not buy. By going about her work in the way she has gone about it the burden of it all has been lightened, and her work has been made truly enjoyable.

Let us take a moment to see how these same conditions would have been met by a person of less wisdom, one not so far-sighted as this dear, good woman has been. For a time possibly her spirit would have been crushed. Fears and forebodings of all kinds would probably have taken hold of her, and she would have felt that nothing that she could do would be of any avail. Or, she might have rebelled against the agencies, against the law which brought about the conditions in which she found herself, and she might have become embittered against the world, and gradually also against the various people with whom she came in contact. Or again, she might have thought that her efforts would be unable to meet the circumstances, and that it was the duty of some one to lift her out of her difficulties. In this way no progress at all would have been made towards the accomplishment of the desired results, and continually she would have felt more keenly the circumstances in which she found herself, because there was nothing else to occupy her mind. In this way the little farm would not have become hers, she would not have been able to do anything for others, and her nature would have become embittered against everything and everybody.

True it is, then, not, What are the conditions in one's life? but, How does he meet the conditions that he finds there? This will determine all. And if at any time we are apt to think that our own lot is about the hardest there is, and if we are able at any time to persuade ourselves that we can find no one whose lot is just a little harder than ours, let us then study for a little while the character Pompilia, in Browning's poem,[1] and after studying it, thank God that the conditions in our life are so favorable; and then set about with a trusting and intrepid spirit to actualize the conditions that we most desire.

Thought is at the bottom of all progress or retrogression, of all success or failure, of all that is desirable or undesirable in human life. The type of thought we entertain both creates and draws conditions that crystallize about it, conditions exactly the same in nature as is the thought that gives them form. Thoughts are forces, and each creates of its kind, whether we realize it or not. The great law of the drawing power of the mind, which says that like creates like, and that like attracts like, is continually working in every human life, for it is one of the great immutable laws of the universe. For one to take time to see clearly the things he would attain to, and then to hold that ideal steadily and continually before his mind, never allowing faith—his positive thought-forces—to give way to or to be neutralized by doubts and fears, and then to set about doing each day what his hands find to do, never complaining, but spending the time that he would otherwise spend in complaint in focusing his thought-forces upon the ideal that his mind has built, will sooner or later bring about the full materialization of that for which he sets out.

There are those who, when they begin to grasp the fact that there is what we may term a "science of thought," who, when they begin to realize that through the instrumentality of our interior, spiritual thought-forces we have the power of gradually moulding

---

[1] "The Ring and the Book," by Robert Browning.

the every-day conditions of life as we would have them, in their early enthusiasm are not able to see results as quickly as they expect, and are apt to think, therefore, that after all there is not very much in that which has but newly come to their knowledge. They must remember, however, that in endeavoring to overcome an old or to grow a new habit, everything cannot be done *all at once*.

In the degree that we attempt to use the thought-forces do we continually become able to use them more effectively. Progress is slow at first, more rapid as we proceed. Power grows by using, or, in other words, using brings a continually increasing power. This is governed by law the same as are all things in our lives, and all things in the universe about us. Every act and advancement made by the musician is in full accordance with law. No one commencing the study of music can, for example, sit down to the piano and play the piece of a master at the first effort. He must not conclude, however, nor does he conclude, that the piece of the master *cannot be* played by him, or, for that matter, by any one. He begins to practise the piece. The law of the mind that we have already noticed comes to his aid, whereby his mind follows the music more readily, more rapidly, and more surely each succeeding time, and there also comes into operation and to his aid the law underlying the action of the reflex nerve system of the body, which we have also noticed, whereby his fingers coördinate their movements with the movements of his mind, more readily, more rapidly, and more accurately each succeeding time; until by and by the time comes when that which he stumbles through at first, that in which there is no harmony, nothing but discord, finally reveals itself as the music of the master, the music that thrills and moves masses of men and women. So it is in the use of the thought-forces. It is the reiteration, the constant reiteration of the thought that grows the power of continually stronger thought-focusing, and that finally brings manifestation.

All life is from within out. This is something that cannot be reiterated too often. The springs of life are all from within. This being true, it would be well for us to give more time to the inner life than we are accustomed to give to it, especially in this Western world.

There is nothing that will bring us such abundant returns as to take a little time in the quiet each day of our lives. We need this to get the kinks out of our minds and hence out of our lives. We need this to form better the higher ideals of life. We need this in order to see clearly in mind the things upon which we would concentrate and focus the thought-forces. We need this in order to make continually anew and to keep our conscious connection with the Infinite. We need this in order that the rush and hurry of our every-day life does not keep us away from the conscious realization of the fact that the spirit of Infinite life and power that is back of all, working in and through all, the life of all, is the life of our life, and the source of our power; and that outside of this we have no life and we have no power. To realize this fact fully, and to live in it consciously at all times, is to find the kingdom of God, which is essentially an inner kingdom, and can never be anything else. The kingdom of heaven is to be found only within, and this is done once for all, and in a manner in which it cannot otherwise be done, when we come into the conscious, living realization of the fact that in our real selves we are essentially one with the Divine life, and open ourselves continually so that this Divine life can speak to and manifest through us. In this way we come into the condition where we are continually walking with God. In this way the consciousness of God becomes a living reality in our lives; and in the degree in which it becomes a reality does it bring us into the realization of continually increasing wisdom, insight, and power. *This consciousness of God in the soul of man is the essence, indeed the sum and substance of all religion.* This identifies religion with every act and every moment of every-day life. That which does not identify itself with every moment of every day and with every act of life is religion in name only and not in reality. This consciousness of God in the soul of man. is the one thing uniformly taught by all the prophets, by all the inspired ones, by all the seers and mystics in the world's history, what. ever the time, wherever the country, whatever the religion, whatever minor differences we may find in their lives and teachings. In regard to this they all agree; indeed, this is the essence of their teaching, as it has also been the secret of their power and the secret of their lasting influence.

It is the attitude of the child that is necessary before we can enter into the kingdom of heaven. As it was said, "Except ye become as little children, ye cannot enter into the kingdom of heaven." For we then realize that of ourselves we can do nothing, but that it is only as we realize that it is the Divine life and power working within us, and it is only as we open ourselves that it may work through us, that we are or can do anything. It is thus that the simple life, which is essentially the life of the greatest enjoyment and the greatest attainment, is entered upon.

In the Orient the people as a class take far more time in the quiet, in the silence, than we take. Some of them carry this possibly to as great an extreme as we carry the opposite, with the result that they do not actualize and objectify in the outer life the things they dream in the inner life. We give so much time to the activities of the outer life that we do not take sufficient time in the quiet to form in the inner, spiritual thought-life the ideals and the conditions that we would have actualized and manifested in the outer life, The result is that we take life in a kind of haphazard way, taking it as it comes, thinking not very much about it until, perhaps, pushed by some bitter experiences, instead of moulding it, through the agency of the inner forces, exactly as we would have it. We need to strike the happy balance between the custom in this respect of the Eastern and Western worlds, and go to the extreme of neither the one nor the other. This alone will give the ideal life; and it is the ideal life only that is the thoroughly satisfactory life. In the Orient there are many who are day after day sitting in the quiet, meditating, contemplating, idealizing, with their eyes focused on their stomach in spiritual revery, while through lack of outer activities, in their stomachs they are actually starving. In this Western world, men and women, in the rush and activity of our accustomed life, are running hither and thither, with no centre, no foundation upon which to stand, nothing to which they can anchor their lives, because they do not take sufficient time to come into the realization of what the centre, of what the reality of their lives is.

If the Oriental would do his contemplating, and then get up and do his work, he would be in a better condition; he would be living a more normal and satisfactory life. If we in the Occident would take more time from the rush and activity of life for contemplation, for meditation, for idealization, for becoming acquainted with our real selves, and then go about our work manifesting the powers of our real selves, we would be far better off, because we would be living a more natural, a more normal life. To find one's centre, to become centred in the Infinite, is the first great essential of every satisfactory life; and then to go out, thinking, speaking, working, loving, living, from this centre.

In the highest character-building, such as we have been considering, there are those who feel they are handicapped by what we term *heredity*. In a sense they are right; in another sense they are totally wrong. It is along the same lines as the thought which many before us had inculcated in them through the couplet in the New England Primer: "In Adam's fall, we sinnèd all." Now, in the first place, it is rather hard to understand the justice of this if it is true. In the second place, it is rather hard to understand why it is true. And in the third place there is no truth in it at all. We are now dealing with the real essential self, and, however old Adam is, God is eternal. This means you; it means me; it means every human soul. When we fully realize this fact we see that heredity is a reed that is easily broken. The life of every one is in his own hands and he can make it in character, in attainment, in power, in divine self-realization, and hence in influence, exactly what he wills to make it. All things that he most fondly dreams of are his, or may become so if he is truly in earnest; and as he rises more and more to his ideal, and grows in the strength and influence of his character, he becomes an example and an inspiration to all with whom he comes in contact; so that through him the weak and faltering are encouraged and strengthened; so that those of low ideals and of a low type of life instinctively and inevitably have their ideals raised, and the ideals of no one can be raised without its showing forth in his outer life. As he advances in his grasp upon and understanding of the power and potency of the thought-forces, he finds that many times through the process of mental suggestion he can be of tremendous aid to one who is weak and struggling, by sending to him now and then, and by continually holding him in the highest thought, in the thought of the highest strength, wisdom, and love.

The one who takes sufficient time in the quiet mentally to form his ideals, sufficient time to make and to keep continually his conscious connection with the Infinite, with the Divine life and forces, is the one who is best adapted to the strenuous life. He it is who can go out and deal with sagacity and power with whatever issues may arise in the affairs of everyday life. He it is who is building not for the years, but for the centuries; not for time, but for the eternities. And he can go out knowing not whither he goes, knowing that the Divine life within him will never fail him, but will lead him on until he beholds the Father face to face.

He is building for the centuries because only that which is the highest, the truest, the noblest, and best will abide the test of the centuries. He is building for eternity because when the transition we call death takes place, life, character, self-mastery, divine self-realization,—the only things that the soul when stripped of everything else takes with it,—he has in abundance. In life, or when the time of the transition to another form of life comes, he is never afraid, never fearful, because he knows and realizes that behind him, within him, beyond him, is the Infinite wisdom and love; and in this he is eternally centred, and from it he can never be separated. With Whittier he sings:

"I know not where His islands lift
Their fronded palms in air;
I only know I cannot drift
Beyond His love and care."

This Mystical Life Of Ours

I

The Fresh Beginning

When one awakes from sleep and so returns to conscious life, he is in a peculiarly receptive and impressionable state. All relations with the material world have for a time been shut off, the mind is in a freer and more natural state, resembling somewhat a sensitive plate, where impressions can readily leave their traces. This is why many times the highest and truest impressions come to one in the early morning hours, before the activities of the day and their attendant distractions have exerted an influence. This is one reason why many people can do their best work in the early hours of the day.

But this fact is also a most valuable one in connection with the moulding of every-day life. The mind is at this time as a clean sheet of paper. We can most valuably use this quiet, receptive, impressionable period by wisely directing the activities of the mind along the highest and most desirable paths, and thus, so to speak, set the pace for the day.

Each morning is a fresh beginning. We are, as it were, just beginning life. We have it *entirely* in our own hands. And when the morning with its fresh beginning comes, all yesterdays should be yesterdays, with which we have nothing to do. Sufficient is it to know that the way we lived our yesterday has determined for us our today. And, again, when the morning with its fresh beginning comes, all tomorrows should be tomorrows, with which we have nothing to do. Sufficient to know that the way we live our today determines our tomorrow.

"Every day is a fresh beginning,
Every morn is the world made new;
You who are weary of sorrow and sinning,
Here is a beautiful hope for you,
A hope for me and a hope for you.

"All the past things are past and over,
The tasks are done, and the tears are shed.
Yesterday's errors let yesterday cover;
Yesterday's wounds, which smarted and bled,
Are healed with the healing which night has shed.

* * * * * * * * * *

"Let them go, since we cannot relieve them,
Cannot undo and cannot atone.
God in His mercy receive, forgive them!
Only the new days are our own.
Today is ours, and today alone.

"Here are the skies all burnished brightly;
Here is the spent earth all reborn;
Here are the tired limbs springing lightly,
To face the sun and to share with the morn,
In the chrism of dew and the cool of dawn.

"Every day is a fresh beginning,
Listen, my soul, to the glad refrain,
And, spite of old sorrow and older sinning,
And puzzles forecasted, and possible pain,
Take heart with the day and begin again."

Simply the first hour of this new day, with all its richness and glory, with all its sublime and eternity-determining possibilities, and each succeeding hour as it comes, but *not before* it comes. This is the secret of character building. This simple method will bring anyone to the realization of the highest life that can be even conceived of, and there is nothing in this connection that can be conceived of that cannot be realized somehow, some-when, somewhere.

This brings such a life within the possibilities of *all*, for there is *no one*, if really in earnest and if he really desires it, who cannot live to his highest for a single hour. But even though there should be, if he is *only earnest in his endeavor*, then, through the law that like builds like, he will be able to come a little nearer to it the next hour, and still nearer the next, and the next, until sooner or later comes the time when it becomes the natural, and any other would require the effort.

In this way one becomes in love and in league with the highest and best in the universe, and as a consequence, the highest and best in the universe becomes in love and in league with him. They aid him at every turn; they seem literally to move all things his way, because, forsooth, he has first moved their way.

In Tune with the Infinite

II

The Supreme Fact Of Human Life

The great central fact in human life is the coming into a conscious, vital realization of our oneness with the Infinite Life, and the opening of ourselves fully to this divine inflow. "I and the Father are one," said the Master. In this we see how He recognized His oneness with the Father's life. Again He said, "The words that I speak unto you I speak not of myself: but the Father that dwelleth in me, He doeth the works." In this we see how clearly He recognized the fact that He of Himself could do nothing, only as He worked in conjunction with the Father. Again, "My Father works and I work." In other words, my Father sends the power, I open myself to it, and work in conjunction with it.

Again He said, "Seek ye first the kingdom of God and His righteousness, and all these things shall be added unto you." And He left us not in the dark as to exactly what He meant by this, for again He said, "Say not Lo here nor lo there; know ye not that the kingdom of heaven is within you?" According to his teaching the kingdom of God and the kingdom of heaven were one and the same. If, then, His teaching is that the kingdom of heaven is in us, do we not clearly see that, putting it in other words, His injunction is nothing more nor less than, Come ye into a conscious realization of your oneness with the Father's life. As you realize this oneness you find the kingdom, and when you find this, all things else shall follow.

* * * * * * * * * *

Again, the Master said, "Call no man your Father upon the earth: for one is your Father, which is in heaven." Here He recognized the fact that the real life is direct from the life of God. Our fathers and our mothers are the agents that give us the bodies, the houses in which we live, but the real life comes from the Infinite Source of Life, God, who is our Father.

One day word was brought to the Master that his mother and his brethren were without, wishing to speak with Him. "Who is my mother and who are my brethren?" said He. "Whosoever shall do the will of my Father which is in heaven, the same is my brother, and my sister, and mother."

Many people are greatly enslaved by what we term ties of re-lationship. It is well, however, for us to remember that our true relatives are not necessarily those who are connected with us by ties of blood. Our truest relatives are those who are nearest akin to us in mind, in soul, in spirit. Our nearest relatives may be those living on the opposite side of the globe,—people whom we may never have seen as yet, but to whom we will yet be drawn, either in this form of life or in another, through that ever working and never failing law of attraction.

When the Master gave the injunction, "Call no man your father upon the earth: for one is your Father, which is in heaven," He here gave us the basis for that grand conception of the fatherhood of God. And if God is equally the Father of all, then we have here the basis for the brotherhood of man. But there is, in a sense, a conception still higher than this, namely, the oneness of man and God, and hence the oneness of the whole human race. When we realize this fact, then we clearly see how in the degree that we come into the realization of our oneness with the Infinite Life, and so, every step that we make Godward, we aid in lifting all mankind up to this realization, and enable them, in turn, to make a step Godward.

The Master again pointed out our true relations with the Infinite Life when He said, "Except ye become as little children ye shall not enter into the kingdom of heaven." When He said, "Man shall not live by bread alone, but by every word that proceedeth out of the mouth of God," He gave utterance to a truth of far greater import than we have as yet commenced fully to grasp. Here He taught that even the physical life can not be maintained by material food alone, but that one's connection with this Infinite Source determines to a very great extent the condition of even the bodily structure and activities.

* * * * * * * * * *

Said the great Hindu sage, Manu, "He who in his own soul perceives the Supreme Soul in all beings, and acquires equanimity toward them all, attains the highest bliss." It was Athanasius who said, "Even we may become Gods walking about in the flesh. The same great truth we are considering is the one that runs through the life and the teachings of Guatama, who became the Buddha. People are in bondage, said he, because they have not yet removed the idea of *I*. To do away with all sense of separateness, and to recognize the oneness of the self with the Infinite, is the spirit that breathes through all his teachings.

* * * * * * * * * *

All the prophets, seers, sages, and saviours in the world's history became what they became, and consequently had the powers they had, through an entirely natural process. They all recognized and came into the conscious realization of their oneness with the Infinite Life. God is no respecter of persons. He doesn't create prophets, seers, sages, and saviours as such. He creates men. But here and there one recognizes his true identity, recognizes the oneness of his life with the Source whence it came. He lives in the realization of this oneness, and in turn becomes a prophet, seer, sage, or saviour.

In Tune with the Infinite

263

III

The Creative Power Of Thought

Of the vital power of thought and the interior forces in moulding conditions, and more, of the supremacy of thought over all conditions, the world has scarcely the faintest grasp, not to say even idea, as yet. The fact that thoughts are forces, and that through them *we have creative power*, is one of the most vital facts of the universe, the most vital fact of man's being. And through this instrumentality we have in our grasp and as our rightful heritage, the power of making life and all its manifold conditions exactly what we will.

Through our thought-forces we have creative power, not in a figurative sense, but in reality. Everything in the material universe about us had its origin first in spirit, in thought, and from this it took its form. The very world in which we live, with all its manifold wonders and sublime manifestations, is the result of the energies of the Divine Intelligence or Mind,—God, or whatever term it comes convenient for each one to use. And God said, Let there be, and there was,—the material world, at least the material manifestation of it, literally spoken into existence, the spoken word, however, but the outward manifestation of the interior forces of the Supreme Intelligence.

Every castle the world has ever seen was first an ideal in the architect's mind. Every statue was first an ideal in the sculptor's mind. Every piece of mechanism the world has ever known was first formed in the mind of the inventor. Here it was given birth to. These same mind-forces then dictated to and sent the energy into the hand that drew the model, and then again dictated to and sent the energy into the hands whereby the first instrument was clothed in the material form of metal or of wood. The lower negative always gives way to the higher when made positive. Mind is positive: matter is negative.

Each individual life is a part of, and hence is one with, the Infinite Life; and the highest intelligence and power belongs to each in just the degree that he recognizes his oneness and lays claim to and uses it. The power of the word is not merely an idle phrase or form of expression. It is a real mental, spiritual, scientific fact, and can become vital and powerful in your hands and in mine in just the degree that we understand the omnipotence of the thought forces and raise all to the higher planes.

The blind, the lame, the diseased, stood before Christ, who said, "receive thy sight, rise up and walk, or, be thou healed;" and lo! *it was so*. The spoken word, however, was but the outward expression and manifestation of His interior thought forces, the power and potency of which He so thoroughly knew. But the laws governing them are the same today as they were then, and it lies in our power to use them the same as it lay in His.

What All the World's A-Seeking

IV

The Drawing Power Of Mind

Each individual life, after it has reached a certain age or degree of intelligence, lives in the midst of the surroundings or environments of its own creation; and this by reason of that wonderful power, *the drawing power of mind*, which is continually operating in every life, whether it is conscious of it or not.

We are all living, so to speak, in a vast ocean of thought. The very atmosphere about us is charged with the thought-forces that are being continually sent out. When the thought-forces leave the brain, they go out upon the atmosphere, the subtle conducting ether, much the same as sound-waves go out. It is by virtue of this law that thought transference is possible, and has become an established scientific fact, by virtue of which a person can so direct his thought-forces that a person at a distance, and in a receptive attitude, can get the thought much the same as sound, for example, is conducted through the agency of a connecting medium.

Even though the thoughts as they leave a particular person, are not consciously directed, they go out; and all may be influenced by them in a greater or less degree, each one in proportion as he or she is more or less sensitively organized, or in proportion as he or she is negative, and so open to forces and influences from without. The law operating here is one with that great law of the universe,—that like attracts like, so that one continually attracts to himself forces and influences most akin to those of his own life. And his own life is determined by the thoughts and emotions he habitually entertains, for each is building his world from within.

266

As within, so without; cause, effect.

A stalk of wheat and a stalk of corn are growing side by side, within an inch of each other. The soil is the same for both; but the wheat converts the food it takes from the soil into wheat, the likeness of itself, while the corn converts the food it takes from the same soil into corn, the likeness of itself. What that which each has taken from the soil is converted into is determined by the soul, the interior life, the interior forces of each. This same grain taken as food by two persons will be converted into the body of a criminal in the one case, and into the body of a saint in the other, each after its kind; and its kind is determined by the inner life of each. And what again determines the inner life of each? The thoughts and emotions that are habitually entertained and that inevitably, sooner or later, manifest themselves in outer material form. Thought is the great builder in human life: it is the determining factor. Continually think thoughts that are good, and your life will show forth in goodness, and your body in health and beauty. Continually think evil and your life will show forth in evil, and your body in weakness and repulsiveness. Think thoughts of love, and you will love and will be loved. Think thoughts of hatred, and you will hate and will be hated. Each follows its kind.

What All the World's A-Seeking

V

Creating One's Own Atmosphere

It is by virtue of this law that each person creates his own "atmosphere"; and this atmosphere is determined by the character of the thoughts he habitually entertains. It is, in fact, simply his thought atmosphere—the atmosphere which other people detect and are influenced by.

In this way each person creates the atmosphere of his own room; a family, the atmosphere of the house in which they live, so that the moment you enter the door you feel influences kindred to the thoughts and hence to the lives of those who dwell there. You get a feeling of peace and harmony or a feeling of disquietude and inharmony. You get a welcome, want-to-stay feeling or a cold, want-to-get-away feeling, according to their thought attitude toward you, even though but few words be spoken. So the characteristic mental states of a congregation of people who assemble there determine the atmosphere of any given assembly-place, church, or cathedral. Its inhabitants so make, so determine the atmosphere of a particular village or city. The sympathetic thoughts sent out by a vast amphitheatre of people, as they cheer a contestant, carry him to goals he never could reach by his own efforts alone. The same is true in regard to an orator and his audience.

Napoleon's army is in the East. The plague is beginning to make inroads into its ranks. Long lines of men are lying on cots and on the ground in an open space adjoining the army. Fear has taken a vital hold of all, and the men are continually being stricken. Look yonder: contrary to the earnest entreaties of his officers, who tell him that such exposure will mean sure death, Napoleon with a calm and dauntless look upon his face, with a firm and defiant step, is coming through these plague stricken ranks. He is going up to, talking with, touching the men; and, as they see him, there goes up a mighty shout,—The Emperor! the Emperor!, and from that hour the plague in its inroads is stopped. A marvellous example of the power of a man who, by his own dauntless courage, absolute fearlessness, and power of mind, could send out such forces that they in turn awakened kindred forces in the minds of thousands of others, which in turn dominate their very bodies, so that the plague, and even death itself, is driven from the field. One of the grandest examples of a man of the most mighty and tremendous mind and will power, and at the same time an example of one of the grandest failures, taking life in its totality, the world has ever seen.

*   *   *   *   *   *   *   *   *   *

We are all much more influenced by the thought-forces and mental states of those around us and of the world at large than we have even the slightest conception of. If not self-hypnotized into certain beliefs and practices, we are, so to speak, semi-hypnotized through the influence of the thoughts of others, even though unconsciously both on their part and on ours. We are so influenced and enslaved in just the degree that we fail to recognize the power and omnipotence of our own forces, and so become slaves to custom, conventionality, the opinions of others, and so in like proportion lose our own individuality and powers.

*   *   *   *   *   *   *   *   *   *

Each is building his world from within, and, if outside forces play, it is because he allows them to play; and he has it in his own power to determine whether these shall be positive, uplifting, ennobling, strengthening, success-giving, or negative, degrading,

269

weakening, failure-bringing.

What All the World's A-Seeking

VI

The Law Of Attraction Works Unceasingly

If one hold himself in the thought of poverty, he will be poor, and the chances are that he will remain in poverty. If he hold himself, whatever present conditions may be, continually in the thought of prosperity, he sets into operation forces that will sooner or later bring him into prosperous conditions. The law of attraction works unceasingly throughout the universe, and the one great and never changing fact in connection with it is, as we have found, that like attracts like. If we are one with this Infinite Power, this source of all things, then in the degree that we live in the realization of this oneness, in that degree do we actualize in our selves a power that will bring to us an abundance of all things that it is desirable for us to have. In this way we come into possession of a power where by we can actualize at all times those conditions that we desire.

As all truth exists now, and awaits simply our perception of it, so all things necessary for present needs exist now, and await simply the power in us to appropriate them. God holds all things in His hands. His constant word is, My child, acknowledge me in all your ways, and in the degree that you do this, in the degree that you live this, then what is mine is yours. Jehovah-jireh,—the Lord will provide. "He giveth to all men liberally and upbraideth not." He giveth liberally to all men who put themselves in the right attitude to receive from Him. He forces no good things upon anyone.

The old and somewhat prevalent idea of godliness and poverty

271

has absolutely no basis for its existence, and the sooner we get away from it the better. It had its birth in the same way that the idea of asceticism came into existence, when the idea prevailed that there was necessarily a warfare between the flesh and the spirit. It had its origin therefore in the minds of those who had a distorted, a one-sided view of life. True godliness is in a sense the same as true wisdom. The one who is truly wise, and who uses the forces and powers with which he is endowed, to him the great universe always opens her treasure house.

* * * * * * * * * *

Are you out of a situation? Let the fear that you will not get another take hold of and dominate you, and the chances are that it may be a long time before you will get another, or the one that you do get may be a very poor one indeed. Whatever the circumstances, you must realize that you have within you forces and powers that you can set into operation that will triumph over any and all apparent or temporary losses. Set these forces into operation and you will then be placing a magnet that will draw to you a situation that may be far better than the one you have lost, and the time may soon come when you will be even thankful that you lost the old one.

Recognize, working in and through you, the same Infinite Power that creates and governs all things in the universe, the same Infinite Power that governs the endless systems of worlds in space. Send out your thought,—thought is a force, and it has occult power of unknown proportions when rightly used and wisely directed,— send out your thought that the right situation or the right work will come to you at the right time, in the right way, and that you will recognize it when it comes. Hold to this thought, never allow it to weaken, hold to it, and continually water it with firm expectation. You in this way put your advertisement into a psychical, a spiritual newspaper, a paper that has not a limited circulation, but one that will make its way not only to the utmost bounds of the earth, but of the very universe itself. It is an advertisement, moreover, which if rightly placed on your part, will be far more effective than any advertisement you could possibly put into any printed sheet, no matter what claims are made in regard to its being "the great advertising medium." In the degree that you come into this realization and live in harmony with the higher laws and forces, in that degree will you be able to do this effectively.

If you wish to look through the "want" columns of the newspapers, then do it, but not in the ordinary way. Put the higher forces into operation and thus place it on a higher basis.

* * * * * * * * * *

If you get the situation and it does not prove to be exactly what you want, if you feel that you are capable of filling a better one, then the moment you enter upon it take the attitude of mind that this situation is the stepping-stone that will lead you to one that will be still better. Hold this thought steadily, affirm it, believe it, expect it, and all the time be faithful, *absolutely faithful* to the situation in which you are at present placed. If you are not faithful to it then the chances are that it will not be the stepping-stone to something better, but to something poorer. If you are faithful to it, the time may soon come when you will be glad and thankful, when you will rejoice, that you lost your old position.

In Tune with the Infinite

VII

The Law Of Prosperity

This is the law of prosperity: When apparent adversity comes, be not cast down by it, but make the best of it, and always look forward for better things, for conditions more prosperous. To hold yourself in this attitude of mind is to set into operation subtle, silent, and irresistible forces that sooner or later will actualize in material form that which is today merely an idea. But ideas have mystical power, and ideas, when rightly planted and rightly tended, are the seeds that actualize material conditions.

Never give a moment to complaint, but utilize the time that would otherwise be spent in this way in looking forward and actualizing the conditions you desire. Suggest prosperity to yourself. See yourself in a prosperous condition. Affirm that you will before long be in a prosperous condition. Affirm it calmly and quietly, but strongly and confidently. Believe it, believe it absolutely. Expect it,—keep it continually watered with expectation. You thus make yourself a magnet to attract the things that you desire. Don't be afraid to suggest, to affirm these things, for by so doing you put forth an ideal which will begin to clothe itself in material form. In this way you are utilizing agents among the most subtle and powerful in the universe. If you are particularly desirous for anything that you feel it is good and right for you to have, something that will broaden your life or that will increase your usefulness to others, simply hold the thought that at the right time, in the right way, and through the right instrumentality, there will come to you or there will open up for you the way whereby you can attain what you desire.

*   *   *   *   *   *   *   *   *   *

Don't fold your hands and expect to see things drop into your lap, but set into operation the higher forces and then take hold of the first thing that offers itself. Do what your hands find to do, *and do it well.* If this work is not thoroughly satisfactory to you, then affirm, believe, and expect that it is the agency that will lead you to something better. "The basis for attracting the best of all the world can give to you is to first surround, own, and live in these things in mind, or what is falsely called imagination. All so-called imaginings are realities and forces of unseen element. Live in mind in a palace and gradually palatial surroundings will gravitate to you. But so living is *not* pining, or longing, or complainingly wishing. It is when you are 'down in the world,' calmly and persistently seeing yourself as up. It is when you are now compelled to eat from a tin plate, regarding that tin plate as only the certain step to one of silver. It is not envying and growling at other people who have silver plate. That growling is just so much capital stock taken from the bank account of mental force."

A friend who knows the power of the interior forces, and whose life is guided in every detail by them, has given a suggestion in this form: When you are in the arms of the bear, even though he is hugging you, look him in the face and laugh, but all the time keep your eye on the bull. If you allow all of your attention to be given to the work of the bear, the bull may get entirely out of your sight. In other words, if you yield to adversity the chances are that it will master you, but if you recognize in yourself the power of mastery over conditions then adversity will yield to you, and will be changed into prosperity. If when it comes you calmly and quietly recognize it, and use the time that might otherwise be spent in regrets, and fears, and forebodings, in setting into operation the powerful forces within you, it will soon take its leave.

Faith, absolute dogmatic faith, is the only law of true success. When we recognize the fact that a an carries his success or his failure with him, and that it does not depend upon outside conditions, we will come into the possession of powers that will quickly change outside conditions into agencies that make for success. When we come into this higher realization and bring our lives into complete harmony with the higher laws, we will then be able so to focus and direct the awakened interior forces, that they will go out and return laden with that for which they are sent. We will then be great enough to attract success, and it will not always be apparently just a little ways ahead. We can then establish in ourselves a centre so strong that instead of running hither and thither for this or that, we can stay at home and draw to us the conditions we desire. If we firmly establish and hold to this centre, things will seem continually to come our way.

* * * * * * * * * *

In Tune with the Infinite

VIII

The Law Of Habit-forming

Have we it within our power to determine at all times what types of habits shall take form in our lives? In other words, is habit-forming, character-building, a matter of mere chance, or have we it within our own control? We have, entirely and absolutely.

* * * * * * * * * *

For there is a simple, natural, and thoroughly scientific method that all should know. A method whereby old, undesirable, earth-binding habits can be broken, and new, desirable, heaven-lifting habits can be acquired,—a method whereby life in part or in its totality can be changed, provided one is sufficiently in earnest to know, and, knowing it, to apply the law.

Thought is the force underlying all. And what do we mean by this? Simply this: Your every act—every conscious act—is preceded by a thought. Your dominating thoughts determine your dominating actions. The acts repeated crystallize themselves into the habit. The aggregate of your habits is your character. Whatever, then, you would have your acts, you must look well to the character of the thought you entertain. Whatever act you would not do,—habit you would not acquire you must look well to it that you do not entertain the type of thought that will give birth to this act, this habit.

It is a simple psychological law that any type of thought, if entertained for a sufficient length of time, will, by and by, reach the motor tracks of the brain, and finally burst forth into action.

Murder can be and many times is committed in this way, the same as all undesirable things are done. On the other hand, the greatest powers are grown, the most God-like characteristics are engendered, the most heroic acts are performed in the same way.

The thing clearly to understand is this: That the thought is always parent to the act. Now, we have it entirely in our own hands to determine exactly what thoughts we entertain. In the realm of our own minds we have absolute control, or we should have, and if at any time we have not, then there is a method by which we can gain control, and in the realm of the mind become thorough masters.

*   *   *   *   *   *   *   *   *   *

Here let us refer to that law of the mind which is the same as is the law in connection with the reflex nerve system of the body, the law which says that whenever one does a certain thing in a certain way it is easier to do the same thing in the same way the next time, and still easier the next, and the next, and the next, until in time it comes to pass that no effort is required, or no effort worth speaking of; but on the contrary, to do the opposite would require the effort. The mind carries with it the power that perpetuates its own type of thought, the same as the body carries with it through the reflex nerve system the power which perpetuates and makes continually easier its own particular acts. Thus a simple effort to control one's thoughts, a simple setting about it, even if at first failure is the result, and even if for a time failure seems to be about the only result, will in time, sooner or later, bring him to the point of easy, full, and complete control.

Each one, then, can grow the power of determining, controlling his thought, the power of determining what types of thought he shall and what types he shall not entertain. For let us never part in mind with this fact, that every earnest *effort* along any line makes the end aimed at just a little easier for each succeeding effort, even if, as has been said, apparent failure is the result of the earlier efforts. This is a case where even failure is success, for the failure is not in the effort, and every earnest effort adds an increment of power that will eventually accomplish the end aimed at.

Character-Building Thought Power

IX

Actualizing One's Ideals

There is nothing more true in connection with human life than that we grow into the likeness of those things we contemplate. Literally and scientifically and necessarily true is it that, "as a man thinketh in his heart, so *is* he." The "is" part is his character. His character is the sum total of his habits. His habits have been formed by his conscious acts; but every conscious act is, as we have found, preceded by a thought. And so we have it—thought on the one hand, character, life, destiny on the other. And simple it becomes when we bear in mind that it is simply the thought of the present moment, and the next moment when it is upon us, and then the next, and so on through all time.

One can in this way attain to whatever ideals he would attain to. Two steps are necessary: first, as the days pass, to form one's ideals; and second, to follow them continually whatever may arise, wherever they may lead him. Always remember that the great and strong character is the one who is ever ready to sacrifice the present pleasure for the future good. He who will thus follow his highest ideals as they present themselves to him day after day, year after year, will find that as Dante, following his beloved from world to world, finally found her at the gates of Paradise, so he will find himself eventually at the same gates. Life is not, we may say, for mere passing pleasure, but for the highest unfoldment that one can attain to, the noblest character that one can grow, and for the greatest service that one can render to all mankind. In this, however, we will find the highest pleasure, for in this the only real pleasure lies.

* * * * * * * * * *

The question is not, What are the conditions in our lives? but, How do we meet the conditions that we find there? And whatever the conditions are, it is unwise and profitless to look upon them, even if they are conditions that we would have otherwise, in the attitude of complaint, for complaint will bring depression, and depression will weaken and possibly even kill the spirit that would engender the power that would enable us to bring into our lives an entirely new set of conditions.

* * * * * * * * * *

Each one is so apt to think that his own conditions, his own trials or troubles or sorrows, or his own struggles, as the case may be, are greater than those of the great mass of mankind, or possibly greater than those of any one else in the world. He forgets that each one has his own peculiar trials or troubles or sorrows to bear, or struggles in habits to overcome, and that his is but the common lot of all the human race. We are apt to make the mistake in this— in that we see and feel keenly our own trials, or adverse conditions, or characteristics to be overcome, while those of others we do not see so clearly, and hence we are apt to think that they are not at all equal to our own. Each has his own problems to work out. Each must work out his own problems. Each must grow the insight that will enable him to see what the causes are that have brought the unfavorable conditions into his life; each must grow the strength that will enable him to face these conditions, and to set into operation forces that will bring about a different set of conditions. We may be of aid to one another by way of suggestion, by way of bringing to one another a knowledge of certain higher laws and forces,—laws and forces that will make it easier to do that which we would do. The doing, however, must be done by each one for himself.

Character-Building Thought Power

X

Faith And Prayer—Their Nature

What, shall we ask, is the place, what the value, of prayer? Prayer, as every act of devotion, brings us into an ever greater conscious harmony with the Infinite, the one pearl of great price; for it is this harmony which brings all other things.

Prayer is the soul's sincere desire and thus is its own answer, as the sincere desire made active and accompanied by faith sooner or later gives place to realization; *for faith is an invisible and invincible magnet, and attracts to itself whatever it fervently desires and calmly and persistently expects.* This is absolute, and the results will be absolute in exact proportion as this operation of the thought forces, as this faith is absolute, and relative in exact proportion as it is relative.

The Master said, "What things soever ye desire, when ye pray, *believe* that ye receive them and ye shall have them." Can any law be more clearly enunciated, can anything be more definite and more absolute than this? According to thy faith be it unto thee. Do we at times fail in obtaining the results we desire? The fault, the failure, lies not in the law but in ourselves. Regarded in its right and true light, than prayer there is nothing more scientific, nothing more valuable, nothing more effective.

This conscious realization of oneness with the Infinite Life is of all things the one thing to be desired; for, when this oneness is realized and lived in, all other things follow in its train, there are no desires that shall not be realized, for God has planted in the human breast no desire without its corresponding means of realization. No harm can come nigh, nothing can touch us, there will be nothing to fear; for we shall thus attract only the good. And whatever changes time may bring, understanding the law, we shall always expect something better, and thus, set into operation the forces that will attract that something, realizing that many times angels go out that archangels.may enter in; and this is always true in the case of the life of this higher realization. And why should we have any fear whatever,—fear even for the nation as is many times expressed? God is behind His world, in love and with infinite care and watchfulness working out His great and almighty plans; and whatever plans men may devise, He will when the time is ripe either frustrate and shatter, or aid and push through to their most perfect culmination,—frustrate and shatter if contrary to, aid and actualize if in harmony with His.

* * * * * * * * * *

These facts, the facts relating to the powers that come with the higher awakening, have been dealt with somewhat fully, to show that the matters along the lines of man's interior, intuitive, spiritual, thought, soul life, instead of being, as they are so many times regarded, merely indefinite, sentimental, or impractical, are, on the contrary, powerfully, omnipotently real, and are of all practical things in the world the most practical, and, in the truest and deepest sense, the only truly practical things there are. And pre-eminently is this true when we look with a long range of vision, past the mere today, to the final outcome, to the time when that transition we are accustomed to call death takes place, and all accumulations and possessions material are left behind, and the soul takes with it only the unfoldment and growth of the real life; and unless it has this, when all else must be left behind, it goes out poor indeed. And a most wonderful and beautiful fact of it all is this: that all growth, all advancement, all attainment made along the lines of the spiritual, the soul, the real life, is so much made forever, and can never be lost.

What All the World's A-Seeking

XI

The Petty Personal And The Larger Universal

When the step from the personal to the impersonal, from the personal, the individual, to the universal, is once made, the great solution of life has come; and by this same step one enters at once into the realm of all power. When this is done, and one fully realizes the fact that the greatest life is the life spent in the service of all mankind, and then when he vitally grasps that great eternal principle of right, of truth, of justice, that runs through all the universe, and which, though temporarily it may seem to be perverted, always and with never an exception eventually prevails, and that with an omnipotent power,—he then holds the key to all situations.

A king of this nature goes about his work absolutely regardless of what men may say or hear or think or do; for he himself has absolutely nothing to gain or nothing to lose, and nothing of this nature can come near him or touch him, for he is standing not in the personal, but in the universal. He is then in God's work, and the very God-powers are his, and it seems as if the very angels of heaven come to minister unto him and to move things his way; and this is true, very true, for he himself is simply moving God's way, and when this is so, the certainty of the outcome is absolute.

How often did the Master say, "I seek not to do mine own will, but the will of the Father who sent me"! Here is the world's great example of the life out of the personal and in the universal, hence

His great power. The same has been true of all the saviours, the prophets, the seers, the sages, and the leaders in the world's history, of all of truly great and lasting power.

He who would then come into the secret of power must come from the personal into the universal, and with this comes not only great power, but also freedom from the vexations and perplexities that rise from the misconstruing of motives, the opinions of others; for such a one cares nothing as to what men may say, or hear, or think, or do, so long as he is true to the great principles of right and truth before him. And, if we will search carefully, we shall find that practically all the perplexities and difficulties of life have their origin on the side of the personal.

Much is said to young men today about success in life—success generally though, as the world calls success. It is well, however, always to bear in mind the fact that there is a success which is a miserable, a deplorable failure; while, on the other hand, there is a failure which is a grand, a noble, a God-like success. And one crying need of the age is that young men be taught the true dignity, nobility, and power of such a failure,—such a failure in the eyes of the world today, but such a success in the eyes of God and the coming ages. When this is done, there will be among us more prophets, more saviours, more men of grand and noble stature, who with a firm and steady hand will hold the lighted torch of true advancement high up among the people; and they will be those whom the people will gladly follow, for they will be those who will speak and move with authority, true sons of God, true brothers of men. A man may make his millions and his life be a failure still.

What All the World's A-Seeking

XII

The Poem Hangs On The Berry-Bush

To live undisturbed by passing occurrences you must first find your own centre. You must then be firm in your own centre, and so rule the world from within. He who does not himself condition circumstances allows the process to be reversed, and becomes a conditioned circumstance. Find your centre and live in it. Surrender it to no person, to no thing. In the degree that you do this will you find yourself growing stronger and stronger in it. And how can one find his centre? By realizing his oneness with the Infinite Power, and by living continually in this realization.

But if you do not rule from your own centre, if you invest this or that with the power of bringing you annoyance, or evil, or harm, then take what it brings, but cease your railings against the eternal goodness and beneficence of all things.

> "I swear the earth shall surely be complete,
> To him or her who shall be complete;
> The earth remains jagged and broken,
> Only to him who remains jagged and broken."

If the windows of your soul are dirty and streaked, covered with matter foreign to them, then the world as you look out of them will be to you dirty and streaked and out of order. Cease your complainings, however; keep your pessimism, your "poor, unfortunate me" to yourself, lest you betray the fact that your windows are badly in need of something. But know that your friend, who keeps his windows clean, that the Eternal Sun may illumine all within and make visible all without,— know that he lives in a different world from yours.

Then, go wash your windows, and instead of longing for some other world, you will discover the wonderful beauties of this world; and if you don't find transcendent beauties on every hand here, the chances are that: you will never find them anywhere.

> "The poem hangs on the berry-bush,
> When comes the poet's eye,
> And the whole street is a masquerade,
> When Shakespeare passes by."

This same Shakespeare, whose mere passing causes all this commotion, is the one who put into the mouth of one of his creations the words: "The fault, dear Brutus, is not in our stars, but in ourselves, that we are underlings." And the great work of his own life is right good evidence that he realized full well the truth of the facts we are considering. And again he gave us a great truth in keeping with what we are considering when he said:

> "Our doubts are traitors,
> And make us lose the good we oft might win,
> By *fearing* to attempt."

There is probably no agent that brings us more undesirable conditions than fear. We should live in fear of nothing, nor will we when we come fully to know ourselves. An old French proverb runs:

> "Some of your griefs you have cured,
> And the sharpest you still have survived;
> But what *torments of pain* you endured,
> From evils that never arrived."

Fear and lack of faith go hand in hand. The one is born of the other. Tell me how much one is given to fear, and I will tell you how much he lacks in faith. Fear is a most expensive guest to entertain, the same as worry is: so expensive are they that no one can afford to entertain them. *We invite what we fear, the same as, by a different attitude of mind, we invite and attract the influences and conditions we desire.* The mind dominated by fear opens the door for the entrance of the very things, for the actualization of the very conditions it fears.

"Where are you going? " asked an Eastern pilgrim on meeting the plague one day. "I am going to Bagdad to kill five thousand people," was the reply. A few days later the same pilgrim met the plague returning. "You told me you were going to Bagdad to kill five thousand people," said he, "but instead, you killed fifty thousand." "No," said the plague, "*I killed only five thousand,* as I told you I would; *the others died of fright.*

Fear can paralyze every muscle in the body. Fear affects the flow of the blood, likewise the normal and healthy action of all the life forces. Fear can make the body rigid, motionless, and powerless to move.

In Tune with the Infinite

XIII

The Influence Of Our Prevailing Mental States Upon Others

Not only do we attract to ourselves the things we fear, but we also aid in attracting to others the conditions we in our own minds hold them in fear of. This we do in proportion to the strength of our own thought, and in the degree that they are sensitively organized and so influenced by our thought, and this, although it be unconscious both on their part and on ours.

Children, and especially when very young, are, generally speaking, more sensitive to their surrounding influences than grown people are. Some are veritable little sensitive plates, registering the influences about them, and embodying them as they grow. How careful in their prevailing mental states then should be those who have them in charge, and especially how careful should a mother be during the time she is carrying the child, and when every thought, every mental as well as emotional state has its direct influence upon the life of the unborn child. Let parents be careful how they hold a child, either younger or older, in the thought of fear. This is many times done, unwittingly on their part, through anxiety, and at times through what might well be termed over-care, which is fully as bad as under-care.

I know of a number of cases where a child has been so continually held in the thought of fear lest this or that condition come upon him, that the very things that were feared have been drawn to him, which probably otherwise never would have come at all.

Many times there has been no adequate basis for the fear. In case there is a basis, then far wiser is it to take exactly the opposite attitude, so as to neutralize the force at work, and then to hold the child in the thought of wisdom and strength that it may be able to meet the condition and master it, instead of being mastered by it.

But a day or two ago a friend was telling me of an experience of his own life in this connection. At a period when he was having a terrific struggle with a certain habit, he was so continually held in the thought of fear by his mother and the young lady to whom he was engaged,—the engagement to be consummated at the end of a certain period, the time depending on his proving his mastery,—that he, very sensitively organized, *continually* felt the depressing and weakening effects of their negative thoughts. He could always tell exactly how they felt toward him; he was continually influenced and weakened by their fear, by their questionings, by their suspicions, all of which had the effect of lessening the sense of his own power, all of which had an endeavor-paralyzing influence upon him.

And so instead of their begetting courage and strength in him, they brought him to a still greater realization of his own weakness and the almost worthless use of struggle.

Here were two who loved him dearly, and who would have done anything and everything to help him gain the mastery, but who, ignorant of the silent, subtle, ever-working and all-telling power of the thought forces, instead of imparting to him courage, instead of adding to his strength, disarmed him of this, and then added an additional weakness from without. In this way the battle for him was made harder in a three-fold degree.

Fear and worry and all kindred mental states are too expensive for any person, man, woman, or child, to entertain or indulge in. Fear paralyzes healthy action, worry corrodes and pulls down the organism, and will finally tear it to pieces. Nothing is to be gained by it, but everything to be lost. Long-continued grief at any loss will do the same. Each brings its own peculiar type of ailment. An inordinate love of gain, a close-fisted, hoarding disposition will have kindred effects. Anger, jealousy, malice, continual fault-finding, lust, has each its own peculiar corroding, weakening, tearing down effects.

We shall find that not only are happiness and prosperity con-comitants of righteousness,—living in harmony with the higher laws, but bodily health as well. The great Hebrew seer enunciated a wonderful chemistry of life when he said,—"As righteousness tendeth to life, so he that pursueth evil, pursueth it to his own death." On the other hand, "In the way of righteousness is life; and in the pathway thereof there is no death." The time will come when it will be seen that this means far more than most people dare *even to think as yet*. "It rests with man to say whether his soul shall be housed in a stately mansion of ever-growing splendor and beauty, or in a hovel of his own building,—a hovel at last ruined and abandoned to decay."

The bodies of almost untold numbers, living their one-sided, unbalanced lives, are every year, through these influences, weak-ening and falling by the wayside long before their time. Poor, poor houses! Intended to be beautiful temples, brought to desolation by their ignorant, reckless, deluded tenants. Poor houses!

In Tune with the Infinite

XIV

Saviours One Of Another

And in the same sense we are all the saviours one of another, or may become so. A sudden emergency arises, and I stand faltering and weak with fear. My friend beside me is strong and fearless. He sees the emergency. He summons up all the latent powers within him, and springs forth to meet it. This sublime example arouses me, calls my latent powers into activity, when but for him I might not have known them there. I follow his example. I now know my powers, and know them forever after. Thus, in this, my friend has become my saviour.

I am weak in some point of character,—vacillating, yielding, stumbling, falling, continually eating the bitter fruit of it all. My friend is strong, he has gained thorough self-mastery. The majesty and beauty of power are upon his brow. I see his example, I love his life, I am influenced by his power. My soul longs and cries out for the same. A supreme effort of will—that imperial master that will take one anywhere when rightly directed—arises within me, it is born at last, and it calls all the soul's latent powers into activity: and instead of stumbling I stand firm, instead of giving over in weakness I stand firm and master, I enter into the joys of full self-mastery, and through this into the mastery of all things besides. And thus my friend has again become my saviour.

With the new power I have acquired through the example and influence of my saviour-friend, I, in turn, stand before a friend who is struggling, who is stumbling and in despair. He sees, he feels, the power of my strength. He longs for, his soul cries out for the same. *His* interior forces are called into activity, he now knows his powers; and instead of the slave, he becomes the master, and thus I, in turn, have become his saviour. Oh, the wonderful sense of sublimity, the mighty feelings of responsibility, the deep sense of power and peace the recognition of this fact should bring to each and all.

God works through the instrumentality of human agency. Then forever away with that old, shrivelling, weakening, dying, and devilish idea that we are poor worms of the dust! We may or we may not be: it all depends upon the self. The moment we believe we are we become such; and as long as we hold to the belief we will be held to this identity, and will act and live as such. The moment, however, we recognize our divinity, our higher, our God-selves, and the fact that we are the saviours of our fellow-men, we become saviours, and stand and move in the midst of a majesty and beauty and power that of itself proclaims us as such.

There is a prevalent idea to the effect that overcoming in this sense necessarily implies more or less of a giving up,—that it means something possibly on the order of asceticism. On the contrary, the highest, truest, keenest pleasures the human soul can know, it finds only after the higher is entered upon and has commenced its work of mastery; and, instead of there being a giving up of any kind, there is a great law which says that the lower always and of its own accord falls away before the higher.

What All the World's A-Seeking

XV

Not Repression, But Self-Mastery

From what has been said let it not he inferred that the body, the physical, material life is to be despised or looked down upon. This, rather let it be said, is one of the crying errors of the times, and prolific of a *vast* amount of error, suffering, and shame. On the contrary, it should be thought all the more highly of: it should be loved and developed to its highest perfections, beauties, and powers. God gave us the body not in vain. It is just as holy and beautiful as the spirit itself. It is merely the outward material manifestation of the individualized spirit; and we by our hourly thoughts and emotions are building it, are determining its conditions, its structure, and appearance.

* * * * * * * * * *

Every part, every organ, every function of the body is just as clean, just as beautiful, just as sweet, and just as holy as every other part; and it is only by virtue of man's perverted ways of looking at some that they become otherwise, and the moment they so become, abuses, ill uses, suffering, and shame creep in.

Not repression, but elevation. Would that this could be repeated a thousand times over! Not repression, but elevation. Every part, every organ, every function of the body is given for *use*, but not for misuse or abuse; and the moment the latter takes place in connection with any function it loses its higher powers of use, and there goes with this the higher powers of true enjoyment.

* * * * * * * * * *

No, a knowledge of the spiritual realities of life prohibits asceticism, repression, the same as it prohibits license and perverted use. To err on the one side is just as contrary to the ideal life as to err on the other. All things are for a purpose, all should be used and enjoyed; but all should be rightly used, that they may be fully enjoyed.

It is the threefold life and development that is wanted,—physical, mental, spiritual. This gives the rounded life, and he or she who fails in any one comes short of the perfect whole. The physical has its uses just the same and is just as important as the others. The great secret of the highly successful life is, however, to infuse the mental and the physical with the spiritual; in other words, to spiritualize all, and so raise all to the highest possibilities and powers.

It is the all-around, fully developed we want,—not the ethereal, pale-blooded man and woman, but the man and woman of flesh and blood, for action and service here and now,—the man and woman strong and powerful, with all the faculties and functions fully unfolded and used, all in a royal and bounding condition, but all rightly subordinated. The man and the woman of this kind, with the imperial hand of mastery upon all,—standing, moving thus like a king, nay, like a very God,—such is the man and such is the woman of power. Such is the ideal life: anything else is one-sided, and falls short of it.

* * * * * * * * * *

What All the World's A-Seeking

XVI

Thoughts Are Forces

Thought is at the bottom of all progress or retrogression, of all success or failure, of all that is desirable or undesirable in human life. The type of thought we entertain both creates and draws conditions that crystallize about it, conditions exactly the same in nature as is the thought that gives them form. Thoughts are forces, and each creates of its kind, whether we realize it or not. The great law of the drawing power of the mind, which says that like creates like, and that like attracts like, is continually working in every human life, for it is one of the great immutable laws of the universe. For one to take time to see clearly the things he would attain to, and then to hold that ideal steadily and continually before his mind, never allowing faith—his positive thought-forces—to give way to or to be neutralized by doubts and fears, and then to set about doing each day what his hands find to do, never complaining, but spending the time that he would otherwise spend in complaint in focusing his thought-forces upon the ideal that his mind has built, will sooner or later bring about the full materialization of that for which he sets out.

There are those who, when they begin to grasp the fact that there is what we may term a "science of thought," who, when they begin to realize that through the instrumentality of our interior, spiritual thought-forces we have the power of gradually moulding the everyday conditions of life as we would have them, in their early enthusiasm are not able to see results as quickly as they expect, and are apt to think, therefore, that after all there is not very much in that which has but newly come to their knowledge. They must remember, however, that in endeavoring to overcome an old or to grow a new habit, everything cannot be done *all at once.*

In the degree that we attempt to use the thought-forces do we continually become able to use them more effectively. Progress is slow at first, more rapid as we proceed. Power grows by using, or, in other words, using brings a continually increasing power. This is governed by law the same as are all things in our lives, and all things in the universe about us. Every act and advancement made by the musician is in full accordance with law. No one commencing the study of music can, for example, sit down to the piano and play the piece of a master at the first effort. He must not conclude, however, nor does he conclude, that the piece of the master *cannot be* played by him, or, for that matter, by anyone. He begins to practice the piece. The law of the mind that we have already noticed comes to his aid, whereby his mind follows the music more readily, more rapidly, and more surely each succeeding time, and there also comes into operation and to his aid the law underlying the action of the reflex nerve system of the body, which we have also noticed, whereby his fingers coordinate their movements with the movements of his mind, more readily, more rapidly, and more accurately each succeeding time; until by and by the time comes when that which he stumbles through at first, that in which there is no harmony, nothing but discord, finally reveals itself as the music of the master, the music that thrills and moves masses of men and women. So it is in the use of the thought-forces. It is the reiteration, the constant reiteration of the thought that grows the power of continually stronger thought-focusing, and that finally brings manifestation.

Character-Building Thought Power

XVII

All Life From Within

All life is from within out. This is something that cannot be reiterated too often. The springs of life are all from within. This being true, it would be well for us to give more time to the inner life than we are accustomed to give to it, especially in this Western World.

There is nothing that will bring us such abundant returns as to take a little time in the quiet each day of our lives. We need this to get the kinks out of our minds and hence out of our lives. We need this to form better the higher ideals of life. We need this in order to see clearly in mind the things upon which we would concentrate and focus the thought-forces. We need this in order to make continually anew and to keep our conscious connection with the Infinite. We need this in order that the rush and hurry of our everyday life does not keep us away from the conscious realization of the fact that the spirit of Infinite life and power that is back of all, working in and through all, the life of all, is the life of our life, and the source of our power; and that outside of this we have no life and we have no power. To realize this fact fully, and to live in it consciously at all times, is to find the kingdom of God, which is essentially an inner kingdom, and can never be anything else. The kingdom of heaven is to be found only within, and is done once for all, and in a manner in which it cannot otherwise be done, when we come into the conscious, living realization of the fact that in our real selves we are essentially one with the Divine life, and open ourselves continually so that this Divine life can speak to and manifest through us. In this way we come into the condition where we are continually walking with God. In this way the consciousness of God becomes a living reality in our lives; and in the degree in which it becomes a reality does it bring us into the realization of continually increasing wisdom, insight, and power. *This consciousness of God in the soul of man is the essence, indeed the sum and substance of all religion.* This identifies religion with every act and every moment of everyday life. That which does not identify itself with every moment of every day and with every act of life is religion in name only and not in reality.

*   *   *   *   *   *   *   *   *   *

It is the attitude of the child that is necessary before we can enter into the kingdom of heaven. As it was said by Jesus of Nazareth, "Except ye become as little children, ye cannot enter into the kingdom of heaven." For we then realize that of ourselves we can do nothing but that it is only as we realize that it is the Divine life and power working, within us, and it is only as we open ourselves that it may work through us, that we are or can do anything. It is thus that the simple life, which is essentially the life of the greatest enjoyment and the greatest attainment, is entered upon.

In the Orient the people as a class take far more time in the quiet, in the silence, than we take. Some of them carry this possibly to as great an extreme as we carry the opposite, with the result that they do not actualize and objectify in the outer life the things they dream in the innerlife. We give so much time to the activities of the outer life that we do not take sufficient time in the quiet to form in the inner, spiritual thought-life the ideals and the conditions that we would have actualized and manifested in the outer life. The result is that we take life in a kind of haphazard way, taking it as it comes, thinking not very much about it until, perhaps, pushed by some bitter experiences, instead of moulding it, through the agency of the inner forces, exactly as we would have it. We need to strike the happy balance between the custom in this respect of the Eastern and Western worlds, and go to the extreme of neither

300

the one nor the other.

* * * * * * * * * *

If the Oriental would do his contemplating, and then get up and do his work, he would be in a better condition; he would be living a more normal and satisfactory life. If we in the Occident would take more time from the rush and activity of life for contemplation, for meditation, for idealization, for becoming acquainted with our real selves, and then go about our work manifesting the powers of our real selves, we would be far better off, because we would be living a more natural, a more normal life. To find one's centre, to become centred in the Infinite, is the first great essential of every satisfactory life; and then to go out, thinking, speaking, working, loving, living, from this centre.

Character-Building Thought Power

XVIII

Heredity And The Higher Power

In the highest character-building, such as we have been considering, there are those who feel they are handicapped by what we
term *heredity*. In a sense they are right; in another sense they are
totally wrong. It is along the same lines as the thought which many
before us had inculcated in them through the couplet in the New
England Primer: "In Adam's fall, we sinned all." Now, in the first
place, it is rather hard to understand the justice of this if it is true.
In the second place, it is rather hard to understand why it is true.
And in the third place there is no truth in it at all. We are now
dealing with the real essential self, and, however old Adam is, God
is eternal. This means you; it means me; it means every human
soul. When we fully realize this fact we see that heredity is a reed
that is easily broken. The life of everyone is in his own hands and
he can make it in character, in attainment, in power, in divine self-
realization, and hence in influence, exactly what he wills to make
it. All things that he most fondly dreams of are his, or may become
so if he is truly in earnest; and as he rises more and more to his
ideal, and grows in the strength and influence of his character,
he becomes an example and an inspiration to all with whom he
comes in contact; so that through him the weak and faltering are
encouraged and strengthened; so that those of low ideals and of a
low type of life instinctively and inevitably have their ideals raised,
and the ideals of no one can be raised without its showing forth in
his outer life. As he advances in his grasp upon and understanding of the power and potency of the thought-forces, he finds that

many times through the process of mental suggestion he can be of tremendous aid to one who is weak and struggling, by sending to him now and then, and by continually holding him in the highest thought, in the thought of the highest strength, wisdom, and love.

The one who takes sufficient time in the quiet mentally to form his ideals, sufficient time to make and to keep continually his conscious connection with the Infinite, with the Divine life and forces, is the one who is best adapted to the strenuous life. He it is who can go out and deal with sagacity and power with whatever issues may arise in the affairs of everyday life. He it is who is building not for the years, but for the centuries; not for time, but for the eternities. And he can go out knowing not wither he goes, knowing that the Divine life within him will never fail him, but will lead him on until he beholds the Father face to face.

He is building for the centuries because only that which is the highest, the truest, the noblest, and best will abide the test of the centuries. He is building for eternity because when the transition we call death takes place, life, character, self-mastery, divine self-realization,—the only things that the soul when stripped of everything else takes with it he has in abundance. In life, or when the time of the transition to another form of life comes, he is never afraid, never fearful, because he knows and realizes that behind him, within him, beyond him, is the Infinite wisdom and love; and in this he is eternally centred, and from it he can never be separated. With Whittier he sings:

> "I know not where His islands lift
> Their fronded palms in air;
> I only know I cannot drift
> Beyond His love and care."

Character-Building Thought Power

XIX

Castles In The Air

In our very laboratory experiments we are demonstrating the great fact that thoughts are forces. They have form, and duality, and substance, and power, and we are beginning to find that there is what we may term a *science of thought*.

* * * * * * * * * *

Everything in the material universe about us, everything the universe has ever known, had its origin first in thought. From this it took its form. Every castle, every statue, every painting, every piece of mechanism, everything had its birth, its origin, first in the mind of the one who formed it before it received its material expression or embodiment. The Very universe in which we live is the result of the thought energies of God, the Infinite Spirit that is back of all. And if it is true, as we have found, that we in our true selves are in essence the same, and in this sense are one with the life of this Infinite Spirit, do we not then see that in the degree that we come into a vital realization of this stupendous fact, *we, through the operation of our interior, spiritual, thought forces, have in like sense creative power?*

Everything exists in the unseen before it is manifested or realized in the seen, and in this sense it is true that the unseen things are the real, while the things that are seen are the unreal. The unseen things are cause; the seen things are *effect*. The unseen things are the eternal; the seen things are the changing, the transient.

The *"power of the word"* is a literal scientific fact. Through the

304

operation of our thought forces we have creative power. The spoken word is nothing more nor less than the outward expression of the workings of these interior forces. The spoken word is then, in a sense, the means whereby the thought-forces are focused and directed along any particular line; and this concentration, this giving them direction, is necessary before any outward or material manifestation of their power can become evident.

Much is said in regard to "building castles in the air," and one who is given to this building is not always looked upon with favour. But castles in the air are always necessary before we can have castles on the ground, before we can have castles in which to live. The trouble with the one who gives himself to building castles in the air is not that he builds them in the air, but that he does not go farther and actualize in life, in character, in material form, the castles he thus builds. He does part of the work, a very necessary part; but another equally necessary part remains still undone.

There is in connection with the thought forces what we may term, the drawing power of mind, and the great law operating here is one with that great law of the universe, that like attracts like. We are continually attracting to us from both the seen and the unseen side of life, forces and conditions most akin to those of our own thoughts.

This law is continually operating whether we are conscious of it or not. We are all living, so to speak, in a vast ocean of thought, and the very atmosphere around us is continually filled with the thought forces that are being continually sent or that are continually going out in the form of thought waves. We are all affected, more or less, by these thought forces, either consciously or unconsciously; and in the degree that we are more or less sensitively organized, or in the degree that we are negative and so are open to outside influences, rather than positive, thus determining what influences shall enter into our realm of thought, and hence into our lives.

In Tune with the Infinite

XX

The Anchor Of The Sensitively Organized

There are those among us who are much more sensitively organized than others. As an organism their bodies are more finely, more sensitively constructed. These, generally speaking, are people who are always more or less affected by the mentalities of those with whom they come in contact, or in whose company they are. A friend, the editor of one of our great journals, is so sensitively organized that it is impossible for him to attend a gathering, such as a reception, talk and shake hands with a number of people during the course of the evening, without taking on to a greater or less extent their various mental and physical conditions. These affect him to such an extent that he is scarcely himself and in his best condition for work until some two or three days afterward.

Some think it unfortunate for one to be sensitively organized. By no means. It is a good thing, for one may thus be more open and receptive to the higher impulses of the soul within, and to all higher forces and influences from without. It may, however, be unfortunate and extremely inconvenient to be so organized unless one recognize and gain the power of closing himself, of making himself positive to all detrimental or undesirable influences. This power everyone, however sensitively organized he may be, can acquire.

This he can acquire through the mind's action. And, moreover, there is no habit of more value to anyone, be he sensitively or less sensitively organized, than that of occasionally taking and holding himself continually in the attitude of mind—I close myself, I make myself positive to all things below, and open and receptive to all higher influences, to all things above. By taking this attitude of mind consciously now and then, it soon becomes a habit, and if one is deeply in earnest in regard to it, it puts into operation silent but subtle and powerful influences in effecting the desired results. In this way all lower and undesirable influences from both the seen and the unseen side of life are closed out, while all higher influences are invited, and in the degree that they are invited will they enter.

* * * * * * * * * *

The fact of life in whatever form, means the continuance of life, even though the form be changed. Life is the one eternal principle of the universe and so always continues, even though the form of the agency through which it manifests be changed. "In my Father's house are many mansions." And surely, because the individual has dropped, has gone out of the physical body, there is no evidence at all that the life does not go right on the same as before, not commencing,—for there is no cessation,—but commencing in the other form, exactly where it has left off here; for all life is a continuous evolution, step by step; there one neither skips nor jumps.

* * * * * * * * * *

We cannot rationally believe other than that those who have laboured in love and with uplifting power here are still labouring in the same way, and in all probability with more earnest zeal, and with still greater power.

"And Elisha prayed, and said, Lord, I pray thee, open his eyes, that he may see. And the Lord opened the eyes of the young man; and he saw: and, behold, the mountain *was full of horses and chariots of fire* round about Elisha."

In Tune with the Infinite

XXI

How We Attract Success Or Failure

As science is so abundantly demonstrating today,—the things that we see are but a very small fraction of the things that are. The real, vital forces at work in our own lives and in the world about us are not seen by the ordinary physical eye. Yet they are the causes of which all things we see are merely the effects. Thoughts are forces; like builds like, and like attracts like. For one to govern his thinking, then, is to determine his life.

Says one of deep insight into the nature of things: "The law of correspondences between spiritual and material things is wonderfully exact in its workings. People ruled by the mood of gloom attract to them gloomy things. People always discouraged and despondent do not succeed in anything, and live only by burdening someone else. The hopeful, confident, and cheerful attract the elements of success. A man's front or back yard will advertise that man's ruling mood in the way it is kept. A woman at home shows her state of mind in her dress. A slattern advertises the ruling mood of hopelessness, carelessness, and lack of system. Rags, tatters, and dirt are always in the mind before being on the body. The thought that is most put out brings its corresponding visible element to crystallize about you as surely and literally as the visible bit of copper in solution attracts to it the invisible copper in that solution. A mind always hopeful, confident, courageous, and determined on its set purpose, and keeping itself to that purpose, attracts to itself out of the elements things and powers favorable to that purpose.

"Every thought of yours has a literal value to you in every possible way. The strength of your body, the strength of your mind, your success in business, and the pleasure your company brings others, depends on the nature of your thoughts. ...In whatever mood you set your mind does your spirit receive of unseen substance in correspondence with that mood. It is as much a chemical law as a spiritual law. Chemistry is not confined to the elements we see. The elements we do not see with the physical eye outnumber ten thousand times those we do see."

*   *   *   *   *   *   *   *   *   *

Faith is nothing more nor less than the operation of the *thought-forces* in the form of an earnest desire, coupled with expectation as to its fulfillment. And in the degree that faith, the earnest desire thus sent out, is continually held to and watered by firm expectation, in just that degree does it either draw to itself, or does it change from the unseen into the visible, from the spiritual into the material, that for which it is sent.

In Tune with the Infinite

XXII

Fear Brings Failure

Nothing is more subtle than thought, nothing more powerful, nothing more irresistible in its operations, when rightly applied and held to with a faith and fidelity that is unswerving,—a faith and fidelity that never knows the neutralizing effects of doubt and fear. If one have aspirations and a sincere desire for a higher and better condition, so far as advantages, facilities, associates, or any surroundings or environments are concerned, and if he continually send out his highest thought forces for the realization of these desires, and continually water these forces with firm expectation as to their fulfillment, he will sooner or later find himself in the realization of these desires, and all in accordance with natural laws and forces.

Fear brings its own fulfillment the same as hope. The same law operates, and if, as our good and valued friend, Job, said when the darkest days were setting in upon him, That which I feared has come upon me,—was true, how much more surely could he have brought about the opposite conditions, those he would have desired, had he had even the slightest realization of his own powers, and had he acted the part of the master instead of that of the servant; had he dictated terms instead of being dictated to, and thus suffering the consequences.

If one finds himself in any particular condition, in the midst of any surroundings or environments that are not desirable, that have nothing—at least for any length of time—that is of value to him, for his highest life and unfoldment, he has the remedy entirely within his own grasp the moment he realizes the power and supremacy of the forces of the mind and spirit; and, unless he intelligently use these forces, he drifts. Unless through them he becomes master and dictates, he becomes the slave and is dictated to, and so is driven hither and thither.

Earnest, sincere desire, sincere aspiration for higher and better conditions or means to realize them, the thought-forces actively sent out for their realization, these continually watered by firm expectation without allowing the contrary, neutralizing force of fear ever to enter in,—this, accompanied by rightly directed work and activity, will bring about the fullest realization of one's highest desires and aspirations with a certainty as absolute as that effect follows cause. Each and every one of us can thus make for himself ever higher and higher conditions, can attract ever higher and higher influences, can realize an ever higher and higher ideal in life. These are the forces that are within us, simply waiting to be recognized and used,—the forces that we should infuse into and mould everyday life with. The moment we vitally recognize them, they become our servants and wait upon our bidding.

*   *   *   *   *   *   *   *   *   *

We are born to be neither slaves nor beggars, but to dominion and to plenty. This is our rightful heritage, if we will but recognize and lay claim to it. Many a man and many a woman is to-day longing for conditions better and higher than he or she is in, who might be using the same time now spent in vain, indefinite, spasmodic longings, in putting into operation forces which, accompanied by the right personal activity, would speedily bring the fullest realization of his or her fondest dreams.

What All the World's A-Seeking

XXIII

Heart Training Through The Animal World

It is an established fact that the training of the intellect alone is not sufficient. Nothing in this world can be truer than that the education of the head, without the training of the heart, simply increases one's power for evil, while the education of the heart, along with the head, increases one's power for good, and this, indeed, is the true education.

Clearly we must begin with the child. The lessons learned in childhood are the last to be forgotten. Let them be taught that the lower animals are God's creatures, as they themselves are, put here by a common Heavenly Father, each for its own special purpose, *and that they have the same right to life and protection.* Let them be taught that principle recognised by all noble-hearted men, that it is only a depraved, debased, and cowardly nature that will injure an inferior, defenceless creature, simply because it is in its power to do so, and that there is no better, no grander test of true bravery and nobility of character than one's treatment of the lower animals.

*   *   *   *   *   *   *   *   *   *

I cannot refrain in this connection from quoting a sentence or two from Archdeacon Farrar which have recently come to my notice:

"Not once or twice only, at the seaside, have I come across a sad

313

and disgraceful sight—a sight which haunts me still—a number of harmless sea-birds lying defaced and dead upon the sand, their white plumage red with blood, as they had been tossed there, dead or half-dead, their torture and massacre having furnished a day's amusement to heartless and senseless men. Amusement! I say execrable amusement! All killing for mere killing's sake is execrable amusement. Can you imagine the stupid callousness, the utter insensibility to mercy and beauty, of the man who, seeing those bright, beautiful creatures as their white, immaculate wings flash in the sunshine over the blue waves, can go out in a boat with his boys to teach them to become brutes in character by finding amusement—I say, again, dis-humanising amusement—by wantonly murdering these fair birds of God, or cruelly wounding them, and letting them fly away to wait and die in lonely places?"

And another paragraph which was sent me by a kind friend to our fellow-creatures a few days ago: "The celebrated Russian novelist, Turgenieff, tells a most touching incident from his own life, which awakened in him sentiments that have coloured all his writings with a deep and tender feeling.

"When Turgenieff was a boy of ten his father took him out one day bird-shooting. As they tramped across the brown stubble, a golden pheasant rose with a low whirr from the ground at his feet, and, with the joy of a sportsman throbbing through his veins, he raised his gun and fired, wild with excitement when the creature fell fluttering at his side. Life was ebbing fast, but the instinct of the mother was stronger than death itself, and with a feeble flutter of her wings the mother bird reached the nest where her young brood were huddled, unconscious of danger. Then, with such a look of pleading and reproach that his heart stood still at the ruin he had wrought,—and never to his dying day did he forget the feeling of cruelty and guilt that came to him in that moment,—the little brown head toppled over, and only the dead body of the mother shielded her nestlings.

" 'Father, father,' he cried, 'what have I done?' as he turned his horror-stricken face to his father. But not to his father's eye had this little tragedy been enacted, and he said: 'Well done, my son; that was well done for your first shot. You will soon be a fine sportsman.'

" 'Never, father; never again shall I destroy any living creature. If that is sport I will have none of it. Life is more beautiful to me than death, and since I cannot give life, I will not take it.' "

And so, instead of putting into the hands of the child a gun or any other weapon that may be instrumental in crippling, torturing, or taking the life of even a single animal, I would give him the field-glass and the camera, and send him out to be a friend to the animals, to observe and study their characteristics, their habits, to learn from them those wonderful lessons that can be learned, and thus have his whole nature expand in admiration and love and care for them, and become thereby the truly manly and princely type of man, rather than the careless, callous, brutal type.

*   *   *   *   *   *   *   *   *   *

Every Living Creature

XXIV

The Secret And The Power Of Love

* * * * * * * * * *

When we fully realize the great fact of the oneness of all life,—that all are partakers from this one Infinite Source, and so that the same life is the life in each individual, then prejudices go and hatreds cease. Love grows and reigns supreme. Then, wherever we go, whenever we come in contact with the fellowman, we are able to recognize the God within. We thus look only for the good, and we find it. It always pays.

There is a deep scientific fact underlying the great truth, "He that takes the sword shall perish by the sword." The moment we come into a realization of the subtle power of the thought-forces, we can quickly see that the moment we entertain any thoughts of hatred toward another, he gets the effects of these diabolical forces that go out from us, and has the same thoughts of hatred aroused in him, which in turn return to the sender. Then when we understand the effects of the passion, hatred or anger, even upon the physical body, we can see how detrimental, how expensive this is. The same is true in regard to all kindred thoughts or passions, envy, criticism, jealousy, scorn. In the ultimate we shall find that in entertaining feelings of this nature toward another, we always suffer far more than the one toward whom we entertain them.

And then when we fully realize the fact that selfishness is at the root of all error, sin, and crime, and that ignorance is the basis of all selfishness, with what charity we come to look upon the acts of all. It is the ignorant man who seeks his own ends at the expense of the greater whole. It is the ignorant man, therefore, who is the selfish man. The truly wise man is never selfish. He is a seer, and recognizes the fact that he, a single member of the one great body, is benefited in just the degree that the entire body is benefited, and so he seeks nothing for himself that he would not equally seek for all mankind.

If selfishness is at the bottom of all error, sin, and crime, and ignorance is the basis of all selfishness, then when we see a manifestation of either of these qualities, if we are true to the highest within us, we will look for and will seek to call forth the good in each individual with whom we come in contact. When God speaks to God, then God responds, and shows forth as God. But when devil speaks to devil, then devil responds, and the devil is always to pay.

I sometimes hear a person say, "I don't see any good in him." No? Then you are no seer. Look deeper and you will find the very God in every human soul. But remember it takes a God to recognize a God. Christ always spoke to the highest, the truest, and the best in men. He knew and he recognized the God in each because He had first realized it in Himself. He ate with publicans and sinners. Abominable, the Scribes and Pharisees said. They were so wrapped up in their own conceits, their own self-centredness, hence their own ignorance, that they had never found the God in themselves, and so they never dreamed that it was the *real life* of even publicans and sinners.

In the degree that we hold a person in the thought of evil or of error, do we suggest evil and error to him. In the degree that he is sensitively organized, or not well individualized, and so, subject to the suggestions of the thought-forces from others, will he be influenced; and so in this way we may be sharers in the very evildoing in which we hold another in thought. In the same way when we hold a person in the thought of the right, the good, and the true, righteousness, goodness, and truth are suggested to him, and thus we have a most beneficent influence on his life and conduct. If our hearts go out in love to all with whom we come in contact, we inspire love, and the same ennobling and warming influences of love always return to us from those in whom we inspire them. There is a deep scientific principle underlying the precept—If you would have all the world love you, you must first love all the world.

In the degree that we love will we be loved. Thoughts are forces. Each creates of its kind. Each comes back laden with the effect that corresponds to itself and of which it is the cause.

> "Then let your secret thoughts be fair—
> They have a vital part, and share
> In shaping words and moulding fate;
> God's system is so intricate."

I know of no better practice than that of a friend who continually holds himself in an attitude of mind that he continually sends out his love in the form of the thought,—"Dear everybody, I love you." And when we realize the fact that a thought invariably produces its effect before it returns, or before it ceases, we can see how he is continually breathing out a blessing not only upon all with whom he comes in contact, but upon all the world. These same thoughts of love, moreover, tokened in various ways, are continually coming to him from all quarters.

* * * * * * * * * *

In Tune with the Infinite

XXV

Then Give To The World The Best You Have, And The Best Will Come Back To You

What a privilege and how enjoyable it would be to live and walk in a world where we meet only Gods. In such a world you can live. In such a world I can live. For in the degree that we come into this higher realization do we see only the God in each human soul; and when we are thus able to see him in everyone we meet, we then live in such a world.

And when we thus recognize the God in everyone, we by this recognition help to call it forth ever more and more. What a privilege—this privilege of yours, this privilege of mine! That hypocritical judging of another is something then with which we can have nothing to do; for we have the power of looking beyond the evolving, changing, error-making self, and seeing the real, the changeless, the eternal self which by and by will show forth in the full beauty of holiness. We are then large enough also to realize the fact that when we condemn another, by that very act we condemn ourselves.

This realization so fills us with love that we continually overflow it, and all with whom we come in contact feel its warming and life-giving power. These in turn send back the same feelings of love to us, and so we continually attract love from all quarters. Tell me how much one loves and I will tell you how much he has seen of God. Tell me how much he loves and I will tell you how much he lives with God. Tell me how much he loves and I will tell you how far into the Kingdom of Heaven,—the kingdom of harmony, he has entered, for "love is the fulfilling of the law."

And in a sense love is everything. It is the key to life, and its influences are those that move the world. Live only in the thought of love for all and you will draw love to you from all. Live in the thought of malice or hatred, and malice and hatred will come back to you.

> "For evil poisons; malice shafts
> Like boomerangs return,
> Inflicting wounds that will not heal
> While rage and anger burn."

Every thought you entertain is a force that goes out, and every thought comes back laden with its kind. This is an immutable law. Every thought you entertain has moreover a direct effect upon your body. Love and its kindred emotions are the normal and the natural, those in accordance with the eternal order of the universe, for "God is love." These have a life-giving, health-engendering influence upon your body, besides beautifying your countenance, enriching your voice, and making you ever more attractive in every way. And as it is true that in the degree that you hold thoughts of love for all, you call the same from them in return, and as these have a direct effect upon your mind, and through your mind upon your body, it is as so much life force added to your own from without. You are then continually building this into both your mental and your physical life, and so your life is enriched by its influence.

Hatred and all its kindred emotions are the unnatural, the abnormal, the perversions, and so, out of harmony with the eternal order of the universe. For if love is the fulfilling of the law, then these, its opposites, are direct violations of law, and there can never be a violation of law without its attendant pain and suffering in one form or another. There is no escape from this. And what is the result of this particular form of violation? When you allow thoughts of anger, hatred, malice, jealousy, envy, criticism, or scorn to exercise sway, they have a corroding and poisoning effect upon the organism; they pull it down, and if allowed to continue will eventually tear it to pieces by externalizing themselves in the particular forms of disease they give rise to. And then in addition to the destructive influences from your own mind you are continually calling the same influences from other minds, and these come as destructive forces augmenting your own, thus aiding in the tearing-down process.

And so love inspires love; hatred breeds hatred. Love and good-will stimulate and build up the body; hatred and malice corrode and tear it down. Love is a savor of life unto life; hatred is a savor of death unto death.

> "There are loyal hearts, there are spirits brave,
> There are souls that are pure and true;
> Then give to the world the best you have.
> And the best will come back to you.
>
> "Give love, and love to *your* heart will flow,
> A strength in your utmost need;
> Have faith, and a score of hearts will show
> Their faith in *your* word and deed."

* * * * * * * * * *

In Tune with the Infinite

XXVI

Hatred Never Ceases By Hatred, But By Love

Love is positive, and stronger than hatred. Hatred can always be conquered by love.

On the other hand, if you meet hatred with hatred, you simply intensify it. You add fuel to the flame already kindled, upon which it will feed and grow, and so you increase and intensify the evil conditions. Nothing is to be gained by it, everything is to be lost. By sending love for hatred you will be able to so neutralize it that it will not only have no effect upon you, but will not be able even to reach you. But more than this, you will by this course sooner or later be able literally to transmute the enemy into the friend. Meet hatred with hatred and you degrade yourself. Meet hatred with love and you elevate not only yourself but also the one who bears you hatred.

The Persian sage has said, "Always meet petulance with gentleness, and perverseness with kindness. A gentle hand can lead even an elephant by a hair. Reply to thine enemy with gentleness. Opposition to peace is sin." The Buddhist says, "If a man foolishly does me wrong I will return him the protection of my ungrudging love. The more evil comes from him, the more good shall go from me." "The wise man avenges injuries by benefits," says the Chinese. "Return good for evil, overcome anger by love; hatred never ceases by hatred, but by love," says the Hindu.

The truly wise man or woman will recognize no one as an

enemy. Occasionally we hear the expression, "Never mind; I'll get even with him." Will you? And how will you do it? You can do it in one of two ways. You can, as you have in mind, deal with him as he deals, or apparently deals, with you,—pay him, as we say, in his own coin. If you do this you will get even with him by sinking yourself to his level, and both of you will suffer by it. Or, you can show yourself the larger, you can send him love for hatred, kindness for ill-treatment, and so get even with him by raising him to the higher level. But remember that you can never help another without by that very act helping yourself; and if forgetful of self, then in most all cases the value to you is greater than the service you render another. If you are ready to treat him as he treats you, then you show clearly that there is in you that which draws the hatred and ill-treatment to you; you deserve what you are getting and should not complain, nor would you complain if you were wise. By following the other course you most effectually accomplish your purpose,—you gain a victory for yourself, and at the same time you do a great service for him, of which it is evident he stands greatly in need.

Thus you may become his saviour. He in turn may become the saviour of other error-making, and consequently care-encumbered men and women. Many times the struggles are greater than we can ever know. We need more gentleness and sympathy and compassion in our common human life. Then we will neither blame nor condemn. Instead of blaming or condemning we will sympathize, and all the more we will:

> "Comfort one another,
> For the way is often dreary,
> And the feet are often weary,
> And the heart is very sad.
> There is a heavy burden bearing,
> When it seems that none are caring,
> And we half forget that ever we were glad.
>
> "Comfort one another
> With the hand-clasp close and tender.

With the sweetness love can render,
And the looks of friendly eyes.
Do not wait with grace unspoken
While life's daily bread is broken—
Gentle speech is oft like manna from the skies."

*   *   *   *   *   *   *   *   *   *

In Tune with the Infinite

XXVII

Thought And Its Intelligent Direction

* * * * * * * * * *

Of all known forms of energy, thought is the most subtle, the most irresistible force. It has always been operating; but, so far as the great masses of the people are concerned, it has been operating blindly, or, rather, they have been blind to its mighty power, except in the cases of a few here and there. And these, as a consequence, have been our prophets, our seers, our sages, our saviours, our men of great and mighty power. We are just beginning to grasp the tremendous truth that there is a *science of thought*, and that the laws governing it can be known and scientifically applied.

* * * * * * * * * *

Thought needs direction to be effective, and upon this effective results depend as much as upon the force itself. This brings us to the will. Will is not, as is so often thought, a force in itself; will is the directing power. Thought is the force. Will gives direction. Thought scattered gives the weak, the uncertain, the vacillating, the aspiring, but the never-doing, the I-would-like-to, but the get-no-where, the attain-to-nothing man or woman. Thought steadily directed by the will gives the strong, the firm, the never-yielding; the never-know-defeat man or woman, the man or woman who uses the very difficulties and hindrances that would dishearten the ordinary person, as stones with which he paves a way over which he triumphantly walks, who, by the very force he carries with him, so neutralizes and transmutes the very obstacles that would bar his way that they fall before him, and in turn aid him on his way; the man or, woman who, like the eagle, uses the very contrary wind that would thwart his flight, that would turn him and carry him in the opposite direction, as the very agency upon which he mounts and mounts and mounts, until actually lost to the human eye, and which, in addition to thus aiding him, brings to him an ever fuller realization of his own powers, or in other words, an ever greater power.

It is this that gives the man or the woman who in storm or in sunny weather, rides over every obstacle, throws before him every barrier, and, as Browning has said, finally "arrives." Take, for example, the successful business man,—for it is all one, the law is the same in all cases—the man who started with nothing except his own interior equipments. He has made up his mind to *one* thing,—success. This is his ideal. He thinks success, he sees success. He refuses to see anything else. He expects success: he thus attracts it to him, his thought-forces continually attract to him every agency that makes for success. He has set up the current, so that every wind that blows brings him success. He doesn't expect failure, and so he doesn't invite it. He has no time, no energies, to waste in fears or forebodings. He is dauntless, untiring, in his efforts. Let disaster come today, and tomorrow—ay, even yet to-day—he is getting his bearings, he is setting forces anew into operation; and these very forces are of more value to him than the half million dollars of his neighbor who has suffered from the same disaster.

We speak of a man's failing in business, little thinking that the real failure came long before, and that the final crash is but the culmination, the outward visible manifestation, of the real failure that occurred within possibly long ago. *A man carries his success or his failure with him: it is not dependent upon outside conditions.*

What All the World's A-Seeking

XXVIII

Will—The Human And The Divine

Will is the steady directing power: it is concentration. It is the pilot which, after the vessel is started by the mighty force within, puts it on its right course and keeps it true to that course.

* * * * * * * * * *

Will is the magnifying glass which so concentrates and so focuses the sun's rays that they quickly burn a hole through the paper that is held before it. The same rays, not thus concentrated, not thus focused, would fall upon the paper for days without any effect whatever. Will is the means for the directing, the concentrating, the focusing, of the thought-forces. Thought under wise direction,—this it is that does the work, that brings results, that makes the successful career. One object in mind which we never lose sight of; an ideal steadily held before the mind, never lost sight of, never lowered, never swerved from,—this, with persistence, determines all. Nothing can resist the power of thought, when thus directed by will.

May not this power, then, be used for base as well as for good purposes, for selfish as well as for unselfish ends? The same with this modification,—the more highly thought is spiritualized, the more subtle and powerful it becomes; and the more highly spiritualized the life, the farther is it removed from base, ignoble, selfish ends. But, even if it can be thus used, let him who would so use it

327

be careful, let him never forget that that mighty, searching, omnipotent law of the right, of truth, of justice, that runs through all the universe and that can never be annulled or even for a moment set aside, will drive him to the wall, will crush him with a terrific force if he so use it.

Let him never forget that whatever he may get for self at the expense of someone else, through deception, through misrepresentation, through the exercise of the lower functions and powers, will by a law equally subtle, equally powerful, be turned into ashes in his very hands. The honey he thinks he has secured will be turned into bitterness as he attempts to eat it; the beautiful fruit he thinks is his will be as wormwood as he tries to enjoy it; the rose he has plucked will vanish, and he will find himself clutching a handful of thorns, which will penetrate to the very quick and which will flow the very life-blood from his hands. For through the violation of a higher, an immutable law, though he may get this or that, the power of true enjoyment will be taken away, and what he gets will become as a thorn in his side: either this or it will sooner or later escape from his hands. God's triumphal car moves in a direction and at a rate that is certain and absolute, and he who would oppose it or go contrary to it must fall and be crushed beneath its wheels; and for him this crushing is necessary, in order that it may bring him the more quickly to a knowledge of the higher laws, to a realization of the higher self.

This brings to our notice two orders of will, which we may term, for convenience' sake, the human and the divine. The human will is the one just noticed, the sense will, the will of the lower self, that which seeks its own ends regardless of its connection with the greater whole. The divine will is the will of the higher self, the God-self, that never makes an error, that never leads into difficulties.

*   *   *   *   *   *   *   *   *   *

It is thus that the Infinite Power works through and for us—true inspiration—while our part is simply to see that our connection with this power is consciously and perfectly kept.

*   *   *   *   *   *   *   *   *   *

What All the World's A-Seeking

XXIX

The Secret Of The Highest Power

The secret of the highest power is simply the uniting of the outer agencies of expression with the Power that works from within. Are you a painter? Then in the degree that you open yourself to the power of the forces within will you become great instead of mediocre. You can never put into permanent form inspirations higher than those that come through your own soul. In order for the higher inspirations to come through it, you must open your soul, you must open it fully to the Supreme Source of all inspiration. Are you an orator? In the degree that you come into harmony and work in conjunction with the higher powers that will speak through you will you have the real power of moulding and of moving men. If you use merely your physical agents, you will be simply a demagogue. If you open yourself so that the voice of God can speak through and use your physical agents, you will become a great and true orator, great and true in just the degree that you so open yourself.

Are you a singer? Then open yourself and let the God within pour forth in the spirit of song. You will find it a thousand times easier than all your long and studied practice *without this*, and other things being equal, there will come to you a power of song so enchanting and so enrapturing that its influence upon all who hear will be irresistible.

When my cabin or tent has been pitched during the summer on the edge or in the midst of a forest, I have sometimes lain awake on my cot in the early morning, just as the day was beginning to break. Silence at first. Then an intermittent chirp here and there. And as the unfolding tints of the dawn became faintly perceptible, these grew more and more frequent, until by and by the whole forest seemed to burst forth in one grand chorus of song. Wonderful! wonderful! It seemed as if the very trees, as if every grass-blade, as if the bushes, the very sky above, and the earth beneath, had part in this wonderful symphony. Then, as I have listened as it went on and on, I have thought, What a study in the matter of song! If we could but learn from the birds. If we could but open ourselves to the same powers and allow them to pour forth in us, what singers, what movers of men we might have! Nay, what singers and what movers of men *we would have*!

* * * * * * * * * *

When we open ourselves to the highest inspirations they never fail us. When we fail to do this we fail in attaining the highest results, whatever the undertaking.

Are you a writer? Then remember that the one great precept underlying all successful literary work is, *Look into thine own heart and write. Be true. Be fearless. Be loyal to the promptings of your own soul.* Remember that an author can never write more than he himself is. If he would write more, then he must be more. He is simply his own amanuensis. He in a sense writes himself into his book. He can put no more into it than he himself is.

If he is one of a great personality, strong in purpose, deep in feeling, open always to the highest inspirations, a certain indefinable something gets into his pages that makes them breathe forth a vital, living power, a power so great that each reader gets the same inspirations as those that spoke through the author. That that's written between the lines is many times more than that that's written in the lines. It is the spirit of the author that engenders this power.

* * * * * * * * * *

The one, on the other hand, who fears to depart from beaten

paths, who allows himself to be bound by arbitrary rules, limits his own creative powers in just the degree that he allows himself so to be bound. "My book," says one of the greatest of modern authors, "shall smell of the pines and resound with the hum of insects. The swallow over my window shall interweave that thread or straw he carries in his bill into my web also." Far better, gentle sage, to have it smell of the pines and resound with the hum of insects than to have it sound of the rules that a smaller type of man gets by studying the works of a few great, fearless writers like yourself, and formulating from what he thus gains a handbook of rhetoric. "Of no use are the men who study to do exactly as was done before, who can never understand that *to-day is a new day.*"

In Tune with the Infinite

XXX

Wisdom: Or Interior Illumination

In order for the highest wisdom and insight we must have absolute confidence in the Divine guiding us, but not through the channel of someone else. And why should we go to another for knowledge and wisdom? With God is no respect of persons. Why should we seek these things secondhand? Why should we thus stultify our own innate powers? Why should we not go direct to the Infinite Source itself? "If any man lack wisdom let him ask of God." "Before they call I will answer, and while they are yet speaking, I will hear."

When we thus go directly to the Infinite Source itself we are no longer slaves to personalities, institutions, or books. We should always keep ourselves open to suggestions of truth from these agencies. We should always regard them as agencies, however, and *never as sources*. We should never recognize them as masters, but simply as teachers. With Browning, we must recognize the great fact that—

> "Truth is within ourselves; it takes no rise
> From outward things, whate'er you may believe.
> There is an inmost centre in us all,
> Where truth abides in fullness."

There is no more important injunction in all the world, nor one with a deeper interior meaning, than "To thine own self be true." In other words, be true to your own soul, for it is through your own soul that the voice of God speaks to you. This is the interior guide. This is "the light that lighteth every man that cometh into the world." This is conscience. This is intuition. This is the voice of the higher self, the voice of the soul, the voice of God. "Thou shalt hear a voice behind thee, saying: This is the way, walk ye in it."

When Elijah was on the mountain it was after the various physical commotions and manifestations that he heard the "still, small voice," the voice of his own soul, through which the Infinite God was speaking. If we will but follow this voice of intuition, it will speak ever more clearly and more plainly, until by and by it will be absolute and unerring in its guidance. The great trouble with us is that we do not listen to and do not follow this voice within our own souls, and so we become as a house divided against itself. We are pulled this way and that, and we are never *certain* of anything. I have a friend who listens so carefully to this inner voice, who, in other words, always acts so quickly and so fully in accordance with his intuitions, and whose life as a consequence is so absolutely guided by them, that he always does the right thing at the right time and in the right way. He always knows when to act and how to act, and he is never in the condition of a house divided against itself.

But someone says, "May it not be dangerous for us to act always upon our intuitions? Suppose we should have an intuition to do harm to someone?" We need not be afraid of this, however, for the voice of the soul, this voice of God speaking through the soul, will never direct one to do harm to another, nor to do anything that is not in accordance with the highest: standards of right, and truth, and justice. And if you at any time have a prompting of this kind, know that it is not the voice of intuition; it is some characteristic of your lower self that is prompting you.

Reason is not to be set aside, but it is to be continually illumined by this higher spiritual perception, and in the degree that it is thus illumined will it become an agent of light and power. When one becomes thoroughly individualized he enters into the realm of all knowledge and wisdom; and to be individualized is to recognize no power outside of the Infinite Power that is back of all. When one recognizes this great fact and opens himself to this Spirit of Infinite Wisdom, he then enters upon the road to the true education, and mysteries that before were closed now reveal themselves to him. This must indeed be the foundation of all true education, this evolving from within, this evolving of what has been involved by the Infinite Power.

There are no new stars, there are no new laws or forces, but we can so open ourselves to this Spirit of Infinite Wisdom that we can discover and recognize those that have not been known before; and in this way they become new to us.

"This is true wisdom. Wisdom is the knowledge of God." Wisdom comes by intuition. It far transcends knowledge. Great knowledge, knowledge of many things, may be had by virtue simply of a very retentive memory. It comes by tuition. But wisdom far transcends knowledge, in that knowledge is a mere incident of this deeper wisdom.

In Tune with the Infinite

XXXI

Let There Be Many Windows In Your Soul

He who would enter into the realm of wisdom must first divest himself of all intellectual pride. He must become as a little child. Prejudices, preconceived opinions, and beliefs always stand in the way of true wisdom. Conceited opinions are always suicidal in their influences. They bar the door to the entrance of truth.

All about us we see men in the religious world, in the world of science, in the political, in the social world, who through intellectual pride are so wrapped in their own conceits and prejudices that larger and later revelations of truth can find no entrance to them; and instead of growing and expanding, they are becoming dwarfed and stunted, and still more incapable of receiving truth. Instead of actively aiding in the progress of the world, they are as so many dead sticks in the way that would retard the wheels of progress. This, however, they can never do. Such always in time get bruised, broken, and left behind, while God's triumphal car of truth moves steadily onward.

When the steam engine was still being experimented with, and before it was perfected sufficiently to come into practical use, a well-known Englishman—well known then in scientific circles—wrote an extended pamphlet proving that it would be impossible for it *ever* to be used in ocean navigation, that is, in a trip involving the crossing of the ocean, because it would be utterly impossible for any vessel to carry with it sufficient coal for the use of its furnace. And the interesting feature of the whole matter was that the very first steam vessel that made the trip from England to America, had among its cargo a part of the first edition of this carefully prepared pamphlet. There was only the one edition. Many editions might be sold now.

This seems indeed an amusing fact; but far more amusing is the man who voluntarily closes himself to truth because, forsooth, it does not come through conventional, or orthodox, or heretofore accepted channels; or because it may not be in full accord with, or possibly may be opposed to, established usages or beliefs. On the contrary—

> "Let there be many windows in your soul,
> That all the glory of the universe
> May beautify it. Not the narrow pane
> Of one poor creed can catch the radiant rays
> That shine from countless sources. Tear away
> The blinds of superstition: let the light
> Pour through fair windows, broad as truth itself
> and high as heaven. . . . Tune your ear
> To all the wordless music of the stars
> And to the voice of Nature, and your heart
> Shall turn to truth and goodness as the plant
> Turns to the sun. A thousand unseen hands
> Reach down to help you to their peace-
> crowned heights,
> And all the forces of the firmament
> shall fortify your strength. Be not afraid
> To thrust aside half-truths and grasp the whole."

There is a great law in connection with the coming of truth. It is this: Whenever a man or a woman shuts himself or herself to the entrance of truth on account of intellectual pride, preconceived opinions, prejudices, or for whatever reason, there is a great law which says that truth *in its fullness* will come to that one from no source. And on the other hand, when a man or a woman opens himself or herself fully to the entrance of truth from *whatever* source it may come, there is an equally great law which says that truth will flow in to him or to her from all sources, from all quarters. Such becomes the free man, the free woman, for it is the truth that makes us free. The other remains in bondage, for truth has had no invitation and will not enter where it is not fully and freely welcomed.

And where truth is denied entrance the rich blessings it carries with it cannot take up their abode. On the contrary, when this is the case, it sends an envoy carrying with it atrophy, disease, death, physically and spiritually as well as intellectually. And the man who would rob another of his free and unfettered search for truth, who would stand as the interpreter of truth for another, with the intent of remaining in this position, rather than endeavoring to lead him to the place where he can be his own interpreter, is more to be shunned than a thief and a robber. The injury he works is far greater, for he is doing direct and positive injury to the very life of the one he thus holds.

Who has ever appointed any man, whoever he may be, as the keeper, the custodian, the dispenser of God's illimitable truth? Many indeed are moved and so are called to be teachers of truth; but the true teacher will never stand as the interpreter of truth for another. The *true teacher* is the one whose endeavor is to bring the one he teaches to a true knowledge of himself and hence of his own interior powers, that he may become his own interpreter. All others are, generally speaking, those animated by purely personal motives, self-aggrandizement, or personal gain. Moreover, he who would claim to have all truth and the only truth, is a bigot, a fool, or a knave.

In Tune with the Infinite

XXXII

As To The Quality Of Our Education

Every child in school until a certain age or until a sufficient equipment to meet the ordinary duties of life is reached, should be the nation's motto.

It is also eminently fitting that something be said of the *quality* of the education it is proposed to make compulsory attendance upon universal. To come at once to the point in mind and briefly—training of the intellect alone is not sufficient; we shall remain a long way off from the ideal until we make moral, humane, heart-training a far more important feature of our educational systems than we have made it thus far. We are advancing in this respect, but we have great advances yet to make. Kindness and consideration, sympathy and fraternity, love of justice—the full and ready willingness to give it as well as to demand it, the clearcut comprehension of the majesty and beauty that escapes into the life of the individual as he understands and appropriates to himself the all-embracing contents of the golden rule. The training of the intellect alone at the expense of the "humanities " has made or has enlarged the power of many a criminal, many a usurper of other men's homes and property, many an oppressor, and has thereby added poison and desolation to his own life as well as to the lives of those with whom he has come in contact and who have felt his blighting and withering influence. It is also chiefly from those without this training, that that great body of our fellow-creatures which we term the animal world, receive their most thoughtless and cruel treatment, and perhaps from among none more than among the rich and fashionable.

I think there is another feature in our educational systems that we would do wisely to give more attention to. In a nation of free institutions, more attention could wisely be given to systematic and concrete instruction in connection with the institutions of government, and in connection with this a training in civic pride that sees to it that our public offices are filled with men of at least ordinary honesty and integrity, men who regard public office as a public trust worthy the service of their highest manhood, rather than with those whose eye is single to the largest amount of loot and graft that comes within the range of their vision and the reach of their hand. Such a system would in time spell the end of Tammany Hall—a Democratic organization in New York City, whose chief object is to make politics a cover to divert the largest possible sums of money from the people of the City of New York to line the pockets, and in great abundance, of those in control of the body of loot. It would in time spell the end of the Republican rings and halls whose object and purpose is identically the same in every city where they have been able to gain control, as well as the Democratic rings in cities other than New York. The methods of the rings of the one are equally black with the methods of the rings of the other; where the motives are the same the resultant action is the same.

Our educational methods are developing. In educational work are some of our noblest, our foremost men and women. There is an element of the practical, the useful, that is now sort of remodelling our earlier methods. It has always seemed to me that not only in our public schools but in our colleges and universities, it is possible to get as great a degree of *training* from branches that are in themselves useful, that will be of actual use later on, as out of those that are used for their training value only. The element of the useful, not at the expense of the training, but combined with it, should be, I think, and is coming to be, the marked feature of our developing educational methods.

The bread and butter problem will be the problem of practically all in our common or public schools to-day. There probably will not be one in a thousand whose problem it will not be. To make our educational systems so that they will be of the greatest *practical aid* to all as they enter upon life's activities should, it seems to me, be one of our greatest aims. That our college courses can be improved to at least from twenty to forty per cent along this same line I am fully persuaded, in addition to the saving of considerable valuable time for those who, contemplating professional careers, will afterwards have to spend a considerable period in years in professional schools.

When we consider that not more than one-tenth of one per cent of those in our common schools ever get as far as the college or university, we can see how important it is that every child be guaranteed what the law of the most ordinary justice demands, that he or she have the benefit at least of what will enable him or her to enter upon the stage of young manhood and young womanhood free from the tremendous handicaps with which so many are entering upon it to-day.

In the Fire of the Heart

XXXIII

A New Order Of Patriotism

A new order of patriotism is coming into being and among us. What was at one time confined to the few brave, independent, advanced men, is now becoming common among the people. We are finding that the elements of justice and righteousness, fraternity and godliness, have a very direct relation to, or rather, that patriotism has a very direct relation to them. War—war and the flag, were at one time supposed to be the *only* agents with which patriotism was linked. To hurrah for the flag and to be eager to go to the front, when the war bugles sounded, or were likely to sound, was for a long period a prevailing idea of patriotism. It may still be a way in which patriotism may be manifested.

The people are learning the real cause of many wars, indeed the great majority of them—the bull-headedness or pig-headedness, the incapacity on the part of those having to do with affairs; and again, the throwing of an entire nation into war by large and powerful though unscrupulous financial interests solely for gain. These two agents are responsible for the great bulk, indeed for nine out of every ten, of all modern wars, even as they have been for all time past. Men are beginning to realize that instead of having anything to do with this type of war, patriotism lies in *refusing absolutely* to aid or abet it and in using one's influence in a similar way among one's neighbours more blunt and with less power of discernment. When we reach a point where the large body of citizens see to it that these men and their agents—for the large financial interests of the unscrupulous type almost invariably work through agents many of whom they place or have the people place in public positions—when, I repeat, the larger body of citizens see to it that these men and their agents are kept out of public office and relegate them to the subordinate place where they rightly belong, then we will witness the full birth of an entirely new and a higher order of patriotism that is soon to be dominant among us.

The highest patriotism that I know is that which impels a man to be honest, kind, hence thoughtful in all his business relations and in his daily life; that impels him to the primary and to give attention to those features of our political institutions that are of even greater consequence than his casting his vote on election day; that impels him to think and to be discriminating in his thought; that enables him to be not afraid to point out and denounce the pure self-seeker and his demagogic ways, be he in public life, in the ranks of high standing financiers, or in the ranks of organized labour, or in the ranks of the common life.

It is this patriotism in the common life that is of the high quality. Men who are industrious and honest in their work; who are faithful to whatever tasks are imposed upon them; who are as eager to give justice as to demand it; who are working industriously and intelligently in order to take care of themselves and those dependent upon them, and thus remain self-supporting members of the community; who remain brave and sweet in their natures and who abide always in faith in face of the hard or uncertain times that come at some time or another and in some form or another into the lives of everyone of us; who are jealous of their country's honour, and of the administration of its internal affairs, for in the life of the nation as in the life of the individual, all life is from within out, and as is the inner so always will be the outer. These, I repeat, are the men and these are the conditions that are giving birth to that new and that higher order of patriotism that is now coming among us, and that is to take captive the hearts of men.

That wars in the past have been, and even at the present time are too frequent, all thinking men and women are agreed. That they are in the great majority of cases entirely inexcusable, and that there is and should be very little use for military forces if any, outside of *purposes of defence*, the highest and most intelligent portion of our citizenship thoroughly believes. And so far as effectiveness is concerned it has been proven time and again, that a *citizen soldiery* is the finest in the world. Neither vast bodies of men drawn off from creative and productive enterprises and made into a professional soldier class, nor bodies of hirelings, but men who are citizens of intelligence and training, and who stand with the ear ready for the call to arms when there is just cause for their hearing this call, such are the intelligent, such are the brave and the daring, such are the most effective. Men will not fight effectively for the little price in money they are paid. They will not fight effectively for the glory of another, nor will they fight effectively for a mere tract of land. But where homes are and institutions that they love and revere and care for, then men will fight with all that triumphant intelligence and all that indomitable daring that it is possible to call forth. With a citizen soldiery ready at the just moment to come from the mine, the mill, the counting-house, the farm, thousands of thousands or millions strong, why should there be a vast professional soldiery, a great non-producing class kept primarily for the glory and to do the bidding of a ruling class, but supported almost entirely by the great common people, that is true of the foolhardy military systems of various European countries today?

So far then as the soldiery of a nation is concerned, let the interests of all the people be equally taken care of, let there be institutions founded upon justice, upon equal opportunities for all and special privileges for no man, let there be homes and sentiment encircling these homes, and the keeping up of a large military system becomes but a fool's dream. There will come from such a people a citizen soldiery more intelligent, more brave and determined, and therefore more effective, than can ever come from any professional fighting class, and at a cost not a hundredth part as great.

Take sentiment from the battle-field and you take its chief source of heroism away. The people of homes and of just institutions are a people of sentiment. Upon every cartridge-box and upon every rifle and upon every field piece of such a soldiery the word "Invincible" could most rightly be stamped.

In the Fire of the Heart

XXXIV

Men Of Exceptional Executive And Financial Ability

The great nation is, again, the nation in which the man of great natural executive or financial ability finds contentment in a smaller amount of possessions for himself, and the larger contentment and satisfaction and joy in using that unusual ability in the service of, for the benefit of, his city, his state, the nation. The wonder is that more are not doing this already. What an influence a few such men could have, what results they could accomplish, what real riches they could bring into their lives through the riches they would bring into the lives of multitudes—What gratitude would go to them!

As men continue to see the small satisfaction there is in the possession of great ability of this nature, and in the possession of great wealth when divorced from an adequate or even from an abundant connection with the interests and the welfare of their fellow-men, and as they catch the undying truth of the great law of life as enunciated by One who though He had not even where to lay His head was greater than them all—He that is greatest among you shall be your servant—then they in company with all men will be the gainers. Think what could be accomplished in the nation along the lines we have been considering in this little volume by a company of such men devoted to such ends. A change is coming and very rapidly. The time has already arrived when we will no longer look upon the possession of mere wealth or the ability to get it as deserving of any special distinction, and especially when the means adopted in its acquirement are other than those of absolute honour and rectitude.

How significant are the following observations from the *Outlook*:

"Those who have fallen most completely under the spell of fortune-hunting, and have been consumed by the fever of a pursuit which dries up the very sources of spiritual life, can no longer be blind to the fact that when great wealth ceases to be associated with character, honour, genius, or public respect, it is a very shabby substitute for the thing men once held it to be. There are hosts of honourable men of wealth, and there are large fortunes which have been honourably made; but so much brutal indifference to the rights of others, so much tyrannical use of power, so much arbitrary employment of privilege without a touch of genius, so much cynical indifference to human ties of all kinds, so much vulgar greed, have come to light, . . . that the lustre has very largely gone and wealth, as a supreme prize of life, has immensely lost in attractive power. There are hosts of young men who are ambitious to be rich, but who are not willing to accept wealth on such terms; the price is too great, the bargain too hard."

Men of exceptional executive and financial ability, raise yourselves to the standing-point of real greatness and use these abilities to noble purposes and to undying ends instead of piling a heap of things together that you'll soon have to leave and that may do those to whom it will go more harm than good. The times are changing, mankind is advancing and ascending to higher standing places, and it will be but a short time when your position if maintained as at present will be a very ordinary one or even a very low one in the public esteem—and so will be your memories.

The Bishop of Exeter voices a well-nigh universal human cry at present when he says:

Give us men!
Strong and stalwart ones:
Men whom highest hope inspires,
Men whom purest honour fires,
Men who trample Self beneath them,
Men who make their country wreathe them
As her noble sons,
Worthy of their sires.
Men who never shame their mothers,
Men who never fail their brothers,
True, however false are others:
Give us Men—I say again,
Give us Men!

In the Fire of the Heart

XXXV

An Example—A Very Young Old Lady

A close observer, a careful student of the power of the thought forces, will soon be able to read in the voice, in the movements, in the features, the effects registered by the prevailing mental states and conditions. Or, if he is told the prevailing mental states and conditions, he can describe the voice, the movements, the features, as well as describe, in a general way, the peculiar physical ailments their possessor is heir to.

There comes to mind at this moment a friend, a lady well on to eighty years of age. An old lady, some, most people in fact, would call her, especially those who measure age by the number of the seasons that have come and gone since one's birth. But to call our friend old, would be to call black white. She is no older than a girl of twenty-five, and indeed younger, I am glad to say, or I am sorry to say, depending upon the point of view, than *many* a girl of this age. Seeking for the good in all people and in all things, she has found the good everywhere. The brightness of disposition and of voice that is hers today, that attracts all people to her and that makes her so beautifully attractive to all people, has characterized her all through life. It has in turn carried brightness and hope and courage and strength to hundreds and thousands of people through all these years, and will continue to do so, apparently, for many years yet to come.

No fears, no worryings, no hatreds, no jealousies, no sorrowings, no grievings, no sordid graspings after inordinate gain, have found entrance into her realm of thought. As a consequence her mind, free from these abnormal states and conditions, has not externalized in her body the various physical ailments that the great majority of people are lugging about with them, thinking in their ignorance, that they are natural, and that it is all in accordance with the "eternal order of things" that they should have them. Her life has been one of varied experiences, so that all these things would have found ready entrance into the realm of her mind and so into her life were she ignorant enough to allow them entrance. On the contrary she has been wise enough to recognize the fact that in one kingdom at least she is ruler,—the kingdom of her mind, and that it is hers to dictate as to what shall and what shall not enter there. She knows, moreover, that in determining this she is determining all the conditions of her life. It is indeed a pleasure as well as an inspiration to see her as she goes here and there, to see her sunny disposition, her youthful step, to hear her joyous laughter. Indeed and in truth, Shakespeare knew whereof he spoke when he said,—"It is the mind that makes the body rich."

With great pleasure I watched her but recently as she was walking along the street, stopping to have a word and so a part in the lives of a group of children at play by the wayside, hastening her step a little to have a word with a washerwoman toting her bundle of clothes, stopping for a word with a laboring man returning with dinner pail in hand from his work, returning the recognition from the lady in her carriage, and so imparting some of her own rich life to all with whom she came in contact.

And as good fortune would have it, while still watching her, an old lady passed her,—really old, this one, though at least ten or fifteen years younger, so far as the count by the seasons is concerned. Nevertheless she was bent in form and apparently stiff in joint and muscle. Silent in mood, she wore a countenance of long-faced sadness, which was intensified surely several fold by a black, sombre head-gear with an immense heavy veil still more sombre looking if possible. Her entire dress was of this description.

By this relic-of-barbarism garb, combined with her own mood and expression, she continually proclaimed to the world two things,—her own personal sorrows and woes, which by this very method she kept continually fresh in her mind, and also her lack of faith in the eternal goodness of things, her lack of faith in the love and eternal goodness of the Infinite Father.

Wrapped only in the thoughts of her own ailments, and sorrows, and woes, she received and she gave nothing of joy, nothing of hope, nothing of courage, nothing of value to those whom she passed or with whom she came in contact. But on the contrary she suggested to all and helped to intensify in many, those mental states all too prevalent in our common human life. And as she passed our friend one could notice a slight turn of the head which, coupled with the expression in her face, seemed to indicate this as her thought,—Your dress and your conduct are not wholly in keeping with a lady of your years. Thank God, then, thank God they are not. And may He in His great goodness and love send us an innumerable company of the same rare type; and may they live a thousand years to bless mankind, to impart the life-giving influences of their own royal lives to the numerous ones all about us who stand so much in need of them.

In Tune with the Infinite

XXXVI

How Mind Builds Body

Would you remain always young, and would you carry all the joyousness and buoyancy of youth into your maturer years? Then have care concerning but one thing,—how you live in your thought world. This will determine all. It was the inspired one, Gautama, the Buddha, who said,—"The mind is everything; what you think you become." And the same thing had Ruskin in mind when he said,—"Make yourself nests of pleasant thoughts. None of us as yet know, for none of us have been taught in early youth, what fairy palaces we may build of beautiful thought,—*proof against all adversity.*" And would you have in your body all the elasticity, all the strength, all the beauty of your younger years? Then live these in your mind, making no room for unclean thought, and you will externalize them in your body. In the degree that you keep young in thought will you remain young in body. And you will find that your body will in turn aid your mind, for body helps mind the same as mind builds body.

You are continually building, and so externalizing in your body conditions most akin to the thoughts and emotions you entertain. And not only are you so building from within, but you are also continually drawing from without, forces of a kindred nature. Your particular kind of thought connects you with a similar order of thought from without. If it is bright, hopeful, cheerful, you connect yourself with a current of thought of this nature. If it is sad, fearing, despondent, then this is the order of thought you connect yourself with.

If the latter is the order of your thought, then perhaps unconsciously and by degrees you have been connecting yourself with it. You need to go back and pick up again a part of your child nature, with its careless and cheerful type of thought.

Full, rich, and abounding health is the normal and the natural condition of life. Anything else is an abnormal condition, and abnormal conditions as a rule come through perversions. God never created sickness, suffering, and disease; they are man's own creations. They come through his violating the laws under which he lives. So used are we to seeing them that we come gradually, if not to think of them as natural, then to look upon them as a matter of course.

The time will come when the work of the physician will not be to treat and attempt to heal the body, but to heal the mind, which in turn will heal the body. In other words, the true physician will be a teacher; his work will be to keep people well, instead of attempting to make them well after sickness and disease comes on; and still beyond this there will come a time when each will be his own physician. In the degree that we live in harmony with the higher laws of our being, and so, in the degree that we become better acquainted with the powers of the mind and spirit, will we give less attention to the body,—no less *care*, but less *attention*.

The bodies of thousands to-day would be much better cared for if their owners gave them less thought and attention. As a rule, those who think least of their bodies enjoy the best health. Many are kept in continual ill health by the abnormal thought and attention they give them.

Give the body the nourishment, the exercise, the fresh air, the sunlight it requires, keep it clean, and then think of it as little as possible. In your thoughts and in your conversation never dwell upon the negative side. Don't talk of sickness and disease. By talking of these you do yourself harm and you do harm to those who listen to you. Talk of those things that will make people the better for listening to you. Thus you will infect them with health and strength and not with weakness and disease.

"Never affirm or repeat about your health what you do not wish to be true. Do not dwell upon your ailments, nor study your symptoms. Never allow yourself to be convinced that you are not complete master of yourself. Stoutly affirm your superiority over bodily ills, and do not acknowledge yourself the slave of any inferior power. . . . I would teach children early to build a strong barrier between themselves and disease, by healthy habits of thought, high thinking, and purity of life. I would teach them to expel all thoughts of death, all images of disease, all discordant emotions, like hatred, malice, revenge, envy, and sensuality, as they would banish a temptation to do evil. I would teach them that bad food, bad drink, or bad air makes bad blood; that bad blood makes bad tissue, and bad flesh bad morals. I would teach them that healthy thoughts are as essential to healthy bodies as pure thoughts to a clean life. I would teach them to cultivate a strong will power, and to brace themselves against life's enemies in every possible way. I would teach the sick to have hope, confidence, cheer. Our thoughts and imaginations are the only real limits to our possibilities. No man's success or health will ever reach beyond his own confidence; as a rule, we erect our own barriers."

In Tune with the Infinite

XXXVII

Soul Radiance

All the frictions, all the uncertainties, all the ills, the sufferings, the fears, the forebodings, the perplexities of life come to us because we are out of harmony with the divine order of things. They will continue to come as long as we so live. Rowing against the tide is hard and uncertain. To go with the tide and thus to take advantage of the working of a great natural force is safe and easy. To come into the conscious, vital realization of our oneness with the Infinite Life and Power is to come into the current of this divine sequence. Coming thus into harmony with the Infinite, brings us in turn into harmony with all about us, into harmony with the life of the heavens, into harmony with all the universe. And above all, it brings us into harmony with ourselves, so that body, soul, and mind become perfectly harmonized, and when this is so, life becomes full and complete.

The sense life then no longer masters and enslaves us. The physical is subordinated to and ruled by the mental; this in turn is subordinated to and continually illumined by the spiritual. Life is then no longer the poor, onesided thing it is in so many cases; but the three-fold, the all-round life with all its beauties and ever increasing joys and powers is entered upon. Thus it is that we are brought to realize that the middle path is the great solution of life; neither asceticism on the one hand nor license and perverted use on the other. Everything is for use, but all must be wisely used in order to be fully enjoyed.

As we live in these higher realizations the senses are not ignored but are ever more fully perfected. As the body becomes less gross and heavy, finer in its texture and form, all the senses become finer, so that powers we do not now realize as belonging to us gradually develop. Thus we come, in a perfectly natural and normal way, into the super-conscious realms whereby we make it possible for the higher laws and truths to be revealed to us. As we enter into these realms we are then not among those who give their time to speculating as to whether this one or that one had the insight and the powers attributed to him, but we are able to know for ourselves. Neither are we among those who attempt to lead the people upon the hearsay of someone else, but we know whereof we speak, and only thus can we speak with authority. There are many things that we cannot know until by living the life we bring ourselves into that state where it is possible for them to be revealed to us. "If any man will do His will, he shall know of the doctrine." It was Plotinus who said, "The mind that wishes to behold God must itself become God." As we thus make it possible for these higher laws and truths to be revealed to us, we will in turn become enlightened ones, channels through which they may be revealed to others.

When one is fully alive to the possibilities that come with this higher awakening, as he goes here and there, as he mingles with his fellow-men, he imparts to all an inspiration that kindles in them a feeling of power kindred to his own. We are all continually giving out influences similar to those that are playing in our own lives. We do this in the same way that each flower emits its own peculiar odor. The rose breathes out its fragrance upon the air and all who come near it are refreshed and inspired by this emanation from the soul of the rose. A poisonous weed sends out its obnoxious odor; it is neither refreshing nor inspiring in its effects, and if one remain near it long he may be so unpleasantly affected as to be made even ill by it.

The higher the life the more inspiring and helpful are the emanations that it is continually sending out. The lower the life the more harmful is the influence it continually sends out to all who come in contact with it. Each one is continually radiating an atmosphere of one kind or the other.

We are told by the mariners who sail on the Indian Seas, that many times they are able to tell their approach to certain islands long before they can see them by the sweet fragrance of the sandalwood that is wafted far out upon the deep. Do you not see how it would serve to have such a soul playing through such a body that as you go here and there a subtle, silent force goes out from you that all feel and are influenced by; so that you carry with you an inspiration and continually shed a benediction wherever you go; so that your friends and all people will say,—His coming brings peace and joy into our homes, welcome his coming; so that as you pass along the street, tired, and weary, and even sinsick men and women will feel a certain divine touch that will awaken new desires and a new life in them; that will make the very horse as you pass him turn his head with a strange, half-human, longing look? Such are the subtle powers of the human soul when it makes itself translucent to the Divine.

In Tune with the Infinite

XXXVIII

Intuition: The Voice Of The Soul

The power of every life, the very life itself, is determined by what it relates itself to. God is immanent as well as transcendent. He is creating, working, ruling in the universe today, in your life and in mine, just as much as He ever has been. We are too apt to regard Him after the manner of an absentee landlord, one who has set in operation the forces of this great universe, and then taken Himself away.

In the degree, however, that we recognize Him as immanent as well as transcendent, are we able to partake of His life and power. For in the degree that we recognize Him as the Infinite Spirit of Life and Power that is today, at this very moment, working and manifesting in and through all, and then, in the degree that we come into the realization of our oneness with this life, do we become partakers of, and so do we actualize in ourselves the qualities of His life. *In the degree that we open ourselves to the inflowing tide of this immanent and transcendent life, do we make ourselves channels through which the Infinite Intelligence and Power can work.*

It is through the instrumentality of the mind that we are enabled to connect the real soul life with the physical life, and so enable the soul life to manifest and work through the physical. The thought life needs *continually* to be illumined from within. This illumination can come in just the degree that through the agency of the mind we recognize our oneness with the Divine, of which each soul is an individual form of expression.

This gives us the inner guiding which we call intuition. "Intuition is to the spiritual nature and understanding practically what sense perception is to the sensuous nature and understanding. It is an inner spiritual sense through which man is opened to the direct revelation and knowledge of God, the secrets of nature and life, and through which he is brought into conscious unity and fellowship with God, and made to realize his own deific nature and supremacy of being as the son of God.... It is, we repeat, a spiritual sense opening inwardly, as the physical senses open outwardly; and because it has the capacity to perceive, grasp, and know the truth at first hand, independent of all external sources of information, we call it intuition. All inspired teaching and spiritual revelations are based upon the recognition of this spiritual faculty of the soul, and its power to receive and appropriate them"

Some call it the voice of the soul; some call it the voice of God; some call it the sixth sense. It is our inner spiritual sense.

In the degree that we come into the recognition of our own *true* selves, into the realization of the oneness of our life with the Infinite Life, and in the degree that we open ourselves to this divine inflow, does this voice of intuition, this voice of the soul, this voice of God, speak clearly; and in the degree that we recognize, listen to, and obey it, does it speak ever more clearly, until by-and-by there comes the time when it is unerring, absolutely unerring, in its guidance.

In Tune with the Infinite

XXXIX

Miracles And The Higher Life

The most powerful agent in character-building is this awakening to the true self, to the fact that man is a spiritual being—nay, more, that I, this very eternal I, am a spiritual being, right here and now, at this very moment, with the God-powers which can be quickly called forth. With this awakening, life in all its manifold relations becomes wonderfully simplified, And as to the powers, the full realization of the fact that man is a spiritual being and a living as such brings, they are absolutely without limit, increasing in direct proportion as the higher self, the Godself, assumes the mastery, and so as this higher spiritualization of life goes on.

With this awakening and realization one is brought at once *en rapport* with the universe. He feels the power and the thrill of the life universal. He goes out from his own little garden spot, and mingles with the great universe; and the little perplexities, trials, and difficulties of life that today so vex and annoy him, fall away of their own accord by reason of their very insignificance. The intuitions become keener and ever more keen and unerring in their guidance. There comes more and more the power of reading men, so that no harm can come from this source. There comes more and more the power of seeing into the future, so that more and more true becomes the old adage,—that coming events cast their shadows before. Health in time takes the place of disease; for all disease and its consequent suffering is merely the result of the violation of law, either consciously or unconsciously, either intentionally or unintentionally. There comes also a spiritual

360

power which, as it is sent out, is adequate for the healing of others the same as in the days of old. The body becomes less gross and heavy, finer in its texture and form, so that it serves far better and responds far more readily to the higher impulses of the soul. Matter itself in time responds to the action of these higher forces; and many things that we are accustomed by reason of our limited vision to call miraculous or supernatural become the normal, the natural, the every-day.

For what, let us ask, is a miracle? Nothing more nor less than this: a highly illumined soul, one who has brought his life into thorough harmony with the higher spiritual laws and forces of his being, and therefore with those of the universe, thus making it possible for the highest things to come to him, has brought to him a law a little higher than the ordinary mind knows of as yet. This he touches, he operates. It responds. The people see the result, and cry out, Miracle! miracle! when it is just as natural, just as fully in accordance with the law on this higher plane, as is the common, the everyday on the ordinary. And let it be remembered that the miraculous, the supernatural of today becomes, as in the process of evolution we leave the lower for the higher, the common-place, the natural, the everyday of tomorrow; and, truly, miracles are being performed in the world today just as much as they ever have been.

The Master never claimed for himself anything that he did not claim for all mankind; but, quite to the contrary, he said and continually repeated, Not only shall ye do these things, but greater than these shall ye do; for I have pointed out to you the way,— meaning, though strange as it evidently seems to many, *exactly* what he said.

What All the World's A-Seeking

XL

The Voice Of The Higher Self

Great should be the joy that God's boundless truth is open to all, open *equally* to all, and that it will make each one its dwelling place in proportion as he earnestly desires it and opens himself to it.

And in regard to the wisdom that guides us in our daily life, there is nothing that it is right and well for us to know that may not be known when we recognize the law of its coming, and are able wisely to use it. Let us know that all things are ours as soon as we know how to appropriate them.

> "I hold it as a changeless law,
> From which no soul can sway or swerve,
> We have that in us which will draw
> Whate'er we need or most deserve."

If the times come when we know not what course to pursue, when we know not which way to turn, the fault lies in ourselves. If the fault lies in ourselves then the correction of this unnatural condition lies also in ourselves. It is never necessary to come into such a state if we are awake and remain awake to the light and the powers within us. The light is ever shining, and the only thing that it is necessary for us diligently to see to is that we permit neither this thing nor that to come between us and the light. "With Thee is the fountain of life; in Thy light shall we see light."

Let us hear the words of one of the most highly illumined men I have ever known, and one who as a consequence is never in the dark, when the time comes, as to what to do and how to do it. "Whenever you are in doubt as to the course you should pursue, after you have turned to every outward means of guidance, *let the inward eye see, let the inward ear hear*, and allow this simple, natural, beautiful process to go on unimpeded by questionings or doubts.... In all dark hours and times of unwanted perplexity we need to follow one simple direction, found, as all needed directions can be found, in the dear old gospel, which so many read, but alas, so few interpret. 'Enter into thine inner chamber and shut the door.' Does this mean that we must literally betake ourselves to a private closet with a key in the door? If it did, then the command could never be obeyed in the open air, on land or sea, and the Christ loved the lakes and the forests far better than the cramping rooms of city dwelling houses; still His counsels are so wide-reaching that there is no spot on earth and no conceivable situation in which any of us may be placed where we cannot follow them.

"One of the most intuitive men we ever met had a desk in a city office where several other gentlemen were doing business constantly and often talking loudly. Entirely undisturbed by the many various sounds about him, this self-centred, faithful man would, in any moment of perplexity, draw the curtains of privacy so completely about him that he would be as fully enclosed in his own psychic aura, and thereby as effectually removed from all distractions as though he were alone in some primeval wood. Taking his difficulty with him into the mystic silence in the form of a direct question, to which he expected a certain answer, he would remain utterly passive until the reply came, and never once through many years' experience did he find himself disappointed or misled. Intuitive perceptions of truth are the daily bread to satisfy our daily hunger; they come like the manna in the desert day by day; each day brings adequate supply for that day's need only. They must be followed instantly, for dalliance with them means their obscuration.

"One condition is imposed by *universal law*, and this we must obey. Put all wishes aside save the one desire to know *truth*; couple with this one demand—the fully consecrated determination to follow what is distinctly perceived as truth immediately it is revealed.

No other affection must be permitted to share the field with this all-absorbing love of *truth* for its own sake. Obey this one direction and never forget that expectation and desire are bride and bridegroom and forever inseparable, and you will soon find your hitherto darkened way grow luminous with celestial radiance, for with the heaven within, all heavens without incessantly cooperate." This may be termed going into the "silence." This it is to perceive and to be guided by "the light that lighteth every man that cometh into the world." This it is to listen to and be guided by the voice of your own soul, the voice of your higher self.

In Tune with the Infinite

XLI

The Soul Must Be Made Translucent To The Divine

The soul is divine and in allowing it to become translucent to the Infinite Spirit it reveals all things to us. As man turns away from the Divine Light do all things become hidden. There is nothing hidden of itself. When the spiritual sense is opened, then it transcends all the limitations of the physical senses and the intellect. And in the degree that we are able to get away from the limitations set by them, and realize that so far as the real life is concerned it is one with the Infinite Life, then we begin to reach the place where this voice will always speak, where it will never fail us, if we follow it, and as a consequence where we will always have the divine illumination and guidance. To know this and to live in this realization is not to live in heaven hereafter, but to live in heaven here and now, *to-day and every day.*

No human soul need be without it. When we turn our face in the right direction it comes as simply and as naturally as the flower blooms and the winds blow. It is not to be bought with money or with price. It is a condition waiting simply to be realized, by rich and by poor, by king and by peasant, by master and by servant the world over. All are equal heirs to it. And so the peasant, if he find it first, lives a life far transcending in beauty and in real power the life of his king. The servant, if he find it first, lives a life surpassing the life of his master.

If you would find the highest, the fullest, and the richest life that not only this world but that any world can know, then do away with the sense of the separateness of your life from the life of God. Hold to the thought of your oneness. In the degree that you do this you will find yourself realizing it more and more, and as this life of realization is lived, you will find that no good thing will be withheld, for all things are included in this. Then it will be yours, without fears or forebodings, simply to do today what your hands find to do, and so be ready for tomorrow, *when it comes*, knowing that tomorrow will bring tomorrow's supplies for the mental, the spiritual, and the physical life. Remember, however, that tomorrow's supplies are not needed until tomorrow comes.

If one is willing to trust himself *fully* to the Law, the Law will never fail him. It is the half-hearted trusting to it that brings uncertain, and so, unsatisfactory results. Nothing is firmer and surer than Deity. It will never fail the one who throws himself wholly upon it. The secret of life then, is to live continually in this realization, whatever one may be doing, wherever one may be, by day and by night, both waking and sleeping. It can be lived in while we are sleeping no less than when we are awake.

In Tune with the Infinite

XLII

Receiving Instruction During Sleep

During the process of sleep it is merely the physical body that is at rest and in quiet; the soul life with all its activities goes right on. Sleep is nature's provision for the recuperation of the body, for the rebuilding and hence the replacing of the waste that is continually going on during the waking hours. It is nature's great restorer. If sufficient sleep is not allowed the body, so that the rebuilding may equalize the wasting process, the body is gradually depleted and weakened, and any ailment or malady, when it is in this condition, is able to find a more ready entrance. It is for this reason that those who are subject to it will take a cold, as we term it, more readily when the body is tired or exhausted through loss of sleep than at most any other time. The body is in that condition where outside influences can have a more ready effect upon it, than when it is in its normal condition. And when they do have an effect they always go to the weaker portions first.

Our bodies are given us to serve far higher purposes than we ordinarily use them for. Especially is this true in the numerous cases where the body is master of its owner. In the degree that we come into the realization of the higher powers of the mind and spirit, in that degree does the body, through their influence upon it, become less gross and heavy, finer in its texture and form. And then, because the mind finds a kingdom of enjoyment in itself, and in all the higher things it becomes related to, *excesses* in eating and drinking, as well as all others, naturally and of their own accord fall away. There also falls away the desire for the heavier, grosser, less valuable kinds of food and drink, such as the flesh of animals, alcoholic drinks, and all things of the class that stimulate the body and the passions rather than build the body and the brain into a strong, clean, well-nourished, enduring, and fibrous condition. In the degree that the body thus becomes less gross and heavy, finer in its texture and form, is there less waste, and what there is is more easily replaced, so that it keeps in a more regular and even condition. When this is true, less sleep is actually required. And even the amount that is taken does more for a body of this finer type than it can do for one of the other nature.

As the body in this way grows finer, in otherwords, as the process of its evolution is thus accelerated, it in turn helps the mind and the soul in the realization of ever higher perceptions, and thus body helps mind the same as mind builds body. It was undoubtedly this fact that Browning had in mind when he said:

> "Let us cry 'All good things
> Are ours, nor soul helps flesh, more now,
> Than flesh helps soul.'"

Sleep, then, is for the resting and the rebuilding of the body. The soul needs no rest, and while the body is at rest in sleep the soul life is active the same as when the body is in activity.

There are some, having a deep insight into the soul's activities, who say that we travel when we sleep. Some are able to recall and bring over into the conscious, waking life the scenes visited, the information gained, and the events that have transpired. Most people are not able to do this and so much that might otherwise be gained is lost. They say, however, that it is in our power, in proportion as we understand the laws, to go where we will, and to bring over into the conscious, waking life all the experiences thus gained. Be this, however, as it may, it certainly is true that while sleeping we have the power, in a perfectly normal and natural way, to get much of value by way of light, instruction, and growth that the majority of people now miss.

If the soul life, that which relates us to Infinite Spirit, is always active, even while the body is at rest, why may not the mind so direct conditions as one falls asleep, that while the body is at rest, it may continually receive illumination from the soul and bring what it thus receives over into the conscious, waking life? This, indeed, can be done, and is done by some to great advantage; and many times the highest inspirations from the soul come in this way, as would seem most natural, since at this time all communications from the outer, material world no longer enter. By charging the mind on going to sleep as to a particular time for waking, it is possible as many of us know, to wake on the very minute.

The mind acting intently along a particular line will continue so to act until some other object of thought carries it along another line. And since in sleep only the body is in quiet while the mind and soul are active, then the mind on being given a certain direction when one drops off to sleep, will take up the line along which it is directed, and can be made, in time, to bring over into consciousness the results of its activities. Some will be able very soon to get results of this kind; for some it will take longer. Quiet and continued effort will increase the faculty.

In Tune with the Infinite

XLIII

The Joseph Type Both Dreams And Interprets

Then by virtue of the law of the drawing power of mind, since the mind is always active, we are drawing to us even while sleeping, influences from the realms kindred to those in which we in our thoughts are living before we fall asleep. In this way we can put ourselves into relation with whatever kinds of influence we choose and accordingly gain much during the process of sleep. In many ways the interior faculties are more open and receptive while we are in sleep than while we are awake. Hence the necessity of exercising even greater care as to the nature of the thoughts that occupy the mind as we enter into sleep, for there can come to us only what we by our own order of thought attract. We have it entirely in our own hands.

And for the same reason,—this greater degree of receptivity during this period,—we are able by understanding and using the law, to gain much of value more readily in this way than when the physical senses are fully open to the material world about us. Many will find a practice somewhat after the following nature of value: When light or information is desired along any particular line, light or information you feel it is right and wise for you to have, as, for example, light in regard to an uncertain course of action, then as you retire, first bring your mind into the attitude of peace and good-will for all. You in this way bring yourself into an harmonious condition, and in turn attract to yourself these same peaceful conditions from without.

Then resting in this sense of peace, quietly and calmly send out your earnest desire for the needed light or information; cast out of your mind all fears or forebodings lest it come not, for "in quietness and in confidence shall be your strength." Take the expectant attitude of mind, firmly believing and expecting that when you awake the desired results will be with you. Then on awaking, before any thoughts or activities from the outside world come in to absorb the attention, remain for a little while receptive to the intuitions or the impressions that come. When they come, when they manifest themselves clearly, then act upon them without delay. In the degree that you do this, in that degree will the power of doing it ever more effectively grow.

Or, if for unselfish purposes you desire to grow and develop any of your faculties, or to increase the health and strength of your body, take a corresponding attitude of mind, the form of which will readily suggest itself in accordance with your particular needs or desires. In this way you will open yourself to, you will connect yourself with, and you will set into operation within yourself, the particular order of forces that will make for these results. Don't be afraid to voice your desires. In this way you set into operation vibratory forces which go out and which make their impress felt somewhere, and which, arousing into activity or uniting with other forces, set about to actualize your desires. No good thing shalt be withheld from him who lives in harmony with the higher laws and forces. There are no desires that shall not be satisfied to the one who knows and who wisely uses the powers with which he or she is endowed.

Your sleep will be more quiet, and peaceful, and refreshing, and so your power increased mentally, physically, and spiritually, simply by sending out as you fall asleep, thoughts of love and good-will, thoughts of peace and harmony for all. In this way you are connecting yourself with all the forces in the universe that make for peace and harmony.

Visions and inspirations of the highest order will come in the degree that we make for them the right conditions. One who has studied deeply into the subject in hand has said: "To receive education spiritually while the body is resting in sleep is a perfectly normal and orderly experience, and would occur definitely and satisfactorily in the lives of all of us, if we paid more attention to internal and consequently less to external states with their supposed but unreal necessities....Our thoughts make us what we are here and hereafter, and our thoughts are often busier by night than by day, for when we are asleep to the exterior we can be wide awake to the interior world; and the unseen world is a substantial place, the conditions of which are entirely regulated by mental and moral attainments. "When we are not deriving information through outward avenues of sensation, we are receiving instruction through interior channels of perception, and when this fact is understood for what it is worth, it will become a universal custom for persons to take to sleep with them the special subject on which they most earnestly desire particular instruction. The Pharaoh type of person dreams, and so does his butler and baker; but the Joseph type, which is that of the truly gifted seer, both dreams and interprets."

In Tune with the Infinite

XLIV

Humaneness In Our Diet

"Is not flesh-eating natural?" I hear it asked. "Does not man in his primitive, savage state make use of flesh *naturally*? Do not animals devour one another?" Yes; but we are not savages, nor are we purely animals, and it is time for us to have outgrown this attendant-of-savage-life custom. The truth of the matter is that considerably more than one-half of the people in the world today are not flesh-eaters. And many peoples, whom large numbers in America and England, for example, refer to as the heathen, and send missionaries to Christianize, are far ahead of us, and hence *more Christian* in this matter. And one reason why missionaries in many parts of India, among the Buddhists and Brahmins, for example, have been so comparatively unsuccessful in their work is because the majority of those keen-minded and spiritually un-folded people cannot see what superiority there is in the religion of the one whom it allows to kill, cook, and feast upon the bodies of his or her fellow-creatures, which they themselves could not do.

In Bombay, to have the carcasses of animals exposed to pub-lic view, as we see them in the stores and markets here, and at times scores of them decorating the windows and entire fronts, is prohibited by law.

We shall find numerous articles of food, as we study the matter, that, so far as body nourishing, building, and sustaining qualities are concerned, contain twice, and in some cases *over* twice, as much as any flesh food that can be mentioned. The liability to mistake in this matter lies in the fact that flesh foods when taken into the stomach burn, oxygenize, more quickly than most other foods do, and this short stimulating effect, resembling more or less the stimulating effects of alcohol, is mistaken for a body nourishing and sustaining effect.

No, experience will teach you that if you do away with flesh-eating and get in its place the other *valuable* foods, the time will quickly come when you will care less and less for it; then again, the time will come when you will have no desire for it, and finally, you will grow positively to dislike it and its effects, and nothing could induce you to return again to the flesh-pots. And as for those who think that the ones who are not flesh-eaters are necessarily weaklings, I should like to match a friend of mine, an instructor in one of our great American universities, who for over eighteen years has eaten no flesh foods,—I should like to match him with any whom they may send forward, when it comes to a test of long continued work and endurance.

In London there are already numbers of restaurants where no flesh foods are served; in Berlin there are already about twenty, and their number in these, as well as in numerous other cities, is continually increasing. It is a matter of but a short time until there will be numbers of such in our own country. The only really consistent humanitarian is the one who is not a flesh-eater.

When one goes into the better restaurants where no flesh foods are served, in England and Germany for example, he is impressed with the foundation less excuse of so many people that it is hard, or even impossible, to get along without flesh foods. In the vegetable realm will be found an abundance, a hundred or a thousand times over, and especially when we begin to give some little attention to the great varieties of most valuable foods there, and to the exceed-ingly appetising ways in which they can be prepared. One reason why such large numbers of people feel that meat is a necessity, or almost a necessity with them as an article of food, is because in our hotels and restaurants and cafes, and, in fact, in the majority of our homes, the meat element forms the chief portion of the foods prepared for our tables, and to it, practically, all the skill in preparation is given; while the other things are looked upon more as accessories, and are many times prepared in an exceedingly careless manner, much as mere accessories would be. But with a decreasing use of flesh foods and with more attention given to the skilful preparation of the large numbers of other still more valuable foods, we shall begin to wonder why we have so long been slaves to a mere custom, thinking it a necessity.

The time will come in the world's history, and a movement is setting in that direction even now, when it will be deemed as strange a thing to find a man or a woman who eats flesh as food, as it is now to find a man or a woman who refrains from eating it. And personally, I share the belief with many others, that the *highest* mental, physical, and spiritual excellence will come to a person only when, among other things, he refrains from a flesh and blood diet.

And there is another matter of grave importance that we should not be allowed to lose sight of in this connection. The brutality to the animal creation, which as a weaker creation we should protect and care for, has its corresponding and balancing element in connection with our duty to those who are hired to do our butchery for us.

Each one who aids in creating the demand for flesh foods is to a greater or less extent, not indirectly but directly, responsible for the degrading and dehumanizing influences at work in the lives of many thousands of their fellow-men. We *are* our brother's keeper whenever it comes to a matter that we are personally involved in, and there are responsibilities that we cannot shift after we are once made acquainted with the facts pertaining to them.

Every Living Creature

XLV

To Be At Peace

A deep interior meaning underlies the great truth, "To be spiritually minded is life and peace." To recognize the fact that we are spirit, and to live in this thought, is to be spiritually minded, and so to be in harmony and peace. Oh, the thousands of men and women all about us weary with care, troubled and ill at ease, running hither and thither to find peace, weary in body, soul, and mind; going to other countries, traveling the world over, coming back, and still not finding it. Of course they have not found it and they never will find it in this way, because they are looking for it where it is not. They are looking for it without when they should look within. Peace is to be found only within, and unless one find it there he will never find it at all.

Peace lies not in the external world. It lies within one's own soul. We may travel over many different avenues in pursuit of it, we may seek it through the channels of the bodily appetites and passions, we may seek it through all the channels of the external, we may chase for it hither and thither, but it will always be just beyond our grasp, because we are searching for it where it is not. In the degree, however, that we order the bodily appetites and passions in accordance with the promptings of the soul within will the higher forms of happiness and peace enter our lives; but in the degree that we fail in doing this will disease, suffering, and discontent enter in.

To be at one with God is to be at peace. The child simplicity is the greatest agency in bringing this full and complete realization, the child simplicity that recognizes its true relations with the Father's life. There are people I know who have come into such a conscious realization of their oneness with this Infinite Life, this Spirit of Infinite Peace, that their lives are fairly bubbling over with joy. I have particularly in mind at this moment a comparatively young man who was an invalid for several years, his health completely broken with nervous exhaustion, who thought there was nothing in life worth living for, to whom everything and everybody presented a gloomy aspect and he in turn presented a gloomy aspect to all with whom he came in contact. Not long ago he came into such a vital realization of his oneness with this Infinite Power, he opened himself so completely to its divine inflow, that today he is in perfect health, and frequently as I meet him now he cannot resist the impulse to cry out, "Oh, it is a joy to be alive."

He who comes into this higher realization never has any fear, for he has always with him a sense of protection, and the very realization of this makes his protection complete. Of him it is true— "No weapon that is formed against thee shall prosper;" "There shall no ill come nigh thy dwelling;" "Thou shalt be in league with the stones of the field, and the beasts of the field shall be at peace with thee."

These are the men and the women who seem to live charmed lives. The moment we fear anything we open the door for the entrance of the actualization of the very thing we fear. An animal will never harm a person who is absolutely fearless in regard to it. The instant he fears he opens himself to danger; and some animals, the dog for example, can instantly detect the element of fear, and this gives him the courage to do harm. In the degree that we come into a full realization of our oneness with this Infinite Power do we become calm and quiet, undisturbed by the little occurrences that before so vex and annoy us. We are no longer disappointed in people, for we always read them aright. We have the power of penetrating into their very souls and seeing the underlying motives that are at work there.

As soon as we are able to read people aright we will then cease to be disappointed in them, we will cease to place them on pedestals, for this can never be done without some attendant disappointment. The fall will necessarily come, sooner or later, and moreover, we are thus many times unfair to our friends. When we come into harmony with this Spirit of Peace, evil reports and apparent bad treatment, either at the hands of friends or of enemies, will no longer disturb us. When we are conscious of the fact that in our life and our work we are true to that eternal principle of right, of truth, of justice that runs through all the universe, that unites and governs all, that always eventually prevails, then nothing of this kind can come nigh us, and come what may we will always be tranquil and undisturbed.

The things that cause sorrow, and pain, and bereavement will not be able to take the hold of us they now take, for true wisdom will enable us to see the proper place and know the right relations of all things. The loss of friends by the transition we call death will not cause sorrow to the soul that has come into this higher realization, for he knows that there is no such thing as death, for each one is not only a partaker, but an eternal partaker, of this Infinite Life. He knows that the mere falling away of the physical body by no means affects the real soul life. With a tranquil spirit born of a higher faith he can realize for himself, and to those less strong he can say:

> "Loving friends! be wise and dry
> Straightway every weeping eye;
> What you left upon the bier
> is not worth a single tear;
> 'Tis a simple sea-shell; one
> Out of which the pearl has gone.
> The shell was nothing, leave it there;
> The pearl—the soul—was all, is here."

And so far as the element of separation is concerned, he realizes that to spirit there are no bounds, and that spiritual communion, whether between two persons in the body, or two persons, one in the body and one out of the body, is within the reach of all. In the degree that the higher spiritual life is realized can there be this higher spiritual communion.

In the degree that we are filled with this Spirit of Peace by thus opening ourselves to its inflow does it pour through us, so that we carry it with us wherever we go. In the degree that we thus open ourselves do we become magnets to attract peace from all sources; and in the degree that we attract and embody it in ourselves are we able to give it forth to others. We can in this way become such perfect embodiments of peace that wherever we go we are continually shedding benedictions. There are people all around us who are continually giving out blessings and comfort, persons whose mere presence seems to change sorrow into joy, fear into courage, despair into hope, weakness into power.

It is the one who has come into the realization of his own true self who carries this power with him and who radiates it wherever he goes—the one who, as we say, has found his center. And in all the great universe there is but one center—the Infinite Power that is working in and through all.

In Tune with the Infinite

XLVI

Courage Begets Strength; Fear Begets Weakness

The one who then has found his centre is the one who has come into the realization of his oneness with this Infinite Power, the one who recognizes himself as a spiritual being, for God is Spirit.

Such is the man of power. Centred in the Infinite, he has thereby, so to speak, connected himself with, he has attached his belts to, the great power-house of the universe. He is constantly drawing power to himself from all sources. For, thus centred, knowing himself, conscious of his own power, the thoughts that go from his mind are thoughts of strength ;and by virtue of the law that like attracts like, he by his thoughts is continually attracting to himself from all quarters the aid of all whose thoughts are thoughts of strength, and in this way he is linking himself with this order of thought in the universe.

And so, "to him that hath, to him shall be given." This is simply the working of a natural law. His strong, positive, and hence constructive thought is continually working success for him along all lines, and continually bringing to him help from all directions. The things that he sees, that he creates in the ideal, are through the agency of this strong constructive thought continually clothing themselves, taking form, manifesting themselves in the material. Silent, unseen forces are at work which will sooner or later be made manifest in the visible.

Fear and all thoughts of failure never suggest themselves to such a man; or if they do, they are immediately sent out of his mind, and so he is not influenced by this order of thought from without. He does not attract it to him. He is in another current of thought. Consequently the weakening, failure-bringing thoughts of the fearing, the vacillating, the pessimistic about him, have no influence upon him. The one who is of the negative, fearing kind not only has his energies and his physical agents weakened, or even paralyzed through the influence of this kind of thought that is born within him, but he also in this way connects himself with this order of thought in the world about him. And in the degree that he does this does he become a victim to the weak, fearing, negative minds all around him. Instead of growing in power, he increases in weakness. He is in the same order of thought with those of whom it is true—"and even that which they have shall be taken away from them." This again is simply the working of a natural law, the same as is its opposite. Fearing lest I lose even what I have I hide it away in a napkin. Very well. I must then pay the price of my "fearing lest I lose."

Thoughts of strength both build strength from within and attract it from without. Thoughts of weakness actualize weakness from within and attract it from without. Courage begets strength, fear begets weakness. And so courage begets success, fear begets failure. It is the man or the woman of faith, and hence of courage, who is the master of circumstances, and who makes his or her power felt in the world. It is the man or the woman who lacks faith and who as a consequence is weakened and crippled by fears and forebodings, who is the creature of all passing occurrences.

What one lives in his invisible, thought world, he is continually actualizing in his visible, material world. If he would have any conditions different in the latter he must make the necessary change in the former. A clear realization of this great fact would bring success to thousands of men and women who all about us are now in the depths of despair. It would bring health, abounding health and strength to thousands now diseased and suffering. It would bring peace and joy to thousands now unhappy and ill at ease.

And oh, the thousands all about us who are continually living in the slavery of fear. The spirits within that should be strong and powerful, are rendered weak and impotent. Their energies are crippled, their efforts are paralyzed. "Fear is everywhere—fear of want, fear of starvation, fear of public opinion, fear of private opinion, fear that what we own today may not be ours tomorrow, fear of sickness, fear of death. Fear has become with millions a fixed habit. The thought is everywhere. The thought is thrown upon us from every direction.... To live in continual dread, continual cringing, continual fear of anything, be it loss of love, loss of money, loss of position or situation, is to take the readiest means to lose what we fear we shall."

By fear nothing is to be gained, but on the contrary, everything is to be lost. "I know this is true," says one, "but I am given to fear; it's natural to me and I can't help it." Can't help it! In saying this you indicate one great reason of your fear by showing that you do not even know yourself as yet. You must know yourself in order to know your powers, and not until you know them can you use them wisely and fully. Don't say you can't help it. If you think you can't, the chances are that you can't. If you think you can, and act in accordance with this thought, then not only are the chances that you can, but if you act fully in accordance with it, that you can and that you will is an absolute certainty. It was Virgil who in describing the crew which in his mind would win the race, said of them—"They can because they think they can." In other words, this very attitude of mind on their part will infuse a spiritual power into their bodies that will give them the strength and endurance which will enable them to win.

Then take the thought that you *can*; take it merely as a seed-thought, if need be, plant it in your consciousness, tend it, cultivate it, and it will gradually reach out and gather strength from all quarters. It will focus and make positive and active the spiritual force within you that is now scattered and of little avail. It will draw to itself force from without. It will draw to your aid the influence of other minds of its own nature, minds that are fearless, strong, courageous. You will thus draw to yourself and connect yourself with this order of thought. If earnest and faithful, the time will soon come when all fear will lose its hold; and instead of being an embodiment of weakness and a creature of circumstances, you will find yourself a tower of strength and a master of circumstances.

In Tune with the Infinite

XLVII

"And What Is Mine Shall Know My Face"

We need more faith in everyday life—faith in the power that works for good, faith in the Infinite God, and hence faith in ourselves created in His image. And however things at times may seem to go, however dark at times appearances may be, the knowledge of the fact that "the Supreme Power has us in its charge as it has the suns and endless systems of worlds in space," will give us the supreme faith that all is well with us, the same as all is well with the world. "Thou wilt keep him in perfect peace whose mind is stayed on Thee."

There is nothing firmer, and safer, and surer than Deity. Then, as we recognize the fact that we have it in our own hands to open ourselves ever more fully to this Infinite Power, and call upon it to manifest itself in and through us, we will find in ourselves an ever increasing sense of power. For in this way we are working in conjunction with it, and it in turn is working in conjunction with us.

We are then led into the full realization of the fact that all things work together for good to those that love the good. Then the fears and forebodings that have dominated us in the past will be transmuted into faith, and faith when rightly understood and rightly used is a force before which nothing can stand.

Materialism leads naturally to pessimism. And how could it do otherwise? A knowledge of the Spiritual Power working in and through us as well as in and through all things, a power that works for righteousness, leads to optimism. Pessimism leads to weakness. Optimism leads to power. The one who is centred in Deity is the one who not only outrides every storm, but who through the faith, and so, the conscious power that is in him, faces storm with the same calmness and serenity that he faces fair weather; for he knows well beforehand what the outcome will be. He knows that underneath are the everlasting arms. He it is who realizes the truth of the injunction, "Rest in the Lord, wait patiently for Him and He shall give thee thy heart's desire." All shall be given, simply given, to him who is ready to accept it. Can anything be clearer than this?

In the degree, then, that we work in conjunction with the Supreme Power do we need the less to concern ourselves about results. To live in the full realization of this fact and all that attends it brings peace, a full, rich, abiding peace—a peace that makes the present complete, and that, going on before, brings back the assurance that as our days, so shall our strength be. The one who is thus centred, even in the face of all the unrest and the turmoil about us, can realize and say:

* * * * * * * * * *

"I stay my haste, I make delays,
For what avails this eager pace?
I stand amid eternal ways,
And what is mine shall know my face.

"Asleep, awake, by night or day,
The friends I seek are seeking me;
No wind can drive my bark astray,
Nor change the tide of destiny.

* * * * * * * * * *

"The waters know their own, and draw
The brooks that spring in yonder height;
So flows the good with equal law
Unto the soul of pure delight.

"The stars come nightly to the sky;
The tidal wave unto the sea;
Nor time, nor space, nor deep, nor high,
Can keep my own away from me."

In Tune with the Infinite

XLVIII

Heredity And Environment—Are We Bound By Them?

The true secret of power lies in keeping one's connection with the God who worketh all things. Whatever can't be done in the physical can be done in the spiritual. And in direct proportion as a man recognizes himself as spirit, and lives accordingly, is he able to transcend in power the man who recognizes himself merely as material. All the sacred literature of the world is teeming with examples of what we call miracles. They are not confined to any particular times or places. There is no age of miracles in distinction from any other period that may be an age of miracles. Whatever has been done in the world's history can be done again through the operation of the same laws and forces. These miracles were performed not by those who were more than men, but by those who through the recognition of their oneness with God became God-men, so that the higher forces and powers worked through them.

For what, let us ask, is a miracle? Is it something supernatural? Supernatural only in the sense of being above the natural, or rather, above that which is natural to man in his ordinary state. A miracle is nothing more nor less than this. One who has come into a knowledge of his true identity, of his oneness with the all-pervading Wisdom and Power, thus makes it possible for laws higher than the ordinary mind knows of to be revealed to him. These laws he makes use of; the people see the results, and by

387

virtue of their own limitations, call them miracles and speak of the person who performs these apparently supernatural works as a supernatural being. But they as supernatural beings could themselves perform these supernatural works if they would open themselves to the recognition of the same laws, and consequently to the realization of the same possibilities and powers. And let us also remember that the supernatural of yesterday becomes, as in the process of evolution we advance from the lower to the higher, from the more material to the more spiritual, the common and the natural of today, and what seems to be the supernatural of today becomes in the same way the natural of tomorrow, and so on through the ages. Yes, it is the God-man who does the things that appear supernatural, the man who by virtue of his realization of the higher powers transcends the majority and so stands out among them. But any power that is possible to one human soul is possible to another. The same laws operate in every life. We can be men and women of power or we can be men and women of impotence. The moment one vitally grasps the fact that he can rise he will rise, and he can have absolutely no limitations other than the limitations he sets to himself. Cream always rises to the top. It rises simply because *it is the nature of cream to rise.*

We hear much said of "environment." We need to realize that environment should never be allowed to make the man, but that man should always, and always can, condition the environment. When we realize this we will find that many times it is not necessary to take ourselves out of any particular environment, because we may yet have a work to do there; but by the very force we carry with us we can so affect and change matters that we will have an entirely new set of conditions in an old environment.

The same is true in regard to "hereditary" traits and influences. We sometimes hear the question asked, "Can they be overcome?" Only the one who doesn't yet know himself can ask a question such as this. If we entertain and live in the belief that they cannot be overcome, then the chances are that they will always remain. The moment, however, that we come into a realization of our true selves, and so of the tremendous powers and forces within—the powers and forces of the mind and spirit—hereditary traits and influences that are harmful in nature will begin to lessen, and will disappear with a rapidity directly in proportion to the completeness of this realization.

"There is no thing we cannot overcome;
Say not thy evil instinct is inherited,
Or that some trait inborn makes thy whole life forlorn,
And calls down punishment that is not merited.

Back of thy parents and grandparents lies
The Great Eternal Will!, that too is thine
Inheritance,—strong, beautiful, divine,
Sure lever of success for one who tries.

Earth has no claim the soul cannot contest;
Know thyself part of the Eternal Source;
Naught can stand before thy spirit's force:
The soul's Divine Inheritance is best."

In Tune with the Infinite

XLIX

Preserving One's Individuality

Again there are many who are living far below their possibilities because they are continually handing over their individualities to others. Do you want to be a power in the world? Then be yourself. Don't class yourself, don't allow yourself to be classed among the *second-hand*, among the they-say people. Be true to the highest within your own soul and then allow yourself to be governed by no customs or conventionalities or arbitrary man-made rules that are not founded upon *principle*. Those things that are founded upon principle will be observed by the right-minded, the right-hearted man or woman, in any case.

Don't surrender your individuality, which is your greatest agent of power, to the customs and conventionalities that have gotten their life from the great mass of those who haven't enough force to preserve their individualities—those who in other words have given them over as ingredients to the "mush of concession" which one of our greatest writers has said characterizes our modern society. If you do surrender your individuality in this way, you simply aid in increasing the undesirable conditions; in payment for this you become a slave, and the chances are that in time you will be unable to hold even the respect of those whom you in this way try to please.

If you preserve your individuality then you become a master, and if wise and discreet, your influence and power will be an aid in bringing about a higher, a better, and a more healthy set of conditions in the world. All people, moreover, will think more of you, will honor you more highly for doing this than if you show your weakness by contributing yourself to the same "mush of concession" that so many of them are contributing themselves to. With all classes of people you will then have an influence. "A great style of hero draws equally all classes, all extremes of society to him, till we say the very dogs believe in him."

To be one's self is the only worthy, and by all means the only satisfactory, thing to be.

"When we appeal to the Supreme and our life is governed by a principle, we are not governed either by fear of public opinion or loss of others' approbation, and we may be sure that the Supreme will sustain us. If in any way we try to live to suit others we never shall suit them, and the more we try the more unreasonable and exacting do they become. The government of your life is a matter that lies entirely between God and yourself, and when your life is swayed and influenced from any other source you are on the wrong path." When we find the kingdom within and become centred in the Infinite, then we become a law unto ourselves. When we become a law unto ourselves, then we are able to bring others to a knowledge of laws higher than they are governed or many times even enslaved by.

When we have found this centre, then that beautiful simplicity, at once the charm and the power of a truly great personality, enters into our lives. Then all striving for effect—that sure indicator of weakness and a lack of genuine power—is absent. This striving for effect that is so common is always an indicator of a lack of something. It brings to mind the man who rides behind a dock-tailed horse. Conscious of the fact that there is not enough in *himself* to attract attention, in common with a number of other weaklings, he adopts the brutal method of having his horse's tail sawed off, that its unnatural, odd appearance may attract from people the attention that he of himself is unable to secure.

But the one who strives for effect is always fooled more than he succeeds in fooling others. The man and the woman of true wisdom and insight can always see the causes that prompt, the motives that underlie the acts of all with whom he or she comes in contact. "He is great who is what he is from nature and who never reminds us of others."

The men and the women who are truly awake to the real powers within are the men and women who seem to be doing so little, yet who in reality are doing so much. They seem to be doing so little because they are working with higher agencies, and yet are doing so much because of this very fact. They do their work on the higher plane. They keep so completely their connection with the Infinite Power that It does the work for them and they are relieved of the responsibility. They are the careless people. They are careless because it is the Infinite Power that is working through them, and with this Infinite Power they are simply co-operating.

In Tune with the Infinite

L

Exclusiveness And Inclusiveness: What They Indicate

When we come fully to realize the great fact that all evil and error and sin with all their consequent sufferings come through ignorance, then wherever we see a manifestation of these in whatever form, if our hearts are right, we will have compassion—sympathy and compassion for the one in whom we see them. Compassion will then change itself into love, and love will manifest itself in kindly service. Such is the divine method. And so instead of aiding in trampling and keeping a weaker one down, we will hold him up until he can stand alone and become the master.

By example and not by precept. By living, not by preaching. By doing, not by professing. By living the life, not by dogmatizing as to how it should be lived. There is no contagion equal to the contagion of life. Whatever we sow, that shall we also reap, and each thing sown produces of its kind. We can kill not only by doing another bodily injury directly, but we can and we do kill by every antagonistic thought. Not only do we thus kill, but while we kill we suicide. Many a man has been made sick by having the ill thoughts of a number of people centred upon him; some have been actually killed. Put hatred into the world and we make it a literal hell. Put love into the world and heaven with all its beauties and glories becomes a reality.

Not to love is not to live, or it is to live a living death. The life that goes out in love to all is the life that is full, and rich, and continually expanding in beauty and in power. Such is the life that becomes ever more inclusive, and hence larger in its scope and influence. The larger the man and the woman, the more inclusive they are in their love and their friendships. The smaller the man and the woman, the more dwarfed and dwindling their natures, the more they pride themselves upon their "exclusiveness." Any one—a fool or an idiot—can be exclusive. It comes easy. It takes and it signifies a large nature to be universal, to be inclusive. Only the man or the woman of a small, personal, self-centred, self-seeking nature is exclusive. The man or the woman of a large, royal, unself-centred nature never is. The small nature is the one that continually strives for effect. The larger nature never does. The one goes here and there in order to gain recognition, in order to attach himself to the world. The other stays at home and draws the world to *him*. The one loves merely himself. The other loves all the world; but in his larger love for all the world he finds himself included.

Verily, then, the more one loves the nearer he approaches to God, for God is the Spirit of Infinite Love. And when we come into the realization of our oneness with this Infinite Spirit, then divine love so fills us that, enriching and enrapturing our own lives, from them it flows out to enrich the life of all the world.

In coming into the realization of our oneness with the Infinite Life, we are brought at once into right relations with our fellowmen. We are brought into harmony with the great law, that we find our own lives in losing them in the service of others. We are brought to a knowledge of the fact that all life is one, and so that we are all parts of the one great whole. We then realize that we can't do for another without at the same time doing for ourselves. We also realize that we cannot do harm to another without by that very act doing harm to ourselves. We realize that the man who lives to himself alone lives a little, dwarfed, and stunted life, because he has no part in this larger life of humanity. But the one who in service loses his own life in this larger life, has his own life increased and enriched a thousand or a million fold, and every joy, every happiness, everything of value coming to each member of this greater whole comes as such to him, for he has a part in the life of each and all.

And here let a word be said in regard to true service. Peter and John were one day going up to the temple, and as they were entering the gate they were met by a poor cripple who asked them for alms. Instead of giving him something to supply the day's needs and then leaving him in the same dependent condition for the morrow and the morrow, Peter did him a real service, and a real service for all mankind by saying: Silver and gold have I none, but such as I have I give unto thee. *And then he made him whole.* He thus brought him into the condition where he could help himself. In other words, the greatest service we can do for another is to help him to help himself. To help him directly might be weakening, though not necessarily. It depends entirely upon circumstances. But to help one to help himself is never weakening, but always encouraging and strengthening, because it leads him to a larger and stronger life.

In Tune with the Infinite

LI

The Nature Of Real Riches

The one who has come into the realization of the higher life no longer has a desire for the accumulation of enormous wealth, anymore than he has a desire for any other *excess*. In the degree that he comes into the recognition of the fact that he is wealthy within, external wealth becomes less important in his estimation. When he comes into the realization of the fact that there is a source within from which he can put forth a power to call to him and actualize in his hands at any time a sufficient supply for all his needs, he no longer burdens himself with vast material accumulations that require his constant care and attention, and thus take his time and his thought from the real things of life. In other words, he first finds the *kingdom*, and he realizes that when he has found this, all other things follow in full measure.

Wealth beyond a certain amount cannot be used, and when it cannot be used it then becomes a hindrance rather than an aid, a curse rather than a blessing. All about us are persons with lives now stunted and dwarfed who could make them rich and beautiful, filled with a perennial joy, if they would begin wisely to use that which they have spent the greater portion of their lives in accumulating.

The man who accumulates during his entire life, and who leaves even all when he goes out for "benevolent purposes," comes far short of the ideal life. It is but a poor excuse of a life. It is not especially commendable in me to give a pair of old, worn-out shoes that I shall never use again to another who is in need of shoes. But it is commendable, if indeed doing anything we ought to do can be spoken of as being commendable, it is commendable for me to give a good pair of strong shoes to the man who in the midst of a severe winter is practically shoeless, the man who is exerting every effort to earn an honest living and thereby take care of his family's needs. And if in giving the shoes I also give myself, he then has a double gift, and I a double blessing.

There is no wiser use that those who have great accumulations can make of them than wisely to put them into life, into character, *day by day while they live.* In this way their lives will be continually enriched and increased. The time will come when it will be regarded as a disgrace for a man to die and leave vast accumulations behind him.

Many a person is living in a palace to-day who in the real life is poorer than many a one who has not even a roof to cover him. A man may own and live in a palace, but the palace for him may be a poorhouse still.

Moth and rust are nature's wise provisions —God's methods— for disintegrating and scattering, in this way getting ready for use in new forms, that which is hoarded and consequently serving no use. There is also a great law continually operating whose effects are to dwarf and deaden the powers of true enjoyment, as well as all the higher faculties of the one who hoards.

Multitudes of people are continually keeping away from them higher and better things because they are forever clinging on to the old. If they would use and pass on the old, room would be made for new things to come. Hoarding always brings loss in one form or another. Using, wisely using, brings an ever renewing gain.

If the tree should as ignorantly and as greedily hold on to this year's leaves when they have served their purpose, where would be the full and beautiful new life that will be put forth in the spring? Gradual decay and finally death would be the result. If the tree is already dead, then it may perhaps be well enough for it to cling on to the old, for no new leaves will come. But as long as the life in the tree is active, it is *neccessary* that it rid itself of the old ones, that room may be made for the new.

Opulence is the law of the universe, an abundant supply for every need if nothing is put in the way of its coming. The natural and the normal life for us is this—To have such a fulness of life and power by living so continually in the realization of our one-ness with the Infinite Life and Power that we find ourselves in the constant possession of an abundant supply of all things needed.

Then not by hoarding but by wisely using and ridding ourselves of things as they come, an ever renewing supply will be ours, a supply far better adapted to present needs than the old could possibly be. In this way we not only come into possession of the richest treasures of the Infinite Good ourselves, but we also become open channels through which they can flow to others.

In Tune with the Infinite

LII

A Method Of Attainment

A living insight into the fact of the essential unity of the human life with the Divine Life is the profoundest knowledge that man can attain to. This as a mere intellectual perception, however, as a mere dead theory, amounts to but little, if indeed to anything at all, so far as bearing fruit in everyday life is concerned. It is the *vital, living realization* of this great transcendent truth in the life of each one that makes it a mighty moving and moulding force in his life.

It is only through this living realization of the essential unity of our life with the Father's life that true blessedness, and even true peace and happiness, can be found. The sooner, then, that we come into it, and thus live the life of the spirit, the better, for neither will they come nor can they be found in any other way, There is, moreover, no time either in this form of life, or in any other form, that we can any more readily come into it, and thereby into all that follows. And when this fountain of Divine Life is once fully opened within us, it can never again be dried up, and we can rest assured that it will at all times uphold us in peace and bear us on safety. And however strange or unaccountable at times occurrences may appear, we can rest in a triumphant security, knowing that only good can come, for in God's life there is only good, and in God's life we are now living, and there we shall live forever.

There is a simple method which will aid us greatly in coming into the realization we have been considering. So simple is it that thousands and indeed millions have passed it by, looking, as is so generally our custom, for agencies of at least apparently greater power; we so frequently and so universally forget that the greatest things in life are the most simple.

The method is this: wherever you are, whatever doing, walking along the street or through the fields, at work of any kind, falling off to or awaking from sleep, setting about any undertaking, in doubt as to what course to pursue at any particular time, in brief, whatever it may be, carry with you this thought: It is the Father that worketh in me, my Father works and I work. This is the thought so continually used by Jesus, who came into the fullest realization of the oneness of his life with the God-life that anyone who has lived in the world thus far has come into, and it is given because it is so simple. From it each can make his own formula. Jesus' term was "the Father." Many will likewise find themselves naturally using the same term and will find it becoming very precious to them. Others will find themselves using other terms for the same conception and thought: It is the Father that worketh in me, my Father works and I work. In other words, It is the Spirit of Infinite Life and Power that is back of all, working in and through all, the life and animating power of all—God—that worketh in me, and I do as I am directed and empowered by It.

In this way we open ourselves, and become consciously awake to the Infinite Life and Power that is ever waiting and ready to direct and work in our lives, if we will merely put ourselves into the attitude whereby It can work in them. In this way we open ourselves so that It can speak and manifest to and through us. This It is ever ready to do if we will but make for It the right conditions. By carrying with us this thought, by holding ourselves in this attitude of mind consciously for awhile, by repeating it even in so many words now and then at first, we will find it in time becoming our habitual thought, and will find ourselves living in it without the conscious effort that we have to make at first, and we will in time find ourselves almost unconsciously living in it continually. Thus God as a living presence, as a guiding, animating power, becomes an actuality in our lives. The conscious presence of God in our lives, which is the essence, indeed the sum and substance of *all* religion, then becomes a reality, and all wisdom and all power will be given us as we are able to appropriate and use then wisely; if for merely selfish, personal ends, they will be withheld; if for the greatest aid and service for the world, we will find them continually increasing.

With this higher realization comes more and more the simple, child-like spirit. With Jesus we realize—Of myself I can do nothing, it is the Father within me that doeth His work. In ourselves we are and can do nothing; in God we can do all things. We never can be in the condition—in God—until through this higher realization God becomes a *conscious, living* reality in our lives.

Faithfulness to this simple method will bring about a complete change in great numbers of lives. Each one for himself can test its efficacy in a very short time. It is the highway upon which many will enter that will by easy stages take them into the realization of the highest life that can be attained to. To set one's face in the right direction, and then simply to travel on, will in time bring him into the realization of the highest life that can be even conceived of—it is the secret of all attainment.

The Greatest Thing Ever Known

A Sort Of Creed

To be observed today, or in part; to be changed to-morrow—or abandoned— if the light is better.

To Live to our highest in all things that pertain to us;

To lend a hand as best we can to all others for this same end;

To aid in righting the wrongs that cross our path by pointing the wrong-doer to a better way, and thus aid him in becoming a power for good;

To remain in nature always sweet and simple and humble, and therefore strong;

To open ourselves fully and to keep ourselves pure and clean as fit channels for the Divine Power to work through us;

To turn toward and keep our faces always to the light;

To do our own thinking, listening quietly to the opinions of others, and to be sufficiently men and women to act always upon our own convictions;

To do our duty as we see it, regardless of the opinions of others, seeming gain or loss, temporary blame or praise;

To play the part of neither knave nor fool by attempting to judge another, but to give that same time to living more worthily ourselves;

To get up immediately when we stumble, face again to the light, and travel on without wasting even a moment in regret;

To love all things and to stand in awe or fear of nothing save our own wrong-doing;

To recognize the good lying at the heart of all people, of all things, waiting for expression, all in its own good way and time;

To love the fields and the wild flowers, the stars, the far-open sea, the soft, warm earth, and to live much with them alone, but to love struggling and weary men and women and every pulsing living creature better;

To strive always to do unto others as we would have them do unto us.

In brief—to be honest, to be fearless, to be just, to be kind. This will make our part in life's great and as yet not fully understood play truly glorious, and we need then stand in fear of nothing—life nor death; for death is life.

Or, rather, it is the quick transition to life in another form; the putting off of the old coat and the putting on of a new; a passing not from light to darkness but from light to light, according as we have lived here; a taking up of life in another form just where we leave it off here; a part in life not to be shunned or dreaded or feared, but to be welcomed with a glad and ready smile when it comes in its *own* good way and time.

The Greatest Thing Ever Known

I

The Greatest Thing Ever Known

The greatest thing ever known—What is it? Full surely the answer must be one that is absolutely universal, both in its nature and in the possibilities of its application. It must be one that can be accepted wholly and unreservedly, not only by a single individual, but even by bodies of individuals, be they the originators of any particular school of Ethics, the followers of any particular system of Philosophy, or even the adherents of any great system of Religion. It must be one so true in itself that it can be accepted by all men alike the world over.

And again, it must be an answer that is true for no particular period of time, but equally true for all time—an answer that was true not only for yesterday, that is true for to-day, that may be true for to-morrow, but one equally true for yesterday, to-day, and forever. In laying our foundation, therefore, it must be laid upon something as true and as certain as Life itself, and as eternal as Everlasting Life.

What is as true and as certain as Life itself? Life, only Life. And what do we mean by this answer? Let us give it for a moment our most careful consideration, for upon what we find here depends and rests all that is to follow. Let us start, then, with that in regard to which all can agree; something taken not from mere tradition, from mere hearsay, but something that comes to us from no source other than our own interior consciousness, our own reason and insight. In other words, let us make our approach, not from the theological standpoint, but from that which is far more certain

406

and satisfactory—the philosophical.

Then, and then only, will we allow pure reason to be our guide, and then by having as the earnest desire of both mind and heart, truth, truth for its own sake, and then for the sake of its influence upon every-day life, we will thus allow pure reason to be illumined by the Light that lighteth every man that cometh into the world. In the degree that we open ourselves to and are true to this are we on sure and safe ground, for thus are we going directly to the source and the only source of all *true* revelation. In the degree, on the other hand, that we close ourselves or become untrue to this are we on uncertain and dangerous ground, and liable to find ourselves hopelessly floundering in the quagmire of theological traditions and speculations and doubts, of which the world has already seen so much. Pure reason, therefore, shall be our guide—pure reason illumined by the Inner Light.

Again, then, What is Life? Being is Life. Life is Being. Being, therefore, is our starting-point, and indeed our very foundation itself.

Each can form his own idea of being, so that in reality it needs no defining. By it we mean that self-existent principle of Life and all that attends it, without beginning and without end, the Power that animates all and so that is the Life of all. In short, we can scarcely define Being, if indeed it can be defined, without using the word Life, and indeed without identifying the two. Being and Life, then, are one and: the same.

It is Being that projects itself into existence. Being, acting through its own intelligence, prompted by love, projected by will, goes out and *takes* form. We cannot say that it enters into form, for until it projects itself into existence *there is no form,* but form comes by virtue of Being, the self-existent Principle of Life and Power, manifesting itself in ex-istence. So in a sense Life, which is one with Being, is the soul and form, of whatever nature the body.

Only as Being projects itself into ex-istence are we able to know it. We can know the fact that Being *is,* but only as it manifests itself in form are we able to know *it itself.*

Being is *one*, not many. As Being is the source of all Life, there is, then, only one Life, and this Being is the Life of all. "The one Divine Being; and this alone is the true Reality in all Existence, and so remains in all Eternity." And there is nothing real that is, or, indeed, that can be, outside of it. True, then, are the words of one of the most highly illumined philosophers of modern times—" Thus we have these two elements: Being, as it is essentially and in itself; and Form, which is assumed by the former in consequence of Existence. But how have we expressed ourselves? What is it that assumes a form? Answer: Being, as it exists in itself, without any change whatever in its inward, Essential Nature. But what, then, is there in Existence? Answer: Nothing else than the One Eternal and Unchangeable Being, besides which there can be nothing."

This Being which is Infinite is in truth, then, the Infinite Being, and this Infinite Being is what we mean by God—each using the term that appeals most to himself. Literally, the I Am, as is signified by the name Jehovah, which is derived in the Hebrew from the word To Be. God, then, is the Infinite Being, the Infinite Spirit of Life which fills all in ex-istence with himself alone, so that all is He, since He is All. If God is all, then all *must* be He, and from this fact there is no escape, and no other conclusion can be arrived at which does not do violence to all rational thought. There are those—and to such these pages are not addressed, for so limited are they in comprehension, or so closed to truth and hence so engrossed in bigotry, that they either can or will see nothing that may be opposed to their present ideas—there are those who say that God is all, and immediately begin to fill up the universe with that which God is not.

Again, there are those open to and eagerly seeking for the highest truth who say: But evil is not God, and how then can God be *all*, for surely there is such a thing as evil. Certainly evil is not God, nor has God anything to do with evil. Evil is simply the result of the temporary perversion of the good, and as such must either cease or in time die at its own hands. As such, then, it has no *essential* reality, for that which has essential reality has neither beginning nor end.

Man is the only one who has to do with evil, he alone is its author; man, who in his thought separates himself from Divine Being, in whom alone true happiness and blessedness can be found. Regarding the mere bodily existence as his real life, he tries to find pleasure and happiness entirely through these channels, and many times by violating the higher laws of his being, and thus what we term evil enters in. But though man has perfect freedom in all his thoughts and acts, God will suffer no such violation. And so, from the pain and suffering that result from the violation of the higher laws of his being, he is pushed on in his thought and through this in his life to the Reality of his being, and finds that only in conscious union with God true pleasure and blessedness lie, as God surely intends. True, then, evil is not God, nor has God anything to do with evil; for man alone has to do with it, so long, and only so long, as he lives his life out of a conscious union with the life of God.

Infinite Being, God, then, is the one and the only Life. You and I in our true selves are Life. It cannot be truly said that we *have* life, for we *are* Life; Life that manifests itself in the form in existence that we denominate by the term body. And as the Infinite Being, the Infinite Life, God, is the I Am, the life of all in existence, then we indeed are parts of the Infinite Being, the Infinite Life, the I Am, the very God himself. And thus it is that your life and mine is one with the life of God. By this we do not mean the mere body, but the Real Self that takes to itself the form—body. It is utterly impossible that there be any real life that is not one with the life of God. And in this sense it is true that the life of man and the life of God are essentially and necessarily one and the same. In essence they are one and the same; they differ not in quality, for this it is impossible rationally even to conceive of. There is a difference—it is a difference simply in *degree,* not in essence or kind. It is only by reason of our own thought that our life is separate from the life of God, only by reason of our own thought that we live in this separation, if indeed we can use the term *live* where the *full* life is not consciously realized and enjoyed. Truly, then, "In Him we live and move and have our being."

We never could have been, and never can be, other than Divine Being. And I fully agree with the thought expressed in a recent letter from Prof. Max Muller in which he says: "I cannot accept Athanasius when he says that we can become gods; man cannot say, become God, because he is God; what else could he be, if God is the. only true and real being?"

How is it, then, I hear it asked, that man has the limitations that he has, that he ' is subject to fears and forebodings, that he is liable to sin and error, that he is the victim of disease and suffering? There is but one reason. He is not living, except in rare cases here and there, in the *conscious realization* of his own true Being, and hence of his own true Self. We must *in thought* be conscious of who and what we are before the qualities and powers of our real being, and hence our real selves, actualize or even manifest themselves. Says one of the most highly illumined seers of modern times: "The True Life and its Blessedness consists in a union with the Unchangeable and Eternal; but the Eternal can be apprehended *only by Thought,* and is in no other way approachable by us."

Thought is the atmosphere, the element, in a sense the very substance, of the phase of Divine Being that we call human life. How much it is likewise that of other forms of Divine Being in existence, as we see it in the various manifestations of life around us, we cannot be so fully certain of. But certain it is that through thought, and through thought alone, we are able to conceive of Divine Being as the Infinite Spirit and Essence of Life, and then to see clearly that it is the Life of our Life, and then to live in the realization of our oneness with it, and in this way allow the Divine Word to become incarnate in us by being thus fully and completely manifest in us, precisely as it became manifest and hence incarnate in the Christ Jesus, as we shall hereafter find.

When Divine Being manifests itself in physical human form, its inward essential nature or reality changes not, for this from its very nature it is impossible for it in any way to do. It does, however, have to manifest itself through the agency of physical senses, and precisely for this reason is it that for a time our real inward Essential Nature and Life is concealed from us, but this again only by reason of our limited comprehension.

When we are born into the world of Nature we see and recognize through and by means of the physical senses, and the natural physical world becomes to us for a time the *real* world. By and by, however, through these very senses we are able to conceive of the One and Eternal Source of Life as our real and therefore our only life, and then through them to hold ourselves in this living realization. Hence, first that which is natural and *then* that which is spiritual is necessarily as well as literally and philosophically true. Happy, however, is the man who dwells not long as the purely natural man, but is early transformed into the spiritual, and so in whom the Divine Word early becomes incarnate.

Blessed state indeed, says the thoughtful and earnest seeker for the best things in life, and more to be prized than all else besides; but if this state is really possible of realization, what can be said regarding the method of entering into it? There is only one thing in all the wide universe that will enable you as well as all the world to do it effectually. "Be ye therefore transformed by the renewing of your minds." This is the force, the transforming power, so far as the form of life we denominate by the term human is concerned, this and this alone.

True, then, and most welcome is the great fact of facts that the world is beginning to become so conscious of today, that "The mind is everything; what you think, you become." Mortal mind? says one. Yes and no. Strictly speaking, there is no such thing as mortal mind—there is only Divine Mind. When in our own thought, and by reason of our limited comprehension, we shut ourselves off and look upon ourselves as individual physical beings, we give birth to a temporary mode of thought that might well be termed mortal mind, or, rather, the product of mortal mind. But it is at first natural, and it is only by using this "mortal mind" that it is able to be transformed, and hence renewed into the Divine

Mind. So by wisely using that which we have, the natural, we are transformed from that which is most apparent, and consequently that which we think we are, the mortal, the physical, into that which from all eternity we in reality are, and never except in our own minds can get away from,—the Spiritual, the Divine.

It is through this instrumentality that the Divine Life within us, the Divine Life with all its ever-ready-to-breakforth glories and powers, is enabled to be changed from a mere passive and hence potential actuality, and to burst forth into the full splendor of conscious, active life. Surely, then, thought rightly directed and rightly used has within it the true regenerating and hence redeeming power; through it and it alone are we able to make for ourselves a new heaven and a new earth, or, rather, by thus finding the kingdom of God, and through it entering into the conscious realization of the heavenly state, are we able to make for ourselves a new earth by actualizing the kingdom of Heaven in our lives while living on the earth, and which, when once truly realized, can never be lost.

The majority of people are not awake; it is only here and there that we find one even partially awake. Practically all of us, as a result, are living lives that are unworthy almost the name of lives, compared to those we might be living, and that lie within our easy grasp. While it is true that each life is in and of Divine Being, hence always one with it, in order that this great fact bear fruit in individual lives, each one must, as we have already said, be conscious of it, *he must know it in thought,* and then live continually in this consciousness.

An eagle has been chained for many months to the perch just outside of his cage; so long has he been conscious of the, fact that he is bound by the little silver chain which holds him that he has given up all efforts to escape, almost forgetting, perhaps, that the power of flight is longer his. One day a link of the little chain opens, but, living so long in the consciousness that he is held in captivity, he makes no effort to escape. The freedom of the heavens is now his, were he only conscious of his power. But day after day he sits sullenly longing for freedom, but remaining a captive still. One morning, however, he ventures a little farther out on his perch than usual, when suddenly a strange consciousness is his—he sets his wings, and the captivity which has held him for months will perchance know him no more forever.

And so it is with man. On account of the false gods that tradition and prevailing theology have brought him he knows not himself, and not knowing himself he knows neither his powers nor his possibilities. The human soul is held captive. An opaque physical structure is about all that he can be said truly to give evidence of. The day comes, however, when in his thought he moves out a little farther than is usual, then a little farther and a little farther. The Inner Light is now moving within, he catches at first a little glimpse of his real Essential Being, then a little more and a little more, and by and by the fact of his essential oneness with the Infinite Life and Power bursts in upon, illumines, and takes possession of his soul. In bewilderment, and almost afraid to utter it at first, he cries aloud, "O God, I am one with Thee!" Enraptured by this new consciousness, he holds to the thought of this oneness, and living continually in this thought his life forever after flows steadily on in one constant realization of his oneness with Divine Being. And so "the first man, [which] is of the earth earthy," is changed into "the second man, [which] is the Lord from Heaven," and thereafter the Christ sits enthroned.

Compared with the new life that he is now continually living, the old life of ignorance with its consequent limitations, which can now know him no more forever, deserved only the name of death, for, strictly speaking, he was indeed dead unto life, and only he who lives in the conscious realization of his oneness with the One and Only Life can be said truly to be born into Life. He is born into the world and lives in the world, but into consciously real and eternal *Life* he has not yet entered. He is born the Adam man, but within him the Christ man has not awakened, or, rather, he has not yet awakened to the Christ within, and so the Christ man is not yet born, and sitting therefore in darkness he knows not yet the glorious realities of life.

"I am thine own Spirit" are the words that the Infinite Father by means of the Inner Voice is continually speaking to every human soul. He who *will* hear *can* hear, and through it step out into fulness of life.

We hear much in the prevailing crude and irrational theology in regard to the "fall of man;" but it is only as man has departed from the Inner Light, and gone after false man-made gods, that anything that might rationally be termed a "fall" has come about. Separating our lives in thought from their oneness with Divine Life is what constitutes, and what alone will ever constitute, the fall of man. But the teaching that has come to us through past generations, which has as its dominant keynote poor worm and miserable sinner, death and the grave, is as false as it is pernicious and therefore damnable in its influences. These old thoughts and words have had the influence of taking heaven out of earth and populating the earth with doubt, and error, and sin, and crime. New and true thoughts and words will make literally a new heaven and a new earth.

Man is essentially Divine, part and parcel of the Infinite God, and so, essentially good. When he severs his connection in consciousness with the Divine, then and then only do doubt, and error, and sin, and crime, with their consequent pain, suffering, disease, and despair, enter into his life. Only a pure and radical infidel—by this we mean one who is in reality such, for there are many who are called infidels, even by many avowed religionists, who live a far truer religion than they themselves live—can rationally hold to the doctrine of original sin, with its consequent poor worm and miserable sinner. The religious teacher who professes to believe in God as the One Divine and Supreme Being, and at the same time holds to this irrational doctrine, is many times more a disciple of the Devil, whom he recognizes and whose power he evidently respects, than he is of the Infinite God in whom he *professes* to believe. He and he alone it is who finds a place for what he and his theology term the Devil. The one who truly believes in God as the only true and real being and the source of all life and power can indeed find no place for the Devil. He sees and recognizes the evil that comes from lives that lose for a time their conscious connection with the Supreme Source of their being, but he can find no place for any other *essential and abiding* Reality.

And as this separation from God is made entirely through the instrumentality of the mind, he sees that making one's conscious connection again with God—the true and only true redemption— must also be made through the instrumentality of the mind. Believing in the God in whom he believes, aye, *knowing the God whom he knows,* he sees no place for an atonement in the sense of appeasing the wrath of an angry God. Knowing the God whom he knows, he shares not in those barbaric, not to say idiotic, notions. He does see, however, that redemption can and must come through living in the conscious at-one-ment with the Father's life. He recognizes it as the natural method that the Adam man be first born with freedom of thought and consequently freedom of action, and that from him the Christ man then comes forth into consciousness. He recognizes that it is God's, and consequently nature's and evolution's, method that "the first man is of the earth earthy, the second man is the Lord from heaven." He recognizes the fact that kittens are born blind, not because their parents or even their grand-parents sinned, but because it is simply *natural* for them to be born blind, and that in process of time their eyes will open. He also recognizes that, on account of our limited comprehension, the "natural" appears first and then the "spiritual," but in reality the spiritual is from the very first incarnated within, and only because it is can it in process of time, either sooner or later, assume the ascendency by changing from potential into active life.

Once in a while there comes into the world one who from the very first recognizes no separation of his life from the Father's life, and who dwells continually in this living realization; and by bringing anew to the world this great fact, and showing forth the works that will always and inevitably follow this realization, he becomes in a sense a world's savior, as did Jesus, who, through the completeness of his realization of the Father's life incarnate in him, became the Christ Jesus. He in this way pointed out to the world how all men can enter into the realization of the Christ-life and thus be saved from all impulse to sin. And so instead of coming to appease the vengeance of an angry God —difficult for one who has any adequate conception of God even to conceive of—he brought to the world, by exemplifying in his own life as well as by teaching to all who will hear his *real message,* the method whereby all of us can enter into the full and complete realization of our oneness with the life of the tender and loving Infinite Father.

Redeemed from the bondage of the senses through which alone sin comes, and born into the heavenly state, into life eternal, is every one who comes into the same relations with the Father, and hence into the same realization of his oneness with the Father's life, that Jesus came into. It is difficult, however, to see how any one will be redeemed from the bondage of sin and enter into the heavenly state simply by believing that Jesus entered into it while here. No amount of believing that he lived the life he lived will take any one into the heavenly state, but *living the life that Jesus lived* will take every one who lives it there, in any age and in any clime, even whether or not he knows that such a man as Jesus ever lived.

The world has less need for a perverted and hence perverting doctrine of "vicarious atonement" that bodies of men have formulated by either intentionally or ignorantly dragging the teachings, as also the life, of the Master down to a purely material interpretation—less need, I repeat, has the world for this diabolical doctrine than it has for the great vitalizing fact of a conscious, living at-one-ment with the Father's life, as every one whose spiritual sense is at all unfolded will inevitably get from the life and teachings of the Master, if indeed he is more interested in the real living truth that he taught than he is in the almost numberless man-made theological theories and dogmas regarding it.

In order that we may ever keep our standing ground clearly in mind, let us now gather into a single view the substance of what we have endeavored thus far to present.

From everlasting to everlasting is Being, self-ex-istent, without beginning and without end. Depending upon nothing outside of itself and the essential essence, the very life of all that through it comes into existence, it is therefore Infinite Being. Existing at first as pure spirit, it is therefore Divine Being. Literally the I Am, the Divine Jehovah, the Infinite God. Then, animated by love and acting through its own volition, it projects itself into existence and assumes the various forms we see in the universe about us, including we ourselves. But by the act of projecting itself into existence, the Infinite Divine Being does not change in the least its essential inner nature, as indeed it would be impossible for it to do. What, then, in reality is there in existence ? Only Divine Being, the Infinite God in all his manifold manifestations; and thus it remains through all eternity, as must necessarily be from its very nature, and otherwise it could not be. God, then, is the Infinite Being, the Infinite Spirit which is the essential essence, the life of all, which therefore fills all the universe with Himself alone, so that all is He, since He is all.

But when Divine Being incarnates itself in flesh and forms for its use a physical body—a human body, as we call it—it necessarily has to manifest through the instrumentality of physical senses, and, though Divine Being is infinite, the vision of man is limited, and for a time his true inner Life (always Divine Being) is concealed from him, for he naturally interprets everything from the standpoint of the physical. First that which is natural, and man knows himself only as a natural physical being, differing not essentially from the material universe about him. As he looks out, however, he sees that he differs from other forms in existence, in that he has a mind through which thought is engendered, a mind that grows by using. Then contemplating himself and longing for the truth of his existence, gradually there dawns upon his consciousness the fact that his life is Divine Being, that other than this it has never been—except in his own mind when in his thought he mistook the mere physical form in existence as the real essential life itself, thus separating his life from the Infinite Divine Life. He thus realizes that in God he lives, moves, and has his being, that God is the life of his life, his very life itself; and thus he comes in time into the conscious, living realization of his oneness with the Infinite Life and Power. And so we find it true—first the natural man, then the spiritual.

Through thought, and through thought alone, the second man, the Lord from Heaven, is gradually evolved out of the first man, which is of the earth earthy. Through a perfectly natural process of evolution, out of the first man Adam—sense perception—is evolved the Christ man —Divine self-realization. Impossible, however, is it for anything to be evolved that was not first involved; and so man finds that the Lord Christ has always been within and he has known it not.

It is the same to-day as it was many years ago with Jacob when he said, " Surely the Lord is in this place; and I knew it not." This and all that followed he found simply by using the stones of the place where he was; for with the stones of the place he made for himself a pillow, and it was while sleeping on this pillow that he beheld the ladder set upon the earth and reaching to the heavens, upon which the angels were ascending and descending, and thus it was that he entered into communion with the life of the heavens. Later, then, he transformed the pillow into a pillar that served as a guide to other men.

And so with every human soul—we must use simply the stones of the place where we are. The only stones with which human life can build is thought. It and it alone is the moulding, the creative power — earnest, sincere thought of the place where we are, this constitutes the stones of the place where we are and with which we can make a pillow upon which for the time being to rest. Through this and this alone will the life of the heavens be opened to us; for angels ascending — aspiration—will in time bring to us angels descending — inspiration. Then with Jacob of old we will cry out, "Behold, the Lord is in this place; and I knew it not." Then our pillow, the thought that gives us the knowledge that the Infinite

Divine Life is always within, the Essential Essence of the human soul itself, we can convert into a pillar, a pillar that will be a guide to lead other men into this same realization and life.

And so the entire problem of human life is wonderfully simple and easy if we are but true to the highest within us, and keep ourselves free from the various perplexing and mystifying theological theories and dogmas, which ordinarily give merely a promise of spiritual awakening, realization, and power in some other form of life, rather than actualizing it here and now in this life.

But only as man becomes conscious of the Lord Christ within, only as he becomes conscious,—realizes in thought that he is one with the Infinite Life and Power,—does this great fact become a moving and mighty force in the affairs of his daily life. Until this is true he remains in the condition of the eagle, which, though unchained, thinking nevertheless that he was still chained, remained in captivity when the freedom of the heavens awaited simply the spreading of his wings.

Although the answer to our title has been given both in lines and between lines long before this, it may be an aid to us, especially in making practical what is to follow, to put it as best we can into a definite form: The greatest thing ever known—indeed, the greatest thing that ever can be known—is that in our real essential nature we are one with the Infinite Life and Power, and that by coming into, and dwelling continually in, the *conscious living realization* of this great fact, we enable to be manifested unto and actualized within us the qualities and powers of the Divine Life, and this in the exact degree of the completeness of this realization on our part.

II

Divine Energies In Every-Day Life

And what, let us ask, is the result and hence the value of this realization? For unless it is of value in the affairs of every-day life, it is then a mere dead theory, and consequently of no real value. *Use* must be the final test of everything, and if it has no actual use, or if no visible results follow its use, we had better not spend time with it, for it is then not founded upon truth.

First, let it be said, it is not the mere intellectual recognition, merely the dead theory, but the conscious vital and living realization of this great truth, that makes it of value, and that makes it show forth in the affairs of everyday life. This it is, and this alone, that gives true blessedness, for this is none other than the finding of the kingdom of God, and when this is once found and lived in, all other things literally and necessarily follow. Through this the qualities and powers of the Divine Life are more and more realized and actualized, and through their leading we are led into the possession of all other things.

He who comes into this full and living realization of his oneness with the Divine Life is brought at once into right relations with himself, with his fellow-men, and with the laws of the universe about him. He lives now in the inner, the real life, and whatever is in the interior must necessarily take form in the exterior, for all life is from within out. There is no true life in regard to which this law does not hold. And if the will of God is done in the inward life, then is it necessarily done in all things of the outward life, and the results are always manifest. Thus and thus alone it is that men have become prophets, seers, and saviors; they have become what the world calls the "elect" of God, because in their own lives they first elected God and lived their lives in His life. And thus it is that to-day men can become prophets, seers, and saviors, for the laws of the Divine Life and the relations of what we term the human life to it are identically the same to-day as they have been in all time past and will be in all time to come. The Divine Being changes not; it is man alone who changes.

It is solely by virtue of man's leaving the inner life of the spirit and thus departing from God, or by virtue of his not yet finding this real life, that sin and error, pain and disease, fears and forebodings, have crept as naturally and as necessarily as that effect follows cause into his life; only by closing his eyes to the inner light, by shutting his ears to the inner voice, that, although he has eyes to see, yet he sees not, and, although he has ears to hear, yet he hears not. And it is only by uniting his life with the Divine Life, and thus living again the life of the spirit, that these things will go, even as they have come.

All the evil, unhappiness, misery, and want in the world are attributable to man, and are the direct results of his taking his life, either consciously or unconsciously, either directly or indirectly, out of harmony with the Power that works for righteousness and consequently for wholeness and perfection. And when our life is lived in the life of God, and God's will therefore becomes our will, all is and necessarily must be well with us, for contrary to His will it is impossible that anything should ever come to pass. And thus it is that he who seeks first the kingdom of God and His righteousness shall have all other things added unto him. The soul, the real life, is Divine, and by allowing it to become translucent to Infinite Spirit by living continually in this conscious union with Divine Being it reveals all things to us. Things become hidden, mysteries fill and uncertainties pervade life only as we turn away from the inner light and life; there is nothing that is hidden of itself; to God all things are known, and he who consciously lives his life in the life of God sees with the Divine vision that reveals all things to him. He who lives continually under this Divine guidance enters thereby into the realm of the highest wisdom, and even in the most trivial things of every-day life he never finds himself in a state of doubt or perplexity, for he always knows what to do and how to do it.

He has no regrets for the past, because before he entered into his present consciousness he was in a sense dead unto life, and all regrets that he might have for the past are now swallowed up in the joys that the new birth that has brought him into fulness of life continually spreads before his every step. He has neither fears nor forebodings in regard to the future, for he knows that contrary to God's will, which is now his will, nothing can ever come to pass. Peace, therefore, a full and abiding peace, is continually his.

As all life is from within out, and as this is absolutely true in regard to the physical body, the fountain of Divine Life that has been opened up within him, which of itself can admit of no disease or imperfection of any kind, will allow only healthy conditions to be externalized in his body; and where unhealthy conditions have been built into it before his entrance into the new life, the life that now courses through it will in time drive them out by entirely replacing the diseased structure with that which is pure and whole.

A continually growing sense of power is his, for he is now working in conjunction with the Infinite God, and with God all things are possible. In material things he is not lacking, for all things are from this one Infinite Source, and, guided by the Divine Wisdom and sustained by the Divine Power that are now his, in a perfectly natural and normal way he finds that an abundance of all things is his, always in hand in sufficient time to supply all his material needs, and never is there lack when the time comes, if he simply does each day what his hands find to do. Sure always of this unfailing source of supply, he does not give himself to the accumulation and the hoarding of great material possessions, thereby robbing and enslaving the real life.

His thoughts grow more and more into the nature of their Divine Source, and as *thoughts are forces,* and as in the degree that they are spiritualized do they become ever more effective in their operations, so through their instrumentality is he able to mould more and more effectively the every-day conditions of life. And so as he enters into this new life he finds that all things of the outer life fall into line; for *as is the inner, so always and necessarily is the outer.*

These truths will come as new revelations to many, and again to many they will come merely as agents to strengthen and possibly to arouse to renewed life the realizations of which they are already more or less conscious. In themselves, however, they are not new, *but as old as the world.* They are the real spirit of true Christianity, not, however, of the Christianity that the majority of people conventionally hold, and which in many respects is as radically inconsistent as it is void of results, but the great transcendent truths of our relations with the Father's life that Jesus taught.

They are likewise the real essential spirit of all the great religions of the world, and as all religions in their purity are from the same source,—God speaking through the minds of those who have come into a sufficient union with Him to hear and to interpret His voice, the one universal source of all true inspiration and all true revelation,—so far as their fundamental principles are concerned they are necessarily the same.

And the great spiritual awakening, the beginnings of which we are witnessing in all parts of the world to-day, is evidence that the Divine Breath is stirring in the minds and hearts of men and women in a manner such as it has rarely if ever stirred before. Men and women are literally finding God. They are breaking through the mere letter and form of an old and too-long-held ecclesiastical theorizing and dogmatism into the real vital spirit of the religion of the living and transcendent God. They are waking here and there and everywhere to the realization of their oneness with the living God. Their lives are being completely filled with

423

this realization, and as a consequence they are showing forth the works of God.

They are leaving the old one-day-in-seven, some-otherworld religion, and they are finding the joys as well as the practicability of an every-day, this-world religion. They are passing out of the religion of death and possible glory hereafter into the religion of life and joy and glory here and now, to-day and every day, as well as hereafter and forevermore. With this new religion of the living God and the spiritual power that through it is being made active in their lives, they are moulding in detail all of the affairs of every-day life, proving thereby that their religion is the religion of life. And any system of religion that does not enable its possessor to do this is simply *not* religion, and we should no longer desecrate the word by applying it to any such hollow mockeries.

To this old semblance of religion those who are thus entering into this new and larger religion of life will never return, nor can they, any more than the chick can enter within the confines of its shell again after it has been once born into life. Having found the pearl, the shell for them must perish; or rather, as it is of no farther value to them, it perishes simply by the operation of natural law. Centred thus in the Infinite, working now in conscious harmony with Divine forces, they ever after rule the world from within.

III

The Master's Great But Lost Gift

The conclusions we have arrived at thus far we have arrived at independently of any authority outside of our own reason and insight. It is always of interest as well as of greater or less value to compare our own conclusions with those of others whose opinions we value. It would indeed be a matter of exceeding great interest to compare those we have reached with those of a number whose opinions come with greater or less authority to all the world. Space does not permit this, however, and I propose that we give the balance of our time to the consideration, though necessarily brief consideration, of two such; one universally-regarded as one of the most highly illumined teachers, if not the most highly illumined, the world has ever known, the Christ Jesus; the other universally regarded as one of the most highly illumined philosophers the world has ever known, the philosopher Fichte. And in these two we have the advantage of the life and teachings of one who lived and taught nearly nineteen hundred years ago, and one who lived and taught a trifle less than a hundred years ago. By selecting these, let it also be said, we have the advantage of two whose lives fully manifested the truth of that which they taught.

In considering the life and teachings of Jesus, let us consider them not as dull expositors interpret and represent them, but as he himself gave them to the world. Certainly Jesus was Divine; but he was Divine, as he himself clearly taught, in just the same sense that you and I and every human soul is Divine. He differed from us, however, in that he had come into a far clearer and fuller realization of his divinity than we have come into, as indeed his life so clearly indicates. Jesus *was* God manifest in the flesh, as indeed every one must be who comes into the full realization of his oneness with God, as Jesus himself again so clearly taught.

In the thoroughly absurd, illogical, and positively demoralizing doctrine of "vicarious atonement," as given us by early ecclesiastical bodies by perverting the real teachings of Jesus even to the extent of calling interpolations in the New Testament to their aid, I certainly cannot believe. I do, however, believe that it has done more harm to the real teachings of Jesus, has been more productive of scepticism and infidelity, than all other causes combined. It is a doctrine that can be formulated only by those who have no spiritual insight themselves, and who therefore drag the teachings of the Master down to a purely material interpretation because of their inability to give them the spiritual interpretation that he intended they should have.

If his mission was not that of vicarious atonement, not for the purpose of appeasing the wrath and indignation of an angry God and thus reconciling Him to His children, what then was it? Clearly his mission was that of a Redeemer as he gave himself out to be—a Redeemer to bring the children of men back to their Father. And how did he purpose to do this? Clearly by having them consciously unite their lives with the Father's life, even as he had united his. The kingdom of God and His righteousness is not only what he came to teach, but what he clearly and unmistakably taught.

That he plainly and unequivocally taught his disciples that this was his mission is evidenced by numerous sentences such as the following, occurring all through the gospels: Matt. IV., 23, "Jesus went about in all Galilee, teaching in their synagogues and preaching the gospel of the kingdom," etc. . . . Luke VIII, 1, "He went about through cities and villages, preaching and bringing the good tidings of the kingdom of God." . . . Luke IV., 43, "But he said unto them: I must preach the good tidings of the kingdom of God to other cities also, *for therefore was I sent.*" . . . Luke IX., 2, "And he sent them forth to preach the kingdom of God and to heal the sick." . . . Matt, XXIV., 14, "And this gospel of the kingdom shall be preached in the whole world, for a testimony unto all nations," etc. . . . In more than thirty places in the first three gospels do we find Jesus thoroughly explaining to his disciples his especial mission—to preach the glad tidings of the coming of the kingdom of God; and even before he entered upon his public work, we hear John the Baptist going before him and saying, "Repent ye; for the kingdom of Heaven is at hand."

What did Jesus mean by the kingdom of God, or, as he sometimes expressed it, the kingdom of Heaven? As an answer, and an answer better than any speculations in regard to it, let us again take his own words: "Neither shall they say, Lo here! or, Lo there! for, behold, the kingdom of God is within you." He taught only what he himself had found, the conscious union with the Father's life as the one and all-inclusive thing. With Jesus from the very first, only in union with God was there reality. And this life in the Father's life seemed nothing at all marvellous to him; it was perfectly natural, and the only life he knew. Hence he could not say otherwise than that he and the Father were one. His vision was so clear, and his already realized Divine life was so full and complete, that he knew that it was utterly impossible for his life to be without the Father's life, as *we* indeed shall know when our vision becomes clear, and we enter into the same fully realized union with it.

This great knowledge came to Jesus not through intellectual speculation and still less through any communication from without; it came to him through his own interior consciousness; to all appearances he was born with it. He was born with a peculiar aptitude for discerning things of the Spirit, the same as among us some are born with a peculiar aptitude for one thing and others for other things. But so great was this power naturally in Jesus that in it we may justly say he had a great advantage over most people born into the world, and for this reason was he all the more able and all the greater reason was there for him to be one of the great world Teachers and hence Redeemers. He was indeed Immanuel—God with us.

Jesus, I repeat, never speaks of his life in any other connection than as one with the Father's life.

In reply to a question from Thomas in the fourteenth chapter of John, he says, "If ye had known me, ye would have* known my Father also: from henceforth ye know him and have seen him." Philip, who was standing near, unable to comprehend the interior meaning of the Master's words, said unto him : "Lord, show us the Father, and it sufficeth us." Jesus, somewhat surprised that he had not made himself clear to them, replied: "Have I been so long time with you, and dost thou not know me, Philip? He that hath seen me hath seen the Father; how sayest thou, Show us the Father? Believest thou not that I am in the Father, and the Father in me? The words I speak unto you I speak not from myself: but the Father abiding in me doeth His work. Believe me that I am in the Father and the Father in me: or believe me for the very works' sake."

But if his especial mission was to preach the good tidings of the kingdom of God, why, I hear it asked, did he claim that only through *him* can we come unto the kingdom, as he indeed says in his conversation with Philip and Thomas immediately preceding the part just quoted: "I am the way, the truth, and the life; no one cometh unto the Father but by me." Simply because it was the living truth that he brought, which was and evermore is to redeem men by uniting them in mind and heart with the Father, His realized oneness with the Father's life was the way, the truth, and the life, and only by going over the same path that he himself had trod can anyone be truly united with the Father. He found this great vital and redeeming truth nowhere else in the world; he had to speak as one standing alone, and in this sense he spoke most truly and most literally when he said, "No one cometh unto the Father but by me." And in order to point out his life, his realized oneness with the Father's life, as the way, the truth, and the life, he spoke and indeed had to speak as he did, even at the risk of being misunderstood and having his words taken in a purely material sense, as was the tendency of the spiritual poverty of the age, and indeed as his very disciples so often interpreted his words, as we have but recently seen. In order to give forth the spiritual teachings which he gave, he had to use the language and the illustrations that their material minds could grasp, and in this way make his teachings doubly liable to a purely material interpretation.

"I am the bread of life," said he to those assembled about him; "your fathers did eat the manna in the wilderness, and they died. This is the bread which cometh down out of heaven, that a man may eat thereof, and not die. I am the *living* bread which came down out of heaven: if any man eat of this bread, he shall live forever: yea, and the bread which I will give is my flesh, for the life of the world." The Jews taking his words in a material sense argued one with another and said: "How can this man give us his flesh to eat?" Jesus simply reaffirmed his statement, saying: "Verily, verily, I say unto you, except ye eat the flesh of the Son of man and drink his blood, ye have not life in yourselves. . . . For my flesh is meat indeed, and my blood is drink indeed." Literally, "My flesh is the true food, and my blood is the true drink. He that eateth my flesh and drinketh my blood abideth in me and I in him. As the living Father sent me, and I live because of the Father, so he that eateth me, he also shall live because of me."

And many of his disciples, even, when they heard him speaking in this way, said among themselves, "This is a hard saying; who can hear him ?"—who can understand him? Jesus, quickly perceiving that they were again dragging his words down to a material interpretation, asked them if what he had just said caused them to stumble, *and then, in order that they get his real meaning,* he said, "It is the spirit that quickeneth; the flesh proiiteth nothing: the *words* that I have spoken unto you are spirit and are life." And so all except those who are wholly spiritually, not to say even mentally, blind can readily see that what Jesus meant to say, and what he actually did say, was, the words that he spoke to them of his oneness with the Father's life were the true meat and the true drink, of which, unless a man ate and drank, he had not life in himself, but that these were able to give him life and life eternal.

"He that eateth my flesh and drinketh my blood abideth in me, and I in him." Or, reversing the expression, He that dwelleth in me and I in him, he it is that eateth my flesh and drinketh my blood. "The words that I have spoken unto you, (they) are spirit and (they) are life." "As the living Father hath sent me, and I live because of the Father, so he that eateth me, he also shall live because of me." In the words of another,[1] "To eat his flesh and drink his blood means to become wholly and entirely he himself; to become altogether changed into his person without reserve or limitation; to be a faithful repetition of him in another personality; to be transubstantiated with him, *i.e.*, as he is the Eternal Word made flesh and blood, to become his flesh and blood, and what follows from that, and indeed is the same thing, to become the very Eternal Word made flesh and blood itself; to think wholly and entirely like him, and so as if he himself thought and not we; to live wholly and entirely like him, and so as if he himself lived in our life. As surely as you do not now attempt to drag down my own words, and reduce them to the narrow meaning that Jesus is only to be imitated, as an unattainable pattern, partially and at a distance, as far as human weakness will allow, but accept them in the sense in which I have spoken them, that we must be transformed into Christ himself, so surely will it become evident to you that Jesus could not well have expressed himself otherwise, and that he actually did express himself excellently well. Jesus was very far from representing himself as that unattainable ideal into which he was first transformed by the spiritual poverty of the afterages; nor did his apostles so regard him."

To live in Christ is to live the life he lived, by living in the truth in which he lived and which he taught. The one great truth in which he continually lived was, as we have seen, that only in conscious union with God is there any real life, and therefore we can readily see why he continually gave out, as the Gospel writers tell us so many times he did, that his especial mission was to preach

---

[1] Fichte in "The Way towards the Blessed Life."

the glad tidings of the kingdom of God. Were it not possible for us to live the same life that he lived, he certainly would not have taught what he taught. This wonderful life of fully realized Divine life Jesus claims not for himself alone, but for all who actually live in the truth that he taught.

It was not to establish any material institution, as the church, that Jesus made his mission, but that the kingdom of God and His righteousness should become actualized and hold sway in the minds and hearts of men—this was his mission, an entirely different thing from the founding of a material organization. Paul and his party, sharing the then prevailing ideas that a material kingdom was to be established, were the originators of the church, not Jesus. We find the word "church" mentioned in the four Gospels by Jesus only once or twice, and then only in an incidental way, while we find the kingdom mentioned over thirty times in the first three Gospels alone.

As we have already pointed out, had it been his purpose to establish a material organization, then he certainly would not have given it out that something else was his especial purpose. But when the material organization, the church, purely a man-made institution, was established, the early church fathers bringing even interpolations of the Holy Word to their aid in establishing it and some of its various observations,—as modern scholarship has already so clearly discovered, and as it is continually discovering,— the following ages, thinking that they had an institution to keep up, gradually lost, to a greater or less extent, the real spiritual teachings of the Master in their zeal to keep up the form of an institution with which he had nothing to do. And those long and bitter persecutions of the church in the early and middle ages, as well as the long list of crimes sanctioned and committed directly by the church of the middle ages, show that they had not the real truth; for those who live in the truth and have it uppermost in their minds and hearts never persecute—only those who are on either uncertain or false ground, and whose endeavor it is to keep up the form of an institution which they feel would otherwise fall to the ground.

No, true religion has never been known either to persecute or to show intolerance of any kind. Throughout the whole history of the churches' heresies and persecutions, the persecuted party has ever occupied a correspondingly higher and the persecuting party a lower position, the persecuting party continually fighting as it were for life. But the *real truth* which Jesus taught will not cause nor will it even permit persecutions—hence we find the latter only where there is the lack of the former.

And again, the *real truth* which Jesus taught will not admit of divisions, much less of intolerance, for all real truth is exact truth, and in regard to it there can be no differences, and our modern theologians and our churches of to-day, which get their form and life from the speculations and theories of the former, certainly have not the real truth that Jesus taught, for they are divided in various directions on practically every dogma that they seek to promulgate. And strange as it may seem, heresy trials, with all their absurd attendant features, are not entirely unknown even yet, to-day. But in Jesus' own words, "A house divided against itself cannot stand." And so if the church of to-day wants to stand as a real power in the world, or if indeed it wants to stand at all, it must either get back to, or it must come up, as the case may be, to the *real living truth* that Jesus lived and taught. Unless it does this it will inevitably lose its hold on the people even more rapidly than it is losing it to-day. And certainly the younger ones whom it does not yet hold will not be drawn to it, when they can turn to that which has a thousand-fold more of truth and hence of life-giving power than it has to offer.

That this is not a mere sentiment on our part is evidenced by the wonderful rapidity with which the "New Thought" movement— would that we could designate what we mean without using any term—which has its underlying truth, this conscious union with the Divine Life and the actualized powers attendant upon it as Jesus taught,—hence not a new discovery, but a recovery,—is growing in America, in England, to be brief, in practically every civilized country in the world. Thousands every year in our own and in other countries are finding in it the joys of the realized Divine Life, and are turning to it from that which but poorly feeds them; and that this also is no mere sentiment on our part is evidenced by the contents of a letter recently sent by a noted divine in high official standing in the church in England to a noted American preacher, in which he said, in substance, that the church in England is literally honeycombed by the "New Thought" movement, and asked that he be sent a list of the best books that had already appeared in America, along the lines indicated.

And so what we need to-day is the same as what the world is eagerly calling for, the life-giving power of the great central truth that the Master taught, and not the various theories and speculations in regard to his origin, his birth, his life, and the meaning of his teachings. And still less, the fabrications of the early fathers in regard to inherited sin, original sin, vicarious atonement, and their believe-and-be-saved doctrine, and the alternative doctrine, fail to believe that which is opposed to all reason, all common sense, all real mercy, as well as all true justice, and be damned, be forever and eternally lost.

Jesus is indeed a lamb of God that taketh away the sins of the world, but he takes them away by bringing to the world the truth that shall make men free. Hence it is through his life and the truth that he lived and taught, not through his death and the observance of the various ceremonies and forms that have grown up around it. Those who are aided by symbols—and I am aware of the fact that for some many hallowed associations are connected with them—may do well to make use of them until they outgrow the need for them. But symbols are of value only where the real thing is not, and those who have the real thing no longer have need for symbols. "But the hour cometh," said Jesus, "and now is " (since I have brought you the real spirit of truth), "when the true worshippers shall worship the Father in spirit and truth; for such doth the Father seek to be His worshippers. God is a Spirit, and they that worship Him must worship in spirit and truth."

Jesus, according to his own words, did not propose to rest satisfied with the mere *historical belief* that he was the Eternal Word made flesh, and much less, as some phases of theology teach, that reconciliation with the Father, as ordinarily understood, was his purpose. God would adopt no methods in connection with His children that are opposed to their own reason. Nor would He adopt any partial, limited, or tribal methods.

And if, as various theologians would have us believe, that reconciliation with the Father can come about only by a belief in the shedding of the material, physical blood of Jesus, that through it the Father may receive satisfaction for His favor, how, then, in regard to the great company of those who cannot accept a theory so absurd, so illogical, and so opposed to the nature of the living God whom they *know,* and whom they no longer have to speculate and theorize in regard to, to say nothing of the millions upon millions of those who never have heard, and other millions who never can hear, of the man Jesus and the story of his blood "shed for the sins of the world," nine-tenths of whom, for good reasons, would not believe it if they did hear it? No, these fabrications cannot be true, for "in every nation, he that feareth God and worketh righteousness is accepted of Him." And so one may be without connection with any church, and even without connection with any *established* religion, and yet be in spirit, hence in reality* a much truer Christian than hosts of those who profess to be his most ardent followers, as indeed Jesus himself so many times says. "By their *fruits* ye shall know them," said he. "Not every one that saith unto me, Lord, Lord, shall enter into the kingdom of heaven; but he that *doeth* the will of my Father which is in heaven."

That which calls itself Christianity must prove itself, and only that that shows forth in its life the works, the power, the influence— the truth that Jesus' life showed forth—is the real, "He that believeth on me," said Jesus,—and shows it by *living* my life,—" the works that I do shall he do also; and greater works than these shall he do because I go unto the Father." And he who would know by what authority Jesus spoke, let him live the life that he lived and he will then know of the doctrine. Thus and thus only can it be known. We may speculate and theorize in regard to it, but only by living the life can we *know it.*

IV

The Philosopher's Ripest Life Thought

Let us now see how the truths we have already set forth stand in reference to the thought of the philosopher Fichte. Truth, the highest truth, and truth for its own sake, was the one supreme object of his life. And in order to discern this clearly himself, that he in turn might point it out clearly to others, he stood erect and alone, free from connection with any institution, organization, or system of thought that would distort or limit his vision and induce him either intentionally or unintentionally to interpret truth by bending it to suit the tenets of the system of thought or the institution to which he might be, even though inadvertently, bound.

It was of Fichte that an eminent English scholar once said: "Far above the dark vortex of theological strife in which punier intellects chafe and vex themselves in vain, Fichte struggles forward in the sunshine of pure thought which sectarianism cannot see, because its weakened vision is already filled with a borrowed and imperfect light."

It is, moreover, always of value to know how the truth that one finds and endeavors to give to others finds embodiment in his own life, for this is the sure and unfailing test of its vitality, if not indeed of its reality. A word or two, therefore, in reference to the life of Fichte may not be inappropriate here, a word or two from the same eminent English scholar quoted above, the translator

436

of his works from the German to the English, for he knew well his life the same as he knew also his philosophy. "We prize his philosophy deeply," says he; "it is to us an invaluable possession, for it seems the noblest exposition to which we have yet listened of human nature and divine truth; but with reverent thankfulness we acknowledge a still higher debt, for he has left behind him the best gift which man can bequeath to man—a brave, heroic human life."

"In the strong reality of his life,—in his intense love for all things beautiful and true,—in his incorruptible integrity and heroic devotion to the right, we see a living manifestation of his principles. His life is the true counterpart of his philosophy—it is that of a strong, free, incorruptible man."

And now to a few paragraphs of Fichte's thought bearing more or less directly upon the theme immediately in hand. After setting forth in a very comprehensive manner the truth in regard to Being, which he identifies with Life much in the same general manner as we have already endeavored to set it forth, and then after making it clear that by God he means this Infinite Being, this Spirit of Infinite Life, he says:

* * * * * * * * * *

"God alone is, and nothing besides him,—a principle which, it seems to me, may be easily comprehended, and which is the indispensable condition of all religious insight."

* * * * * * * * * *

"But beyond this mere empty and imaginary conception, and as we have carefully set forth this matter above, God enters into us in his actual, true, and immediate life,—or, to express it more strictly, we ourselves are this his immediate Life. But we are not conscious of this immediate Divine Life ; and since, as we have also already seen, our own Ex-istence—that which properly belongs to us —is that only which we can embrace in consciousness, so our

Being in God, notwithstanding that at bottom it is indeed ours, remains nevertheless forever foreign to us, and thus, in deed and truth, *to ourselves* is not our Being; we are in no respect the better of this insight, and remain as far removed as ever from God. We know nothing of this immediate Divine Life, I said; for even at the first touch of consciousness it is changed into a dead World. . . . The form forever veils the substance from us; our vision itself conceals its object; our eye stands in its own light. I say unto thee who thus complainest: 'Raise thyself to the standing-point of Religion, and all these veils are drawn aside; the World, with its dead principle, disappears from before thee, and the Godhead once more resumes its place within thee, in its first and original form, as Life, —as thine own Life, which thou oughtest to live and shalt live.'"

In setting forth how universally Divine Being incarnates itself in human Life, he says: "From the first standing-point the Eternal Word becomes flesh, assumes a personal, sensible, and human existence, without obstruction or reserve, in all times, and in every individual man who has a living insight into his unity with God, and who actually and in truth gives up his personal life to the Divine Life within him, — precisely in the same way as it became incarnate in Jesus Christ."

Speaking, then, of the great fundamental fact of the truth that Jesus himself perceived and gave to the world, and also of the manner whereby he came into the perception of it, he says: "Jesus of Nazareth undoubtedly possessed the highest perception containing the foundation of all other Truth, of the absolute identity of Humanity with the Godhead, as regards what is essentially real in the former."

"His self-consciousness was at once the pure and absolute Truth of Reason itself, self-existent and independent, the simple fact of consciousness."

* * * * * * * * * *

Then in showing that Jesus as he is presented to us by the apostle

438

John never conceived of his life in any other light than as one with the Father's Life, he says:

"But it is precisely the most prominent and striking trait in the character of the Johannean Jesus, ever recurring in the same shape, that he will know nothing of such a separation of his personality from his Father, and that he earnestly rebukes others who attempt to make such a distinction; while he constantly assumes that he who sees him sees the Father, that he who hears him hears the Father, and that he and the Father are wholly one; and he unconditionally denies and rejects the notion of an independent being in himself, such an unbecoming elevation of himself having been made an objection against him by misunderstanding. To him Jesus was not God, for to him there was no independent Jesus whatever; but God was Jesus, and manifested himself as Jesus."

To show, then, that this is a universal truth, brought in its fulness, and with a living exemplified vitality, first to the world by Jesus, but by no means applicable to him alone, he says: "An insight into the absolute unity of the Human Existence with the Divine is certainly the profoundest Knowledge that man can attain. Before Jesus this Knowledge had nowhere existed; and since his time, we may say, even down to the present day, it has been again as good as rooted out and lost, at least in profane literature."

That we must come into the same living realization of this great transcendent truth that Jesus came into, either through his teaching and exemplified realization of it, or through whatever channel it may come, he clearly indicated by the following: "The living possession of the theory we have now set forth—not the dry, dead, and merely historical knowledge of it—is, according to our doctrine, the highest, and indeed the only possible, Blessedness."

"The Metaphysical only, and not the Historical, can give us Blessedness; the latter can only give us understanding. If any man be truly united with God, and dwell in him, it is altogether an indifferent thing how he may have reached this state; and it would be a most useless and perverse employment, instead of living in the thing, to be continually repeating over our recollections of the way. Could Jesus return into the world, we might expect him to be thoroughly satisfied, if he found Christianity actually reigning in the minds of men, whether his merit in the work were recognized or overlooked; and this is, in fact, the very least that might be expected from a man who, while he lived on earth, sought not his own glory, but the glory of him who sent him."

And what in the eyes of Fichte are the results that follow and hence the tests of the genuineness of this higher realization, this True Religion, as he sometimes terms it? His words in this connection are: "True Religion, notwithstanding that it raises the view of those who are inspired by it to its own region, nevertheless retains their Life firmly in the domain of action, and of right moral action. The true and real Religious Life is not alone percipient and contemplative, does not merely brood over devout thoughts, but is essentially active. It consists, as we have seen, in the intimate consciousness that God actually lives, moves, and perfects his work in us. If therefore there is in us no real Life, if no activity and no visible work proceed forth from us, then is God not active in us. Our consciousness of union with God is then deceptive and vain, and the empty shadow of a condition that is not ours; perhaps the general, but lifeless, insight that such a condition is possible, and in others may be actual, but that we ourselves have, nevertheless, not the least portion in it."

"Religion does not consist in mere devout dreams, I said: Religion is not a business by and for itself, which a man may practise apart from his other occupations, perhaps on certain fixed days and hours; but it is the inmost spirit that penetrates, inspires, and pervades all our Thought and Action, which in other respects pursue their appointed course without change or interruption. That the Divine Life and Energy *actually lives in us* is inseparable from Religion, I said."

To show, then, how completely at one in his or her consciousness this truly religious man or woman becomes, how his or her own personal will is lost in, and so transmuted into, the Divine Will, as also the calmness and tranquillity with which his or her life forever thereafter flows along, he says: "The expression of the constant mind of the truly Moral and Religious man is this prayer: 'Lord! let but thy will be done, then is mine also done; for I have no other will than this — that thy will be done."

"This Divine Life now continually develops itself within him, without hindrance or obstruction, as it can and must develop itself only in him and his individuality; this alone it is that he properly wills; his will is therefore always accomplished, and it is absolutely impossible that anything contrary to it should ever come to pass."

"Whatever comes to pass around him, nothing appears to him strange or unaccountable—he knows assuredly, whether he understand it or not, that it is in God's World, and that there nothing can be that does not directly tend to Good. In him there is no fear for the future, for the absolute fountain of all Blessedness eternally bears him on towards it; no sorrow for the Past, for in so far as he was not in God he was nothing, and this is now at an end, and since he has dwelt in God he has been born into Light; while in so far as he was in God, that which he has done is assuredly right and good. He has never aught to deny himself, nor aught to long for; for he is at all times in eternal possession of the fulness of all that he is capable of enjoying. For him all labor and effort have vanished; his whole Outward Existence flows forth, softly and gently, from his Inward Being, and issues out into Reality without difficulty or hindrance."

Speaking, then, of how we may at once enter into and live in the full realization of this real life, and also of those who, instead of entering immediately into the Kingdom and thus finding the highest happiness and joy here and now, are expecting to find it in its completeness after the transition we call death, he says: "Full surely indeed there lies a Blessedness beyond the grave for those who have already entered upon it here, and in no other form or way than that by which they can already enter upon it here in this moment; but by mere burial man cannot arrive at Blessedness— and in the future life, and throughout the whole infinite range of all future life, they would seek for happiness as vainly as they have already sought it here, if they were to seek it in aught else than in that which already surrounds them so closely here below that throughout Eternity it can never be brought nearer to them—in the Infinite. And thus does the poor child of Eternity, cast forth from his native home, and surrounded on all sides by his heavenly inheritance which yet his trembling hand fears to grasp, wander with fugitive and uncertain step throughout the waste, everywhere laboring to establish for himself a dwelling place, but happily ever reminded, by the speedy downfall of each of his successive habitations, that he can find peace nowhere but in his Father's house."

Finally, speaking of how completely doubt and uncertainty are eliminated from the life of him who through the realization of the truth we have set forth becomes thereby centred in the Infinite, he says: "The Religious man is forever secured from the possibility of doubt and uncertainty. In every moment he knows distinctly what he wills, and ought to will; for the innermost root of his life—his will — forever flows forth from the Divinity, immediately and without the possibility of error; its indication is infallible, and for that indication he has an infallible perception. In every moment he knows that in all Eternity he shall know what he shall will, and ought to will; that in all Eternity the fountain of Divine Love which has burst forth in him shall never be dried up, but shall uphold him securely and bear him on forever."

Such, then, in general, are fragments of the thought, and, let it be added, the ripest thought, of one who has exerted perhaps as great a direct influence upon the life of his own immediate as well as succeeding ages as any man who has ever lived. It is to Fichte that, to a very great extent, the German Empire owes the splendid educational system it has to-day. His thought began to exert its influence at the time when its educational system was falling into a state of chaos, and even the Empire itself by virtue of its recent losses was in a more or less uncertain condition. And, acting to a greater or less extent through the minds of Froebel and Pestalozzi, his thought has aided in giving to the world the truest type of education it has yet seen, that that we know under the name kindergarten, which is slowly but surely working to revolutionize our present educational methods, which stand so sadly in need of a change even so radical.

If the truth and vitality of a man's thought are to be judged by its permanent as well as its immediate influence, surely the thought of Fichte found its life in the realms of the highest truth, through which alone real vitality comes, for it has exerted and is still exerting a most powerful life-giving influence, an influence, indeed, that will never end.

V

Sustained In Peace And Safety Forever

At what now have we arrived, and what has been the process? From our own reason and insight, independently of all outside authority, we have found the great truth that a living insight into the fact of the essential unity of the human life with the Divine Life is the profoundest knowledge that man can attain to. This as a mere intellectual perception, however, as a mere dead theory, amounts to but little, if indeed to anything at all, so far as bearing fruit in every-day life is concerned. It is the vital, living realization of this great transcendent truth in the life of each one that makes it a mighty moving and moulding force in his life.

Then we have also found that this same great truth was the great central fact of both the life and the teachings of one who comes as authority to practically all the world, the Christ Jesus. That this was the one great truth in which he continually lived, that it was the secret of his unusual insight and power, and that it was also the great truth that he came to bring to the world, he distinctly tells us. That it was not only what he proclaimed he came to teach, but also what he distinctly taught, we have likewise found.

We have found also that the ripest life thought of the philosopher Fichte—he whose spiritual vision was so fully unfolded as to enable him to give to the world such a remarkable blending of the intellectual and the spiritual in his philosophy—was almost if not identically the same in reference to this great truth, as was also his thought in regard to the life and the power as well as the mission of Jesus.

And when I see day after day the wonderful results that follow in the lives of those who have entered into this living realization, then I know that Jesus knew whereof he spoke when he gave the injunction, "Seek ye first the kingdom of God and His righteousness, and all these things shall be added unto you." Moreover, I do not believe, but *I know,* that whoever through this realization thus finds the kingdom of God will find his words—that all else will follow—literally and absolutely as well as necessarily true. All will follow in a perfectly natural and normal manner, in full accordance with natural spiritual law.

He who goes thus directly to the mountain top will find all things spread out before him in the valley below. He who thus becomes centred in the Infinite will find that to the same centre whence his inner life issues, all things pertaining to his outer material life will in turn be drawn. The beauty of holiness is one with the beauty of wholeness. To know but the One Life is to live in the fact and the beauty of wholeness; and where wholeness is, there no lack of anything will be found.

If what we ordinarily term our Christian churches, and if the preachers who stand in their pulpits, would fully and universally give themselves to the real message that Jesus gave to the world, then we would find that "the common people" would go to and would hear them gladly; there would then be no hard pressing social situation to face, for the people would then have a living knowledge of the one great truth through which all other things would come.

This great transcendent truth, however, that was the very essence of the life and the teachings of Jesus, has been even in our churches as good as rooted out and lost. And shall we conclude that because it is practically lost the greater part of the time and attention of the preacher in the large majority of them is given to the empty, barren, inconsequential themes it is given to? Or is it because

445

so much time and attention is given to the latter that there is no time left for the former? However this may be, it certainly is true that to a greater or less extent to-day we find identically the same conditions that Jesus found, and that he continually tried so hard to do away with. "Full well," said he, "ye reject the commandment of God, that ye may keep your own tradition."

Many a student comes from our theological schools so steeped in theological speculations and in denominational dogmas that he hasn't the slightest conception of what the real mission of Jesus was. What wonder, then, that the church to which he goes soon becomes a dead shell from which the life has gone, into which those in love with life will no longer enter, a church whose chief concern very soon is, how to raise the minister's salary? But once let these minor and inconsequential, not to say at times petty, foolish, and absurd, things be dropped, and let all time and attention be given to the great central truth that Jesus brought to the world, and we shall find that during the next one hundred years, aye, during the next fifty years, what will then be real Christianity will make more progress than what is now termed Christianity has made during all the nineteen hundred years it has been in the world. The fact that during all these hundreds of years it has not accomplished more than it has is quite good evidence that something essential is lacking in it.

The real soul-cry even of all Christendom to-day is the same as the injunction given by the native ministers of Japan to a noted representative of the Christian religion as he was leaving there not long ago: "Send us no more doctrines: we are tired of them. Send us Christ." And the only way that Christ can be sent is by sending the great central truth that he brought to the world, a truth so *world-wide*, so *universal*, that, so far even as the so-called various great religions are concerned, in regard to it there can be up differences, for from its very nature it is at the very foundation, indeed the very life essence, of them all. And so it is true in this sense that there is essentially but one religion, the religion of the living God. For to live in the conscious realization of the fact that

God lives in us is indeed the life of our life, and that in ourselves we have no independent life, and hence no power, is the one great fact of all true religion, even as it is the one great fact of human life. Religion, therefore, at its purest, and life at its truest, are essentially and necessarily one and the same.

It is only through this living realization of the essential unity of our life with the Father's life that true blessedness, and even true peace and happiness, can be found. The sooner, then, that we come into it, and thus live the life of the spirit, the better, for neither will they come nor can they be found in any other way. There is, moreover, no time either in this form of life, or in any other form, that we can any more readily come into it, and thereby into all that follows, than we can at this very moment. And when this fountain of Divine Life is once fully opened within us, it can never again be dried up, and we can rest assured that it will at all times uphold us in peace and bear us on in safety. And however strange or unaccountable at times occurrences may appear, we can rest in a triumphant security, knowing that only good can come, for in God's life there is only good, and in God's life we are now living, and there we shall live forever.[1]

---

[1]For suggestions as to the method of entering into this higher realization, as also for a much fuller portrayal of its results in every-day life, the reader is directed to the volume by the same author entitled, "In Tune with the Infinite, or, Fulness of Peace, Power, and Plenty."

Made in United States
Troutdale, OR
07/25/2023